Revolt

THE ARCHAEOLOGY OF COLONIALISM IN NATIVE NORTH AMERICA

Revolt

An Archaeological History of Pueblo
Resistance and Revitalization in 17th
Century New Mexico

Matthew Liebmann

THE UNIVERSITY OF
ARIZONA PRESS

TUCSON

The University of Arizona Press
© 2012 Matthew Liebmann and the Pueblo of Jemez
All rights reserved
First issued as a paperback edition 2013

www.uapress.arizona.edu

Library of Congress Cataloging-in-Publication Data
Liebmann, Matthew, 1973–
   Revolt : an archaeological history of Pueblo resistance and revitalization
in 17th century New Mexico / Matthew Liebmann.
     p.   cm. — (The archaeology of colonialism in native North America)
   Includes bibliographical references and index.
   ISBN 978-0-8165-2865-3 (cloth : alk. paper)
   ISBN 978-0-8165-3086-1 (pbk. : alk. paper)
   1. Pueblo Revolt, 1680. 2. Pueblo Indians—Colonization.
3. Pueblo Indians—Government relations. 4. Pueblo Indians—
Antiquities. 5. Social archaeology—New Mexico. 6. Ethnoarchaeology—
New Mexico. 7. New Mexico—History—To 1848. I. Title.
   E99.P9L45   2012
   978.9'02—dc23   2011052051

Author's proceeds from the sale of this book will be donated to the Pueblo of
Jemez for the preservation of cultural resources.

Published in cooperation with the William P. Clements Center for Southwest
Studies, Southern Methodist University

Manufactured in the United States of America on acid-free, archival-quality
paper and processed chlorine free.

17   16   15   14   13   12   6   5   4   3   2   1

Dedicated to the Hemish *of the past, present, and future.*
T'ebànõ:pa

Contents

Illustrations

Figures

Tables

Acknowledgments

IF YOU PESTER, BORE, AND IMPOSE YOURSELF on people often enough, eventually you need to thank them for putting up with you. Archaeologists bore, pester, and impose on a lot of people, and for this reason we tend to write long acknowledgments sections at the beginnings of our books. Unfortunately I'm no exception in this regard. This book is the end result of more than a decade of pestering, boring, and imposing on a host of people whose names do not appear on the cover. The contents are based largely on their collective wisdom, assistance, and generosity, and I am lucky to call them colleagues and friends.

First and foremost I thank the people of Jemez Pueblo. They have offered me their hospitality, support, and counsel throughout the years, and have taught me more than I could ever learn in any classroom. Collaborating together on the research for this book was both a privilege and a pleasure. Their generosity has been nothing short of tremendous, and I thank them for putting up with yet another in the long line of nosy *bileganush* from back East who become interested in the rich and storied history of the Jemez. I will be forever grateful to the people of Walatowa for opening their doors to me, particularly the members of the Cultural Resource Advisory Committee, the Tribal Council, Tribal Administration, and the staff of the Department of Resource Protection, including (in no particular order) Chris Toya, Tom Lucero, John D. Romero, T. J. Loretto, Aaron Tosa, Wilma Baca Tosa, Paul A. Chinana, Carrie Gachupin, Rolanda Casiquito, Audrey Gachupin, Alberta Vigil, James Gachupin, Pete Toya, Joshua Madalena, Ray Gachupin, Stuart Gachupin, Vince Toya, Michael Toledo, Paul S. Chinana, Raymond Loretto, Leonard Shendo, Greg Gachupin, and Matthew Gachupin. Thanks as well to project interns Gorman Romero, Marlon Magdalena, Jeremiah Starr, Dominic Toya, Daniel Madalena, Monica Magdalena, Allen Chinana, Shane Toledo, Javin Sandia, Derrick Toledo, Kerwin Tsosie, Cedric Fragua, and Maurice Shendo, who all managed to keep smiles on their faces after climbing the mesas countless times. T'ebànõ:pa.

Bob Preucel has been instrumental in this research from the beginning. It was Bob who pioneered the archaeology of the Pueblo Revolt, first introduced me to the Southwest, and suggested that I conduct research in the Jemez region. He was about the best Ph.D. advisor that any struggling graduate student could ask for, and he continues to be a fantastic teacher, mentor, role model, advocate, and friend. Those familiar with Bob's work will undoubtedly recognize his influence throughout the pages that follow, and I will always be indebted to him for his support and inspiration. Additionally, Clark Erickson, Barbara Mills, and Wendy Ashmore contributed not only to the improvement of this work in its earliest stages, but also to my development as an archaeologist. I have learned more from each of them than they know, and I am truly grateful for the knowledge, advice, and encouragement they have proffered. A special note of thanks to Tony Wallace for taking the time to discuss revitalization studies with me and offering his insights into my research.

Any archaeologist working in the Jemez Province today owes a huge debt of gratitude to Mike Elliott, who laid the foundations for modern archaeological studies in the region. It is no exaggeration to say that this book would not have been possible without Mike's previous work. Similarly, Jeremy Kulisheck selflessly shared his expertise into the archaeology of the area throughout the research process as well, and his perceptive insights continue to shape my thinking regarding ancestral Jemez history. Mike Bremer of the Santa Fe National Forest also deserves many thanks for facilitating and encouraging much of this research. The directors of the Jemez Department of Resource Protection, including Bill Whatley, Mehrdad Khatibi, Steve Blodgett, and Greg Kaufman, all provided crucial assistance and support throughout the process. Erma Ruth, Jack Condon, Judith Isaacs, and Anne Leslie have repeatedly provided great lodging, great food, and great conversation during my repeated stays in New Mexico.

A research fellowship at the William P. Clements Center for Southwest Studies at Southern Methodist University in 2010 allowed me to bring this project to fruition and offered an intellectually challenging, creative, and supportive home during the writing process. The staff of the Clements Center—Ben Johnson, Andrea Boardman, Ruth Ann Elmore, and Sherry Smith—provided an ideal atmosphere in which to write and think. While in Dallas I received valuable feedback on an early version of this manuscript from James Brooks, David Hurst Thomas, Matt Babcock, Scott Cassingham, Alan Covey, Sunday Eiselt, David Rex Gallindo, Sami Lakomäki, Jason Mellard, Lauren O'Brien, and Chris Roos, all of whom I thank for helping me to improve the final product. Steve Silliman, Bob Preucel, and two anonymous reviewers also read the complete manuscript and offered their insights, for which I am truly grateful. Any remaining mistakes, errors, and shortcomings exist despite their best efforts. At the University of Arizona Press, Allyson Carter and her able staff guided the manuscript through the editing and production process. Thanks to Jack Rummel for copyediting assistance, and to

Landis and Kat Bennett of 360 Geographics for drafting many of the figures. Jason Garcia created the fantastic original work of art that appears on the cover.

Over the years many scholars have shared their knowledge, advice, and support regarding the research that appears herein, among them Woody Aguilar, Trish Capone, Tom Cummins, Kathy Deagan, Jennifer Dyer, T. J. Ferguson, Dick Ford, Michael Frachetti, Charles Golden, John Kessell, Thanik Lertchanrit, Richard Leventhal, Diana Loren, Derek Miller, Melissa Murphy, Ann Ramenofsky, Uzma Rizvi, Cal Riley, Jeremy Sabloff, Andrew Scherer, Robert Sharer, James Snead, Adam Stack, Ana Steffen, Chris Stiles, Jennie Sturm, Radhika Sundararajan, Barb Voss, John Weeks, and Mike Wilcox. Special thanks to Phil King for getting me into archaeology when I was still a wide-eyed undergrad who didn't know any better and for teaching me the secrets to his success. My colleagues and friends at the College of William and Mary and Harvard University have encouraged me throughout this endeavor as well, particularly Martin Gallivan, Danielle Moretti-Langholtz, Mary Voigt, Fred Smith, Ofer Bar-Yosef, David Carrasco, Bill Fash, Rowan Flad, C. C. Lamberg-Karlovsky, Peter der Manuellian, Richard Meadow, Jeff Quilter, Jason Ur, and Gary Urton.

Numerous organizations and institutions have sustained my research over the past ten years. The Louis J. Kolb Foundation, the University of Pennsylvania Department of Anthropology, the University of Pennsylvania Museum of Archaeology and Anthropology, the College of William and Mary, and the Peabody Museum of Archaeology and Ethnology all provided support at crucial stages of this research. Fieldwork was funded by the National Science Foundation (BCS-0313808) and the Wenner-Gren Foundation for Anthropological Research. Additionally, the students of the Pecos Pathways program (jointly sponsored by the Robert S. Peabody Museum, Phillips Academy Andover; the Pueblo of Jemez; and Pecos National Historical Park) provided helping hands and much-needed optimism during the data collection phases of this research.

Finally I owe a special debt of gratitude to my family, who to be honest weren't really much help in the writing of this book but have proven themselves useful in a myriad of other ways over the years. Thanks to the extended Liebmann and Dal Barco clans, but especially to the two Herberts, Diane, Marie, Joey, and Harper for all your support and encouragement.

Chronology

1300s	Ancestral Pueblo people migrate into the Jemez Province
1539–41	Pueblo peoples' first encounters with Europeans
1598	First permanent Spanish settlements and missions established in New Mexico
1675	Arrest and imprisonment of forty-seven Tewa medicine men
1675–80	Po'pay retreats to Taos Pueblo; receives prophecy
August 1680	Pueblo Revolt; Spaniards withdraw from New Mexico
1681	Po'pay deposed; Regime of Luis Tupatú and Alonso Catití begins
late 1681	Otermín's attempted reconquest; Jemez move to Patokwa
1683	Ute raid at Patokwa; Boletsakwa constructed
1684	Alonso Catití dies, pan-Pueblo alliance begins to break down
1687	Reneros attacks Tamaya (Santa Ana Pueblo)
1689	Jironza attacks Zia Pueblo; Zias and Santa Anas move to Cerro Colorado
1692	Vargas's ritual repossession of New Mexico ("Bloodless Reconquest")
1693	Colonial resettlement of New Mexico
early 1694	Residents of Patokwa and Boletsakwa move to Astialakwa
April 1694	Battle at Kotyiti
July 1694	Battle at Astialakwa
September 1694	Battle at Tunyo (Black Mesa)
1695	San Diego del Monte Mission constructed at Patokwa
1696	Second Pueblo Revolt

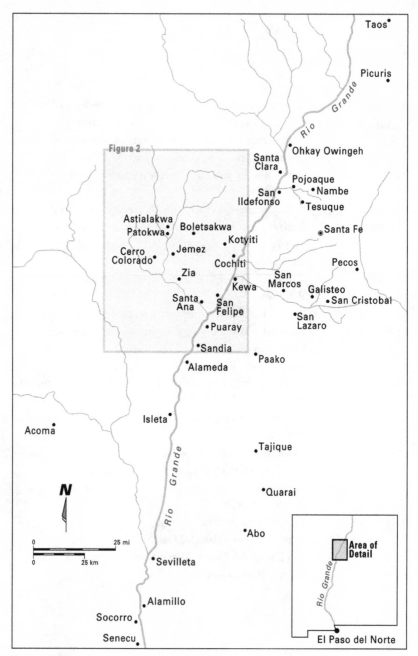

FIGURE FM.1. The seventeenth-century Pueblo world, showing locations mentioned in the text.

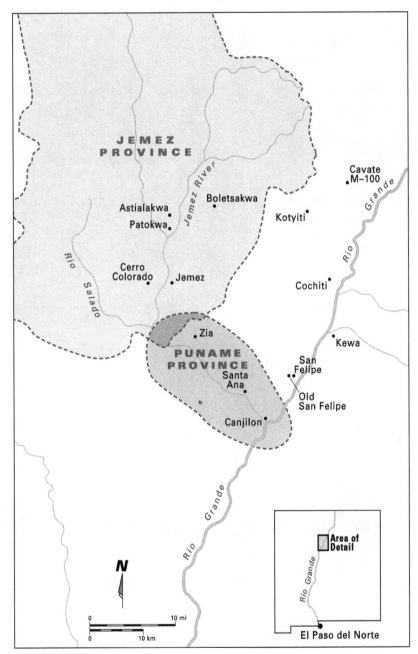

FIGURE FM.2. The Jemez and Puname provinces, 1680–1696.

Revolt

I

Introduction

ARCHAEOLOGY, ANTHROPOLOGY, AND THE PUEBLO REVOLT

JULY 24, 1694. WITH THEIR HOMES IN FLAMES, enemy soldiers advancing, and all escape routes blocked, the Pueblo Indian warriors of the Jemez village of Astialakwa were out of options. The acrid smoke and gunpowder that smeared the air was pierced by the screams of their wives, mothers, and children. The Jemez warriors inched backward until their heels teetered at the edge of the cliffs surrounding the mesa-top pueblo. As their eyes darted back and forth between the armor-clad Spaniards marching toward them and the canyon floor that loomed a thousand dizzying feet below their backs, the warriors made a final, fateful pact. Surveying the towering walls of the mesa that dropped beneath their feet, they choose death over surrender. One by one the Jemez men stepped to the brink and jumped off the precipice, limbs flailing as they plummeted headlong into the abyss. They seemed to hang in the air for a long, still moment before the silence was shattered by a sickening crunch as they smashed into the jumbled boulders at the base of the cliffs. Better to die with dignity, they must have thought as their feet left the ground, than in defeat staring down the barrel of a Spanish harquebus.

Twelve hours earlier the Jemez had been preparing for the impending battle by staging a ritual dance in the plaza at Astialakwa. They were well aware that the Spaniards were coming to attack the mesa-top refuge because General don Diego de Vargas, the self-proclaimed "restorer, conqueror, settler, governor, and captain general of the kingdom and provinces of New Mexico," had publicly announced his plans in the plaza of the colonial capital of Santa Fe four weeks earlier. "The present campaign is necessary," he had declared, "because of the rebellion and backsliding of the Jemez nation." What the residents of Astialakwa may not have been aware of, however, was the fact that Vargas was coming with formidable reinforcements.

In addition to the 120 presidial soldiers and militiamen he had mustered in Santa Fe, don Diego had enlisted the aid of 100 Pueblo allies from the neighboring villages of Zia, Santa Ana, and San Felipe to fight against their Jemez brethren. Just five years earlier these villages had been resolutely opposed to colonial rule, taking up arms against the Spaniards in defense of their freedom. But when the colonizers returned in 1692, the Zias, Santa Anas, and San Felipians shifted their allegiances, casting their lots in with their former enemies. Now these pro-Spanish Pueblo warriors marched under the leadership of Bartolomé de Ojeda, a Zia war captain who had been recruited to the Spanish cause after being captured and held as a prisoner of war.[1]

Vargas gave the signal to begin the assault when the morning star appeared in the early hours of July 24. Splitting his force into two units, the colonial men-at-arms ascended the front of the mesa while the allied Pueblo troops circled around to the back. As the light of dawn broke, the opening volley from a Spanish musket cracked the morning silence and the Jemez warriors scrambled to defend their village against both wings of the attack. The people of Astialakwa rained arrows, slingstones, boulders, and anything else they could get their hands on down on the enemy troops, with the Spaniards forced to dismount their horses and scramble up the steep paths on foot. As the sun climbed high in the summer sky, the attacking forces breached the fortifications surrounding the acropolis and the Jemez found themselves hemmed in by the pincer strategy of their aggressors. When the colonial militia began setting fire to the village room-by-room, the Jemez knew that the tide had turned. The women and children could only watch as their fathers and brothers launched themselves off the crags, dropping from the sky like hailstones.

At least seven Pueblo bodies were later found splashed across the rocks in the valley below Astialakwa. Following the battle the Spaniards reported 77 further Jemez casualties, including 5 seared alive in their houses. In addition to those killed, colonial forces captured 361 Jemez prisoners of war. The Spaniards later attributed their victory over the Indian rebels to the intervention of the saints. They had marched under the protection of *La Conquistadora* (Our Lady of the Conquest) and Santiago (St. James the Greater, patron saint of Spain and the *conquistadores*), with the battle occurring on the eve of the latter's feast day.[2]

Ironically, Jemez oral traditions of this battle recall the intercession of the saints as well—not on the side of the Spaniards, but rather in aid of their own cause. According to Native accounts, not all the warriors who jumped from the cliffs died on that tragic July day. Local legends assert that the apparition of a saint materialized just as the Pueblo men leapt from the rock face, saving them from certain death. "At that moment a likeness of San Diego appeared on the cliff," writes Jemez historian Joe Sando, "and the people who had jumped simply landed on their feet and did not die." Other accounts attribute the salvation of the Jemez to the Virgin of Guadalupe, who report-edly eased the jumpers gently through the air, allowing them to "float like butterflies" into the valley below.[3]

Po'pay's Prophecy

The invocation of saintly intercession by the Jemez and the alliance of neigh-boring Pueblos with the Spaniards was a conspicuous departure from the anti-colonial, anti-Catholic agenda that had been set forth in the previous decade. Fourteen years earlier, a charismatic Pueblo prophet named Po'pay had emerged from an underground kiva at Taos Pueblo declaring that he had received a revelation from the spirits. His back still bore the scars from a Spanish whip, a reminder of his imprisonment after being branded a *hechicero* (sorcerer) by the colonial governor in 1675. On his release Po'pay retreated to Taos, located at the northernmost edge of the Spanish American empire and the outer limits of the colonizers' grasp. There he vowed revenge against the foreign intruders and took refuge in the smoky womb of the kiva. While in seclusion he claimed to have been visited by supernatural beings who delivered to him a fateful mes-sage: the Spaniards must die.[4]

Some accounts claim that Po'pay was visited by a triumvirate of spirits with the power to shoot fire from their fingertips. Others say he conversed directly with *Po'se yemu,* the powerful rain-giver himself. No one knows for sure as the spirits never revealed themselves to the outside world. They appeared to Po'pay alone and spoke through Po'pay alone. According to the furtive Tewa mystic their message was clear: a better life awaited the Pueblo peoples in the future, one like that enjoyed by their ancestors in the age before the Europeans arrived. The rains that had been absent would return to soak the parched Pueblo lands. The corn would grow tall again, and the fields would give birth to plentiful melons, squash, and chiles for their feasts. The Pueblo people were guaranteed renewed health and happiness, the likes of which they had not seen since before the arrival of the foreigners, but only if they would heed the spirits' call. This new world would not come to pass until the Pueblos had eradicated all remnants of the Spaniards and their Christian God from their villages, returning to traditional, pre-Hispanic ways of life.[5]

On August 10, 1680, Po'pay's prophecy was realized. Pueblo Indians throughout northern New Mexico united with their Navajo and Apache allies in an armed revolt, killing 380 colonial settlers and 21 Franciscan missionaries. Native forces sacked Spanish *estancias,* burned the churches, shattered the mis-sion bells, and laid siege to the colonial capital of Santa Fe. As they set fire to the cathedral the Pueblo warriors were heard to declare, "Now the God of the Spaniards, who was their father, is dead." Santa Maria and the saints, they proclaimed, were nothing but "rotten wood."[6] Freedom was returned to the Pueblo peoples, just as the spirits had predicted. The colonists who survived the initial uprising fled Pueblo lands, limping three hundred miles down the Rio Grande to El Paso del Norte, where they remained in exile for more than a dozen years.

For the Jemez, the saga of the Pueblo Revolt began with the apparition of traditional Pueblo spirits in a kiva and ended with the apparition of a Catholic saint on the battlefield. How are we to make sense of this curious arc? How was a united indigenous rebellion transformed into divisive Pueblo-on-Pueblo warfare in the span of just fourteen short years? What are we to make of flame-throwing spirits appearing before a cloistered prophet? Why would nativist, anti-Catholic "apostates" appeal to saints for protection against their zealous Christian enemies? And why did some Native rebels choose to ally themselves with imperial forces on the Spaniards' return, ultimately fighting against their Pueblo brethren?

Like all colonial histories, the story of the Pueblo Revolt era (1680–96) is filled with apparent ironies and contradictions. This book attempts to make sense of these paradoxes, tracing the ways in which Pueblo peoples remade their world as they negotiated the changes brought on by European colonialism. With a chronological span of just sixteen years, the era in question is the archaeological equivalent of batting an eyelash. But the consequences of this blink continue to reverberate among the people of New Mexico today, more than three centuries after the fact. Narrowly conceived, the chapters that follow discuss the historical archaeology of a particular place and time—northern New Mexico between 1680 and 1696. Yet while focusing on a relatively small group of people in just one corner of the Spanish American empire, this book examines larger processes that are common to anticolonial revolutions the world over. Viewed more broadly, then, *Revolt: An Archaeological History* can be seen as a work of historical anthropology, investigating the recurrent phenomena of subaltern resistance, cultural revitalization, and the manipulation of colonial signs that characterize colonized populations more generally.

Pariahs and Paladins: The Romance and Tragedy of Native Revolts

Native American revolts occupy a unique place in the American consciousness. Less than a century ago they were commonly marginalized as anomalous and unsettling footnotes to the story of Manifest Destiny, proof of the supposedly inherent violence and "savagery" of American Indian peoples. In more recent years, however, they have been recast as heroic sagas, documenting the valiant resistance of the human spirit to oppression (Sayre 2005:1–3). In an age of unprecedented institutional hegemony, audiences today live vicariously through the Native freedom fighters of the past, celebrating the underdogs of history who dared to challenge the churning engine of Euro-American expansion. The names of these rebellions and their noble leaders, once cursed as obstacles to national "progress," now evoke notions of perseverance and liberty: Powhatan; King Philip's War; Tecumseh; the Battle of the Little Big Horn; Sitting Bull; Crazy Horse; Geronimo; Pontiac's Rebellion; Quanah Parker; the Pueblo Revolt of 1680. All are honored in chronicles of stage and screen, on posters and T-shirts, on public monuments, and in countless books and scholarly articles. In each case, the revolutionaries involved have been transformed from pariahs into paladins over the course of the past century.

Yet Native American revolts embody a series of curious contradictions in the modern American mind. Their celebration is a clear example of "imperialist nostalgia," wherein colonial societies mourn the indigenous cultural formations that they themselves destroyed (Rosaldo 1989:107–08). And even as they are celebrated as tales of valiant resistance, the Native revolts of the past are simultaneously lamented as heartbreaking examples of futility and reminders of what might have been. Contemporary writers tend to label indigenous rebellions as either successes or failures, with "successful" revolts resulting in the establishment of liberty and self-rule. Any insurrection falling short of this lofty goal is deemed to have "failed." Because anything less than permanent decolonized independence is considered a defeat, modern-day audiences tend to regard the Native revolts of the past as disappointments in the final analysis. The fact that the indigenous peoples of North America live today as colonized subjects, legally (and oxymoronically) defined as domestic dependent nations, is cited as proof of the eventual futility of indigenous insurgencies. Thus in the twenty-first century, Indian uprisings and their iconic leaders are both lionized as inspirational and dismissed as ineffectual; they are acclaimed and admired, yet ultimately bemoaned as futile.

In truth, anticolonial rebellions were rarely unambiguous in either victory or defeat. Even the most triumphant revolts were tinged with bitter setbacks, while those that were brutally suppressed sometimes provided the impetus for future gains. Success and failure are relative propositions, the establishment of which tells us more about the perspective of the evaluator than about the events in question. And as value judgments masquerading as objective, empirical facts, conclusions of "success" and "failure," or of "winners" and "losers," can muddy the waters more than they clarify. In many cases, these assessments are based on models drawn from classic Western examples. The very word *revolution* calls to mind the great modern prototypes: the American Revolution; the French Revolution; the Russian Revolution. These impose a model of what revolution should be—of expected actions, results, and stages to which revolutionary developments conform (E. Weber 1974:4). By comparison, Native American revolts are frequently considered "failures" because they do not correspond to these Eurocentric templates. Today's audiences are disappointed when the Native protagonists of yesterday fail to live up to modern expectations, often through accommodation, syncretism, cooperation, or alliances forged with colonial powers. In the realm of twenty-first century storytelling, we like our warriors to be brave, our savages noble, and our Indians uncompromising.

Following from this penchant to appraise indigenous resistance movements as either successes or failures, chronicles of Native American revolts tend to follow two basic plotlines: that of romance or tragedy (see Dawdy 2008:xviii, 10–11). Modern colonial romances often document the triumph of the colonized over their colonizers, while tragedies recount the folly of Indians' futile attempts to redirect the course of history in the face of the irresistible forces of colonial expansion. Frequently these tales begin as romances and conclude as tragedies, with the Indians winning in the opening pages, only to be defeated in the final chapter. In the pages that follow I attempt to resist both genres, offering neither a romanticized celebration of valiant Native resistance, nor a tragic lament for the loss of an imagined utopia. The Pueblo Revolt of 1680 was not, as we shall see, an unqualified, patriotic "success," nor was it a short-lived, incompetent "failure." Rather, the picture that emerges here is complex, filled with caveats and seeming contradictions. There are no unambiguous heroes or villains in this story. As historians consistently remind us, the past is a messy place. Seventeenth-century New Mexico was no exception.

¡Viva la Revolución!: A Metahistory of the Pueblo Revolt

As celebrated Borderlands historian David Weber notes, the Pueblo Revolt of 1680 "marked one of the rare moments in more than three hundred years of colonial rule in the Americas that Spaniards suffered a thorough defeat by Natives whom they had long subjected" (1999b:8). Yet for many years this pivotal event received little attention from scholars of American history, who tended to look to the Atlantic coast when studying the colonization of the lands that came to be known as the United States. So too did Southwestern archaeologists long overlook the 1680 uprising, more inclined as they were to investigate pre-Hispanic contexts and large-scale cultural processes than short-term historical events (Preucel 2002b:9). In recent decades, however, interest in Native American experiences and the Spanish colonial era in American history has piqued as studies have become consciously less Anglocentric. As a result, over the past half-century historians, anthropologists, journalists, and popular writers have all penned versions of the Pueblo Revolt story, retelling this narrative over and over again (Hackett and Shelby 1942; Forbes 1960; Spicer 1962; Dozier 1970; Silverberg 1970; Folsom 1973; John 1975; Kessell 1979, 2002, 2008; Sando 1979a; Gutiérrez 1991; Knaut 1995; Baldwin 1995; Riley 1999; Weber 1999a; Preucel 2002a; Roberts 2004; Sando and Agoyo 2005; Sálaz 2008; Wilcox 2009).[7]

So why, you might ask, would anyone bother to write—and more importantly, should you bother to read—yet another account of what Joe Sando and Herman Agoyo (2005) call "the first American revolution"?[8] The version that follows differs from previous investigations of the Pueblo Revolt era in two major respects: the data it uses to tell the story, and the models employed to interpret those data. More specifically, this account uses archaeological evidence and anthropological perspectives to provide new insights into the events that occurred between 1680 and 1696 in New Mexico. Not coincidentally, these aspects frame the core arguments of this book: (1) that material culture constitutes the very acts and signs of social life, thus providing crucial insights into Native experiences during this period; and (2) that our understandings of the Pueblo Revolt and its aftermath are greatly enhanced through the comparative perspectives provided by anthropology. As a result, the study that follows is not a simple recapitulation of the same information contained in previous accounts. It draws on new evidence and novel theoretical perspectives to recount a distinctively different chronicle of this tumultuous period in the history of the American Southwest.

Because the Pueblos did not record their versions of the events of the late seventeenth century in writing, conventional histories of the Pueblo Revolt era are based primarily on Spanish colonial journals and Franciscan ecclesiastical correspondence.[9] Yet these texts are limited in scope and contain distinctive biases, written as they were by missionaries and colonial officials who were often attempting to rationalize their defeat and justify the reconquest of the region. The Spanish authors of these documents were largely unconcerned with conveying the experiences of their colonized subjects, and thus the documentary record provides a primarily one-sided perspective on the events of the 1680s and 1690s in New Mexico, a fact against which scholars have struggled for decades. Recent accounts of the Pueblo Revolt have attempted to reanalyze these texts from Native perspectives, explicitly trying to "make the Pueblo experience speak" (Knaut 1995:xii; see also Roberts 2004:3–8). But relying on the documentary record alone results in histories of the Pueblo Revolt that are filtered through Spanish pens, in which Pueblo voices are included only via European interlocutors, and even then only rarely (D. Weber 1999b:9).

This book utilizes a different strategy. In addition to its attempt to read between the lines and against the grain of the existing texts, the account that follows also employs material culture—artifacts, architecture, and rock art—as essential sources of data to supplement the documentary record, providing new perspectives on the Pueblo Revolt and its aftermath. Historical archaeology can complement and enhance the textual record in important ways: it can supply information regarding times, places, and peoples not recorded in written documents (or remembered in oral traditions). It can provide a window into the minutiae of daily life not preserved in official histories, investigating the taken-for-granted, seemingly mundane activities that constitute and transform social life. And it can correct the biases of written documents, challenging the master narratives woven into accounts penned by the "winners" of history (Brumfiel 2003:207; Johnson 1998:34). In short, archaeology provides a new perspective on the Pueblo Revolt that is independent of the Spanish chronicles.

Yet it would be a mistake to claim that this book provides a Pueblo perspective on the Revolt era. While oral traditions and Native versions of events are included whenever possible, I remain wary of attempts to speak for colonized Others hundreds of years in the past from the considerable distance of the twenty-first century. More often than not this becomes an exercise in historical ventriloquism, with contemporary researchers throwing their own voices and opinions into the mouths of people in the past. However, the account that follows does offer *archaeological* perspectives into the events of 1680–96 in New Mexico. It builds on the growing body of research into the archaeology of the Pueblo Revolt era that has been conducted in recent years, which has demonstrated the potential of artifacts and architecture to reveal new and substantial information regarding this tumultuous chapter in New Mexican history (Ferguson 1996; Snead and Preucel 1999; Preucel 1998, 2000a, 2000b, 2002a; 2006; Preucel et. al. 2002; Liebmann et al. 2005; Liebmann 2006, 2008, 2011; Liebmann and Preucel 2007).

The incorporation of material culture in the investigation of the Pueblo Revolt era also yields another distinctive aspect of this book: its temporal scope. Due to their reliance on the documentary record, previous accounts have tended to concentrate on the "bookends" of this particular chapter of

New Mexican history, detailing the incidents of 1680–81, then jumping ahead more than a decade to the Spaniards' ritual reconquest in 1692, often with the turn of a single page. Scholars have previously made little attempt to reconstruct the intervening years of Pueblo liberation, primarily because the Spaniards made only a few short and poorly documented forays into New Mexico during this time. Even so, considering the amount of ink that has been spilled regarding the Pueblo Revolt, the social and cultural contexts of Pueblo life during the Spanish interregnum remain poorly understood. This is particularly true of the Jemez Province (the central focus of this book), which played host to some of the crucial events of the Pueblo Revolt era but has been largely overlooked in previous chronicles. One of the unique contributions of *Revolt: An Archaeological History* is the attention paid to the events that occurred in the decade between 1681 and 1691 in the northern Rio Grande generally, and in the Jemez Province specifically (part II). Although the period being examined is on a much narrower time scale than that of typical archaeological investigations—and more akin to the traditional realm of history—there are substantial benefits to be gleaned by looking at this short but momentous era from an archaeological perspective. Material culture allows us to explore the changes that occurred among the Pueblos during this crucial period of independence, in addition to the new information archaeology offers regarding the opening and closing phases of the Pueblo Revolt era (which are documented by historical texts as well as archaeology and are detailed in parts I and III respectively). In this way, I hope that this book serves as yet another example of the fact that historical archaeology is not merely a "handmaiden to history" (Noel Hume 1964), but provides valuable and original insights into the processes and events of the past.

Historical Anthropology/Anthropological History

The chronicle that follows attempts to add depth, texture, and detail to the well-worn tale of the Pueblo Revolt through the inclusion of archaeological data. In doing so, it also raises some curious paradoxes. The account that emerges may not be quite what readers have come to expect from previous histories of the Revolt. The subtle differences that appear in the interstices between text and artifact—between what has been written and the objects people left behind—present an interpretive challenge. What do these differences mean? How are we to make sense of the wrinkles in the fabric, of the confusing and seemingly incongruous elements of the Pueblo Revolt story? Presented in isolation, some of the artifacts and behaviors of this period may seem strange to modern readers. And interpreted in isolation, the story of the Pueblo Revolt stands in danger of remaining just that, another curious story, full of exotic and peculiar details. But as Jean and John Comaroff note, to become more than just a story, tales of anticolonial resistance "have to be situated in wider worlds of power and meaning that give them life" (1992:17). It is in this contextualization where history and anthropology can inform one another, and where sense can be made of the apparent contradictions of the past.

Bringing the events of the 1680s and 1690s in the Pueblo world into dialogue with more general studies of colonial phenomena is one of the primary goals of this book. Through this comparative perspective, the pages that follow seek to identify patterns in the Pueblo Revolt story that are characteristic of anticolonial liberation movements worldwide. This anthropological perspective can help to shed light on some of the seemingly alien elements of this story, explaining in part why things happened as they did. Why, for example, were fire-spewing spirits necessary to provoke the Pueblos to finally rise up? Why did some Pueblos ally themselves with the Spaniards and fight against their Native brethren at the end of the Revolt era? And why did the Jemez call on saints for protection against the Christian Spaniards in battle? On one level, these historical details are necessarily particular to late-seventeenth-century New Mexico. Yet they are also emblematic of larger processes of colonialism and anticolonial resistance that have repeatedly characterized the encounters between Europeans and colonized Others over the past five hundred years.

This is not simply a matter of anthropology coming to the aid of history, however. The anthropology of colonialism needs specific historical studies at least as much as the opposite is true. Studies of colonial processes must be grounded in historically specific accounts and localized contexts, lest the varied articulations of "colonialism" be melded into a monolithic, totalizing entity. Nicholas Thomas (1994:iv) draws attention to the danger of de-contextualizing colonialism, criticizing studies that would "put Fanon and Lacan (or Derrida) into a blender and take the result to be equally appetizing for premodern and modern; for Asian, African, and American; for metropolitan, settler, indigenous, and diasporic subjects." This book takes the opposite approach, starting from the specifics of indigenous life in colonial New Mexico and looking to a wider literature in an attempt to make sense of these events.

Claude Lévi-Strauss, one of the patriarchs of modern anthropology, famously opined that history and anthropology share similar goals. Both disciplines are "concerned with societies *other* than the one in which we live. Whether this *otherness* is due to remoteness in time . . . or to remoteness in space, or even to cultural heterogeneity, is of secondary importance compared to the basic similarity of perspective." Anthropologists and historians share a struggle to discern systems of representation different from their own, a fact which guarantees that "the best ethnographic study will never make the reader a Native," nor will the best history ever be an exact reproduction of past events. "All that the historian or ethnographer can do," writes Lévi-Strauss, "is to enlarge a specific experience to the dimensions of a more general one" (1963:16–17).

The larger implication of this otherness is that we cannot interpret the cultural logics of historical and ethnographic subjects simply by appealing to "common sense." This is where anthropological theory can help. Although often portrayed (and despised) by nonacademics and scholars alike as confusing, impenetrable, and unnecessarily filled with jargon, social theory can aid in the interpretation of cultural and chronological Others by questioning commonsense views about the meanings of past events and actions. According to modern Western rationality, the Native revolts of the past were virtually all unsuccessful, doomed to fail due to the "backward" behavior of the insurgents. Anthropology helps us to see these events very differently. In the pages that follow, I attempt to understand the cultural phenomena of the Pueblo Revolt era in new ways by bringing this history into a larger dialogue with anthropological theory, focusing on three core themes: subaltern resistance, cultural revitalization, and the importance of signs in colonial relations.

Subaltern Resistance

In order to better understand the actions of Pueblo peoples during the Pueblo Revolt era, this book draws on a larger literature investigating the role of subalterns in shaping history. In brief, subalternity refers to the condition of people who are systematically excluded from power, public discourse, and as a result, from official versions of history. Originally derived from a military term denoting "those of inferior rank," the word *subaltern* was adopted by the nineteenth-century philosopher Antonio Gramsci to designate "groups in society who are subject to the hegemony of the ruling classes" (Ashcroft et al. 2000:215). Subaltern groups commonly include peasants, laborers, and, in colonial situations, colonized and indigenous populations. Gramsci introduced the term as a substitute for "proletariat," but in the hands of postcolonial scholars the concept has assumed a more limited meaning over the past thirty years.[10] Subalternity is not, warns Gayatri Chakravorty Spivak, "just a classy word for oppressed, for Other, for somebody who's not getting a piece of the pie" (quoted in de Kock 1992:45). More accurately, *subaltern* is used today to refer to those persons who are unable to access dominant forms of representation. It denotes people who are systematically and institutionally barred from speaking for themselves, or who are unable to be heard by those in power. As a result, subalterns are structurally written out of official histories. In the context of Pueblo Revolt historiography, subalternity characterizes most of the Native peoples of New Mexico, but not all. As we shall see, some Pueblo elites did manage to insert their voices into official chronicles—all males, and mostly colonial sympathizers (but including a few others who bitterly opposed the Spaniards' rule). The rest, however, have been silenced by what historian E. P. Thompson (1963:12) famously termed "the enormous condescension of posterity."

Giving voice to the subalterns of history was the primary aim of a cadre of postcolonial historians known as the Subaltern Studies Group, from whom I draw inspiration. In a series of texts published throughout the 1980s and 1990s, these scholars attempted to rectify the tendency of official historiography to focus on elites and elite culture (Guha 1982). Their goal was to rewrite colonial history "from the distinct and separate point of view of the masses, using unconventional or neglected sources" (Said 1988:vi), a desire clearly shared by much of contemporary historical archaeology. Of particular interest was the history of subaltern resistance and rebellion. An earlier generation of British Marxist historians, led by Eric Hobsbawm (1959), had characterized forms of "primitive rebellion" (banditry, jacquerie, millenarian outbreaks, etc.) as groundwork for later political revolutions and, eventually, the formation of modern states. The genius of the Subaltern Studies Group (led by historian Ranajit Guha) was their attempt to understand subaltern rebellion on its own terms. This was more than merely the appropriation of Marxist history-from-below by "Third World" scholars (Dirlik 1997; see Chakrabarty 2000:9). Rather, Guha and his colleagues sought to understand the emic tactical and political logic of peasant rebellion, and in so doing, to give voice to the subalterns of colonial history.

Contemporaneous with the development of subaltern studies, historical archaeology has shifted its attention over the past thirty years from a predominant focus on the material culture of colonists to documenting the (literally) buried histories of marginalized groups—women, children, ethnic minorities, disenfranchised groups, enslaved persons, nonliterate members of society, and indigenous peoples, among others. Historical archaeologists have only recently begun to adopt the insights of postcolonial theorists, however. Importantly, members of the Subaltern Studies Group sought not only to document the experiences of subalterns, but to rescue them from the categories of "backwardness" to which non-Western practices are so often relegated. This book attempts the same, aspiring to new understandings of subaltern motivations and actions during the Pueblo Revolt era. Rather than appealing to contemporary Western models of revolution (that rely on notions of success or failure), *Revolt: An Archaeological History* attempts to understand the cultural logics of Native actors through a grammar based in subalternity. Furthermore, inspired by the work of the Subaltern Studies Group, this book seeks to rewrite the history of the Pueblo Revolt using a similarly unconventional and previously neglected source: material culture.

Historical examinations of subaltern resistance are not without their critics, however. Most famously, Spivak questioned the ability to give voice to the subalterns of history in a now-famous essay entitled "Can the Subaltern Speak?" (1985), in which she asserted that the exercise of representing subalterns in the past is an impossible task. By definition subalterns do not represent themselves in historical texts, so according to Spivak they only become a medium through which competing discourses about history represent their own claims—they can never, by their very nature, be "given a voice." Subaltern women, she claims, are often doubly hidden in colonial history, silenced first by their own cultures, and again by that of the colonizer. In her view, we are fooling ourselves if we assert that we can recover subaltern voices, because in truth we are only projecting our voices into their mouths. Thus Spivak ultimately answers her interrogative in the negative, insisting that "the subaltern cannot speak." Yet her point is not to stifle the investigation of subalternity entirely, noting that ignorance of subalterns continues the colonialist project of silencing the oppressed and marginalized of history. Furthermore, in some cases it is precisely what *cannot* be said about the past that becomes important.

In historical archaeology the situation is more complex—unlike documents, which tend to be written by single authors or members of specific social classes, material culture is left behind by persons at all levels of society. In many cases, a record attesting to the life of the subalterns ignored by official histories does exist. However, this record does not speak for itself. It must be given a voice by archaeologists. Claiming to speak for—rather than about—subaltern groups in the past (or present) runs the risk of perpetuating colonial representations. The goal of this book, then, is not only to draw out the experiences of Pueblo peoples through the artifacts that constituted their daily lives, but to use material culture to access the story of those Pueblo persons who go unmentioned in historical texts.

Revitalization Movements

The second core theme of this book is the investigation of cultural revitalization. While Po'pay's call to arms was a distinctive episode in the history of the American Southwest, the events of that fateful August in New Mexico were far from unique. The Pueblo Revolt of 1680 was a classic example of the recurrent anthropological phenomenon known as a *revitalization movement*— a calculated, methodical effort to reform culture and society that frequently occurs in colonial situations. Anthropological literature is filled with examples of charismatic leaders attempting to rapidly (and sometimes violently) transform societies, most famously embodied in the Ghost Dances that swept across the western United States in the nineteenth century and the "Cargo Cults" that cropped up in the South Pacific following World War II. Similar phenomena have been documented in countless anthropological studies of millennialism, apocalypticism, utopian communities, nativistic movements, and messianic sects (Linton 1943; Worsley 1957; Lanternari 1963, 1974; Adas 1979; Osterreich 1991; Lindstrom 1993; Stewart and Harding 1999; Harkin 2004a; Robins 2005; Cave 2006). Anthony F. C. Wallace (1956) was the first to identify the similarities in these seemingly diverse events, coining the term *revitalization movement* to describe "deliberate, organized attempts by some members of a society to construct a more satisfying culture by rapid acceptance of a pattern of multiple innovations" (1970:188).[11]

Over the past half-century, revitalization movements have gained notoriety among anthropologists and the general public because they are commonly considered strange and anomalous events. Yet their characterization as bizarre and atypical overlooks one of the fundamental assertions of Wallace's theory: revitalization movements are remarkably common. Cultural revitalization is not limited to fringe cults, exotic locales, or supposedly 'simple' societies, but is a frequent occurrence among diverse groups around the world and at all levels of social complexity. As Wallace notes, "revitalization movements are evidently not unusual phenomena, but are recurrent features in human history. Probably few [persons] have lived who have not been involved in an instance of the revitalization process. They are, furthermore, of profound historical importance" (Wallace 1956:267).

Despite their proposed ubiquity and significance, interest in revitalization movements has waned among anthropologists in recent years. To be sure, the revitalization movement model is not without problems (Nicholas 1973:73–74; Roth 1992:219–226; Harkin 2004b:xxix; 2004c:143; Siikala 2004:88–89; Wallace 2004:viii). Built on the dominant paradigm of its day—the linear systems theory of the 1950s and 1960s—revitalization is sometimes regarded as "a concept whose time has come and gone" (Harkin 2004b:xviii). Wallace's groundbreaking 1956 study employs an "organismic" model of culture, which includes notions of cultural equilibrium and distortion that are widely questioned today (Wallace 1956:265–266, 2004:vii). Additionally, the original model can be criticized for homogenizing the variety

of political and economic contexts underlying differing cases of revitalization. Why then, it may be asked, in this age of post-isms—postmodernism,
poststructuralism, postcolonialism, and postprocessualism—(or as Sahlins
[1999:404] calls it, "afterology") should anthropologists and historians con-
cern themselves with a fifty-year-old model that to many seems quaint at
best, outdated and irrelevant at worst (Harkin 2004b:xviii)?

Yet to summarily dismiss the revitalization concept as obsolete risks throwing the theoretical baby out with the bathwater. Over the past half-century
the revitalization model has proven remarkably successful in the analysis of
recurring patterns of human behavior among diverse peoples in various times
and places (Harkin 2004b:xix)—so successful, in fact, that professional evan-
gelists have adopted Wallace's archetype as a blueprint for effective conversion
techniques (Peach 2001). Moreover, revitalization movements have proven to
be of profound historical importance, not just in Native North America, but
throughout the world (Wallace 1956:267). Christianity, Islam, Buddhism,
and the Church of Jesus Christ of Latter-Day Saints are probably the best-
known examples of successful revitalization movements, and the significance
of these religions in the formation of the modern world would be difficult to
overstate. Revitalization movements can and do have profound impacts on
cultures and histories, as did Po'pay's rebellion on the formation of modern
Pueblo society, which proved crucial to the development of the contemporary
American Southwest (Liebmann and Preucel 2007).

Consider, for example, the parallels between Po'pay and the Christian
Messiah he so vehemently denounced. Both were itinerant prophet-preachers
who claimed to communicate with supernatural powers. We know little (if
anything) about their upbringings and early years; each steps onto the pages
of history as an adult, and today we read primarily about their short public lives. Each was a rabble-rouser who inveighed against repressive colonial
regimes, challenging the authority of local leaders. Both Po'pay and Jesus
developed a following of loyal disciples who spread their message throughout the region. And each was publicly flogged by state officials for fomenting rebellion among a disgruntled populace. These similarities are not mere
coincidences. Both the Pueblo Revolt and early Christianity are archetypal
examples of revitalization movements.

Revitalization movements adhere to a distinctive pattern. Commonly
arising out of situations of stress or rapidly shifting power relations (Wallace
1956:269; Thornton 1981, 1982, 1986, 1990a; Martin 2004:67; McMullen
2004:267), they are typically inaugurated when a charismatic leader emerges
from the masses. This prophet is frequently the recipient of a revelation from
supernatural entities and speaks to a disenfranchised community suffering

under a system of oppression, exploitation, and chronic poverty. The leader
delivers a message of hope, a vision of better days ahead, and a promise of
improved lives for those who will heed the call. A small following develops
around the magnetic preacher at first, a core group of disciples who spread
the message to the larger populace. Over time believers grow in number and
zeal. In some cases the changes they promote become institutionalized and
a new religion or political system is established; more often the movement
loses momentum as the promised utopia is not realized, and the leader fades
into the shadows of history (Wallace 1956; Graziano 1999:11–13). Occasionally however, the transformations wrought by revitalization movements have
substantial and even world-changing consequences, as did the revitalization
of Pueblo culture that occurred in late seventeenth-century New Mexico.

Considering the proposed importance and prevalence of these events
throughout human history, the conspicuous absence of documented revitalization movements in archaeological contexts is surprising (Fry 1985:126–
128; Liebmann 2008:360). By any account, the number of published studies
utilizing Wallace's revitalization model to explain rapid transformations in
material culture is meager at best (Turnbaugh 1979; Fry 1985; Dahlin 1986;
Scott 1991; Bradley 1996; Preucel 2000a; Mills and Ferguson 2008; Liebmann 2008). This dearth of archaeological studies is ironic, as ethnographic
accounts of revitalization detail the distinctive roles frequently played by
material culture in these movements (see also Wagner 2006, 2010; Weisman
2007). The lack of identified instances of revitalization in the archaeological record is fueled in part by the assumption that the core characteristics
of these phenomena—charisma, revelation, and prophecy—are immaterial,
and therefore archaeologically invisible. Max Weber (1947:358–59) defines
charisma as "a certain quality of an individual personality, by virtue of which
he is set apart from ordinary men and treated as endowed with supernatural,
superhuman, or at least specifically exceptional powers or qualities." More
recently, Pierre Bourdieu (1987 [1971], 1991) has refined Weber's description, noting that charisma does not in fact reside within an individual (as
is often assumed), but is ascribed to that person from without by a community of believers. In other words, charisma is not a metaphysical quality,
but manifests itself only through the practices of a social group. In turn,
these practices are often mediated by material culture and inscribed into
the archaeological record. Consequently charisma (and revitalization) can be
discerned from the remains of the past, if archaeologists only learn to identify
the signatures of these practices (Fry 1985:128–29; Liebmann 2006:51).

By comparing the Pueblo Revolt to other revitalization movements and
weighing these analogies against archaeological and documentary data,

we can begin to fill in some of the gaps in the historical record and draw a more complete picture of the 1680 uprising and its aftermath. Conversely, by looking at the Pueblo Revolt era through the lens of revitalization movements, we stand to learn not only about the specific events that occurred in New Mexico during these years, but also about colonialism more generally. Over the past fifty years the revitalization concept has proven particularly useful in the investigation of colonial contexts, where Wallace's model presaged the postcolonial scholarship of today by emphasizing the hybrid nature of cultural formations and their underlying "chains of causality" that cross ethnic, linguistic, geographical, and political boundaries (Wallace 1956:265, 267; Harkin 2004b:xviii). This book builds on recent investigations of the archaeology of colonialism (Lightfoot 1995, 2005; Lyons and Papadopoulos 2002; Given 2004; Gosden 2004; Silliman 2004, 2005, 2009; Stein 2005; Trigg 2005; Voss 2005, 2008; Frink 2007; Loren 2008; Ferris 2009; Dietler 2010), and by employing the revitalization model it seeks to move beyond the examination of colonialism as a monolithic process to the investigation of a specific but recurring aspect of colonial encounters. Thus the application of Wallace's model to late-seventeenth-century New Mexico seems appropriate not only for what it can tell us about the Pueblo Revolt, but also because it can tell us about revitalization movements and colonialism more generally.

Signs of Struggle and the Struggle over Signs

The third theme that shapes this study is the attention paid to the central role of signs and symbols in Native revolts. To paraphrase Russian linguist Valentin Voloshinov (1973:23), the struggle between colonizer and colonized "is always carried out in an arena of signs." The manipulation and control of signs is at the core of colonial relationships, with negotiations regarding who gets to possess certain signs—and who determines their meaning— permeating all aspects of colonial life (Todorov 1984). Historical ethnographies of anticolonial resistance demonstrate that signs take on particular significance in the context of open rebellion. Colonial revolts are deeply semiotic processes, and although underpinned by environmental and material factors, they are energized and mediated through signs and metaphors (Comaroff and Comaroff 1991:4; Ranger 1975:166–177). This is not to deny the brute material realities of colonial subjugation, but rather to emphasize that signs of anticolonial resistance are not "merely symbolic"—they are the threads from which subaltern rebellion is woven.

Yet archaeologists are often uncomfortable with the interpretation of signs (or more accurately, the interpretation of symbolism). In a field fraught with inherent ambiguity, archaeologists gravitate toward aspects of material culture that are more easily quantifiable and less equivocal. Nonetheless, ethnographic and ethnohistoric studies of both revitalization and subaltern resistance have established the primary role of the world of signs in motivating indigenous revolts. For this reason, the study that follows pays particular attention to the role of signs in social life, as they appear in both the documentary and archaeological records. During the Pueblo Revolt era, many of the signifiers of the colonizing culture became unfixed. They were seized by the Pueblos and sometimes destroyed, sometimes revered, sometimes inverted, and sometimes redeployed. Nearly all were put to symbolic ends that were previously unforeseen (and certainly unintended, at least by the Franciscans). Conversely, by the end of the era some of the signs of the Pueblos were detached, reformulated, transformed, and utilized by the Spaniards as well.

In the Spaniards' absence, the Pueblos used signs to redefine themselves. In many cases, this involved the creation of entirely new forms of representation. In others, the reinterpretation of previously existing signs (both Native and foreign in origin) occurred. These signs were used in the Pueblos' attempts to formulate a distinctive, nativist culture in increasing opposition to that of the Spaniards. In seeking to document and investigate these practices, this book explores processes that, while situated in colonial New Mexico, have analogues throughout the post-colonial world. Colonized subjects the world over attempt to liberate themselves from the colonial yoke by escaping the constraints imposed on them through the signs and values of the dominant system. In doing so, they reconstruct new worlds that hearken back to idealized better days before their colonizers appeared. And yet, even as they attempt to free themselves from the trappings of colonialism, newly liberated peoples often seize its symbols and reconstruct them in their own image (see also Wagner 2010). The study that follows draws attention to these struggles, presenting a new reading of historical documents and the archaeological record that affords a primary role to signs in late-seventeenth-century Pueblo social life.

Collaborative Archaeology in the Jemez Province of New Mexico

The story that unfolds in part II of this book is grounded in the history of a particular Pueblo. Specifically, it pays attention to the events of 1680–96 in the Jemez Province of north-central New Mexico (see figure FM.2). The Jemez

Province has been the home of the Towa-speaking communities west of the Rio Grande—the Jemez people—from at least the early fourteenth century down to the present day (Reiter 1938; Ellis 1956; Elliott 1982, 1986; Kulisheck 2005; Liebmann 2006:117–119). A stalwart center of indigenous resistance throughout the Spanish colonial period, this region was a primary hub of revitalization activities during the Pueblo Revolt era. During the late seventeenth century, Native peoples from throughout the Southwest flocked to the Jemez Province for refuge and protection, and to aid in armed resistance against colonial occupation. This region is particularly appropriate for an archaeological study of the Pueblo Revolt and its aftermath because it contains the remains of four large Pueblo villages that were all constructed, occupied, and vacated between 1680 and 1696, providing a unique opportunity to examine the materiality of the Revolt-era revitalization movement. These sites share a distinctive combination of temporal control, clearly discernable architectural elements, and associated surficial ceramic assemblages. Furthermore, they provide a unique glimpse into multiple phases of the Pueblo Revolt era, with two villages founded during its early years (between 1680 and 1683), one during the middle stage (1689), and one during its denouement (1693–94). The archaeological record of the Jemez Province thus documents the drastic changes in settlement patterns, architecture, ceramic production, and trade that characterize the tumultuous period between the Revolt of 1680 and the Spanish reconquest of the 1690s.

The archaeology that is presented in this book is not, however, "traditional" in most senses of the word. Not a single trowel of dirt was excavated in the research process. No collections were made and stored on the shelves of a museum. And contemporary members of the Jemez Pueblo tribe participated in all phases of the research, from planning an appropriate research methodology, to collection of the data, to the interpretation of the results. In this way, the research presented here is representative of a new breed of collaborative archaeology that has developed over the past twenty years (McDavid 2002; Kerber 2006; Little and Shackel 2007; Colwell-Chanthaphonh and Ferguson 2006, 2008; Ferguson and Colwell-Chanthaphonh 2006; Silliman 2008; Philips and Allen 2010). And like much of the collaborative archaeology performed today in the United States, the origins of this project can be traced back to the 1990 passage of the Native American Graves Protection and Repatriation Act (NAGPRA).

NAGPRA is legislation enacted by the U.S. Congress that requires all museums receiving federal funding to conduct inventories of their collections and notify federally recognized tribes of the human remains and sacred objects stored on their shelves, and allows those tribes to determine the ultimate disposition of the human remains and objects in question (Mihesuah 2000; Bray 2001). It also establishes Native American ownership and control over the human remains and sacred objects discovered on federal lands after 1990, dramatically changing the relationships among Native Americans and archaeologists. Following the passage of this law, more than a few archaeologists predicted the demise of American archaeology as a result. They feared that not only would NAGPRA empty American museums, leaving cabinets bare and exhibition halls desolate, but also that Native American archaeology as a field of study would dry up, with researchers fleeing to conduct research in other places where they could once again excavate with impunity (Meighan 1996:212–13; see also Clark 1998, 1999, 2001, 2003). To these scholars, NAGPRA is a fundamentally negative force, destructive to the creation of archaeological knowledge and resulting in a diminution of our understandings of the Native American past.

In one sense the opponents of NAGPRA were right. It did cause the demise of archaeology in Native American contexts as it had been practiced for the previous 150 years. But they were wrong in predicting the death of the field. NAGPRA did not end archaeological research into the Native American past, but it did drastically change the way in which that research is conducted, as well as the relationships among Native Americans and archaeologists. And while NAGPRA resulted in the reburial of some human remains and artifacts, it was not antithetical to the creation of new archaeological knowledge. In many ways, NAGPRA has fostered the production of new understandings about the Native American past that would never have occurred in the absence of this law (Morgan 2010a). This book is one example. The study that follows was made possible not in spite of, but as a direct result of the passage of NAGPRA, and thus stands as a testament to the constructive aspects of the act.

In 1999, the Pueblo of Jemez reburied more than 2000 of their ancestors' remains at Pecos National Historical Park (PNHP) in the single largest reburial under NAGPRA on record. The human remains and funerary objects from Pecos Pueblo had been excavated by A. V. Kidder from 1915 to 1929 and were housed primarily at two museums: Harvard's Peabody Museum of Archaeology and Ethnology, and the Robert S. Peabody Museum at Phillips Academy in Andover, Massachusetts. During the long consultation process leading up to the repatriation, representatives from Jemez Pueblo, Phillips Academy Andover, and PNHP teamed up to found an educational and cultural exchange program that would bring together students from Jemez, Phillips Academy, and the Pecos community during the summers to learn more about each others' cultures and histories, creating a relationship of amity rather than enmity among these institutions. The program was dubbed

Pecos Pathways, and each year since 1998 students from these three entities have gathered together in the Southwest and New England.

At about the same time that the Pecos Pathways program was established, I entered graduate school to pursue a Ph.D. in Anthropology at the University of Pennsylvania. My advisor, Bob Preucel, had begun conducting research with Cochiti Pueblo on their Pueblo Revolt–era refuge, Kotyiti, and he suggested that I contact Jemez Pueblo to gauge their interest in launching a similar investigation of ancestral Jemez Revolt–era villages. I sent an e-mail to the director of the Jemez Department of Resource Protection, William Whatley, who was at the same time looking for a project that could involve the students of the Pecos Pathways program in archaeological research near Jemez Pueblo. It was a serendipitous turn of events, to be sure. As a result, in the summer of 2001 I traveled to Jemez and began talks with the tribal administration regarding my proposed research.

Jemez tribal representatives were understandably leery to engage in academic research, after enduring a series of fraught and troublesome encounters with anthropologists and archaeologists over the course of the past century. Most notably, Kidder's (1958) excavation of Pecos and Elsie Clews Parsons's (1925) ethnographic study of Jemez (which reproduced ritual paraphernalia and sacred knowledge deemed inappropriate for publication) had damaged the reputation of anthropologists at Jemez irreversibly. Given this rocky history, the Jemez wanted to ensure that their concerns would be addressed before approving any additional investigations. However, the tribal administration also had a newfound appreciation for archaeology in the context of NAGPRA as a result of the Pecos repatriation, and they were interested in my proposal in part because they saw it as a possible aid in establishing cultural affiliation with these archaeological sites. Before beginning any fieldwork, I met with tribal representatives to establish a research protocol. I wanted this project to be a true collaboration from the beginning, so I welcomed the opportunity to work together to establish a culturally appropriate research design.

We agreed immediately that it would be a completely noninvasive investigation. That is, no soil would be disturbed and no excavations of any sort would be performed. The goal, we decided, was to leave the archaeological sites we would investigate essentially untouched—to learn more by digging less. The sites would remain exactly the same when we left them as they had been when we arrived. Even the broken potsherds and lithic remains we studied would be returned to the sites after our investigations. I would work with the Department of Resource Protection to secure a permit from the U.S Forest Service (who currently manage the lands on which many ancestral Jemez sites were built), and to hire and train a crew of interns from the Pueblo to assist me in my investigations. We would collect two primary types of data: architectural/spatial information, recorded with a total station (an optical surveying instrument) and ground-penetrating radar; and ceramic data from the pottery scattered across the surface of each site. At the end of each season I would update the governor of the Pueblo, the Tribal Council, and the Tribal Administration regarding the status and results of my research. The Pueblo would be given the chance to review and comment on all resulting publications (including this book).

I must not have said anything particularly offensive in that first season, because when I contacted the governor of the Pueblo and the Department of Resource Protection the next spring they invited me to once again work with the Pecos Pathways program. After my third field season, the Jemez Department of Resource Protection hired me as their tribal archaeologist and NAGPRA program coordinator. In this capacity I continued my research, making regular presentations to the Tribal Council and the Pueblo's Cultural Resource Advisory Committee, and visiting archaeological sites with tribal members to seek their input. In all, I conducted five seasons of fieldwork in the summers of 2001–2005, lived in the Jemez Valley between 2003 and 2005 (working for the tribe), and returned for three more summers of fieldwork between 2006 and 2008 to augment my dissertation data. The results of this research are contained in this book.

When discussing collaborative archaeological research with colleagues, I am frequently asked whether I see an inherent conflict between what is perceived as tribal control of information and objective scientific inquiry. How can you produce good scholarship (i.e., disinterested research), the argument goes, while at the same time adhering to restrictions placed on that research by tribal collaborators? In theory such a conflict could indeed prove problematic. In practice, however, this is an obstacle that never presented itself in the course of our research. In fact, tribal collaboration has been instrumental in improving the quality of the archaeology presented here, as it served as an additional form of peer-review. Often the vetting process provided by tribal members was far more rigorous and critical than that of my academic colleagues. Through these critical reviews of our research and my conclusions, the opinions and information provided by tribal members have proven crucial in enhancing and enriching the final product that appears between these covers.

Surface Archaeology

Our choice of a noninvasive research strategy was appropriate for multiple reasons. First and foremost, it ensured that there would be absolutely no disturbance of graves or human remains interred at any of the sites in question, an unconditional prerequisite for any new archaeological research from the Pueblo's perspective. Second, it was ethically responsible from a preservation perspective, as it meant that there would be no destruction of the precious, nonrenewable archaeological resources of the Jemez Province. And third, the sites under consideration were by their very nature amenable to surface studies. Each had relatively brief, late-seventeenth-century occupations (ranging from a matter of months to sixteen years), and their architectural plans are generally not obscured by earlier or later settlement. All exhibit highly visible surficial architectural remains (including standing walls), and abundant ceramic assemblages are evident on the surface at most of these villages. Furthermore, the surficial records of these sites offered appropriate and sufficient evidence to answer our proposed research questions.

Noninvasive (or "surface") archaeology has gained credence in recent years as a viable and valuable research strategy in a broad range of archaeological contexts the world over (Sullivan 1998a; Neuzil et al. 2007). This has not always been the case; in fact, the interpretive potential of surface remains has been a point of contention among archaeologists for decades (Lewarch and O'Brien 1981). In the past, archaeologists often ignored or denied the analytic value of the surface artifact assemblage. Surface remains were considered contaminated at best, an obstacle to be removed in order to access "pristine" (i.e., subsurface) data at worst. The research potential of the superstratum was often thought to be limited to simply locating subsurface archaeological remains. In contrast, proponents of noninvasive archaeology have maintained that, in the words of Alan Sullivan, "the value of surface archaeological phenomena neither depends upon nor derives from characteristics of subsurface archaeological phenomena" (1998b:xi). Furthermore, they point out that the majority of the underground archaeological record is ultimately formed out of surficial depositional events and processes (Dunnell and Dancey 1983:269). Surface remains are thus worthy of archaeological attention not only because they are accessible and economical to study, but because of their inherent potential to improve our understanding of the human past (Tainter 1998:169). This is particularly so when that past involves behaviors and events likely to produce surficial (as opposed to deeply stratified) remains, such as high mobility, short-term sedentism, warfare, and rapid evacuation.

There are, of course, limits to the interpretive potential of noninvasive archaeology. What you see on the surface is not necessarily what exists underground (Simmons 1998:159). Surface archaeology has the potential to make a significant contribution to our understanding of the human past only if archaeologists critically assess the surficial archaeological record. Part of this evaluation process includes a determination of the degree to which the origins of artifacts and features discernable on the surface can be reliably ascertained (Lewarch and O'Brien 1981:298). Furthermore, the research questions addressed by surface remains must be appropriate in terms of focus and scale. Noninvasive archaeology cannot answer every question about the past, nor does it provide a complete picture of all earlier times (but neither does excavation). Yet when applied to appropriate contexts and research questions, surface archaeology has proven to be an indispensable tool for advancing our understanding of the human past.

Organization of This Book

Revolt: An Archaeological History of Pueblo Resistance and Revitalization in 17th Century New Mexico examines the Pueblo Revolt era from its roots in the initial colonization of New Mexico down to its most recent consequences in the present day. But its primary focus examines the transformations that occurred between 1680 and 1694 in the Pueblo world (and more specifically, in the Jemez Province). Accordingly, this book is divided into three parts, detailing three stages roughly corresponding with what historian John Kessell has termed "the Pueblo-Spanish War": the era leading up to and including the Pueblo Revolt of 1680; the twelve-year period of Pueblo independence that followed; and the events of the Spanish reconquest (Kessell and Hendricks 1992:11; Kessell 2008:130). Part I examines Pueblo life during the early days of Spanish colonization, with chapter 2 detailing the transformations and violent subjugation that occurred between 1598 and 1680 in New Mexico. This chapter draws on historical (documentary) and archaeological sources to draw a picture of Pueblo life in the seventeenth century in an attempt to answer the question, "Why did the Pueblos revolt in 1680?" As such, it details a variety of factors that contributed to Pueblo discontent, ultimately providing fertile grounds for a revitalization movement and the impetus for Po'pay's revolution. Chapter 3 focuses more specifically on the events of Po'pay's rebellion. It details the organization of the insurgency in the years and months leading up to the fateful events of August 1680, the execution of the uprising, the subsequent siege on Santa Fe, and the ultimate expulsion of the Spaniards from New Mexico.

Part II chronicles the period of Pueblo independence (also known as the Spanish interregnum) from 1680 to 1692. It opens with the events that occurred during the earliest phase of this post-colonial liberation, describing Po'pay's reign in the immediate absence of the Spaniards. Chapter 4 goes on to detail Governor Otermín's abortive attempt to reconquer the Pueblos in 1681, and the removal of Po'pay, who was ousted from power within a year of the uprising. Chapter 5 considers the ways in which Pueblo peoples physically rebuilt their world during this period through an investigation of the construction of new villages in the Jemez Province and elsewhere, and the resulting factionalism that occurred in numerous Pueblo communities during this period.

Chapter 6 investigates the various ways in which nativism and revivalism shaped and were shaped by the material culture of the Jemez Province during this period, investigating these phenomena in the light of recent anthropological research on social memory. An examination of the ceramics and architecture of the Jemez villages of Patokwa and Boletsakwa reveals some of the changes in settlement patterns, social organization, and identities that occurred after the Revolt. This theme continues in (and is complicated by the findings of) chapter 7, which examines the phenomenon of postcolonial catachresis (the appropriation and deployment of the signs and symbols of the colonizer by colonized peoples). It details the creative ways in which Spanish ideology, technology, and innovations were transformed and redeployed to serve the purposes of the Native peoples of New Mexico in their colonizers' absence.

Part II concludes with an examination of the latter years of Pueblo independence (chapter 8), when Pueblo factionalism degenerated into inter-Pueblo warfare, and repeated incursions by the Spaniards forced further population shifts and the construction of new villages. This chapter examines the profound ambivalence of the Puname Pueblos of Zia and Santa Ana toward Spanish rule, a common response of colonized peoples in decolonizing (and recolonizing) contexts. The Puname Pueblos entered the late 1680s strongly opposed to Spanish attempts to regain the region but emerged as the Spaniards' strongest allies when the foreigners returned to New Mexico in the early 1690s.

Part III explores the final violent phase of the Pueblo-Spanish War, from the so-called "Bloodless Reconquest" of 1692 to the closing battles of the *reconquista* in 1694. Chapter 9 recounts the return of the Spaniards under Diego de Vargas in 1692, the resettlement of the colony in 1693, and the battles of 1694 that closed the curtain on the Pueblo Revolt era. The arrival of a new crop of colonists stimulated further shifts in Pueblo settlement and alliances and helped to incite new inter-Pueblo animosities, as various villages either resisted or allied with the returning Spaniards. By 1694 the anticolonial Pueblos were offering armed resistance to the Spaniards and their allies, and chapter 9 describes the construction of a final new village by the Jemez in anticipation of the penultimate military encounter of the Pueblo

Revolt era. Jemez oral traditions, Spanish military records, and archaeology are combined to reveal the details of this battle. The chapter goes on to examine the impacts of this skirmish on Jemez revitalization, as well as Jemez-Spanish relations and the further breakdown of inter-Pueblo alliances that characterized the final act of the Pueblo Revolt saga.

In the conclusion I examine the implications of this study for the anthropological study of subaltern resistance and revitalization movements more generally. The book closes with a brief assessment of the enduring legacy of the Pueblo Revolt for the people of Jemez and the other Pueblos today, suggesting that the Revolt should not be viewed as a "failed" attempt at revitalization or revolution. In fact, the cultural formations forged in the 1680s and 1690s continue to shape Pueblo culture and society in the twenty-first century. The conclusion goes on to situate the specific historical example of the Pueblo Revolt within the larger anthropological phenomena of subaltern resistance and revitalization movements more generally.

Following the conclusion, a brief epilogue details the events of the Pueblo Revolt of 1696 (also known as "the Second Pueblo Revolt") in the Jemez Province, providing the coda to the symphony of archaeology, anthropology, and history that comprises the Pueblo Revolt story.

Part I

The Genesis of a Prophecy: 1598–1680

2

Life under the Mission Bell

WHY DID THE PUEBLOS REVOLT IN 1680, driving Spanish colonists out of northern New Mexico? Investigators have debated this question for more than three centuries. In the days and weeks immediately following the uprising, the newly exiled friars framed their inquiries in theological terms, asking whether the uprising was the work of God or that of the devil. But as the years passed, investigators expanded their queries into the secular realm. Was it inspired by outside agitators, or did the impetus for rebellion come from within the Pueblos? Did the Spaniards bear any responsibility, or was this wholly the work of the Indians? Did it result from short-term environmental factors or long-term ethnic miscegenation? What were the relative roles of religion versus economics? Did a single leader make the Revolt possible, or was it the work of a larger body (D. Weber 1999a; Liebmann 2006:53–59)?

There are no simple answers to these questions. According to philosopher Louis Althusser, revolutions such as this are "overdetermined" (2005 [1962]:106–107). That is, these social upheavals result from a combination of heterogeneous factors, no one of which can be isolated as the single cause of the rebellion. The choice to take up arms against their oppressors must have been an agonizing one for the Pueblo warriors. It meant risking not only their own lives but also those of their loved ones. Both sides suffered casualties in the hundreds over the course of two violent weeks, with 401 deaths reported on the Spaniards' side and more than 350 among the Pueblos. What then caused the Native people of New Mexico to risk it all that fateful August? In order to answer these questions, the pages that follow sketch out some of the major causes of Pueblo distress under Spanish rule. As such this chapter does not provide a comprehensive chronicle of Pueblo-Spanish relations in the sixteenth and seventeenth centuries. Rather it attempts to establish the main factors behind the Pueblos' discontent, in order to provide insight into the rationale behind their decision to heed Po'pay's call in 1680.

Northern New Mexico on the Eve of Colonization

The seeds of the Pueblo Revolt were sown nearly a century and a half earlier, when mounted Spaniards first set foot and hoof into the sands of the Rio Grande valley, accompanied by numerous enslaved Africans and thousands of indigenous Mexican auxiliaries (Flint 2008). The earliest conquistadores and Catholic priests to venture into Pueblo territory in the sixteenth century were members of exploratory parties that did not intend to settle among the Pueblos permanently (including the expeditions of de Niza [1539], Vasquez de Coronado [1540–42], Rodriguez and Chamuscado [1581–82], Espejo [1582–83], and Castaño de Sosa [1590–91]). These early *entradas* were often cruel in their treatment of the indigenous population as they searched for souls and new sources of wealth. But their presence was temporary and as such it was endured, if not welcomed, by the Natives of the northern Rio Grande.

This is not to suggest that the pre-Hispanic Pueblo world was a united, integrated entity. Prior to the Spaniards' arrival it is doubtful that the Pueblos thought of themselves as inhabiting a single shared region. At the time the people who came to be known as "Pueblo Indians" first encountered the strangers with hairy faces in the mid-1500s, they lived in an estimated seventy-five to one hundred different villages located throughout modern-day New Mexico and northeastern Arizona (Schroeder 1979; Pratt and Snow 1988). These settlements generally consisted of multistoried masonry or adobe dwellings bordering on central plazas, varying in size from just a few rooms to numbers in the thousands, with multiple plazas and numerous kivas (Haas and Creamer 1992). Although these peoples shared broad similarities in material culture, subsistence strategies, religious practices, and political organization, they differed in many significant ways as well. They spoke seven separate, mutually unintelligible languages, each with multiple dialects. (Six of these are still spoken today.) As a result, the village-dwelling Natives of the northern Rio Grande did not think of themselves as a unitary ethnic group. Rather, sixteenth-century Pueblo villages were loosely organized into a series of dispersed settlement clusters, each with broadly defined, separate ethnolinguistic identities (Adams and Duff 2004; Snead et al. 2004:27). When the first European explorers ventured up the Jemez River in 1541, for example, they recorded a cluster of seven pueblos whose inhabitants identified themselves as ethnically "Hemes," distinct from the neighboring Tewa Province of Yunque-yunque.[1]

Neither was the Pueblos' pre-Hispanic existence a paradisiacal utopia. While it is true that on the eve of contact with Europeans the Pueblos were yet to be plagued by the ills associated with exploitation and colonization, their lives were not without hardship. The haunting specter of recurrent droughts contributed to repeated migrations and general population decline in the late 1400s–early 1500s. Pueblo populations suffered from chronic malnutrition as well as vitamin and mineral deficiencies in the century before the Spaniards arrived, with anemia ubiquitous in late pre-Columbian times (Stodder and Martin 1992:58–59; Stodder et al. 2002; Kellner et al. 2010:82). Conflict appears to have affected Pueblo settlement and social life to a significant degree in the century before the Spaniards' arrival as well, with settlement layouts and population consolidation apparently structured in large part by defensive concerns. In fact, the Spaniards commented on the ubiquity of warfare among the Pueblos almost immediately on their arrival in the 1540s. The newcomers noted both the sophisticated battle tactics employed by the Pueblos and the number of burned villages they encountered while traveling through the region, indicating that they had not crossed into a world of indigenous peace and harmony (LeBlanc 1999:44–54; Walker 2002:167; Kantner 2004:255).

The Gathering Storm, 1598–1680

The difficulties faced by the Pueblos in pre-Hispanic times were different in both degree and kind from those instigated by Spanish exploration and colonization, however. When Spaniards laid the foundations of the first mission churches and colonial settlements into New Mexican soil in 1598, the peoples they had labeled "Pueblo Indians" began to experience significant changes in the lifestyles they had cultivated for centuries. Spanish programs of taxation, forced labor, and evangelization—in addition to the introduction of epidemic diseases, drought, famine, and increased raiding by neighboring tribes—caused enduring and extensive stresses on Pueblo peoples throughout the seventeenth century.

The initial colonization effort in New Mexico was carried out under the auspices of don Juan de Oñate in 1598 (M. Simmons 1991a). Its effects on Pueblo peoples were immediate and largely deleterious. On their arrival Oñate's party evicted members of the winter moiety from a Tewa village which they promptly renamed "San Juan Pueblo" before moving into the newly "vacant" homes (Ellis and Ellis 1992; Riley 1999:75). The Spaniards reported this displacement to have been voluntary, but anthropologist and Ohkay Owingeh Native Alfonso Ortiz (1979:281) wonders "how many Spanish harquebuses the San Juan people were staring at when the request was made?" Shortly thereafter Spaniards took up residence in Pueblo

communities across the Southwest, establishing missions and colonial out-
posts throughout the region.

Repartimiento *and* Encomienda

The economic burden of supporting these newcomers fell immediately onto
the backs of the Pueblos. As vassals of the Spanish crown, all Pueblo households were required to pay tribute to the governor of the colony in the form
of clothing and maize. These taxes, and the manner in which they were levied, disrupted the economic systems the Pueblos had established over the
preceding centuries. Initially each Pueblo household was required to supply
one cotton blanket, tanned buckskin, or buffalo robe and one *fanega* (approximately 140 pounds) of maize per year.[2] But the Spaniards quickly com-
pounded the abuse of this system, increasing their tribute demands. Writing
in 1601, Fray Lope Izquierdo complained that "during the winter . . . our
men, with little consideration, took blankets away from the Indian women,
leaving them naked and shivering with cold. Finding themselves naked and
miserable, they embraced their children tightly in their arms to warm and
protect them." His contemporaries observed that clothing was collected with
such severity that the Pueblos were left with "nothing but what they had
on." As early as 1609, the Viceroy of New Spain noted that this tribute was
excessive and caused "much vexation and trouble" to the Natives.[3]

The increasingly harsh tribute demands levied by the Spaniards are reflected
in the archaeological record of seventeenth-century mission pueblos. Katherine Spielmann's investigations in the Salinas District document an increase
in antelope hunting at Pueblo Blanco during the early colonial era, likely
related to Spanish demands for animal hides. The faunal assemblage of the
nearby pueblo of Gran Quivira records a corresponding increase in hide pro-
cessing during the same period, suggesting that the residents of that pueblo
may have developed a specialization in tanning during this period in order to
meet the escalating tribute demands of the colonial government (Spielmann
et al. 2009:107–112).

During the first eighty years of Spanish rule many Pueblos fell under
the jurisdiction of the encomienda system, whereby favored subjects of the
Spanish crown (*encomenderos*) were extended the privilege of extracting tribute from a specified village or group of Indians, theoretically in exchange
for educating the neophytes in the ways of Christianity (Snow 1983; Anderson 1985; Trigg 2005:136–39). But the encomienda system did more than
simply burden the Pueblos with excessive tariffs. It weakened the economic

foundations of Pueblo society. In 1630, Fray Alonso de Benavides denounced the encomenderos' virtual enslavement of orphaned Pueblo children under the guise of charitable care. "Spanish governors . . . issue warrants or permits to take Indian boys and girls from the pueblos on the pretext that they are orphans," he wrote, "and take them to serve permanently in houses of the Spaniards where they remain as slaves." Others accused the encomenderos of grazing their herds in Pueblo fields, destroying crops and crippling the Pueblo economy in the process.[4]

Documents dating to the early seventeenth century record that in the fall of 1606 Oñate granted the pueblo of "Santiago de Jemez" in encomienda for three generations (Scholes 1944:340). To which ancestral Jemez village this refers is unclear,[5] but the establishment of the encomienda seems to have had little effect on the Jemez initially. Roof beams recovered from pueblos in the Jemez Valley suggest that construction continued in the region throughout the first decade of the 1600s (Reiter 1938:181; Ivey 1991:13). And if the inhabitants of the Jemez Province were being instructed in the ways of Christianity by an encomendero during this period it appears to have had little effect, as they were referred to as *infieles* (infidels) in a 1614 document. Yet even if they managed to escape the virtual enslavement of the encomienda system and the accompanying evangelization efforts in the first generation of Spanish colonization, they could not escape Spanish suzerainty entirely. Early seventeenth-century records indicate that the Jemez were subject to the payment of tribute in the form of the repartimiento.[6]

Repartimiento was a system that forced Pueblo workers to provide labor for Spanish farms and estancias. The stress of increased labor demands was inscribed indelibly on Pueblo bodies. Bioarchaeological studies detect increased stress on the shoulders and arms of Pueblo men during the colonial period, markers consistent with an increase in burden-bearing. Older women appear to have been drawn into the labor pool in increasing numbers as well, judging from the musculoskeletal stress markers on their spines, hands, and forearms (Morgan 2010b:37; Spielmann et al. 2009:118). Under the repartimiento system the Pueblos commonly complained of being forced to toil in Spanish fields during the weeks when they were most needed at home: planting and harvest season. This caused a decline in the amount of foodstuffs gathered annually by the Pueblos, reducing their reserves to dangerously low levels.

Even worse was the blatant sacking of Pueblo stores of maize by the colonists. In the early seventeenth century the Spaniards reported sending "people out every month in various directions to bring maize from the pueblos. The feelings of the Natives against supplying it cannot be exaggerated . . . for they weep and cry out as if all their descendants were being killed." Archaeological studies suggest that Spanish demands for corn depleted reserves in the Salinas pueblos to such an extent that it disrupted long-standing Native trade networks (Spielmann et al. 2009:109). As the century progressed, the colonial government resorted to increasingly harsh and forceful methods to exact this tribute, including the use of violence, torture, and threats of military engagement (Hammond and Rey 1953, 2:608–610, 680; Anderson 1985:366). This increasingly harsh treatment of the Pueblos may be reflected in the skeletal remains from mission villages, which show an increase in violent injuries after the arrival of the Spaniards (Stodder et al. 2002:493; Bruwelheide et al. 2010:150–55).

The tribute levied on the Pueblos quickly depleted Native reserves. Within the first three years of colonial occupation Pueblo people were reported to be subsisting on "tomatoes mixed with sand and dirt . . . as they had nothing else to live on." By their own admission, the Spaniards had "taken away from them by force . . . what they had saved up for many years." This severe taxation resulted in an inversion of the New Mexican subsistence economy. Whereas on their arrival the Spaniards initially depended on the Pueblos for sustenance, by the end of the first decade of colonization the Natives were forced to rely on the Spaniards for access to food. Pueblo women are reported to have regularly followed the carts in which maize tribute was transported from the pueblos to the capital, in hopes of scavenging any stray cobs that might fall off.[7]

Evangelization and Conversion

The reduction of Pueblo food surpluses had the added effect of aiding the Franciscan missionary effort. The newly established churches served as access points for the redistribution of foodstuffs, storing the spoils of taxation and reallocating them to sufficiently subservient subjects. With their reserves exhausted, Pueblo peoples increasingly turned to the friars for access to maize. Fray Izquierdo reports of a woman "asking for aid in the best manner she knew, to keep from starving. She offered, if given food, to accept baptism for herself and her eight-year-old son. They were so weak, however, that the medicine and attention given them were not sufficient to save them from dying." By establishing missions as centers of redistribution, the Franciscans gained valuable capital in the New Mexican political economy as well. During times of hardship, mission silos became the sole source of subsistence, with the clergy serving as the gatekeepers of the storehouses.[8]

The Franciscan missionary program was not secondary to the colonization of New Mexico, but rather an essential and motivating factor. The Spanish claim to the New World was staked on papal bulls of 1493 that required the monarchs of Castile and Aragon to ensure the instruction of Natives in the Christian faith. Additional bulls in 1501 and 1508 left no doubt that the Crowns' primary responsibility (if not their principal ambition) was the salvation of indigenous souls. In fact, the official declarations of Spanish sovereigns unequivocally affirmed that conversion of Native populations was the fundamental aim of their colonial enterprise. This was reemphasized in New Mexico after 1608, when the territory changed from a proprietary venture funded by Oñate to a royal colony funded by the imperial treasury.[9]

Although the missions and the secular colonial administration existed in a symbiotic relationship, the political climate of New Mexico was characterized by significant church-state tensions for much of the seventeenth century. Franciscans, colonial officials, and encomenderos battled repeatedly during the early colonial period, with the Pueblos often caught in the middle. The friars and governors frequently fought over control of the Native labor pool, leaving the Pueblos in a precarious position—forced to choose between being good Christians in the service of God or loyal vassals in service of the Crown. Pleasing the governor might earn the friars' reprobation, while at other times secular officials punished the Pueblos for serving the Franciscans. In the 1660s, for example, the *alcalde mayor* (district officer) of the Salinas district was accused of whipping twenty Indians from the Pueblo of Quarai for the crime of singing in the choir during the celebration of a neighboring village's patron saint. The alcalde had ordered the residents not to "assist in the service of the convent, not even voluntarily," at the behest of the governor. The next day the priest preached a sermon stressing that there was only one power to whom the Indians were obliged, that of God, his church, and the pope. He further explained that the fifth commandment dictated that they honor not only their natural parents but their spiritual fathers as well, and thus they owed their support to the friars. The alcalde interrupted the priest's homily to reiterate an alternative perspective, suggesting that it was not only possible but also necessary to serve two masters. Cases such as this illustrate the point that in seventeenth-century New Mexico, there was often no way to be a "good Indian." Obeying one branch of the colonial system frequently meant defying the other.[10]

The friars were apparently blinded to the fact that, like the encomienda and repartimiento, the missions contributed to the pressures weighing on Pueblo society as well. The result was often more affliction than comfort among the Natives. In 1662 a Spanish soldier complained that the friars were not content with just a few helpers, but rather wanted "the Indians of the entire pueblo, for gathering piñon, weaving, painting, and making stockings. . . . And in all this, they greatly abused the Indians, men and women." Adding even more stress were the Spaniards' efforts to eradicate traditional Pueblo religion. Franciscans regularly attempted to drive the devil from the pueblos through destruction of Pueblo ceremonial chambers, confiscation of masks and ritual paraphernalia, prohibition of kachina dances, and periodic arrests of religious leaders (who they referred to as "sorcerers"). Typical of this fanatical zeal was the behavior of a young friar stationed at Pecos, who in 1620 ordered all the implements of Native religion to be smashed, including "many idols" of clay, stone, and wood, as well as other ceremonial paraphernalia. A decade later, Fray Benavides boasted that he had burned "more than a thousand idols of wood" in a single blaze while their shocked Pueblo warden looked on in dismay. Twenty years before the Revolt, the Franciscan leadership decreed an unconditional prohibition of kachina dances, and missionaries were instructed to collect and destroy all materials of "idolatry." Shortly thereafter, priests reportedly incinerated sixteen hundred kachina masks.[11]

Iconoclastic practices such as these are documented in the archaeological record as well. The dean of Southwestern archaeology, A. V. Kidder, unearthed caches of Pueblo ceremonial artifacts that had been "subjected to violent misuse" in seventeenth-century contexts at Pecos Pueblo, along with painted stone slabs that had been intentionally shattered, and smashed "idols" that were later reverently reassembled and curated. At the mission pueblos of Awat'ovi, Hawikku, Pecos, Abó, and Quarai, excavations have documented the backfilling and sometimes burning of kivas in the early seventeenth century, all presumably under the direction of the newly arrived friars. These activities are further corroborated by Pueblo oral traditions, which recount the destruction of altars and burning of ceremonial items in the plazas of villages.[12]

The Franciscans did not restrict their abuses solely to inanimate objects, however. Many turned their fervor on Pueblo persons directly. On learning that long hair was of great importance to Pueblo men, missionaries began to cut the Natives' tresses for even trivial transgressions. Loss of their hair was not only a great indignity to Pueblo people, but a foreboding omen. For the Pueblos, long hair represents the rain. To cut someone's hair is akin to cutting off the blessings of the spirits. So disturbing was this punishment that a colony of newly shorn, disgruntled, and unconverted Puebloans formed for a time at Acoma in the second decade of the 1600s. Shortly thereafter the Spanish government outlawed forcible hair cutting, although the practice continued throughout the seventeenth century.[13]

More common were the violent physical abuses enacted on Pueblo people by the priests. Corporal punishment was an accepted practice among the Franciscans, and whippings were carried out regularly in mission communities throughout the seventeenth century. Among the more brutal disciplinarians was Fray Salvador de Guerra, who in 1655 whipped a Hopi man for worshipping idols until "he was bathed in blood." Later the same day Guerra beat him again, doused him in turpentine and set him aflame. When interrogated regarding this incident, Guerra testified that he had in fact used beating and larding with turpentine to punish idolaters and children.[14] These statements are corroborated by the testimony of Pueblo witnesses who had seen "sinners" who were marked by burns:

> [Guerra] took from the Indians a great amount of cloth and tribute. The Indians went to the custodian to complain, or else to the governor. When the Indians returned to the said places, Fray Salvador had them brought to him, and he went to their homes to search them. He found some feathers or idols, and consequently seized [their owners] and ordered turpentine brought so as to set fire to them. . . . One of them he sent to [the witness's] pueblo. The Indian was about to die of his burns and could not walk.[15]

On another occasion, a man who had been set on fire by Guerra "got up, and desiring to go by a certain road where there is a tank of water, to throw himself in it. . . . Guerra mounted a horse, thinking that the Indian was going to complain to the government . . . and rode over him with his horse until he killed him." Such killing of Pueblo persons under the Spanish program of evangelization was unfortunately common. One witness testified that it was "considered a jest for the *doctrineros* [missionaries] to kill the Indians." Public executions of "idolaters" were commonplace as well: twenty-nine were hanged at Jemez in the 1640s, nine in the 1650s, and in the late 1660s "some were hanged and burned in the pueblo of Senecú as traitors and sorcerers."[16]

Reports of sexual abuse by clergymen abound as well. Documents from the Holy Office of the Inquisition dating to the 1660s are filled with sordid accounts of sexual exploitation in New Mexico, although considering the context in which these accusations were made they must be evaluated with a critical eye. Still, many of these accounts are corroborated by multiple sources (sometimes including the accused themselves) and attest to the fact that sexual abuse of Pueblo people by clergymen did occur in seventeenth-century missions. Among the more famous examples are the testimonies of twenty-two women from Tajique who accused a missionary of rape. A man charged that the same friar had "taken his wife away from him, and had obliged her every night to arise from her husband's side to go and sleep with him." The accused Franciscan admitted to having a child with this woman, and that "as a man, he had enjoyed" the mother. At Awat'ovi, a friar allegedly "had improper relations" with a woman, and then ordered a man who knew about it killed.

A similar charge was brought against a priest at Taos for the "crime of forcing a woman, splitting her throat, and burying her in his cell." Sexual relations between Franciscans and their parishioners were apparently common enough that in 1660, a priest matter-of-factly reported that "all the pueblos are full of friars' children," and that many of his fellow missionaries had concubines. In the 1630s, two women at Taos accused Fray Nicolas Hidalgo of murdering their husbands, raping them, and raising the children of these encounters as Spaniards with him in the mission. Hidalgo was also indicted for regularly sodomizing and castrating Pueblo men as a form of punishment.[17]

Although the accuracy and veracity of these inquisitional testimonies can be questioned, the abusive nature of the Spaniards is corroborated in Pueblo oral traditions. Hopi accounts of early Spanish contacts refer to the priests as *Tota'tsi*, a term which translates literally as "tyrant or dictator."[18] These histories tell of priests "who intimidated the people into slave labor under the threat 'that they would be slashed to death or punished in some way'" (Wiget 1982:185–86). In fact, scenes from this period may be depicted in petroglyphs near the Hopi village of Awat'ovi (Dongoske and Dongoske 2002). These oral traditions also detail "a deliberate ruse on the part of the priests to separate husbands and fathers from their families, thus permitting the priests free access to illicit affairs with the women." Oral traditions regarding missionaries at Shungopovi state that:

> the priests would send the husbands to the Little Colorado or to Moencopi for water. The men were not long deceived, however, and many went only a few miles before they returned to surprise the priest in their wives' sleeping chambers. They were punished for this, and as an alternative to visiting the women the priest began to bring the young girls to his house. One of the girls had a brother who found out about this and who confronted the priest with his knowledge and threatened to kill him, but the priest scared him away. The boy went to Awat'ovi and there learned that the abuse of the women was widespread.[19]

Other Hopi oral traditions detail various Spanish attempts to eradicate aspects of Native religion, including the suppression of kiva rituals, forbidding kachina dances, banning the production and use of *pahos* (prayer sticks), and compulsory attendance of Catholic masses (Wiget 1982:184–86).

Spanish missionary activities among the Pueblos sometimes included policies of *congregación* or *reducción*—attempts to move Native populations living in dispersed communities into fewer settlements to facilitate proselytization and instruction in European methods of farming. Although apparently not carried out systematically throughout New Mexico, in some areas these efforts produced a significant shift in settlement patterns, aiding in the attrition of the pueblos (Barrett 2002b:141; Rothschild 2003:96–119). The Jemez Province was affected by these policies more than any other Pueblo region. While the Jemez occupied between 10 and 15 primary pueblos on the eve of contact, missionary efforts reduced them to two main villages by the 1620s, and just one by 1680 (Kulisheck 2001; Kulisheck and Elliott 2005:5). According to the 1634 memorial of Benavides, because the priests "recogniz[ed] the impossibility of administering well to those Indian mountaineers," the friar who was stationed among the Jemez in the 1620s "induced them to live in a pueblo, which with their help he founded in a very suitable place."[20] The movement and disruptions caused by these policies almost certainly brought additional tensions into the lives of many Puebloans, as well as facilitating another major cause of stress in seventeenth-century Pueblo villages: disease.

Disease and Demographic Decline

Of all the stresses that Spanish colonization imposed on the Pueblo world, one of the most pernicious was the introduction of Old World diseases such as smallpox, measles, typhus, and influenza. Many regional Native American populations were decimated following prolonged contact with Europeans after 1492, and the Pueblos were no exception. As Ann Ramenofsky notes, "The virgin-soil status of native New Mexicans, coupled with a settlement form that was pre-adapted for disease contact, created an ideal setting for the transmission of infectious agents" (1996:177). While most scholars agree there was a general decline in population among the Pueblos during the Spanish colonial period, the degree, nature, and timing of this crash is widely debated (Scholes 1930; Schroeder 1972; Zubrow 1974; Reff 1991:228–230; Palkovich 1994; Ramenofsky 1996; Riley 1999:203; Barrett 2002a, 2002b; Kulisheck 2003, 2005, 2010; Ramenofsky et al. 2009; Wilcox 2009; Ramenofsky and Kulisheck in press). Accurate estimates of pre-Revolt Pueblo populations are hampered by the paucity of demographic evidence contained in historical records. Precious little data exists in the documentary record relating to the population of New Mexico between 1600 and 1680, largely due to the fact that the Natives destroyed most church records, including accounts of births, marriages, and deaths, in the wake of the Revolt.[21] Furthermore, the calculations made by missionaries during this period were sometimes grossly exaggerated in a deliberate bid to impress royal authorities and generate additional support from the government. Nevertheless, Franciscan records do indicate a general decline in population throughout the eight decades from 1600 to 1680, a period when overstating population estimates would often have been to the friars' benefit.[22]

Although documentary evidence regarding epidemic disease among the seventeenth-century Pueblos is meager, a few references do indicate that outbreaks occurred with sufficient frequency to negatively impact Pueblo populations. Oñate estimated the total Pueblo population at the turn of the seventeenth century to be around sixty thousand.[23] An epidemic in 1636 reduced this population by as much as one-third, causing the Franciscan commissary-general to estimate that by 1638 the total number had declined to forty thousand or less due to "the very active prevalence during these last years of smallpox and the sickness of which the Mexicans called *cocolitzli* [typhus]."[24] While these figures may be neither precise nor accurate, they nonetheless document a perceived reduction in population due to the arrival of what the Pueblos termed the *Kliwah* ("refuse wind," a spirit who visits sickness on the village [Parsons 1939, 2:938]). Ann Palkovitch (1994:93) estimates Pueblo population losses of up to 60–70 percent for the years 1606 to 1638. Another scourge of smallpox struck in 1640 killing an estimated 3,000, or nearly 10 percent of the Pueblo population at that time. Between 1622 and 1641, the Pecos population is estimated to have declined by 40 percent, from just over 2,000 to 1,189 (Kessell 1979:163, 170). Moreover, the destruction wrought by disease is evident in the number of pueblos vacated throughout the sixteenth and seventeenth centuries. Between 1540 and 1643, the number of Pueblo villages was reduced from an estimated seventy-five to a hundred pueblos to a total of just forty-five (Schroeder 1972:55, 1979; Barrett 2002a:62; Rothschild 2003:60).

Recent scholarship by Jeremy Kulisheck and Ann Ramenofsky suggests that the greatest losses, both in terms of population and number of villages, were sustained during the years following 1650 (Kulisheck 2005, 2010; Ramenofsky and Kulisheck in press). Writing in 1697, Fray Augustín de Vetancurt suggested that between 1638 and 1660 the population declined by 42 percent to approximately twenty-four thousand. In 1671 another outbreak—whether caused by measles, smallpox, or typhus is unclear—struck the Pueblos. By the end of the 1670s only approximately seventeen thousand Puebloans remained (Frank 1998:66; Rothschild 2003:62). Even cautious estimates suggest that the Pueblo population decline during the first eight decades of the seventeenth century was drastic: for every three Puebloans in 1600, only one was left by 1680. Less conservative calculations reckon population losses at as high as 80 percent or more (Upham 1982; Reff 1991:229; Riley 1999:202).

Michael Wilcox has recently questioned the notion that Pueblo populations declined precipitously during the seventeenth century. He calls studies
of indigenous depopulation during the colonial period "terminal narratives,"
specifically invoking the "narratives of disease and abandonment deployed
by archaeologists" (2009:11). Wilcox criticizes these investigations as inherently Eurocentric and colonialist, suggesting that archaeologists and historians should emphasize the persistence of Native communities rather than
their supposed decline during the colonial period.[25] To support his argument
he cites the archaeological record of the Jemez Province, which he claims
provides evidence to "challenge the population crash models so frequently
deployed in historic period studies" (2009:175). While his questioning of
the politics behind these "terminal narratives" and the reliability of the Spanish documentary record in establishing absolute population estimates for the
Pueblos is laudable, the archaeological evidence Wilcox presents to refute
these narratives is largely inconclusive regarding seventeenth-century Jemez
demography.[26] Kulisheck's research on field houses in the Jemez Province
suggests that while the local population may have remained relatively stable
through the first half of the seventeenth century, large-scale depopulation
likely occurred after 1650 (Kulisheck 2001, 2003, 2005, 2010).

Wilcox acknowledges that drought and famine "compromised the health
of the Pueblos" during the seventeenth century, contributing to the depopulation of the region (2009:208), and that "a dwindling supply of Indian
labor" (2009:139) plagued the Spaniards during this period. However, he
locates the causes of this decline in the violent policies and brutal actions of
the Spaniards, and not in the passive realm of unintentionally introduced diseases. He concludes that the Pueblos revolted in 1680 out of fear for "the total
destruction of their cultures, religions, and communities" (2009:152) not
due to disease, but because of the cruel and sadistic practices of the colonists.

While violence clearly played a central role in Pueblo population decline, it
appears to have worked in concert with multiple waves of epidemic disease. On
the whole, then, the preponderance of the current available evidence—both documentary and archaeological—supports the notion that large-scale population
decline occurred among the Pueblos sometime between 1600 and 1680, and
it had a particularly devastating effect on the populace of the Jemez Province.

Raiding and Slaving

Prior to Spanish colonization, the Pueblos engaged in considerable interaction with their nomadic and seasonally mobile neighbors (the ancestors

of today's Ute, Navajo, and Apache tribes). Contacts among these groups date back to at least circa AD 1200, but archaeological research suggests that trade between Pueblos and Plains peoples intensified significantly after 1450, probably coinciding with an influx of Athapaskan-speaking peoples into the Southwest (the ancestors of the modern day Navajo and Apache). While instances of hostility and raiding undoubtedly occurred between these groups, archaeological studies suggest that the Pueblos had negotiated a delicate but relatively stable commercial relationship with nomadic hunters in the pre-Contact era based on trade and mutual benefit (Spielmann 1983, 1986, 1989, 1991; Spielmann et al. 2009; Baugh 1991; Habicht-Mauche 1991; Lintz 1991; Speth 1991). Thus when the Coronado expedition reached Pecos in 1540, they noted the uneasy truce that had evolved between the people of Pecos and the bison hunters of the southern Plains. Plains Apaches were said to spend the winter camped in the shadow of the pueblo, but were not fully trusted by those who lived within its walls. "Although they are received as friends, and trade with them," noted Coronado's chronicler, "[the Apaches] do not stay in the villages over night, but outside under the eaves."[27] Spanish colonization changed the dynamics of these relationships considerably.

The introduction of Old World domesticates such as cattle, sheep, and chickens to the Pueblos disrupted exchange by devaluing Plains trade items, particularly protein-rich foodstuffs such as bison meat. Spielmann's investigations documented a marked decrease in access to bison at Salinas pueblos during the mission period, presumably a by-product of the disruption in trade that resulted from Spanish incursions (Spielmann et al. 2009:109). This eventually contributed to a dramatic increase in the frequency and degree of hostilities between the Pueblos and proximate nomadic tribes. Possibly even more significant was the introduction of the horse. By the mid-seventeenth century, Plains Apaches had adopted an increasingly equestrian lifestyle, utilizing horses to dramatically improve the efficiency of hunting and raiding expeditions. Whereas previously the impacts of Ute and Athapaskan raiding parties were limited by what could be carried away on foot, the appropriation of the horse allowed these parties to seize substantially more loot per person, more frequently, and with greater speed. In fact, their mastery of horsemanship led the Spaniards to dub one group of Apaches "Los Faraones" because they resembled the swift cavalry of the biblical Pharaohs depicted in the Book of Exodus (John 1975:59; Lange 1979:202; Riley 1999:197; Brooks 2002:52–55). As early as 1607, these Apache incursions had become so problematic that a friar dispatched to Mexico City reported that the "peaceful Natives of New Mexico are frequently harassed by the attacks of the Apache Indians, who destroy and burn their pueblos, waylay and kill their people by treachery, steal their horses, and cause other damages."[28] That same year the encomendero of the Jemez Province was leading attacks against "Apaches" in retribution for raids on the Pueblos (Barrett 2002a:72).

These attacks seem to have contributed to the bouts of famine that plagued the Pueblos in the seventeenth century as well. In 1640, for example, Apache raids reportedly burned more than 20,000 fanegas (about 2.8 million pounds) of maize, which added insult to an injurious lack of rainfall and resulted in widespread famine and the death of three thousand Puebloans throughout the province. Similarly, in 1659 a Franciscan reported that "bands of heathen" had raided the pueblos of the Salinas District, Jemez, San Ildefonso, and San Felipe, killing Pueblo neophytes and taking others captive. Shortly thereafter, the Pueblos suffered so serious a famine that the Natives were reduced to eating grasses and even the earth itself (*tierra blanca*) in order to sustain themselves.[29]

In many cases, the hostilities of the nomadic hunters were carried out in retribution for Spanish slaving expeditions, which had captured Athapaskans to be sold in central Mexico or the mining towns of Nueva Vizcaya. Historian Andrés Reséndez notes that parish records from San José de Parral record the baptisms of enslaved Indians from New Mexico in steadily increasing numbers during the mid-seventeenth century, peaking in the five years leading up to 1680 (Table 2.1). Unfortunately for the Pueblos, their close association with the Spaniards made them prime targets for Athapaskan reprisals, and their villages bore the brunt of the Apaches' wrath (Scholes 1942:17; Brooks 2002:50–53). Simultaneous with this increase in raiding, the Spanish and Pueblo worlds became increasingly integrated (Knaut 1995:161). Whether

Table 2.1. Indians from New Mexico in baptismal records from Parral, Nueva Vizcaya (Griffen 1969:102)

Years	Apaches	Apaches from New Mexico	Indians from New Mexico	Quiviras	Total
1640–1644	0	0	0	0	0
1645–1648	2	0	5	0	7
1649–1655	9	4	8	0	21
1656–1660	14	1	34	0	49
1661–1665	20	0	8	1	29
1665–1670	4	2	95	1	102
1671–1675	45	0	22	2	69
1676–1680	100	1	15	5	121

this merger developed as a result of Athapaskan aggressions (i.e., the Pueblos became dependent on the Spaniards for military protection) or vice versa (i.e., the Athapaskans took to raiding because the Spaniards disrupted traditional trade relations with the Pueblos) is open to debate. In any case, Athapaskan raiding of Pueblo villages escalated in lockstep with an increase in Spanish slaving during the period from 1600 to 1680, adding to the growing stresses on Pueblo life that developed in the wake of Spanish colonization. Considering the fact that these slaving expeditions took a particularly large toll on Athapaskan tribes, it is easy to see why Apaches and Navajos supported Po'pay's call to arms with such vigor in 1680.

1663–1680: On the Razor's Edge

The pressures introduced into Native life by the colonization of New Mexico—taxation and encomienda, evangelization and religious repression, disease, slavery, and increased raiding—coalesced in the period immediately preceding the Revolt to squeeze the Pueblos like never before. Beginning in 1663 famine once again stalked New Mexico, and the priests resorted to handing out weekly rations in the hopes of keeping their parishioners from fleeing the missions.[30] The following year New Mexico entered one of the most severe periods of climatic stress on record. Tree-ring chronologies suggest that the period between 1664 and 1678 witnessed not only one of the most severe droughts in 1000 years (Salzer 2000; Grissino-Mayer et al. 2002), but also launched New Mexico into a harsh cold snap with devastating consequences. This cold drought combined shortened growing seasons with insufficient moisture, making desiccated stalks and shoots particularly vulnerable to crop-killing frosts (Van West et al. in press).

By 1668 the Rio Grande itself was running at a mere trickle, further straining the Pueblos that had come to depend on irrigation agriculture (Ivey 1994:82). Adding insult to injury was a "plague of locusts that laid waste [to] the fields" that same year. In the first half of 1669, Apache raids killed another 373 Puebloans, removing more than four thousand cattle, sheep, horses, and mules (Kessell 1979:218–219). The increasingly dire situation prompted the Franciscan commissary-general to write:

> This kingdom is seriously afflicted, suffering from two calamities, cause enough to finish it off, as is happening in fact with the greatest speed.
>
> The first of these calamities is that the whole land is at war with the very numerous nation of the heathen Apache Indians, who kill all the

Christian Indians they encounter. No road is safe. They are a brave and bold people. They hurl themselves at danger like people who know not God, nor that there is a hell.

The second calamity is that for three years no crop has been harvested. Last year 1668, a great many Indians perished of hunger, lying dead along the roads, in the ravines, and in their hovels. There were pueblos, like Las Humanas, where more than 450 died of hunger. The same calamity still prevails, for, because there is no money, there is not a fanega of maize or wheat in all the kingdom.[31]

By the 1670s the cycle of famine, raiding, and disease was spinning out of control. Apache attacks in the autumn of 1670 reduced the Pueblos to eating animal hides and the leather straps off their carts. Another bout of epidemic disease followed, afflicting the already weakened population with "a great pestilence [that] carried off many people and cattle." Still more mounted raids came in 1672, as the "province was totally sacked and robbed by attacks and outrages." Months later Athapaskans struck again at the Zuni mission of Hawikku, killing two hundred, taking a thousand captives, stealing all the livestock, and burning the village. By 1675 at least six pueblos were deserted and the rest were left in dire straits.[32]

It was clear to the Pueblos that praying to the Spaniards' tripartite God and the saints was ineffective in bringing back the rains and keeping the frosts at bay. They blamed the drought on the friars' forced cessation of rain-making dances, disrupting their delicate balance with nature. As a result, Pueblo peoples returned to the kachinas in droves between 1666 and 1675. Spanish civil and ecclesiastical authorities in turn united to suppress traditional Native religious practices in the most brutal campaign to date, compounding the misery of the Pueblos. Under the administration of Governor Juan Francisco Treviño (1675–77) Pueblo altars, prayer sticks, and masks were seized; dances forbidden; the gathering of assemblies in kivas outlawed; and many of the sacred chambers destroyed.[33]

Cultural Distortion

In his explication of the revitalization process, Wallace (1956:269, 1970, 1972) notes that periods of extreme stress such as this often produce situations of "cultural distortion." Under these conditions long-held cultural practices begin to change or are abandoned completely. At the same time aberrant behaviors increase. Traditional sexual and kinship mores are suddenly disregarded. The defiance of authority becomes commonplace. Intragroup violence increases. Not surprisingly, just such a period of "distortion" appears to have occurred among the Pueblos in the 1670s. However, Spanish records do not detail the internal strife that occurred within Pueblo communities prior to the Revolt, so it is admittedly difficult to assess the degree of social deviance prior to 1680 based on historical documents alone.

Pueblo oral traditions, on the other hand, clearly document cultural distortion in the late seventeenth century. An unambiguous example comes from Hopi accounts of the late seventeenth century, when the people were said to have entered a state of *koyaanisqatsi* (a "social disease of turmoil and corruption which affects the community").[34] Their licentious behavior included contempt and disregard for traditional authority figures, aberrant violence, and pervasive sexual deviance. "People began to change in their ways," recalls one Hopi man. "There was no mutual respect any more. They were constantly arguing and fighting with one another. People were robbed of their food." The males raped the women and girls, he reported. "People seemed to be blind to what they were doing. They got worse and worse. For example, if children encountered an old person relieving himself, they would smear excrement all over him." The lives of the people were, in his words, "completely insane" and in "utter chaos." Even the religious leaders, the keepers of sacred traditions, grew negligent in their duties. "Their minds were focused on bad things only. Wasting and undoing things was what they paid attention to." Their debauchery had ramifications for the natural world, too:

> Before long the rainfall became sparser and sparser. Although the crops were still growing, they did not grow as lushly any more. The harvests, too, were not as large as in prior years. The sorcerers who were responsible for these changes did not listen to anyone, neither their fathers nor their uncles. They also paid no attention to their religious beliefs. The words of their kachina godfathers and Powamuy godfathers meant nothing to them. . . . For this reason, all kinds of evil things took place in the village. People were even bewitching each other. The situation was as grave as it had been long ago in the underworld. People were on their own. They became more and more scared of the sorcerers and preferred to stay inside their homes.

"Life was out of joint," the narrator succinctly concludes.[35] By 1680, then, it had become abundantly clear to Pueblo people that theirs was a world out of balance.

A Legacy of Rebellion

The picture of Pueblo life in the early colonial period drawn here could be critiqued as partial, tendentious, and selective, emphasizing only the negatives that accompanied the arrival of the Spaniards. To be sure, Wallace's revitalization model draws more attention to the cultural trauma and social strains that preceded these movements than to the purported benefits of colonialism (possibly disproportionately so). This raises the question of whether the Spanish presence in New Mexico was entirely detrimental to Pueblo peoples. Van Hastings Garner (1999) has argued the contrary, contending that European colonialism provided "a feeling of security, well-being, and peace" as well as "a degree of prosperity" to the Pueblos, and that "there developed in New Mexico a degree of tolerance and many mutually advantageous accommodations" in the seventeenth century. Garner summarizes Pueblo-Spanish relations prior to 1680 as "a fairly stable arrangement . . . since it lasted for nearly three-quarters of a century" (1999:67–69). Certainly the introduction of Spanish crops and technologies provided some benefits to the Pueblos. Nevertheless, overly optimistic assessments of Pueblo life under colonial rule such as Garner's neglect to account for the long history of indigenous resistance to Spanish colonialism that occurred throughout the 1600s in the northern Rio Grande.

No less than eight Native revolts occurred among the Pueblos before the more famous and successful uprising of 1680. Many of these insurrections had their origins in the Jemez Province, where the first in this long series was initiated in 1623. Branded infidels a decade earlier, the Jemez burned two mission churches in an apparent protest against the Franciscan's persecution of their "idolatry," forcing the governor to dispatch a group of soldiers into the province in an abortive attempt to restore order. This coup was followed by a series of rebellions at other pueblos: at Zuni in 1632, at Taos in 1639, and again at Jemez sometime between 1644 and 1647. In this second Jemez rebellion the Pueblos allied with neighboring "Apaches" in plotting to overthrow the Spaniards, killing one colonist. For this plot the Jemez were punished "with just severity" when the governor of New Mexico hanged twenty-nine of their leaders, whipping others and sending some into forced servitude. A few years later the Jemez were again implicated in the planning of a rebellion in league with their Keres, southern Tiwa, and Apache neighbors, for which nine of the conspirators were executed. In 1665–68 the Piros and their Apache allies ambushed and killed five Spaniards (including the alcalde mayor of the district), and a short while later another charismatic Pueblo leader, Esteban Clemente of the Salinas District, organized a pan-Pueblo alliance that presaged Po'pay's coalition by more than a decade. The nature and frequency of all these revolts call into question Garner's assertion that Pueblo-Spanish relations were characterized by "a degree of tolerance . . . a feeling of security, well-being, and peace" throughout the 1600s (1999:68). Rather, these repeated uprisings suggest that relations among New Mexican colonists and the Pueblos during the seventeenth century were uneasy in the best of times, hostile and violent in the worst.[36]

The most important of these revolts in relation to the 1680 rebellion was the penultimate uprising that occurred in 1675. Originating in the Tewa region, it began with the alleged "bewitching" of Spanish colonists and missionaries by Pueblo holy men, supposedly resulting in ten deaths and the infliction of a Franciscan with an incurable sickness. The plot to curse the Spaniards quickly spread from Acoma to Pecos and north to Taos, ultimately resulting in the arrest of the forty-seven hechiceros. Four of these "sorcerers" were sentenced to death for conspiring against the Crown, with one hanged in each of the plazas of Tewa-speaking Nambe Pueblo, Keres-speaking San Felipe, and Towa-speaking Jemez. (The fourth committed suicide before his punishment could be meted out.) Some of the remaining conspirators were flogged, others were sold into slavery, and the rest were imprisoned.

Rather than quelling this challenge to colonial authority, the Spaniards' heavy-handed punishments provoked an unprecedented response among the Puebloans. More than seventy armed Native warriors stormed the governor's house in Santa Fe, demanding the release of their religious leaders. Had they been denied, these warriors planned to execute not only the governor but all the residents of Santa Fe (with the help of additional forces amassed outside the capital). Sensing the precarious nature of the situation, the governor assented to their demands, releasing the holy men and diffusing the immediate threat.[37] But the larger implications of this episode were not lost on the Natives. For the first time, the colonial subjects had been able to intimidate their colonizers through a show of force. This demonstrated to the Pueblos the viability of armed resistance, laying the foundations for the successful Native uprising that was to transpire five years later.

By the summer of 1680 the Pueblos were teetering on the edge of rebellion. They had demonstrated to themselves that they were not the pawns of the Spaniards. Po'pay was ensconced in the kiva at Taos, communing with the spirits. And then, sometime between June and August, unseasonably cold weather gripped the fields of northern New Mexico. Tree-ring chronologies suggest that two nights of sub-freezing temperatures were visited on the Pueblos like a biblical plague in the summer of 1680, destroying the crops in the fields (Van West et al. in press). It was too late in the growing season to replant. The harvest was lost. Starvation loomed. This was the last straw. In Pueblo minds, all their afflictions and tribulations could be attributed to a single source: the Spaniards. The foreigners had upset the delicate stability that the Pueblos struggled to maintain between themselves and their environment. Something drastic had to be done to restore balance.

3

"Apostatizing from the Holy Faith"

THE PUEBLO REVOLT OF 1680

OVER THE PAST THREE HUNDRED YEARS Po'pay has been characterized in various and often contradictory ways by many different people: holy
man and agent of Satan; passive priest and fierce warrior; cruel despot and
benevolent chief; devoutly religious recluse and rabble-rousing field marshal;
traditional Pueblo war captain and one who ruled in the manner of a Spanish
governor.[1] Po'pay seems to be all things to all people, eminently malleable
and ever-changing. Ironically, the degree of speculation regarding his identity
is inversely proportional to our meager knowledge about his background.
Written records reveal only his name, the fact that he hailed from Ohkay
Owingeh, and that he was arrested in the Spaniards' sweep of 1675 and subsequently sought refuge at Taos Pueblo. These skimpy hints have spawned considerable debate among modern scholars regarding Po'pay's identity (Chávez
1967; Ortiz 1980; Beninato 1990; Sando and Agoyo 2005). Nonetheless, by
combining the few scraps of evidence contained in Spanish records with contemporary Pueblo ethnography and oral traditions, we can begin to sketch a
preliminary picture of the main organizer of the Pueblo Revolt of 1680.

Anthropologist Alfonso Ortiz has looked to Po'pay's name for clues
regarding his social position. He notes that the name "Po'pay," which translates from the original Tewa as "ripe cultigens" or "ripe pumpkin," is laden
with meaning (Ortiz 1980:19–20). Tewa naming is a complex process, with
each child receiving two names during the initial year of life. The appellation
Po'pay does not follow the established rules for bestowing either of these birth
names, however. According to Ortiz, because the name Po'pay "is generic,
and therefore potent, it could not be conferred on an infant." Such a name
had to be earned in adulthood, typically through service in religious ritual.
In modern Tewa pueblos, these achieved names are commonly emblematic of
seasonal concepts or events. And because *Po'pay* refers to the time of harvest,
an event associated exclusively with the summer moiety among the Tewa,

this name suggests to Ortiz that Po'pay was "very likely a member of the summer moiety," and possibly the leader of the summer priesthood at Ohkay Owingeh (Ortiz 1969:30–35, 100–101, 1980:19–20).

Edward Dozier, an anthropologist from the Tewa pueblo of Santa Clara, similarly ventures that based on Po'pay's arrest as an accused hechicero, he could have occupied "any one of a number of positions in Tewa socioceremonial organization." He may indeed have been a moiety priest; alternatively, he may have been a member of a healing society, "or a member of the hunt association; or even a member of the warrior association." The initiates of these societies, he notes, comprise the elite social classes of the Tewa pueblos (Dozier 1970:56, 189). Alternatively, Joe Sando, a historian from Jemez Pueblo, suggests that Po'pay was not a priestly leader but rather a war captain (in part because members of Pueblo priesthoods are banned from taking life, an act in which Po'pay is reported to have engaged). Contemporary war captains hold positions involving the supervision of social and religious activities within their pueblo, policing the village, and protecting tribal lands. In the past, war captains' primary duties were to assemble and organize warriors, something Po'pay accomplished par excellence in 1680 (Sando 1982:65–66, 1992:177, 2005:15).

Heralding the Spirits

It may have been his role as a religious leader in his home village that gained Po'pay access to the inner sanctum of the kiva at Taos (a Tiwa-speaking pueblo), from where he professed to receive visitations from various spirits. Pueblo witnesses captured in the wake of the Revolt reported that Po'pay claimed to communicate directly with supernatural beings. According to Ortiz, this bold assertion could only be legitimately invoked by a person holding an important position of leadership within a Pueblo. These same captives told the Spaniards that the plot had originated with "an Indian *teniente* [lieutenant] of *Po he yemu*," presumably referring to Po'pay's interactions with the Tewa culture hero *Po'se yemu*—the rain-giving spirit whose name translates as "he who scatters mist before him." The messengers reported receiving a letter from this teniente, who lived in the north and was described as black, yellow-eyed, and very tall. Another witness from San Felipe Pueblo revealed that Po'pay met in the Taos kiva with three spirits named *Caudi* (or *Caydi*), *Tleume*, and *Tilini*, and that they had the ability to shoot fire from their extremities. Although it is unclear to which members of the Pueblo pantheon the two former names refer, Ortiz identifies Tilini as

"Tinini Povi, or 'Olivella Flower Shell Youth,' one of the most revered figures in the Tewa tradition."[2]

Through his summoning of these spirits, Po'pay appealed to mythical figures of authority who crossed the linguistic and ethnic boundaries separating the Pueblos. Po'se yemu is one of the few figures appearing in the mythology of virtually every Pueblo (albeit under various different but equivalent names), making him a natural specter to invoke in an attempt to unify the disparate villages in a pan-Pueblo rebellion. By claiming to communicate with Po'se yemu, Po'pay legitimated his plan of action not only to his Tewa followers or the Tiwa-speakers of Taos, but also to Pueblo speakers of Keres, Towa, Zuni, and Hopi alike. Furthermore, Po'se yemu's role as a guardian, protector, and teacher of traditional Pueblo practices made him the logical choice for Po'pay to invoke to bolster his nativist and revivalist agenda. In several Pueblo legends Po'se yemu is said to have introduced new rituals to the people. In others he orders kachina dances to be held underground, out of sight of the Spaniards. He often acts as a go-between among the Pueblo and non-Pueblo worlds, directly opposing Christianity. According to Tewa legends recorded by Ortiz in the 1960s, for example, Po'se yemu was said to have challenged Jesus in a contest for control over the Pueblo people, in which Po'se yemu emerged victorious. In conjuring this spirit in the Taos kiva, Po'pay appealed to a pan-Pueblo deity who not only mediated between the Pueblo and Spanish worlds, but one who opposed Christianity directly. Po'pay's instructions to the Pueblos thus mirrored that of this mythical culture hero when he told the people to reject the Spaniards' religion and to revive traditional Pueblo rituals. Additionally, some variants of Pueblo mythology maintain that Po'se yemu had put an end to intertribal fighting in the past, making him the natural specter to invoke in support of a unified, pan-Pueblo resistance movement (Parmentier 1979:609–614; Parsons 1939, 1:245).

The Devil in the Details

Descriptions of Po'pay's interactions with Po'se yemu and the other spirits brim with tantalizing but cryptic details. These supernaturals and their teniente are variously described as residing far away in the mountains to the north, traveling underground, having black skin and yellow eyes, communicating via letters, and shooting fire from their extremities.[3] In a controversial 1967 article, Franciscan historian Fray Angelico Chávez employed the references to black skin and yellow eyes to assert that the primary leader of the 1680 Revolt was not Po'pay at all, but rather a mulatto from Santa Clara named Naranjo. (This problematic argument has failed to win widespread scholarly support; see Beninato 1990). Chávez noted that descriptions of a tall, dark-skinned man seem a puzzling way to describe "the average small and not-too-tawny" native of Ohkay Owingeh, begging for further explication. But interpreting these descriptions literally, as accurate portraits of a veritable historical personage (Po'pay, Naranjo, or otherwise), is probably a mistake. Rather, contextualized within the complex semiotic environment of seventeenth-century Spanish Catholicism, the descriptions of black-skinned, yellow-eyed, fire-spewing figures seem far less perplexing.

Similar imagery abounds in Spanish counterreformation descriptions of the devil and his minions. Ethnohistorian Daniel Reff (1995) notes that the most common depiction of Satan in late medieval Europe was that of a black-skinned being, often with large yellow eyes, frequently emitting fire. He was generally believed to live either in the north or in the center of the earth (i.e., underground), and was said to employ the "Devil's Letter" in carrying out his evil works. Viewed in this light, the descriptions of Po'pay and the spirits recorded by the Spaniards seem not to have been intended as naturalistic portrayals, but were probably something more allegorical in nature. Furthermore, the tradition of invoking satanic intervention to explain indigenous rebellions in colonial New Spain dates back more than a century before the Pueblo Revolt. A Jesuit priest's description of the 1616 Tepehuan rebellion in northwest Mexico, for example, ascribed the uprising to the work of the devil, who had frequently appeared to the Indians "in the form of a black man who spouted fire."[4]

Colonial New Mexicans not only considered the devil to be a real and active participant in human affairs, but the missionaries envisioned themselves as soldiers in constant war against this enemy. No Christian—whether Indian, mestizo (mixed-blood), or *peninsular* (native-born Spaniard)—was immune to Satan's influences. The friars of New Mexico commonly held the belief that the devil had ruled over Native Americans throughout the New World prior to the Spaniards' introduction of Christianity (Morrow 1996:46). According to Fray Francisco de Ayeta, the Revolt of 1680 was caused by a reversion to this state of satanic dominion, wherein the Pueblos gave "themselves over to blind idolatry, worshiping the devil and living according to and in the same manner as when they were heathen."[5] Thus it comes as no surprise that in their attempt to make sense of the Pueblo Revolt and justify the reconquest of the region, the Spaniards may have inferred that Po'se yemu was a guise of Satan himself, and that Caudi, Tleume, and Tilini were his minions (lesser demons who delivered the devil's instructions and false promises). It is unclear whether the Pueblo captives believed similarly

themselves, were simply telling the Spaniards what they wanted to hear, or
had their statements embellished by overzealous translators.[6]

Lieutenants of the Teniente

Po'pay may have conjured the spirits in the Taos kiva in isolation, but he was
not alone in planning the Revolt itself. After receiving his visions from the
spirits, the Tewa mystic began to meet with leaders from many of the other
Pueblos. At these juntas, Po'pay presumably began by telling the others of
his communiqué from the spirits. Together they formulated a plot to expel
the Spaniards and usher in a new age of prosperity and happiness, like that
they imagined their ancestors had enjoyed before the arrival of the Spaniards.
Pueblo testimonies speak of a core group of twenty-two war captains who
helped to plan the rebellion, many of whom were named in various Spanish
records: Luis Tupatú of Picuris; Alonso Catití of Kewa; El Saca and El Chato of
Taos; Francisco (El Ollita) of San Ildefonso; El Taqu of Ohkay Owingeh; Luis
Cunixu of Jemez; the Zia leader Antonio Malacate; Pedro Situ and Diego Misu
of Tesuque; and Tano leaders Cristobal Yope of San Lazaro and Antonio Bolsas.[7]

The formation of such a core group of disciples around a charismatic leader
is a common element of revitalization movements the world over. These cliques
frequently include individuals influential within their respective home communities (Wallace 1956:273). That Po'pay would have gathered war captains
as his apostles rather than the holders of other traditional Pueblo offices (caciques, moiety chiefs, or society heads, for example) makes sense, given that war
captains were traditionally charged with coordinating and directing military
activities. War captains were in essence the lieutenants of seventeenth-century
Pueblo armies, and as such their support and cooperation was crucial to the
success of any coordinated military action.

Curiously, the men who formed Po'pay's entourage were not the pure-
blooded "traditional" Puebloans we might expect to lead a nativist/revivalist
revolution like the Pueblo Revolt. Although the spirits had called for the
expulsion of all things Spanish, many of Po'pay's closest collaborators were of
ethnically mixed ancestry: mestizos (persons of Indian and European descent)
and *coyotes* (those born of a Native American and African union). Others were
indios ladinos, Spanish-speaking Natives who had been educated in the missions by the friars. The participation of these bicultural persons in the 1680
Revolt caused one priest to later lament that the Indians who caused the
greatest harm were "those who have been most favored by the religious and
who are most intelligent."[8] One such indio ladino was Juan of Galisteo,

a Christian Indian who had been entrusted by the Spaniards to reconnoiter the Pueblos during the initial stages of the uprising. He returned a few days later having shifted his allegiances, transforming into a leader of the Pueblo forces. Juan appeared in the plaza of the besieged capital dressed not as a traditional Pueblo warrior, however, but as a Spaniard on horseback, "with harquebus, sword, dagger, leather jacket, and all the arms of the Spaniards," a testament to the training he had received at the feet of his colonizers.[9]

Another Spanish-speaking leader of the Revolt was Alonso Catití, a mestizo from the Pueblo of Kewa (Santo Domingo). Catití had served as an interpreter for the Franciscans prior to the uprising, and his half-brother succeeded him in this position after the Revolt. Catití later went so far as to hatch a plot to kill his sibling and his Spanish companions when they returned to New Mexico in 1681 (see chapter 4).[10] Francisco "El Ollita" swore he would do the same to his siblings. He too was a coyote and an indio ladino, with brothers who had enlisted with the Spaniards after the uprising. One of the other members of Po'pay's inner circle was known simply as "El Chato" from Taos, an epithet meaning "flat nosed" in Spanish. Stefanie Beninato (1990:429) suggests that this name likely relates to El Chato's "negroid features," revealing the miscegenation in his family tree.[11]

Racial and ethnic admixture was the norm in seventeenth-century New Mexico, whose population was characterized by one friar as consisting of "so many *mestizos, mulattos,* and bastards . . . that I am sometimes confused."[12] The fact that these persons played a central role in the Revolt should come as no surprise. Previous rebellions had been planned by "half-breeds" and indios ladinos as well: a mestizo named Diego Martín led the Taos uprising of 1639,[13] while a literate, Franciscan-educated polyglot and onetime governor of the Salinas pueblos, Esteban Clemente, coordinated the abortive pan-Pueblo uprising of 1670.[14] This pattern was repeated in 1680, when Po'pay conspired with many of the Puebloans who were closest to the Spaniards in plotting their colonizers' demise. In addition to their intimate knowledge of Spanish culture and the colonizers' strengths and weaknesses, these mestizos, coyotes, and indios ladinos spoke a common language—the tongue of the Spaniards—which may have further facilitated inter-pueblo communication during the prelude to the 1680 Revolt (Dozier 1970:69).

Knotted Cords and Dissent from Within

In the weeks leading up to the rebellion, Po'pay and his inner circle formulated a more detailed blueprint for the revolution. On a predetermined day of Po'pay's choosing all the Pueblos were to rise up, attacking the Spaniards in their midst and killing as many as possible. Having robbed the settlers' estancias, driven off their horses and cattle, burned the mission churches and destroyed their sacred contents, the Puebloans were to close all roads and block every escape route. The villa of Santa Fe was to be isolated from the more populous Spanish settlements to the south, and in a final act of violent nativism, Pueblo warriors from around the province would descend on the Governor's Palace, slaughtering all its inhabitants.

Po'pay's disciples began to spread word of this plan throughout the realm. In order to coordinate the timing of the Revolt among the more than thirty different villages he enjoined to participate, Po'pay employed an ingenious mnemonic device: a knotted rope. According to Pueblo informants, "he took a cord made of maguey fiber and tied some knots in it that indicated the number of days until the perpetration of the treason. He sent it to all the pueblos as far as that of La Isleta . . . under strict charge of secrecy, commanding that the War Captains take it from pueblo to pueblo."[15] Along with these cords, runners carried instructions for those receiving the ropes to untie one hitch each day. On the morning the last knot was loosed they were to rise up in unison, driving the Spaniards from their midst. Each village was further instructed to send up smoke signals as a sign of their intent to participate.[16]

But as the war captains began to disseminate the plan within their home villages it became clear that not all of the Pueblo people agreed with the proposed course of action. In particular, many of the secular leaders of the Pueblos—those who had been appointed by the Spaniards—were clearly opposed to the uprising, which they considered mutinous. At Pecos, a pro-Spanish faction warned the Spaniards when they received word of the impending rebellion nearly three weeks in advance. This alarm was echoed by the leaders of the nearby Pueblos of the Galisteo Basin in the days immediately preceding the Revolt.[17] Dissension within the native ranks was not limited to the eastern periphery of the Pueblo world, however. Po'pay faced opposition even within his home village—and within his own family. At Ohkay Owingeh, the (Spanish-appointed) native governor of the Pueblo, Nicolas Bua, made his objection to the planned rebellion known. Bua also happened to be married to Po'pay's daughter, and when he threatened to reveal his father-in-law's plot to the Spaniards, Po'pay took drastic action. In order to prevent Bua from warning the colonizers, Po'pay reportedly killed his son-in-law in his own home, lest the Pueblos lose the crucial element of surprise and sacrifice months of advanced planning.[18] If he had indeed been a religious leader before this time, it was at that moment that the leader of the

Revolt must have renounced his ritual position, as Pueblo priests are traditionally prohibited from taking life of any kind (Ortiz 1980:21).

In order to further protect his plot, Po'pay excluded one group of Pueblos from the planning entirely. He forbade his messengers from visiting the Piro district (the southernmost linguistic/ethnic group among the Rio Grande Pueblos), or to speak of his revelations to any of its inhabitants for fear that they too would tip off the Spaniards.

At the rest of the Pueblos, reports indicate that those who received the knotted cords sometimes complied as much out of fear of Po'pay as a desire to oust the Spaniards. Pueblo witnesses later claimed that Po'pay and his retinue promised to "impose severe penalties on them if they should disobey," and threatened to "destroy the Indian or pueblo that refused to rebel." One declarant claimed that those who did not obey were threatened with beheading. Many of the people reportedly "held [Po'pay] in terror, obeying his commands although they were contrary to the orders of the señores governors, the prelate and the religious, and the Spaniards."[19] And indeed, there is evidence to suggest that Po'pay ruled in an increasingly despotic manner as the rebellion progressed (see chapter 4).

Despite Po'pay's promises and threats, he was ultimately unsuccessful in keeping his plan completely under wraps. Details of the plot leaked to the Spaniards in the days before the uprising. Rumors of an impending insurrection began streaming into Governor Otermín's office in Santa Fe on the morning of August 9, 1680. First came three different messages, one from Pecos, one from Galisteo, and one from the colonial officials of the Taos region, warning the governor that "the Christian Indians of this kingdom are convoked, allied, and confederated for the purpose of rebelling, forsaking obedience to his Majesty, and apostatizing from the holy faith; and that they desire to kill the ecclesiastical ministers and all the Spaniards, women, and children, destroying the whole population of this kingdom."[20] Later the same day the Pueblo governors of San Marcos, La Cienega, and the nearby Tano pueblos (comprising the villages of San Cristobal, San Lazaro, and Galisteo) journeyed to Santa Fe to inform Governor Otermín of the imminent attack. They reported that two messengers from Tesuque Pueblo named Nicolás Catua and Pedro Omtua had visited them, carrying a knotted cord. Otermín immediately ordered the runners arrested.

Otermín's men tracked down the runners and brought them before the governor that same day. When Otermín asked the youths what they intended to do with the knotted thong in their possession, they testified that the war captains at Tesuque had ordered them to carry the cord to the pueblos southeast of Santa Fe.[21] Otermín's journals do not reveal the conditions under which this interrogation took place, but the threat of persecution must have hung heavy in the air, if in fact these statements didn't result from outright torture itself. Otermín was known to employ particularly creative means when wringing testimony out of captives. One of his favored interrogation techniques involved crushing a deponent's fingers in the screws of the nearest blunderbuss until they cracked.[22] Whatever happened in the Governor's Palace that day, Catua and Omtua divulged to the governor all they had sworn to keep secret. The old men had been planning the uprising for months, they said. The leader of the rebellion lives in the north. He has black skin and yellow eyes, communicates with Po'se yemu, and threatens to kill anyone who refuses to join in the plan. The two knots in the cord? They signified the two days that remained before the Pueblos would rise up in unison to do away with the Spaniards.[23]

Back at Tesuque, the arrest of the young emissaries sent the headmen into a panic. They presumed (correctly) that Catua and Omtua would let slip the details of the uprising, rendering their months of strategizing worthless. The Spanish backlash would be swift and brutal. Even worse would be the wrath of Po'pay, who had sworn vengeance and death on all those responsible for revealing his plans. Their only hope, they decided, was to launch the attack immediately, retaining at least a modicum of the element of surprise. When an unsuspecting Hispanic settler named Cristóbal Herrera wandered into Tesuque that evening, he became the first casualty of the Pueblo Revolt of 1680.

There would be no turning back now. That night the war captains sent out a second group of runners to tell the nearby villages (and Po'pay) that plans had changed. The Revolt would commence in earnest at dawn.[24]

The Making of Martyrs

When the sun rose over New Mexico on the morning of Saturday, August 10, it sparked a fuse of nativist fury that exploded first among the Pueblos north of Santa Fe. Later in the day they would be joined by the Pueblos to the west, south, and east of the capital, when word of the change in date reached those areas. The first ecclesiastical victim was Fray Juan Pío, who arrived at Tesuque to say mass shortly after dawn, as he did every Saturday morning. He was surprised to find the men of the congregation armed to the hilt and smeared with war paint. Alarmed, he reportedly called out to them: "What is this children, are you mad? Do not be disturbed. I will help you and die a thousand deaths for you." In fact he only had one death to give, and the interpreter of the pueblo, an indio ladino named Nicolás, took it on the spot.

Nicolás emerged from the fracas covered in the blood of the fallen priest.[25] The Pueblo Revolt of 1680 had officially begun.

Later that morning, word of the uprising reached the pueblo of Kewa, which, as the custodial seat of the Franciscan order in New Mexico, housed the headquarters of the missionaries.[26] The five presidial soldiers who had been stationed there rushed to protect the three resident priests, taking refuge in the *convento* (priests' quarters). But the warriors of Kewa broke in and a skirmish ensued as the Spaniards struggled in vain to fend off their attackers. The Puebloans killed all five soldiers, dumping their bodies unceremoniously in a pile behind the church. The three priests fared no better. The men of Kewa executed them as well, with their corpses dragged into the church where they were buried in a large grave dug in front of the altar.[27]

When the news that the rebellion had begun in the other pueblos reached Acoma later in the day, the warriors of the Sky City seized Fray Lucas Maldonado and Fray Juan de Val (who was visiting from his station at Zuni), binding the two with rope, along with a particularly zealous Christian mestiza. All three were stripped naked, beaten, and paraded through the village before finally being stoned to death at the entrance of the convento of St. Esteban del Rey. A short while later the Acomas and their Zuni allies encountered Fray Augustín de Santa María on the road. He too was beaten to death, his corpse left to be picked over by buzzards in the desert sun.[28]

According to Hopi oral traditions, the warriors of Orayvi stormed the house of Fray José de Espeleta, breaking down the door to find him cowering in the corner. They quickly dispatched him with a knife to the throat. At Shungopovi, Hopi warriors broke into Fray José Trujillo's house as well. There the friar defended himself, grabbing a sword and cutting down one of his attackers. He was swiftly overpowered, however, and the warriors tied his hands behind his back, hung him from the church vigas, and burned him alive.[29] Other accounts claim that a group of Hopis approached Fray José de Figueroa at Awat'ovi armed with weapons seized from their colonizers. But a Hopi man named Francisco, whom the friar had reared, rose to his defense. The assassins reportedly gave Francisco a choice: kill the priest or be killed himself. Francisco reluctantly agreed to act as executioner. He took up a musket and shot the priest repeatedly. Following this, the Hopis reportedly rounded up the bodies of the clergymen, carried them to a church, and burned them within the chapel.[30]

Like lambs to the slaughter, their hagiographers tell us, the friars faced death bravely. Ramon Gutiérrez suggests that they craved martyrdom, yearning to be crucified in order to be closer to their Christ (Gutiérrez 1991:127–130). On that fateful day in 1680, two-thirds of the ecclesiastical personnel on the northern Spanish frontier got their wish. All told, twenty-one of the thirty-three Franciscans stationed in New Mexico were martyred on August 10.

In some pueblos the nativist cleansing extended beyond the execution of the priests to include the plunder and destruction of mission facilities. At Sandia the anti-Spanish fervor was particularly intense. There the people ripped the church doors from the hinges, shattered Christian statues, smashed the mission bells, and removed the priest's vestments and sacred accoutrements from the sacristy, burying two chalices in a basket of manure. The people of Sandia symbolically crippled the friars by hacking the arms off a full-length figure of Francis of Assisi with an axe, displaying the now-impotent saint on the church altar for all to see. A crucifix was whipped with such ferocity that every last bit of paint and varnish was removed from its surface. They stoned an altarpiece depicting the Immaculate Conception, gouging out the Virgin's eyes. The Sandias were careful to leave the dragon at her feet untouched, however (possibly because it bore a striking resemblance to the horned serpent of Pueblo mythology known as the *awanyu*). Finally, in the ultimate act of desecration, someone defecated on the main altar of the church, smearing the holy statues with excrement before filling the choir loft with hay and setting it ablaze.[31]

The Persistence of Churches, Chalices, and Priests

The desecration and destruction of the churches was not universal among the Pueblos during the opening days of the Revolt, however. At many villages the mission structures and ecclesiastical paraphernalia were left intact. At the mission of Santo Domingo at Kewa, for example, the church, convento, and sacristy were initially unharmed. All the statuary, altarpieces, and altars were left in place, and the sacred ornaments stored in the sacristy (including chalices, vessels for wine and water, an incensario, and a lamp, all made of silver) were reverently ignored. When the priests were killed, the people of Kewa simply piled their bodies at the base of the altar and carefully closed the door to the church behind them.[32] Similarly, the Zunis respectfully preserved all the "ornaments of divine worship" from their mission church, including two bronze images of the crucified Christ; silver chalices, patens, and monstrances; candlesticks and bells; an oil painting of Saint John the Baptist; and a small library of 18 books, missals, and instructional manuals.[33]

A few friars managed to survive the uprising without harm to even a single hair of their tonsured heads. The congregants at the mission of Nuestra Señora de la Asunción de Zia did not kill Fray Nicolàs Hurtado or destroy the village church on that fateful August morning. Rather, the Zias directed their wrath on the nearby estancias of colonial settlers. When Fray Nicolàs later fled with a contingent of Spanish settlers and soldiers that had come to his aid, the Zias rang the mission bells and mocked the Spaniards in derision, but left them untouched.[34]

The most famous alleged Spanish survivor of the uprising was Fray Juan Greyrobe, or as his Zuni parishioners called him, *kwan tatchui lok'yana* ("Juan Grey-robed-father-of-us").[35] While not mentioned in any Spanish record detailing the events of the Pueblo Revolt, the story of Father Greyrobe survives in Zuni oral traditions, seventeen separate versions of which were recorded between 1857 and 1988 (Wiget 1996). This remarkable story maintains that a priest stationed at one of the Zuni missions (likely La Purísima Concepción de Halona) was neither killed nor did he flee during the 1680 uprising, but rather he remained among the Zunis after the Revolt, adopting their manners of dress and custom, growing his hair long, and even taking a Zuni wife. According to these oral traditions his life was spared either because of his benevolent and caring demeanor (which contrasted distinctly with those of his predecessors) or for use as a bargaining chip in the event of Spanish reprisals.[36] "He had a Zuni heart and cared for the sick and women and children" and did not meddle in their traditional religious practices, recalled one nineteenth-century Zuni. "Therefore, in that time of evil, they spared him on condition . . . that he eschew the vestment and usages of his people and kind, and in everything, costume and ways of life alike, become a Zuni."[37] These traditions state that the Zunis gathered for mass that August morning just as they did every week, with one exception: on this day, they concealed weapons in their clothes. At a prearranged signal, the Zuni warriors rose up against the Spaniards who had been stationed among them for the protection of the priest, killing the soldiers and sparing the friar's life— but only on the condition that he agreed to "go native," living as a Zuni.[38]

The Revolt in the Countryside: The Sacking of Estancias

Although the massacre of the priests of New Mexico receives the lion's share of attention in most histories of the Pueblo Revolt, a far greater toll (in terms of the total number of persons killed) was exacted on the secular residents of the colony. Initially, Natives attacked the estancias of the Tewa and Taos regions, pillaging stores of grain, capturing horses and cattle, seizing women and children, and burning the Spaniards' homes. Settlers of all stripes were massacred as they attempted to flee—men and women, young and old, masters and servants. Pueblo warriors fanned out along the roads of northern New Mexico, ambushing *vecinos* and presidial soldiers as they scrambled to seek safety in Santa Fe. By the end of the day, 380 colonial settlers would be executed throughout the colony.[39]

Early on the morning of August 10, at the northern edge of the Spanish empire, forty-four-year-old Sebastián de Herrera set out from his home with his family. His wife, son, brother-in-law, and mother accompanied him on a visit to the mission pueblo of San Geronimo de Taos. Along the way they heard news of a Native rebellion, and were accordingly relieved to be leaving the lands of the "heathen" Utes (who they assumed to be the perpetrators of the uprising) to stay among the Christian Indians of Taos. Along the way, Herrera met up with Fernando de Chávez, ten years his junior, who was seeking refuge for his young family at Taos too. As they approached the pueblo they saw its church and convent in flames, along with many of the nearby estancias of colonial settlers. A group of Taos warriors surrounded them, accompanied by the Indian governor of the pueblo, who shouted to them that the Native forces had killed the colonial settlers throughout New Mexico, punctuating his statement with the proclamation: "Now there are no more Spaniards, and we shall kill you." Herrera and Chávez dropped their possessions to defend themselves and their families, but they were only partially successful. The two Spaniards escaped, along with Herrera's young son. But their wives and other children all perished, along with Herrera's in-laws. In total, more than seventy Spanish settlers were killed in the Taos valley that day.[40]

The picture was much the same among the estancias and haciendas of the Tewa district, surrounding the junction of the Rio Grande and the Rio Chama. At dawn, a group of eight Spaniards set out from Santa Clara Pueblo under the command of their captain, a graying native of New Mexico named Francisco de Anaya. As they left the village they were approached by a group of Pueblo men who asked to speak with them. The Natives were armed, raising Anaya's suspicions. Nervously he agreed to parley, on the condition that the Santa Clara warriors would guarantee safe passage to the Spaniards. They agreed, but their promises soon proved empty. The warriors attacked, killing two young Spaniards who had been sent to serve as an escort. The other six managed to escape, but as they looked back Anaya was forced to watch helplessly as Pueblo warriors stormed his house, carrying off his wife and child. His eldest son, Francisco the younger, was executed later that day at Galisteo Pueblo, where he was serving as a military escort.[41]

By Saturday afternoon mounted squadrons of Pueblo men were scouring the countryside, gathering horses, cattle, sheep, and property from the houses of the Spaniards. At Santa Clara, Tewa and Jemez warriors piled the spoils of war in the plaza, divvying up the Spaniards' effects. They set up sentries on the main roads, intercepting the straggling colonists who had survived the initial uprising and were now desperately scrambling to Santa Fe to seek shelter inside the Governor's Palace. By nightfall, the roads and fields of northern New Mexico were littered with the bodies of fleeing Spaniards.

Throughout the kingdom small groups of colonists who had managed to survive the initial uprising gathered together in (often futile) attempts to protect themselves. In the Keres district south of Santa Fe, a dozen settlers gathered in the house of Cristóbal de Anaya for an anxious night. On Sunday, the estancia was sacked and raided. The Natives left nothing behind but the twelve naked bodies of the settlers. Less than one kilometer (a little more than half a mile) away, the house of Pedro de Cuellar was destroyed as well, and a little farther on Captain Augustín de Carbajal was killed, along with his wife, a daughter, and another woman, their corpses left to rot in the empty house.[42]

A larger group of survivors gathered at the Pueblo of Isleta. In contrast with their Tiwa neighbors at Sandia, Puaray, and Alameda, the Isletas did not take part in the initial uprising, leaving their priest and the surrounding estancias untouched. Five survivors of the uprising at Jemez made their way to Isleta (picking up the friar and three settlers at Zia on the way). Over the course of the next three days, a small force of armed soldiers ventured out to gather the men, women, and children who remained alive in the Rio Abajo (the region south of Santa Fe). All in all, about fifteen hundred settlers managed to assemble at Isleta, including seven missionaries. No doubt their survival was aided by the fact that the rest of the Pueblos had turned their attention on the colonial capital in the days after the rebellion. When a small group of refugees stopped at Sandia on their way to Isleta, they found all the men absent. On asking the women of the pueblo where the men had gone, they replied "very volubly and boldly that they had gone to kill the Spaniards."[43] More specifically, the warriors of Sandia were probably part of the force that was laying siege to Santa Fe at that very moment in an attempt to sever the head of the colonial snake.

"Now God and Santa Maria Are Dead": The Siege of Santa Fe

As the mission bell at the hermitage of San Miguel in Santa Fe struck seven times on the morning of August 10, Governor Otermín received his first warning that something was amiss. Fray Juan Pío had been murdered at

Tesuque, his companion barely escaping with his life. Over the next few hours reports began streaming in, telling of the missionaries and settlers who had been slain in and around the pueblos of Taos, Picuris, Nambé, San Ildefonso, Pojoaque, Santa Clara, Kewa, Pecos, and Galisteo.[44] As news of the killings and devastation in the outlying districts flooded his office, Otermín instructed the residents of the villa of Santa Fe to seek sanctuary inside the thick adobe walls of the Governor's Palace. He ordered all the weaponry of the royal armory—harquebuses, blunderbusses, swords, daggers, shields, and ammunition—to be issued to the young men who had none, drafting them into His Majesty's royal service. Finally, he directed sentries to be posted around the *casas reales* (royal offices) and sent a squadron to the church in order to protect the holy sacrament. In just four hours, the guards were in place and the royal magazine had been distributed.[45]

For the next four days, reports of apostasy and atrocities continued to filter in as approximately a thousand residents of the surrounding area poured into the capital to seek refuge in Santa Fe. Hispano settlers and their families— men and women, young and old—gathered along with Mexican Indians, pre-sidial soldiers, mixed-blood mestizos, *genizaros* (Indian servants and slaves), the governor, and his staff inside the royal villa, crowded cheek-to-jowl with cattle, sheep, goats, and horses. All told, the governor estimated that he had fewer than a hundred men capable of fighting at his disposal. He prepared for the worst. On August 13, Otermín ordered a friar "to consume the most holy sacrament, and take the images, sacred vessels, and things appertaining to divine worship, close the church and convent, and bring everything to the palace."[46] They then maneuvered two small cannon behind the main gate of the casas reales, aiming the barrels at the streets of Santa Fe in anticipation of the impending attack.

The governor's fears were realized that morning when five hundred Tano, Keres, and Pecos warriors, "armed and giving war whoops," amassed just one league (about 4.2 kilometers/2.6 miles) outside the capital. Messengers reported that the Pueblo forces were "on the way to attack [Santa Fe] and destroy the governor and all the Spaniards, so that the whole kingdom might be theirs, and they might profit at the expense of the Spaniards and their haciendas. They were saying that now God and Santa Maria were dead, that they were the ones whom the Spaniards worshipped, and that their own God whom they obeyed never died." The warriors proceeded onto the plains and fields surrounding the church of San Miguel, and into the houses of the Mexi-can Indians in the barrio de Analco, on the outskirts of the colonial capital. They sacked many of the houses of Analco, lodging in others as they prepared to besiege the Governor's Palace.[47]

At the head of the Pueblo forces was Juan of Galisteo, the Spanish-speaking Tano Indian who had grown up in Santa Fe among the Spaniards. Otermín had sent him to Galisteo Pueblo a few days earlier to parley with his disgruntled brethren. In the interim the Tanos had designated him as their leader, and now he approached the casas reales on horseback, wearing a sash of red taffeta that had been taken from a missal at the convent of Santa Cruz de Galisteo. The governor summoned him, under promise of safety, to discuss his recent switching of allegiance. He entered the plaza of the villa armed to the hilt with Spanish weapons and dressed in leather armor. When asked by the governor "How it was that he had gone crazy too?" Juan replied "that there was now no help for it . . . and that the Indians who were coming with him and those they were awaiting were coming to destroy the villa." They brought with them a pair of crosses, one red, the other white. The governor was instructed to choose: the red signaled war, the white that the Spaniards would abandon the kingdom.

Otermín replied that he wanted to avoid violence, and offered a complete pardon to the Pueblos if they would lay down their arms. He appealed to their burgeoning sense of Catholic guilt, asking how they intended to live without the guidance of the friars? Still the Pueblos refused to step down, laughing openly at his demands and mocking the Spaniards by ringing the bells of their church, blowing trumpets, and "giving loud shouts in sign of war." To add insult to injury, they set fire to the church and the houses of the barrio. In an attempt to dislodge them from their hold in Analco before reinforcements arrived, Otermín sent a contingent of soldiers out of the Palace to attack. The Pueblo warriors met them with such fury that the governor himself was forced to join the fray along with all his remaining forces. The battle raged all day; the Pueblo warriors entrenched themselves in the houses of Analco, and in response the Spaniards attempted to smoke them out by setting the homes on fire. Just as the tide appeared to be turning in favor of the Spaniards, Tewa reinforcements arrived to aid the Tano, Keres, and Pecos warriors, driving the colonial forces back into the Governor's Palace.

A tense two days passed in which the Spaniards engaged the Indian forces in minor skirmishes, while the Pueblo army was fortified with additional reinforcements. By Friday, August 16, their numbers had swelled to more than twenty-five hundred. Now they struck the villa with all their might, setting fire to the casas reales. It was all the Spaniards could do to hold their fortifications. The Pueblos then cut off the water supply to the Governor's Palace, damming the irrigation canals. For two days and two nights the colonists were unable to quench their thirst, breathing in the dusty air of the plaza. The livestock began to die of dehydration, their parched tongues hanging limp from dry mouths. The situation was dire. In Otermín's words, they were "perishing with thirst . . . surrounded by such a wailing of women and children, with confusion everywhere" that they had no choice but to engage the enemy once more. Better to perish fighting, they decided, than to die of hunger and thirst, penned up inside the royal villa like animals caught in a hunter's snare.

On the morning following their second night without water, the resident friar said mass for the soldiers at dawn. Believing that "the best strength and armor were prayers to appease the divine wrath," the governor enjoined the women to pray with a fervor the likes of which they had never before raised. Finally, the priests offered the sacrament of reconciliation to all, exhorting them to repent for their sins and to accept the divine will, come what may.

In a desperate, last-ditch effort to save the withering citizenry, Otermín's forces charged the Pueblos with everything they had on the morning of August 20. The pitched battle raged until noon. Otermín claimed to kill three hundred of his Native enemy. Forty-seven Pueblo warriors were captured, and after a brief interrogation in which they declared that they had acted "on the mandate of an Indian who lives a very long way from this kingdom, toward the north . . . and who is the lieutenant of Pose'yemu," they were summarily executed. The Spaniards suffered the loss of five soldiers and numerous casualties. Otermín himself took two arrows to the face and a musket ball to the chest, piercing his deerskin jacket. The bold gambit succeeded, driving the Pueblos from their lodgings around the Palace of the Governors.

Taking stock of the situation, Otermín recognized that even with the Pueblos gone for the moment the Spaniards remained in perilously dire straits. They were fatigued, out of provisions, and still threatened by the enemy. His meager forces had only a few horses left, and even those would not last if the water supply was cut yet again. Furthermore, nearly every house in Santa Fe had been destroyed; those of the Spaniards as well as the Mexican Indians had all been burned to the ground, along with the church. For all these reasons, "looking to the better service of the two Majesties [King Carlos II and Christ] and the safety of the people, arms, horses, and cattle," Otermín ordered the Spaniards to withdraw. The tortuous nine-day siege of Santa Fe was over.[48]

On the twenty-first day of August the column of tattered colonists made their way out of Santa Fe. Under the watchful eyes of Pueblo warriors perched on the surrounding hilltops, the straggling remnants of the once-proud colony now limped down the Rio Grande half-starved and half-naked. Over the next four weeks they dragged themselves more than five hundred kilometers (three hundred miles) south to El Paso del Norte, where they would establish a colonial capital-in-exile.

The kingdom of New Mexico was lost. In the eyes of the Spaniards, the Pueblos were guilty of "conspiracy, alliance, and rebellion . . . apostatizing from the holy faith, forsaking royal obedience, burning images and temples, killing atrociously priests, soldiers, women, and children, taking possession of all the things pertaining to divine worship, of haciendas, and of everything in the kingdom they could, [and] returning to the blind idolatry and super-stitions of their ancient days."[49]

For the Pueblos, however, the siege was the culmination of "a holy war" (as Herman Agoyo [2002:xiv] has termed it) that needed to be fought in order to return balance and harmony to their world, and the victory could hardly have been sweeter. After eighty-two years they had finally succeeded in ridding the Pueblo world of the burdens of colonialism. Po'pay's plan had worked to perfection. As the spirits had predicted, the Spaniards were gone, and the Pueblos were once again free to live as their ancestors had, in the days before the men wearing metal first arrived in their lands.

Part II

The Era of Pueblo Independence: 1680–1692

4

The Aftermath of Revolution

WITH THE SPANIARDS GONE AND THE WEIGHT of the colonial yoke lifted from their necks for the first time in more than eight decades, the Pueblos celebrated their newfound freedom. In plazas throughout the northern Rio Grande the kachinas danced again and people gathered in kivas without fear of reprisals. Pueblo men and women rushed to collect the spoils of war behind the fleeing Spaniards, swarming the estancias and mission facilities that remained standing. Tewas, Tiwas, and Tanos streamed into the Palace of the Governors in Santa Fe and ransacked the casas reales, laying claim to the belongings that Otermín and his staff had left behind.[1]

Within two weeks, even the Pueblos that had been excluded from the organization and execution of the uprising were brought into the fold. While the people of Isleta opted not to attack the Spaniards on August 10, they were apparently in communication with the rest of the Pueblos during the uprising and joined the resistance by August 24. And although the Piro pueblos of Senecú, Socorro, Alamillo, and Sevilleta were initially left out of the planning of the rebellion, emissaries were sent to enlist their aid during the siege of Santa Fe, when many apparently took up the cause of their northern brethren.[2]

Po'pay reveled in his victory. When the leaves of the cottonwoods along the Rio Grande began to change from green to gold, he and his retinue made a tour of the newly liberated Pueblos. As they passed from village to village Po'pay instructed the people in the proper ways to complete the prophecy that had been revealed by the spirits. In addition to a general edict instructing the Pueblos to live "in accordance with the law of their ancestors," Po'pay espoused a message of nativism and revivalism that included six core directives. He ordered the churches burned and the destruction of all Christian accoutrements, with rosaries, crucifixes, and statues of the saints set aflame. Kivas and shrines were to be constructed anew, with ritual reconsecrations and masked dances performed accordingly. Po'pay himself provided instruction in the intricate steps of the old ceremonial dances, and required the people to spend long hours in traditional prayer and ritual activities. Furthermore, the waters of baptism were to be washed away from all Pueblo heads, with former converts ordered to wade into the Rio Grande and scrub themselves with yucca root. "He who might still keep in his heart a regard for the priests, the Governor, and the Spaniards," Po'pay warned, "would be known from his unclean face and clothes." As part of this ritual, the Tewa prophet also ordered the revocation of baptismal names, with indigenous monikers to be used exclusively thereafter. Banned as well was the use and teaching of the Castilian language—above all, any utterance of the names of Christ or Santa Maria. Finally, Po'pay proposed the dissolution of all Christian marriages, advocating a return to the traditional Puebloan practice of serial monogamy.[3]

But even as Po'pay and his entourage were advocating an agenda of strict nativism, they consciously perpetuated the memory of their Spanish overlords. At times, this was done for the personal aggrandizement of the leaders of the rebellion, who took to wearing the vestments of the priests as a conspicuous display of their own status. As they travelled throughout the northern Rio Grande, the leaders took possession of whatever ecclesiastical finery was left in the churches that hadn't been destroyed already. Po'pay reportedly "took from the churches the ornaments and holy vessels which he wished, and divided the rest among the captains and inferior governors." At Isleta, an "Indian captain" appeared a few weeks after the Revolt "dressed in alb and surplice with a scarlet band over it, and a maniple for a crown." Alonso Catití's house was said to be decorated with carpets and cushions looted from a mission church. He dressed "as if he were a priest vested for Mass," sat on a cushioned seat, and drank from a chalice. As for Po'pay, he reportedly took to wearing a bull's horn strapped to his forehead as a symbol of his status as the supreme leader of the Pueblos.[4]

At other times, the Revolt leaders' appropriation of Spanish material culture was used to parody and ridicule their former colonial masters. When Po'pay's victory tour reached Santa Ana, he and Catití staged an elaborate feast mocking the twin pillars of the colonial enterprise, the Spanish governor and the head of the Franciscan Order in New Mexico:

> In the pueblo of Santa Ana [Po'pay] had prepared an invitation feast of the viands which the priests and the governors were accustomed to use; and a great table, according to the manner of the Spaniards. He seated himself at the head, and opposite to him he had Alonso Catití sit, seating the others in the remaining places. He ordered to be brought two chalices, one for himself and the other for the said Alonso, and both began to

drink, ridiculing and scoffing the Spaniards and the Christian religion. And Po'pay, taking his chalice, said to Alonso, as if he were the father custodio: "To your Paternal Reverence's health." Alonso took his chalice and rising said to Po'pay: "Here is to your Lordship's health, Sir Governor."[5]

This type of ritual parody is a long-established tradition among the Pueblos, used to instruct younger members of society in the boundaries, norms, and values of Pueblo cultures. Here Po'pay and Catití drew on that tradition in order to mock the reviled Spanish officials, both sacred and secular (Kessell 2002:148).

But the line between colonial mockery and mimicry is a fine one (Bhabha 1994:86), and Po'pay seems to have crossed it during his tour. Even while admonishing the Pueblos to purge their world of Spanish influence, Po'pay ruled his people, in the words of historian John Kessell, "as only a Spaniard would" (1979:238). The tour itself was a custom appropriated from the Spaniards. When a new governor was appointed to New Mexico it was typical to begin his term by visiting all the pueblos within his jurisdiction (Riley 1999:163). Maybe most shockingly, Po'pay attempted to institute a Spanish-style system of taxation while on his victory tour, demanding that the Pueblos pay annual tribute to him consisting of wool and cotton.[6] Like the porcine dictators on Orwell's *Animal Farm*, Po'pay lived above the rules after the revolution. If all Pueblo people were equal in the wake of the Revolt, Po'pay was more equal than others.

Yet doctrinal manipulations such as these, both intentional and unconscious, are common elements of revitalization movements the world over. At some point most (if not all) organized revitalization phenomena undergo a stage in which the founding prophecy is adapted to fit changing conditions. According to Wallace, in the majority of revitalization movements "the original doctrine is continually modified by the prophet, who responds to various criticisms and affirmations by adding to, emphasizing, playing down, and eliminating selected elements of the original visions" (1956:274–75). Even with these inconsistencies, Po'pay still adhered to his policies of radical nativism more strictly than most. As opposed to the other leaders of the Revolt named in Spanish documents, Po'pay alone seems to have abided by his command to "discard the names given them in holy baptism and call themselves whatever they liked."[7] The other leaders continued to be identified by their Spanish names after the 1680 uprising, including Luis Tupatú, Alonso Catití, Francisco "El Ollita," Luis Cunixu, Antonio Bolsas, and Cristobal Yope. And although the concept of a single ruler with authority over multiple Pueblos does not seem to have been indigenous in origin (this too was borrowed from Spanish colonial institutions), there is precedent for "despotic rule by the religious-political hierarchy" among contemporary Pueblos (Dozier 1970:54; see also Sando 1992:179). Although Po'pay was identified as "captain general of the kingdom . . . who ruled the pueblos despotically and supremely,"[8] and he may have adapted elements of his leadership style from the Spaniards, his reign had an equally strong foundation in the traditional political economy of the Pueblos.

Fulfillment of the Prophecy: 1680–81 on the Rio Grande

There was one element of Po'pay's initial vision to which he would not allow exception, however: in Pueblos where the mission facilities remained intact, he ordered the churches and Christian paraphernalia destroyed. As one Pueblo informant described it: "Po'pay came down in person, and with him El Saca and El Chato from the pueblo of Los Taos, and other captains and leaders and many people who were in his train, and he ordered in all the pueblos through which he passed that they instantly break up and burn the images of the Christ, the Virgin Mary and the other saints, the crosses, and everything pertaining to Christianity, and that they burn the temples, [and] break up the bells."[9] Across the former colony churches were sacked and destroyed at Taos, Picuris, Ohkay Owingeh, Santa Clara, San Ildefonso, Pojoaque, Tesuque, Nambé, Kewa, Pecos, Jemez, San Felipe, Isleta, Senecú, Socorro, Alamillo, Sevilleta, and among the villages of Hopi and Zuni.[10]

The people of Isleta expressed their contempt for the Spaniards' religion by converting the burned husk of the church into a cowpen, but carefully curated the priests' vestments, candlesticks, bells, and missals. At other villages the response to Po'pay's call was heeded with more vigor. In the church of Nuestra Señora del Socorro, the Natives unearthed the sacred objects that had been buried by the Spaniards in a desperate attempt to ensure their protection. They smashed and burned a statue of the Christ and scattered the pieces throughout the pueblo. They also cut down a large pine cross that stood in the cemetery and carried it into the main plaza, where it was unceremoniously reduced to ashes. At Senecú they scalped a figure of Jesus on the cross, the hair and crown of thorns cast on the ground in a vivid display of Po'pay's victory over the Christian religion. They smashed the Catholic altar into pieces. And like their neighbors to the north, the people of Senecú felled the large cross that the Franciscans had erected in their midst. But rather than hauling it from the cemetery into the pueblo they did the opposite, removing the cross from the main plaza and disposing of it by dumping it in the graveyard—a powerful sign that indeed, as Po'pay had proclaimed, now the God of the Spaniards was dead.[11]

Archaeological investigations at Pecos suggest that the church was filled with kindling and set ablaze in the aftermath of the Revolt (Ivey 2005:346–47). (The inhabitants of Pecos would later blame the destruction of the church on the Tewas, possibly because it occurred at the insistence of Po'pay and his retinue.) The massive vigas of the roof quickly caught fire, creating a draft through the nave that blew hot ash out the front doors like a blast furnace. Burning embers must have filled the night air like orange fireflies. The following morning the people of Pecos awoke to find the massive buttressed walls of the church still standing. The scalped roof lay smoldering on the floor, blue sky pouring in from above to illuminate the charred murals. Hellbent on its demolition, the people of Pecos charged the obstinate walls. They clambered to the top, ripping them apart brick by brick, dismantling the massive edifice they had been forced to toil thousands of hours to create under the watchful eyes of the friars. The anti-Spanish faction at Pecos must have cheered when the facade, free-standing after the supporting walls had been laid low, teetered and finally fell on its face like a drunk in the mud (Kessell 1979:239; Hayes 1974:22–23, 32).

The Puebloans particularly loathed the mission bells, which were frequent targets of Native fury during indigenous revolts throughout the Spanish American empire (Thomas 1988:104). Bells held special, albeit very different meanings to everyone who lived within the range of their peals in colonial New Spain. For the friars, bells occupied a special category that blurred the lines between persons and things. Bells began their lives in any mission community through a baptismal ceremony in which they were consecrated and blessed with holy water and oils. They were then bestowed an individual name (typically after a specific saint) and assigned godparents. This new identity stayed with the bell throughout its life and even after— broken bell fragments were sometimes reverently collected and ultimately recast. Through this ceremony bells became full-fledged members of the mission community (Thomas 1988:104; Walsh 1934:32; Foster 1960:159). Native neophytes' associations with bells were probably not quite so rosy. Mission bells organized every facet of their lives. Their toll ordered the Christian Indians to wake, to sleep, to eat, to work, to attend mass, to penance, and to daily prayer. By the time of the Pueblo Revolt, mission bells had been clanging over the Puebloans' heads for more than eight decades. Most of the revolutionaries had lived their entire lives under their sway. When the opportunity to silence their ringing presented itself they seized it with abandon.

Throughout the province, bells were torn from their towers in the autumn of 1680. The San Felipians smashed a hole in the side of one, sinking it in the Rio Grande. The Zias followed suit, drowning theirs in the Jemez River. At Hawikku, Sandia, and Senecú they shattered multiple bells, disposing of the remnants in their respective cemeteries. Bell fragments have also been found in post-Revolt archaeological contexts at the Hopi pueblo of Awat'ovi, as well as San Lazaro, San Marcos, and San Cristóbal in the Galisteo Basin. At Senecú, Alamillo, and Zuni the destruction was elegantly simple: the bells were castrated through the removal of their clappers.[12]

For those who dared to harbor sympathy for the Franciscans' religion the consequences could be dire. At Taos, a mestizo known as "El Portugués" was discovered secreting away a carved image of the Virgin in order to prevent its desecration at the hands of the rebels. When the headmen learned of this they confiscated the figure, setting it in the plaza along with a chalice and a paten. Then they reportedly propped up the corpses of five dead Spaniards in a line behind the holy artifacts. According to one witness, the warriors of Taos staged a mock battle with the cadavers, charging at them "as if they were attacking the corpses and the Most Holy *Capitana* of the Spaniards." The Taoseños took turns shooting and lancing the statue and the corpses until finally they "broke the most holy image into pieces. And they buried these along with the chalice and paten, and burned the bones of the corpses upon the grave." The fate of El Portugués remains unknown.[13]

As they attempted to rid their world of Spanish contagion, the Pueblos simultaneously began to revive their traditional culture in fulfillment of Po'pay's prophecy. From Pecos in the east to the Hopi pueblos in the west, they resurrected traditional religious practices through the construction of new kachina masks and the revival of traditional dances. New kivas (or as the Spaniards called them, *estufas*) were constructed by the peoples of Cochiti, Kewa, Jemez, San Felipe, Puaray, Sevilleta, Alameda, and in the Governor's Palace in Santa Fe.[14] New shrines were erected as well, at which traditional offerings could be made. When the Spaniards briefly returned to New Mexico in 1681 in an abortive attempt at reconquest, they noted that in the preceding year: "In all of [the pueblos] estufas had been erected . . . and around all the pueblos in the four cardinal directions were circular piles of stone, and others in the middle of the plazas, where it was seen that they had made a great many offerings of grain and other things which they use; and a great many masks, powdered herbs, feathers, and other idolatrous things were found in the said estufas."[15] The would-be reconquerors also found kachina masks and other indigenous religious paraphernalia in nearly every pueblo they visited.[16] At Sevilleta, they found particularly disturbing signs of the revival of Pueblo culture. The mission sacristy was demolished, with the roof removed and used in the construction of a new kiva. Nearby were storage cysts filled with corn and squash, topped with a ritual offering in a curious vessel that had been carved, in the words of the Spaniards, "with the face of an Indian and the body of a toad. Inside it were many idolatrous herbs, two pieces of human flesh, feathers, and other superstitious things made by the idolaters, who offer them to that figure so that it will guard their maize."[17] In this way, the Pueblos heeded their prophet's instructions after his tour—they traded the saints for kachinas, the Virgin for the Corn Mothers, and the Pope for Po'pay. And with the revival of pre-Hispanic lifeways and the eradication of the Spaniards and their religion, the Pueblos eagerly anticipated the millennial existence that had been prophesied to follow soon thereafter.

Po'pay's Reign—and Demise

As the snow began to collect on the ends of vigas throughout the northern Rio Grande in the winter of 1680–81, the Pueblos settled into routines that were dictated not by the toll of the mission bells, but by the drums that echoed again from the kivas. Po'pay's commitment to the extinction of his former overlords burned as strong as ever. Even with the Spaniards living more than five hundred kilometers to the south, the prophet never stopped scheming to bring about their total annihilation. The only group for which he reserved more loathing than the odious, hairy-faced white men was the traitorous Pueblo turncoats who had informed the Spaniards of his plans.

In early 1681 the Pueblos encountered the first unwelcome visitors from the colonial capital-in-exile to journey back into the heart of the Pueblo world. Four Native men who had thrown their lot in with the retreating Spaniards the previous August made a courageous but ill-advised foray back to the northern Rio Grande. Their leader was Alonso Shimitihua, a Spanish-speaking colonial sympathizer from Isleta who planned to persuade the Pueblos to surrender and return to Christianity. He was joined by two other Tiwas (named Baltasar and Tomás) and an unidentified man from Jemez. When the group arrived at Isleta they were immediately taken prisoner, bound, and delivered to Alonso Catití's residence at Kewa. Catití had been negotiating peace with a Navajo captain when they arrived. His Athapaskan guest was clothed in Catholic vestments and sipping from a chalice. When Shimitihua informed Catití of his intentions, he was met with a bitter response. "Why do you come now with that?" Catití demanded. "God no longer exists!"

The Keres captain then ordered Shimitihua to be detained in a kiva while he sent for Po'pay, who was living once again at Ohkay Owingeh.

Po'pay arrived a few days later. Informed of Shimitihua's plans, the prophet seethed. He lunged at the Tiwa defector with a dagger hidden beneath his clothes, stabbing at Shimitihua again and again. "There is no longer a God!" Po'pay shrieked. "Will praying bring us the *mantas* [cotton cloth] and other things we need?" Catití stepped between them, wrestling Po'pay away. Next Po'pay turned his attention to Baltasar and Tomás, who now claimed to be double agents. They were not there to urge the Pueblos to surrender, they alleged. Rather they wanted Po'pay's help in fomenting another rebellion, this one among the Tiwas and Piros who had fled the province with the Spaniards and were living in El Paso. The Puebloans in El Paso had sent them to ask the Indians of New Mexico to join them in a second uprising, "for they wanted to have done with [the Spaniards] and all return to New Mexico." They had not yet been able to incite such an uprising themselves because they were opposed by some of the leaders of the El Paso pueblos, including a troublesome Jemez man named Lorenzo Muza.

Muza (whose name means "cat" in Towa) had alerted the Spaniards of the imminent uprising at the Jemez mission on August 10. He escaped, along with one lucky friar and four Spaniards, accompanying the colonists to El Paso. Po'pay hated Muza because of this betrayal, and now he saw his chance to exact revenge. He allotted Baltasar and Tomás whatever reinforcements they needed, instructing them "by whatever deceit necessary" to take Muza from El Paso, "and bring him here, so we can gouge out his eyes." As a last resort, if they weren't able to extract him from El Paso, they were to assassinate Muza and his supporters along with any of the Spanish colonial officers and all the remaining friars.[18] Muza's ultimate fate is not recorded.

Yet even as Po'pay plotted to complete his nativist vision, it gradually dawned on the people of the northern Rio Grande that the Revolt had not, in fact, achieved their liberation. Instead, the uprising had merely succeeded in swapping one form of oppression for another, replacing their colonial overlords with an indigenous one. Po'pay continued his heavy-handed reign, maintaining his demand for tribute from all his followers. His insistence on zealous prayer bordered on fanaticism, requiring the people to spend what even their religious leaders considered excessive hours in the kivas and making offerings at the shrines. The justification for his authoritarian rule was self-evident, at least to Po'pay. "This was the better life and the one they desired," explained the prophet, "because the God of the Spaniards was worth nothing and [ours] was very strong, the Spaniards' God being rotten wood." Those who did not comply with his directives were punished accordingly—

the few who dared to express their sympathies for Christianity he ordered killed. In one case, when a Pecos warrior named Domingo was recognized to have fought on the side of the Spaniards during the siege of Santa Fe, he was dispatched immediately.[19]

Although dictatorial and oppressive rule was nothing new to the Pueblos, Po'pay had taken it too far, alienating himself from even his closest followers with his sanctimonious demands. Sometime between March and November of 1681, the Pueblos collectively staged a coup d'état. Po'pay was deposed and stripped of his horn of leadership. Luis Tupatú was installed in his place as the new leader of the pan-Pueblo resistance movement. Tupatú chose Alonso Catití to be his right-hand man. He charged Catití with the administration of the pueblos of the Rio Abajo ("lower river," the Pueblos from Cochiti south) while Tupatú handled day-to-day matters in the Rio Arriba ("upper river," roughly the settlements from Santa Fe north).[20]

Otermín's Attempted Reconquest, 1681

Less than a year after the visitation of Shimitihua and his companions, a more sinister force reappeared in the northern Rio Grande. In mid-November of 1681 word reached the Pueblos that a column of Spaniards had left El Paso and was journeying upstream from the south. Led by Governor Otermín, the force was composed of 146 soldiers and 112 Indian allies. Yet it was clear even to the Native spies who tracked their progress that this troop consisted largely of novices and untrained recruits. Only a few carried a full set of arms and cavalry equipment; most made do with little more than a shield and a dagger.[21] The average Pueblo warrior was better equipped than these ruffians. Through a system of smoke signals and runners, Native lookouts cautioned the Pueblos to be wary of the ragtag procession. Hidden among the arroyos and hills surrounding the Rio Grande, Pueblo scouts observed as Otermín's force inspected the now-vacant Piro pueblos of Senecú, Socorro, Alamillo, and Sevilleta (all of which had been abandoned in previous months, probably due to raiding by nomadic tribes). On leaving each of these settlements the Spaniards set them aflame, a scorched earth policy that sent a clear message to the "apostate rebels" who still inhabited the pueblos to the north.

The residents of Isleta slept fitfully on the night of December 5, 1681. The events of recent days had them stuck between a rock and a hard place. On the one hand the Spaniards were reportedly making their way up from the south, with Isleta targeted as their next logical stopping place. On the other hand, they were under increasing pressure from the Pueblos to the north,

who had been unhappy with them ever since the Isletas' lackluster performance in the Revolt. Now, with feeble harvests among the Tewas, Tanos,
Jemez, and Keres, the northern warriors were threatening to attack Isleta and
sack their granaries.

The tension broke at dawn with the sound of Spaniards "extolling the most
holy sacrament in loud voices" just outside the village walls. The people of
Isleta rushed to their battle stations and released a few volleys at their attackers. But even as the arrows flew, there was probably an internal debate raging
among the inhabitants. Was it better to expend their energy fighting the
Spaniards first only to be faced by their Native brethren later? Or should they
lay down their arms and ally with the Spaniards now in order to bolster their
defenses against the attack of the Pueblos looming on the horizon? In the
end the Isletas decided that discretion was the better part of valor. They surrendered to the Spaniards by once again offering their obedience to Governor
Otermín before a single shot had been fired from any Spanish harquebus.
Apologizing for the arrows that had sailed over the Spaniards' heads, the people of Isleta explained to Otermín that it had all been a misunderstanding—
they had thought they were being ambushed by some bothersome Apaches.[22]

With Isleta once again a vassal of the Spanish crown, the other Pueblos
in the Rio Abajo took evasive actions. The people of San Felipe, Kewa, and
Cochiti left their former mission villages to take refuge on a high mesa near
Cochiti. The Jemez followed suit, taking to the high ground near their own
pueblo, where they were joined by the Zias and Santa Anas. The remaining
southern Tiwa pueblos of Alameda, Puaray, and Sandia fled to the Sandia
mountains. (A few days later these last three would join the others on the
mesa near Cochiti.) Otermín sent a regiment of seventy men upstream to
inspect the pueblos along the Rio Grande south of Santa Fe. They found the
first two villages empty, but with conspicuous signs of the Pueblos' return
to "idolatry" and their recent evacuation. As the Spaniards approached the
third settlement, Sandia, they were initially reassured by the smoke they saw
rising from the chimneys. Surely this was a sign that the inhabitants were
awaiting their arrival peacefully. Only when they drew closer did they realize
that the smoke was issuing not from placid hearths but rather from the roof
of the church, which was engulfed in flames. Clearly, subduing the rest of the
Pueblos would not be as easy as Isleta. The column continued on through
Kewa to Cochiti, where they found hundreds of Pueblo warriors fortified on
nearby Horn Mesa, itching for a fight.[23]

Peering over the edge, the Indians watched warily as the Spaniards
appeared in the valley below. Calling down to them, they asked the Spaniards
why they had returned. "In order that your souls might not be lost," came

the reply from below. The Pueblo warriors laughed, calling the white men imposters and "bleating, horned goats" (*unos cornudos cabrones llorones*). "You are a bunch of hypocrites!" they shouted, all the while making lewd and perverse gestures. The Spaniards responded by preparing for the worst, arming themselves for battle.[24]

On top of the mesa, the leaders of the Pueblos—many of whom had comprised Po'pay's inner circle—met to decide their next step. A sizeable contingent of older men recommended making peace. After all, they reasoned, the latest reports seemed to indicate that the Spaniards had done no harm at Isleta.[25] Others believed that the Spaniards' newfound amiability was a ruse. As one witness surmised: "Perhaps they are deceiving us in order to take us peacefully and kill us." The advocates for fighting were primarily the council of war captains, headed by Tupatú and Catití. Francisco "El Ollita," the Spanish-speaking coyote leader from San Ildefonso, gave a stirring speech to rally the assembled troops: "No one should surrender in peace," he growled, "all must fight! Although some of my brothers are coming with the Spaniards, if they fight on the side of the Spaniards I will kill them, and if they come over to the side of the Indians I will not harm them." Finally Catití addressed the crowd, announcing that he had already put into motion a plan to destroy the Spaniards with a feigned peace—and a Trojan horse of sorts:

> He had arranged to send to [the Spaniards' encampment] all the prettiest, most pleasing, and neatest Indian women so that, under pretense of coming down to prepare food for the Spaniards, they could provoke them to lewdness, and that night while they were with them, the said coyote Catití would come down with all the men of the Keres and Jemez nations, only the said Catití attempting to speak with the said Spaniards, and at a shout from him they would all rush down to kill the said Spaniards.

Catití briefed the women regarding the plan while they bathed and dressed themselves in all their finery. But as they began to descend the mesa, the women spied a column of Spanish reinforcements approaching the encampment. Losing their nerve, they returned to the mesa top. Catití would have to formulate another plan to do away with the Spaniards. He sent word throughout the region calling all warriors to rise to the occasion. He even called on his predecessor, telling Po'pay that if he was man enough to rebel the previous year, he should be man enough to come now and defend their freedom, even if he was no longer recognized as their leader.[26]

Over the next three days, the Spaniards nervously cooled their heels at Cochiti. Messengers from above visited the camp daily, assuring the Spaniards that the Pueblos were indeed preparing to come down. As the second day lapsed into the third and the Spaniards had still seen no signs of movement, Otermín's troops became increasingly wary. Unbeknownst to them, reinforcements had been streaming onto the mesa top from all corners of the Pueblo world: Tewas, Tanos, Jemez, Pecos, Taos, and Picuris warriors joined the junta with the intent of finishing the job they had started sixteen months prior. While they waited they were visited by two Indians who sympathized with the Spanish cause. They warned the Spaniards that the peace had not been made in good faith, and that the Pueblos were planning an attack. There is some evidence to suggest that these informants were spies sent to intimidate the Spaniards into fleeing without a battle. If this was in fact the case, they were eminently successful. The Spaniards broke camp and retreated that very day, reconnoitering with Otermín and the rest of the column. All continued south, pausing just long enough to put flame to the Pueblo of Isleta. The Spaniards took 385 Isletas with them as they left the blazing village and returned to El Paso. Otermín's attempted reconquest had failed.

The Spaniards' disappointment, as well as the state of the Pueblos after their first year of independence, was duly summarized in the words of Fray Francisco de Ayeta on December 23, 1681:

> at the present writing it has not been possible to perceive the slightest action, vestige, or sign from which can be inferred anything else except only that [the Pueblos] have been and are exceedingly well satisfied to give themselves over to blind idolatry, worshiping the devil and living according to and in the same manner as when they were heathen . . . they have been found to be so pleased with liberty of conscience and so attached to the belief in the worship of Satan that up to the present not a sign has been visible of their ever having been Christians. There have been only proofs of their false Christianity and of their having accepted and embraced the commands of the first leader and captain-general, Po'pay.[27]

5

Rebuilding the Pueblo World, 1681–1683

FOLLOWING OTERMÍN'S SECOND RETREAT, the documentary record concerning events in the Pueblo world goes cold. Spanish chronicles have passed on just a few meager sentences about life in the northern Rio Grande during the eleven-year gap between 1681 and the colonizers' reconquest of 1692. Not surprisingly, the writings of the Spaniards during this period focus on events in El Paso del Norte, not those among the Pueblos. And for the most part, Native oral traditions regarding this era of Pueblo independence (also known as the Spanish interregnum) have not been shared with outsiders. We are left with archaeology to fill in the blanks, providing a window into the events that occurred among the Pueblos between 1681 and 1692.

Accordingly, the focus here turns to the archaeology of the Jemez Province, the traditional homeland of Towa-speaking peoples west of the Rio Grande. The Jemez Province (see figure FM.2) is particularly appropriate for this task as no less than four new pueblo villages were constructed in this region between 1681 and 1694. It retains the most extensive material record of the Spanish interregnum of any of the subregions of the American Southwest. Although events in other parts of the Pueblo world were undoubtedly unique, the Jemez Province serves as the best available proxy for establishing what transpired among the Pueblos between the Revolt and the reconquest. Based on the archaeology of these four sites, we can start to infer not only what happened among the Jemez during the era of Pueblo independence but also glimpse some of the large-scale processes that occurred throughout the Pueblo world during this period.

Conflagration and Migration

Around noon on August 10, 1680, a pueblo messenger arrived at the Jemez mission village, called San Diego de la Congregación by the Spaniards and

Walatowa by the Jemez (known today to the anglophone world as Jemez Pueblo). Pulling up the reigns on his horse, he announced that the Revolt had already begun at the other pueblos, two days earlier than originally planned. "We have killed them all from Los Taos to the pueblo of Santo Domingo," he gleefully declared, enjoining the Jemez to "take up arms and kill these Spaniards and friars who are here."[1] While the Spanish alcalde mayor of the district managed to escape along with Lorenzo Muza and four others, Fray Juan de Jesus did not. After the rest had fled on horseback, the Franciscan locked himself in the convento to await his fate in quiet prayer. Fray Juan, who was renowned throughout New Spain for his gift of prophecy, had reportedly experienced ominous forebodings of his own martyrdom between 1677 and 1680.[2] His premonitions were realized late that Saturday night. Near midnight, the warriors of Jemez reportedly dragged the priest from his cell out into the churchyard. A 1689 account suggests that they stripped Fray Juan naked, tied him to the back of a pig, and paraded him through the plaza of the pueblo, castigating and beating him all the while. Later they removed him from the swine, forced him onto his hands and knees, and took turns riding on his back, spurring his haunches like a horse. Finally they shot Fray Juan with arrows and buried his body next to a kiva in the main plaza at Walatowa (where his remains were discovered a dozen years later, an arrowhead still lodged in the spine).[3]

In the months that followed Po'pay undoubtedly visited the mission village on his victory tour, encouraging the Jemez to destroy the vestiges of Christianity that remained in their midst and turn back to the ways of their ancestors. In response, the residents of Walatowa sacked the church and destroyed the effigies of the Virgin and her Son along with the church bells, but not before the leaders of the Pueblo collected some of the chapel's furnishings and other sacred objects, storing them securely in a chest.[4]

In November 1681 word reached the Jemez that the column of Spanish troops led by Governor Otermín was inching up the Rio Grande. Although they never entered the Jemez Province, the presence of the colonizers among the other Pueblos made the people of Walatowa understandably nervous. Their leaders decided that everyone should withdraw from the mission village and take to higher ground, seeking refuge among the more defensible mesas north of the pueblo as a precautionary measure.[5] They would not leave behind a vacant and abandoned mission pueblo, however. Instead, the Jemez took this opportunity to purge the final remnants of the colonizers once and for all. They burned the entire village to the ground, destroying even their own homes. Jemez oral traditions report that the men of Jemez "held blazing torches to the vigas of the houses" at Walatowa, "while the women and children stood across the river and watched the terrible fire" as the mission village was consumed in flames.[6] They apparently reduced the church to ashes at this time as well, as later documents speak of the Jemez being forced to rebuild the ruined church and priest's dwelling.[7]

Given the nature of the commands handed down by Po'pay, the destruction of the church and priest's quarters at Walatowa is unsurprising. But why would the Jemez destroy their own homes? This seemingly peculiar act was probably related to the unique history of the settlement. The seventeenth-century missions of New Mexico were typically established in the midst of existing Pueblo villages that had often been occupied for centuries prior to the Spaniards' arrival. Unlike the other Pueblo missions, however, San Diego de la Congregación was not built at such a previously existing settlement. Instead, the Spaniards founded an entirely new village, independent of the existing pre-Hispanic Jemez pueblos. In 1622 the Franciscans established the mission of San Diego de la Congregación in the wide, flat floodplain at the southern end of the Jemez valley. As its name suggests, this village was intended to facilitate congregación, inducing the Jemez who lived among the rugged mesas to settle at this more accessible—and more easily monitored—location. Fray Benavides wrote in 1630 of "San Diego de la Congregación, which for our purposes we founded anew, taking to it the Indians . . . We gave them houses already built, along with food and sustenance for several days and plowed fields for their seed plots."[8] Given this history, it seems likely that the Jemez would have associated this village more with their Spanish colonizers than with their pre-Hispanic ancestors. Following Po'pay's directives, then, they torched the entire mission pueblo to rid their world of the things they associated with the Spaniards.

Patokwa: Village of the Turquoise Moiety

After razing their mission village, the Jemez struck out for the safety of the mesas to the north. There they would start their lives over again, living in accordance with the directives of the spirits. They migrated approximately seven kilometers (4.4 miles) up the valley, following the winding course of the Jemez River to the north (Elliott 2002:57). There they settled on a low, peninsular mesa near the confluence of two streams, where they built a new pueblo known as *Patokwa* (LA 96; translation: "turquoise-moiety place" [figure 5.1]).[9] No tree-ring dates have yet been recovered from Patokwa,[10] but Jemez oral traditions and ceramic evidence suggest that this was the place they settled following their departure from Walatowa after the Revolt.

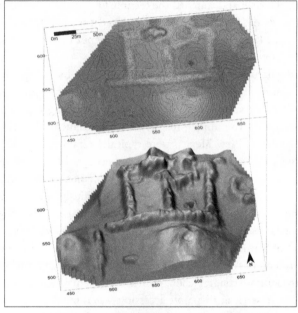

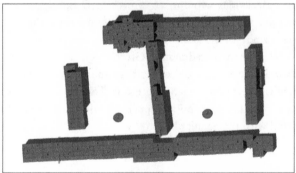

FIGURE 5.1. Patokwa (LA 96), surface map and reconstruction circa 1681.

Furthermore, when the Spaniards returned to New Mexico in 1692, this is where they found the Jemez living.[11] Thus all available lines of evidence—oral tradition, historical documents, and archaeology—converge to establish Patokwa as the place to which the Jemez moved in 1681.

This was not the first time that Jemez people had lived on this landform, which they called *Weshulekwa* (translation: "place where they both are," referring to the confluence of canyons and rivers surrounding the mesa [Harrington 1916:397]). The remains of an earlier village, dating to the AD 1300s, are clearly visible on the mesa top as well.[12] Mounds indicating the location of Rio Grande Classic period (AD 1325–1600) roomblocks are still conspicuous on the ground surface, with thousands of pieces of broken pottery, remains of stone tools, and animal bones littering the area nearby. Northeast of these mounds is a large circular depression, almost certainly the remnants of an ancient kiva. These remains would have been obvious to the Jemez migrants of the seventeenth century as well, and when they came to this area in 1681 they chose to settle directly next to the vestiges of their ancestors' homes (see chapter 6). Here they began to build the village that came to be known as Patokwa.

The seventeenth-century component of Patokwa consists of two large rectangular plazas, surrounded by mounded roomblocks in all four of the cardinal directions. A fifth, central roomblock bisects the two plazas, with additional detached, smaller groups of rooms located to the east, northeast, southwest, and south of the main village. Beneath the ground's surface the tabular masonry walls of the pueblo still stand up to three meters tall, encased in centuries of accumulated dust and sand. In a few areas the top courses of these walls are visible, with the brick-red sandstone blocks revealing the alignments of the original rooms. In the east plaza the remains of a kiva are plainly apparent (due to the presence of walls exposed when a looter attempted to unearth buried treasure here in recent years). There is probably a kiva located in the west plaza too, as suggested by a slight depression in the southern end. (Ground-penetrating radar surveys in 2003 and 2010 confirmed the remains of stone masonry below the surface here, but were inconclusive regarding the form of the buried structure.) The northern and central roomblocks were vandalized sometime prior to the mid-1960s, when looters used a bulldozer to raze rooms in this area.[13] Additionally, the remains of a Franciscan mission complex constructed between 1694 and 1696 are clearly discernable in the northwest corner of the pueblo (for more information on this structure, see the Epilogue).

From the plazas of Patokwa, one has the sense of standing on an island in the middle of a wide, low bowl. Although the site is located on a rise, the mesa itself sits at the end of two canyons. To the south and west loom the peaks of the Nacimiento Mountains, while the volcanic mesas of the Jemez Province rise to the north and east. Two notches have been cut in the rim of this bowl by the two rivers that flow down the canyons past the mesa. Cottonwood trees line the riverbanks below, while cholla cactus and sagebrush push up through the dusty soil on the mesa top, interspersed by the occasional piñon or juniper pine. The mesa itself consists of layered red Permian sandstone with a surface like 40-grit sandpaper. This sandstone served as the building material for the pueblo itself, and admittedly, to the untrained eye Patokwa is not much to look at today. ("It's just piles of rocks," was the way an astonished visitor once described the remains of the village, employing a remarkable economy of words.) Yet despite its modest appearance, the archaeology of Patokwa reveals a wealth of information about the composition of Jemez society in the early 1680s.

Mapping Patokwa

In 2003 and 2004 I conducted a mapping and survey project focused on Patokwa, aided by interns from the Pueblo of Jemez. The mapping of the site was, like most archaeology, a tedious and uncomfortable process. The work took place primarily between June and August, so on most days the sun was intense and the air was hot. There is no tree cover to speak of at Patokwa, making shade a precious and rare commodity. When we started our morning climb up the mesa with forty-pound packs on our backs, we were sometimes blessed with a few clouds. But these usually dissipated by 9:00 a.m., leaving us to roast on the mesa top like chiles on a cooking stone. The typical work crew consisted of four of us: me and a rotating crew of interns from Jemez Pueblo that included Marlon Magdalena, Daniel Madalena, and Gorman Romero.

Our goal was to create a high-resolution topographic map of the surface of Patokwa, in keeping with the noninvasive objectives of our research program. The primary tool we used to accomplish this was a total station, an electronic surveying instrument that records the precise location of points across the landscape. This requires one person to look through the eyepiece of the instrument (a job usually performed by me) and center its crosshairs on a prism (usually held by one of the interns). The total station then emits an infrared signal, which it uses to detect and record the exact location of the prism. Because the prism sits on the end of a long aluminum staff, the intern holding the pole often looked like a modern-day Moses making his way across the site, pausing every step or two to take a measurement. (And at times we felt like the proverbial Hebrews wandering on a seemingly endless journey in the desert.)

In order to ensure consistent coverage across the surface of the site we instituted a standard system of data collection. First we established a 20 × 20 meter grid over the entirety of Patokwa, pounding garden stakes into the ground at each node in order to orient ourselves as we worked our way across the site. Within each 20 × 20 meter unit, we recorded the precise locations of individual points in the landscape on both the horizontal (N-S-E-W) and vertical (elevation) axes by positioning the prism poles accordingly. To guarantee that we didn't miss any area within each unit we used a system of marked ropes to guide our data collection. Ropes were oriented along the north and south boundaries of each grid unit, labeled at 0.25-meter intervals. A third rope, also labeled every 0.25 meters, was then stretched across the unit perpendicular to the north and south lines to serve as a guide for the recording of individual points. We moved the third rope across the grid as measurements were taken along transects within each unit, with its marks providing a reference point for persons holding the prism poles. Three people typically surveyed each grid unit, with me calling out directions from behind the total station to the interns regarding where to place their prism poles. The distance between each measurement and the density of recorded points within each unit varied depending on the microtopography of the area in question—areas exhibiting greater topographic relief were recorded with a higher density and greater overall number of points. In some areas survey density was greater than one point per 0.25m^2. In flatter areas, such as the plazas, points were recorded every 2.5 meters along transects spaced 2.5 meters apart, averaging one point per 6.25m^2. On a good day, we might complete three or four units of the grid. Other days we completed just one, depending on the complexity of the microtopography. All told we recorded 5,303 individual points across the surface of the site.

In 2004 we returned to sample the pottery at Patokwa as well. We chose to collect all the surface ceramic sherds from four 5 × 5 meter units. We selectively placed these units in the areas of highest artifact density in the north, south, east, and west middens (refuse areas) at the site. The southern unit was chosen for its proximity to the aforementioned Classic Period remains, while the other three were located in close proximity to the 1680s settlement in an attempt to isolate the Revolt-era assemblage and minimize the mixing between the two components. Students from the Pecos Pathways program assisted in the collection of approximately two thousand ceramic sherds. This pottery was then washed and analyzed (see chapter 6). Following this analysis, all the sherds were returned to their original locations, leaving the site exactly as it had been prior to our analysis.

The Process of Construction

The spatial organization of Patokwa reveals a wealth of information regarding the construction of the village, and more importantly, regarding the people who built and occupied it. Patokwa's roomblocks are arranged in what has been termed the "linear plaza" form. That is, the village consists of multiple

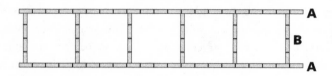

FIGURE 5.2. Ladder construction: A = axial walls, B = cross walls.

long, narrow rows of rooms that define proportionally large, enclosed plazas. This distinctive type of site layout results from coordinated, suprahousehold construction activities in which many rooms are built at the same time by erecting two or more parallel axial (long) walls first, then subdividing the space between them with multiple (shorter) cross walls to form individual rooms (figure 5.2). This technique, termed "ladder-type" construction, results in rooms of similar size and walls with shared azimuths. It is a highly efficient method of building a new pueblo quickly and suggests that inhabitants moved into Patokwa in a large group (or groups) rather than one family at a time.[14] Ladder construction requires coordination and control of labor above the household level because it is typically undertaken by cooperative communal work groups rather than individual family units (Kidder 1958:63; Lange and Riley 1966:97; Hill 1982:73; Robinson 1990; Cordell 1998:27; Cameron 1999b:207).

The linear plaza form has been contrasted with "agglomerative" layouts, characteristic of pueblos formed by dense clusters of individually constructed rooms surrounding relatively small plazas. Agglomerative construction does not require a suprahousehold coordination of labor; it is accomplished by building one room at a time, presumably by members of individual households or extended families (Mills 1998; Cameron 1999b:207–08). Agglomerative pueblos display a lack of shared walls and variable wall azimuths, resulting in roomblocks without the long, unbroken, shared azimuths displayed at Patokwa. In contrast to agglomerative layouts, linear plaza pueblos such as Patokwa tend to make use of proportionally larger plazas because these areas result from preconstruction planning and demonstrate a shared understanding by the community residents regarding the size and organization of the plaza space. Linear plaza pueblos are typically expanded through the addition of new rooms and roomblocks displaced from the original plan, preserving the central plazas (Cameron 1999b:227–230), as was the case with the construction of the detached roomblocks to the northeast, east, southwest, and south at Patokwa. Conversely, agglomerative pueblos can more easily accommodate small groups of immigrants through the addition of individual rooms adjacent to the plaza-oriented construction as new households join the community.

Linear plaza layouts are associated primarily with the Eastern (Rio Grande) Pueblos, patrilineal descent, and patrilocal or neolocal residence patterns, whereas agglomerative layouts have been linked to Western pueblos (Hopi and Zuni in particular) and matrilineal descent patterns (James 1997:435; Cameron 1999b:206–207, 226). Furthermore, linear plaza designs are thought to result from large-scale, well-organized communal migrations because of their evidence for planned and organized construction.

Just such a large-scale, well-organized communal migration took place in the Jemez Province following the destruction of Walatowa in 1681. The planned nature of Patokwa's architecture suggests that the Jemez people migrated to this mesa en masse. When they reached the ruins of the earlier site, a community leader (or group of leaders) must have outlined the plans for construction and assigned tasks to various work groups. Some of the men would have been sent to cut the masonry blocks from the red sandstone cliffs at the edges of the mesa; others felled trees for the vigas (roof beams) and *latillas* (smaller cross timbers) needed for the roofs; yet another group would have prepared the masonry and mortar. Ultimately, however, it was the women who typically laid up the walls among the Pueblos. ("If we force some man to build a wall," wrote Fray Alonso de Benavides in 1630, "he runs away from it, and the women laugh.")[15] Others prepared the food that would support the work crews. This was a communal effort, and everyone pitched in.

After the work groups had been established, the first step in the construction of Patokwa was to lay out the plazas. Both plazas are roughly equal in size (approximately sixty meters N-S by forty meters E-W) and are bounded by roomblocks in all four cardinal directions, forming right angles at the corners. Their identical design indicates that this plan was no accident, and it did not occur haphazardly or organically. Rather, the Jemez leader(s) designed the "negative space" of Patokwa prior to the construction of the roomblocks. Indeed, Pueblo oral traditions suggest that plazas were typically the first element of a new village to be planned following a communal migration. In the early twentieth century, Franz Boas recorded an oral tradition of Pueblo migration and construction among the Keres neighbors of the Jemez that detailed the steps of construction of a new village: "Then there they stopped. First they made the plaza. After [that] they made the chief's house. Then they made four entrances to the plaza, and there they lived" (Boas 1928:70). The Jemez people followed a similar pattern in the construction of Patokwa. After first establishing the layout of the plazas, the residents of Patokwa began construction on their dwellings.

The reference to the building of the "chief's house" recorded by Boas hints at the centralized leadership that is necessary in such instances of organized migration and planned construction. And while we do not know where the elite residences were located at Patokwa (or if indeed there were any), we can identify two conspicuous elements of communal construction in each of the plazas: the kivas. The placement of the kivas in corresponding areas of each of the plazas further hints at the planning and intentional design that went into in the construction of the village. The final element in the aforementioned oral tradition—the entrances to the plazas—were also included in the initial plan of Patokwa. In the northeast, northwest, southeast, and southwest corners of the pueblo, gateway entrances were left open to provide access to the plazas.[16] Robert Preucel has linked similar gateway entrances at the Keres Revolt-era pueblo of Kotyiti to the homes of supernatural beings believed to dwell at the corners of the Pueblo world, suggesting that these open gateways emphasize important elements of Pueblo cosmology (Snead and Preucel 1999:188; Preucel 2006:227–228; see also Ortiz 1969:13–28).

Rooms and People at Patokwa

Although some wall alignments are visible on the ground surface at Patokwa today, it is not possible to determine an exact count of the number of rooms, nor the dimensions of discrete rooms, that were constructed during this initial phase based solely on the surficial investigations that have thus far been conducted at Patokwa.[17] However, in some areas looting and vandalism have exposed wall alignments enough to enable an approximation of average room size. Based on these exposed walls, I estimate the interior dimensions of a conjectural average room at Patokwa to measure 2.5 meters wide by 5.0 meters long, resulting in an average floor area of 12.5 m². This seems a reasonable estimate, based on analogies with two other early Pueblo Revolt era dual-plaza pueblos: Kotyiti (LA 295; average floor area: 14.6 m² [Preucel 1998]), and Boletsakwa (LA 136, average floor area: 11.1 m² [see below]). These figures enabled us to make a hypothetical reconstruction of Patokwa (see figure 5.1) and prove useful for estimating the population of the village.[18]

The estimation of population based on archaeological data is a notoriously difficult task, often more akin to alchemy than science (Cook 1972; Hassan 1981; Nelson et al. 1994:114; Ferguson 1996:42). Over the past half-century many different techniques have been applied to ancestral Puebloan archaeological sites in an effort to determine past populations, including examples based on ethnographic analogy, the volume of rubble, numbers of rooms, floor area, area of roofed architecture, and amount of refuse, to name just a few (Naroll 1962; Hill 1970b; LeBlanc 1971; Clarke 1974; Sumner 1979; Brown 1987; Dohm 1990; Hill et al. 2004; Duwe 2010; Ortman 2010). In order to estimate the founding population of Patokwa, I utilized two sources of evidence gleaned from the architectural survey of the site, the estimated number of rooms and the total estimated floor area.

One of the most common methods of estimating past Pueblo populations via archaeological remains is based on the estimated number of occupied rooms at a site. In order to apply this method the proportion of rooms occupied at a given time must first be determined, but this is a particularly difficult task to accomplish based solely on surficial data. Previous studies in the Zuni area circumvented the issue by assuming that between 50 and 80 percent of a pueblo was occupied at any given time (Smith et al. 1966:12; Watson et al. 1980:207). Keith Kintigh (1985:22) takes the median of these, assuming that an average of 65 percent of the rooms were occupied in a pueblo village at any given time. The situation at Patokwa in 1681 is different from that of typical pre-Hispanic pueblos, however, as it was occupied solely by the founding population, living in newly constructed architecture. (Rooms that appear to have been added subsequent to this initial construction event have been factored out of the following estimates.) Therefore it seems safe to assume that all of the newly constructed architecture at Patokwa was occupied simultaneously in 1681.

Another factor that complicates the estimation of Patokwa's population based on room counts is the fact that previous studies utilizing this technique have relied heavily on the assignation of function to rooms (i.e., storage versus habitation), a determination that is impossible to make in the absence of excavations (J. B. Hill et al. 2004:692). Thus James N. Hill's oft-cited figure of 2.8 persons per habitation room based on ethnographic observations among the Hopi (1970a:75–77) is not particularly useful in relation to the Patokwa data set.

Alternatively, estimates based on the total number of rooms per person, such as Karen Dohm's study of twenty-five historic pueblos, can be useful in estimating the population of Patokwa. Dohm recorded a range from 0.219 to 1.344 rooms per person, with a mean of 0.60 rooms per person, noting that the number of rooms per person increased with increasing site aggregation (1990:212). Assuming for the moment that the 1681 room estimate at Patokwa (including second and third story rooms, but not including the kivas) of 359 is not wildly inaccurate, a maximum estimate—that is, one that assumes the entire site to be occupied contemporaneously—based on Dohm's assumptions yields a population of 598 persons (359 rooms divided by 0.60 rooms per person).

Another measure on which to base population estimates is the internal floor area of rooms, which may be more accurately predicted based solely on surficial data than the total number of rooms (although the problems of room function and number of rooms occupied at any given time still apply). Unfortunately, there is no consensus regarding the amount of floor area typically utilized per person. Previous estimates of population based on floor area have attempted to provide a general figure applicable cross-culturally, and while revised estimates have been suggested for use in the Southwest and elsewhere, this method has not been widely applied in the archaeology of ancestral pueblos. Furthermore, as Dohm has demonstrated, this figure is likely to vary among differing pueblos, regions, and time periods (Naroll 1962; LeBlanc 1971; Cook 1972; Casselberry 1974; Clarke 1974; Brown 1987; Dohm 1990; Cameron 1999b:210).

Preucel's study of the Revolt-period village of Kotyiti provides some baseline evidence from a contemporaneous site with a very similar layout from which an estimation of population at Patokwa can be drawn. Based on documentary sources, he estimates the population at Kotyiti to have been at least 454 persons (Preucel 1998:74). The total floor area of all rooms at Kotyiti, including second story rooms, is 2,304.6 m^2, resulting in an average of 5.1 m^2 of floor area per person. Based on the assumptions described above, the total floor area at Patokwa in 1681 (including second and third story rooms, but not including kivas) is approximately 4,487.5 m^2. Applying the figure of 5.1 m^2 per person yields an estimate of 880 persons living at Patokwa in the initial days after its founding.

Both the population estimates based on number of rooms (598) and that based on floor area (880) are a far cry from the 1697 figure reported by the Franciscan historian Fray Augustín de Vetancurt, who claimed that on the eve of the Pueblo Revolt of 1680 the Jemez mission of San Diego de la Congregación harbored a population of 5,000 persons.[19] Either Vetancurt's estimate is wildly inaccurate or the majority of the Jemez population did not make the journey to Patokwa, choosing instead to emigrate elsewhere. In the absence of any known oral traditions, archaeological data, or historical evidence supporting the latter proposition, I suspect that the former is actually the case. Vetancurt, who never visited San Diego de la Congregación (nor even New Mexico) personally, may have derived this figure from his notion that the population of the Jemez mission brought together the inhabitants of five pre-Hispanic pueblos through the policy of congregación. He seems to have assumed a figure of one thousand occupants at each of those prior villages (again, likely an inflated estimate), tallying a total of five thousand. Yet based on the available archaeological data, it seems probable that the founding population of Patokwa (and thus a more reasonable approximation of the population of San Diego de la Congregación/Walatowa in 1680) numbered somewhere between six hundred and nine hundred persons.

Raids and Factionalism, 1681–1683

The plaza-oriented layout of Patokwa is more than merely an artifact of the ladder-construction technique and mass migration. Defensibility was probably a major factor in the architectural planning of the village as well. A Tiwa witness captured by Otermín in 1681 reported that many of the Pueblos had moved to new villages after the Revolt "in order to be together and in a strong defensive position."[20] Steven LeBlanc describes linear-plaza pueblos such as Patokwa as the archetypal defensive pueblo layout (1999:56–66). With central, enclosed plazas surrounded on all sides by inward-facing roomblocks, Patokwa could have been fortified relatively quickly in the event of an enemy attack. Traditional rooftop entrances into the rooms would have allowed the populace to take refuge within the secure living spaces. After the nonwarriors were safely ensconced inside, the ladders could be raised to thwart the enemy's access, while rooftop perches provided a position of strategic advantage to Pueblo archers and artillerymen, who could fire down on their attackers.

But exactly who did the people of Patokwa anticipate would attack their new pueblo? When the Jemez decamped from their mission village in 1681, it was ostensibly due to the threat of the returning Spaniards. In December of that year, a Tesuque man testified that earlier in the month "the news spread from pueblo to pueblo, it being said that the Spaniards had killed all the natives of the Pueblo of La Isleta and had captured all the outsiders from other pueblos who had come to seek maize. As a result of this . . . the Jemez [went] to a high mesa which is near the pueblo of Los Jemez."[21] Presumably that mesa was where they constructed Patokwa. But Otermín's forces never advanced up the Jemez River to verify this statement, and Jemez concerns about an immediate attack by the Spaniards proved unwarranted (for the moment).

While the initial impetus for the construction of Patokwa may have been to protect themselves from the bearded ones they called *Castyilash* (Castilians), the Jemez quickly found that the Spaniards were not their only threat. They also had to worry about attacks from neighboring nomadic tribes, typically referred to in the documentary record as *Apaches* (Brooks 2002:52; Schaafsma 2002:199). *Apache* (derived from the Zuni word *apachú*, meaning enemy) was a catch-all term used by the Spaniards to refer to any and all of

the nomadic and semisedentary Athapaskan speakers throughout the kingdom of New Mexico, not only the tribes we today call Apaches.[22] Included
in this group were the ancestors of the modern-day Diné (Navajo), who the
Spaniards often referred to as "Apaches de Navajo."[23]

Prior to the Spanish colonization of New Mexico, Jemez relations with
some of their Athapaskan neighbors appear to have been quite amicable.
Ancestral Navajo peoples were some of the most reliable and consistent trading partners of the Jemez. Lori and Paul Reed present evidence suggesting
strong Jemez-Navajo alliances based on the prevalence of Jemez Black-on-
white pottery on Navajo sites dating to AD 1500–1690 (1992:100–101).
Thus while Jemez interactions with their Pueblo neighbors seem to have
been limited during this period, in contrast, trade among Jemez and Navajo
peoples apparently flourished prior to Spanish colonization (Liebmann and
Preucel 2007:204). Indeed, of the Pueblo ceramic types typically found
at sixteenth- and seventeenth-century Navajo sites, Jemez Black-on-white
is the most common. Some of these amicable relationships appear to have
continued into the Colonial period, with strategic alliances forged between
the Jemez and some of the "Apaches" (in all likelihood, ancestral Navajos),
sometimes in opposition to the Spaniards (Brugge 2002). In 1614 the Jemez
colluded with their Athapaskan neighbors in the murder of an Indian from
Cochiti, and in 1645 a Jemez-Apache alliance was implicated in the death
of a Spaniard.[24]

Yet even while the Jemez traded, allied, and conspired with some of
their nomadic neighbors, instances of "Apache" hostility against the Jemez
punctuated the early mission era as well. As noted in chapter 2, the arrival
of the Spaniards not only disrupted Athapaskan-Pueblo trade throughout
the Southwest, but also supplied the nomadic peoples with horses, which
encouraged increased raids on the Pueblos (John 1975:59). Furthermore,
there was no unitary Navajo Nation or unified Apache tribe(s) (analogous to
the modern political entities of today) during this era; rather the Athapaskan
residents of New Mexico comprised separate bands of peoples who spoke
related languages—some of whom were likely allied with the Jemez, others
who were enemies and hostile raiders. A Navajo attack on Walatowa resulted
in the death of a priest in 1639, while in the mid-1650s another Athapaskan raid killed nineteen Jemez with thirty-four captives spirited away by
Navajo aggressors. And in 1659 a Franciscan reported that "bands of heathen . . . have entered the pueblos of . . . Hemes [Jemez], San Ildefonso, and
San Felipe. They have killed some Christian Indians and have carried off
others alive to perish in cruel martyrdom."[25] (Violence among the Athapaskans, Pueblos, and Spaniards during this era was not initiated solely by the

"Apaches," however. Under the administration of Governor Bernardo López de Mendizábal [1659–61], fifteen Navajos who were visiting Jemez peaceably, presumably to trade, were killed at the governor's orders, with an expedition sent out to enslave their families.)[26]

It seems reasonable to assume that in building Patokwa the Jemez strove to protect themselves not only from future Spanish attacks but also from the assaults of Native enemies as well. When the colonizers returned to the northern Rio Grande a decade later, Pueblo people told the Spaniards that "the Apaches from other rancherias . . . came from afar to rob and kill them" during the interregnum between 1681 and 1692.[27]

Navajo/Apache assaults were not the only threat to the Jemez living at Patokwa, however. With the ouster of the Spaniards, the Pueblos suffered from an increase in attacks by Ute raiders as well. Prior to the Spaniards' arrival, Ute peoples existed primarily as small bands of hunter-gatherers living beyond the northern boundaries of the Pueblo world. They engaged in only occasional trade with northern Pueblos such as Taos, Picuris, and Ohkay Owingeh. Because the Utes lacked a dependable surplus, their hunters typically procured only enough meat and hides for the immediate needs of their families. But a significant shift in Ute lifestyles accompanied the introduction of equestrian culture in the early 1600s. On horseback, they became more successful hunters, venturing onto the plains to slay buffalo in increasing numbers. Their social organization changed as well, shifting from isolated family bands to groupings of larger, well-organized camps that stretched for a kilometer or more along the river valleys of the San Miguel, La Plata, and San Juan ranges of northern New Mexico and southwest Colorado (John 1975:117–119).

Unlike their fellow nomadic gatherer-hunters, however, at least some of the Utes decided to pursue peaceful trade relations with the Spaniards rather than encountering them on the warpath. By the 1630s, both Spaniard and Pueblo were venturing to the Ute camps on the northern frontier in order to trade for pelts. When the Pueblos revolted in 1680 the Utes were not entirely happy with the outcome, as just two years prior they had negotiated a peace with Otermín at Taos. Thus in contrast to the "Apaches," who had suffered from deprivation and enslavement under Spanish rule, the Utes "were sorely inconvenienced by the Spaniards' expulsion" in 1680 (John 1975:120; Walz 1951:181). Accordingly, the disgruntled Utes took out their frustrations on the Pueblos in the wake of the Revolt, with attacks on the corn growers' villages becoming more and more common between 1681 and 1692. The situation was exacerbated by Pueblo incursions into Ute territory, where Pueblo hunters stalked buffalo, sometimes masquerading as Spaniards. Dressed in

leather jackets, metal helmets, and wearing the finery they had captured
during the Revolt, the Puebloans announced their presence by blowing the
bugles and horns they had seized from the governor's residence in Santa Fe.
Their transparent ruse annoyed the Utes, who punished the Pueblos with
increasing severity during their years of independence, with particular venom
focused on the northern Tiwa, Tewa, and Jemez pueblos.[28]

In the summer of 1683 the Utes turned their fury on the newly constructed pueblo of Patokwa.[29] The details of this attack are unknown, but
Jemez casualties were probably limited. For a substantial portion of the residents, however, the Ute raid served as a bellwether of things to come. This
new village was not as safe as they had hoped. For one thing, the mesa on
which it was built is relatively low in comparison with the surrounding landscape, rising only sixty-seven meters above the valley floor. Furthermore, it
could be accessed from virtually any direction, exposing the Jemez to simultaneous attacks from multiple sides. While they were lucky to survive the
Ute raid, many of the inhabitants must have doubted that the pueblo would
hold against the more formidable Spanish forces, should they return to the
Jemez Valley. As a result, the people of Patokwa split into two factions.
One group advocated the abandonment of their new home in order to build
another village on a more defensible landform, preferably one of the higher,
sheer-sided mesas nearby. The other group disagreed. Confident that their
warriors could repel any enemy who dared challenge them, they held their
ground and vowed to remain at Patokwa, come what may.

Factionalism in the Early 1680s

In retrospect, the fact that the attack of 1683 opened a rift in the Patokwa
community is not entirely surprising. Factionalism is a remarkably common
and persistent condition among Pueblo societies, particularly those navigat-
ing the minefield of colonial relations.[30] Dozier links this factionalism to the
"authoritarian, totalitarian characteristics" of Pueblo societies, noting that
"opposition to the compulsory dictates of the Pueblo authorities . . . [has]
resulted in frequent factional disputes" from pre-Hispanic through modern
times (Dozier 1966:175). As noted previously, it seems clear that between
the Revolt and the summer of 1683 some Pueblo leaders behaved despotically, most notably Po'pay. It is easy to imagine other leaders at individual
pueblos (such as Patokwa) following suit, considering the likelihood that
many of these same leaders were part of Po'pay's entourage before he was
deposed.

Furthermore, the unique history of the Jemez in the years leading up to the Revolt probably made leadership a highly contested issue at Patokwa, creating conditions ripe for a factional dispute. In the half-century between 1630 and 1680 the Jemez had endured a wholesale reconfiguration of their settlement patterns, resulting in a dramatic reduction in the total number of inhabited villages—a situation that must have correspondingly altered the political landscape of Jemez society radically. As mentioned in chapter 2, prior to the establishment of Franciscan mission facilities in the Jemez Province, the Jemez people lived in 10 to 15 large, self-governing pueblos. Between 1630 and 1680 they were reduced to one primary settlement (San Diego de la Congregación/Walatowa, the mission pueblo they burned in 1681). The coalescence of so many previously autonomous groups into a single community in a matter of a few generations provided a context in which power struggles would be expected. But the simultaneous imposition of colonial rule may have partially mitigated disputes regarding the legitimacy of leadership prior to 1680. The Spanish system of civil government established in the early seventeenth century, with its designated governor and staff of assistants selected annually from among the population at each of the Pueblos, may have served to repress or mask conflicts concerning political leadership (Dozier 1970:189–191). After the Spaniards' ouster in 1680, however, the system that had served to alleviate those tensions was dismantled, with conflicts likely resulting among rival leaders. As a result, the factionalism that appears to have characterized Patokwa in 1683 probably wasn't solely a result of the Ute raid; preexisting political rifts would have created conditions promoting the development of factions within the Patokwa community.

The Jemez were not the only Pueblo group to split into factions in the wake of the 1680 uprising. Factionalism seems to have characterized Isleta and Kewa during this period, too.[31] The divided nature of post-Revolt Pueblos was most clearly evident at Pecos, where a pro-Spanish faction had opposed a group of anticolonialists since the time of Coronado in the 1540s. By the mid-seventeenth century the rift had cleaved the residents of Pecos into two distinct settlements, with the Christian contingent perching in the shadow of the mission church while the more conservative, "traditional" bloc remained in the old north section of the village. During the Revolt the Pecos "friendlies" smuggled the resident friar out of harm's way, while the "hostiles" killed a second priest. Even after the Spaniards were gone, Pecos seems to have remained a pueblo divided.[32]

The conflicted nature of the Pueblos during the Spanish interregnum was perhaps best summed up by a Tewa man from Tesuque Pueblo who the Spaniards captured in late 1681. When asked about the Pueblo peoples'

attitudes regarding the possible return of their former colonizers, he confided
that "they were of different minds regarding it, because some said that if the
Spaniards should come [the Pueblos] would have to fight to the death, and
others said that in the end [the Spaniards] must come and gain the kingdom
because they were sons of the land and had grown up with the natives."[33]
This incipient factionalism was based initially around pro- and anti-Spanish
contingents. But as time passed, these communal rifts were often exacerbated
by the raids of Utes, Navajos, and Apaches. As the testimony of one indio
ladino indicated to the Spaniards in the early 1680s:

> he said that it is true that there are various opinions among them, most of
> them believing that they would have to fight to the death with the said
> Spaniards, keeping them out. Others, who were not so guilty, said, "We
> are not to blame, and we must await [the Spaniards] in our pueblos." And
> he said that when the hostile Apaches came they denounced the leaders
> of the rebellion, saying that when the Spaniards were among them they
> lived in security and quiet, and afterwards with much uneasiness.[34]

Such seems to have been the case at Patokwa, where the 1683 Ute raid ultimately resulted in the fissioning of the pueblo into two separate settlements.
The process of one village splitting into two (termed "schismatic factionalism")
appears to have been a particularly common response to intrapueblo dissent
in pre-Hispanic times, when migration and settlement were unencumbered
by the shackles of colonialism (Siegel and Beals 1960:394, Dozier 1966:172).
Still, schismatic factionalism has persisted among the Pueblos into modern
times, exemplified in the famous Orayvi split of 1906 at Hopi (Whiteley 1988,
2008; Cameron 1999a). This pattern was reestablished in the 1680s when, in
apparent response to the Ute raid of 1683, the dissident group from Patokwa
split off to found a second new pueblo.

Boletsakwa: Pueblo of the Abalone Shell

The splinter group left Patokwa, probably in the autumn of 1683, and travelled approximately 10 kilometers (6.2 miles) to the east where they settled
on a higher, steeper mesa—what the Spaniards referred to as a *peñol*, nearly
150 meters tall. The Spaniards called this the peñol of San Juan, the name by
which it is still known today.[35] San Juan Mesa is more than twice the height
of the mesa on which Patokwa was built, and is surrounded by deep, narrow
canyons. Here the Jemez refugees would be better suited to defend themselves

from enemy raids, whether their attackers be Ute, Apache, Navajo, or Spaniard. In a flat spot on a narrow, peninsular spur of the mesa, surrounded by Ponderosa pines, the Jemez émigrés built a new village known as Boletsakwa (LA 136; translation: "pueblo of the abalone shell," figure 5.3).[36]

The landscape surrounding Boletsakwa is strikingly different from that of its sister site. While the hues around Patokwa are dusty desert reds, Boletsakwa sits amidst the lofty greens of Ponderosa pines and Gambel oaks. The verdant vegetation results from its higher elevation, with the latter located 425 meters (nearly 1,400 feet) above that of the former. Like Patokwa, Boletsakwa exhibits two distinct spatial and temporal components. A late Coalition/early Classic period (AD 1250–1400) settlement is located in the northern half of the site. No standing walls are visible today in this older section, and much of the masonry from the earlier settlement appears to have been borrowed and reused in the construction of the Revolt-era pueblo (Elliott 2002:53). Adjacent and just to the south of this is the later, architecturally distinct Pueblo Revolt–era village. The 1680s component of Boletsakwa consists of two roughly identical square plazas (measuring approximately 32 m along the north-south axis and 34 m east-west) delineated by roomblocks, and bisected by a central roomblock. The original walls of many of these rooms remain standing today, sometimes more than 1.5 meters in height. These walls were constructed of simple biflagged, semi-coursed tuff masonry (*tuff* being rock formed from welded volcanic ash, the material that comprises San Juan mesa). Like Patokwa, Boletsakwa is a linear plaza pueblo, with long narrow roomblocks defining two proportionally large, enclosed plazas. Open "gateway" passages into the plazas are located in the southeast and southwest corners of the south plaza, as well as in the middle of the eastern side of the north plaza. This last gateway provided easy access for residents of the north plaza to the large subterranean kiva located just outside the eastern roomblocks.

Tree-ring dates collected from roof beams at Boletsakwa confirm that the Revolt-period component of the site was constructed between 1680 and 1683, with a cluster of vigas dating to 1683 (table 5.1). A 1694 reference in a Spanish military journal describes the residents of Boletsakwa as those "from the Jemez who had separated themselves from that pueblo and gone to the [San Juan] mesa in years past,"[37] suggesting that the site was indeed founded as a result of a factional rift. And the 1683 testimony of an indio ladino who had recently fled the Pueblos claimed that "in order to live as they had in ancient times . . . the people of Jemez would go to live in the old strong pueblo of San Juan, where they could defend themselves."[38] (Here the "old strong pueblo of San Juan" appears to refer to San Juan Mesa, rather than the village of Ohkay Owingeh.)

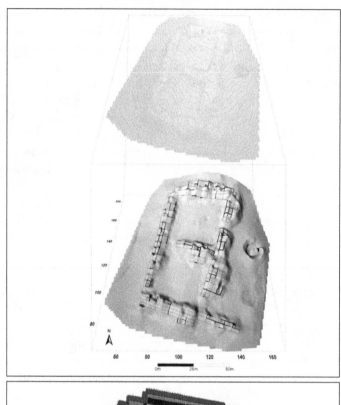

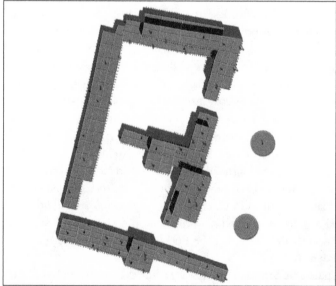

FIGURE 5.3. Boletsakwa (LA 136), surface map and reconstruction circa 1683.

Table 5.1. Tree-ring dates from Boletsakwa (Robinson et al. 1972:45)

Catalog Number	Species	Date
RG-379	Ponderosa pine	1492p–1656v
RG-766	Ponderosa pine	1472p–1663v
RG-764	Ponderosa pine	1621p–1680v
RG-763	Ponderosa pine	1646p–1680v
RG-765	Ponderosa pine	1647p–1680cG
RG-768	Ponderosa pine	1641p–1681vv
RG-757	Ponderosa pine	1650p–1681r
RG-758	Ponderosa pine	1650p–1682vv
RG-758	Ponderosa pine	1628p–1683v
RG-767	Ponderosa pine	1647p–1683v
RG-758	Ponderosa pine	1658p–1683v
RG-758	Ponderosa pine	1653p–1683r
RG-758	Ponderosa pine	1650p–1683r

Key: p = pith ring present; v = subjectively near a cutting date; vv = no way of determining actual cutting date; c = outermost ring is continuous around the entire section; G = beetle galleries present; r = outermost ring is not continuous around the entire section

As they had done two years earlier at Patokwa, the Jemez refugees worked together to raise the walls of Boletsakwa, again employing the ladder-construction technique. Patterns of corner bonding (where the masonry of intersecting walls is tied together) confirm that many of the rooms at Boletsakwa were built in episodes of simultaneous construction (Liebmann 2006:429–33). And like Patokwa, Boletsakwa exhibits traits consistent with a high degree of architectural planning, such as shared wall azimuths, room-blocks arranged at approximately right angles, and plazas of nearly identical size. These traits indicate that construction activities were organized and coordinated above the household level, suggesting that a degree of centralized leadership was present in the Boletsakwa community in 1683.

Mapping Boletsakwa

We used very similar mapping techniques at Boletsakwa to those we had implemented at Patokwa, relying primarily on a total station and the help of a group of interns from Jemez Pueblo. The major difference between the two sites is the significantly higher visibility of many of the rooms and walls at Boletsakwa. While Patokwa's architecture is generally mounded over, Boletsakwa retains numerous standing walls and intact foundations visible on the ground surface today, more than 325 years after the village was constructed. Unfortunately much of this visibility is due to the fact that many of Boletsakwa's rooms have been looted over the past century, leaving the masonry walls exposed to the elements. Additionally, Benny Hyde and W. S. Stallings carried out some partially controlled (but largely undocumented) excavations in the 1930s to collect tree-ring samples from the site (Elliott 2002:54). In the 1960s a local Girl Scout "Archaeology Unit" conducted a series of small-scale excavations, including some in the northern kiva (Bohrer 1968). The partially exposed walls of this kiva reveal an interior floor area of nearly 60 square meters (diameter: 8.7 m, circumference 27.3 m). The fact that these and other excavations were apparently never backfilled helped to establish a more accurate sense of the number and size of individual rooms at Boletsakwa (particularly when compared with Patokwa).

The topographic mapping we conducted also emphasized some of the more ephemeral signatures of archaeological features that are not immediately apparent to the naked eye. In particular, it identified a subtle depression located in the southeast quadrant of the site (south of the exposed kiva), a feature that had previously been noted by Michael Elliott (2002:54). This depression suggested the possibility of a subterranean feature in this area, and seemed to be about the size and shape of a typical kiva. However, the dimple in the landscape was far more subtle than that of a typical kiva depression. Thus we were left to speculate about its nature: was it natural or cultural? Was it architectural? A reservoir? The remnants of a long-dead tree root system? A swale formed by erosion?

To answer these questions we enlisted the aid of Jennie Sturm of TAG Research, a specialist in ground-penetrating radar (GPR) and geophysical analyses in archaeology. Using GPR, we could peer beneath the ground virtually to see whether or not there were any architectural remains below the surface. In August of 2010, Sturm and I dragged a small plastic orange sled—a box about the size of a small carry-on suitcase—back and forth over the ground in the area of this depression. The sled contained two 400 MHz radar antennas, which sent a radar signal into the ground and recorded any reflections that bounced back. The reflected radar amplitudes measured the degree of physical and chemical differences in subsurface materials. Strong (or high amplitude) reflections often indicate denser or different buried materials, such as archaeological features. The GPR instrument recorded these amplitudes, which Sturm later processed to remove background noise generated from internal system interference, ultimately producing a series of "slice-maps," graphic depictions of the radar reflections (figure 5.4).

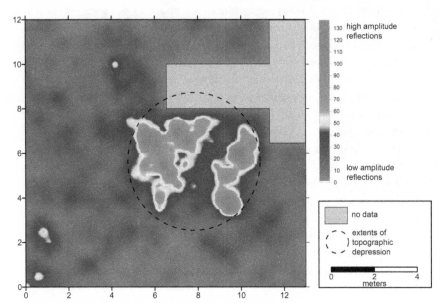

Boletsakwa GPR slice map: 12-15 ns (60-75 cm below ground surface)

FIGURE 5.4. GPR slice map of probable south kiva at Boletsakwa (LA 136).

GPR slice maps are the Rorschach test of modern archaeology, heavily dependent on the interpretation of the viewer. But the reflections that bounced back from under the ground at Boletsakwa clearly show a circular subterranean anomaly in the area of this depression, approximately 8 meters in diameter, buried to a depth of 1.5 meters below the surface. In the realm of archaeological GPR, these images are about as clear as it gets. Of course, without excavation we cannot be absolutely certain as to the cause of this anomaly. But all indications suggest that it represents the remains of a second, buried kiva.

Rooms at Boletsakwa

Our investigations documented 168 ground-floor rooms at the Revolt-era component of Boletsakwa.[39] We derived this estimate by first recording in-situ wall remnants and standing walls, then using these data to infer the probable location and extent of walls that are not presently visible. In areas where wall segments were either completely degraded or not visible, intrasite microtopography and the dispersion of wall fall and rubble were utilized to determine the probable extent of walls and rooms.

In order to account for multistory architecture, I examined the microtopography within individual room blocks. By applying the same techniques
and analogies used in determining the height of room blocks at Patokwa (see
note 18) to the topographic data collected at Boletsakwa, it is possible to infer
the height of individual rooms. These techniques indicate that there were
forty-seven second-floor rooms in the Revolt-era architecture of Boletsakwa,
resulting in a total estimate of 215 rooms. The average floor area at Boletsakwa is 11.1 m^2 (3.6 m^2 sd), with an average room length of 4.9 m (1.1 m sd)
and an average width of 2.2 m (0.5 m sd) (Liebmann 2006:252–56).

Interestingly, the size of the rooms at Boletsakwa differs significantly from
those occupied by the Jemez in the pre-Hispanic era. A comparison of the
floor area of Boletsakwa with that of the pre-Hispanic Jemez village of Unshagi (constructed between 1402 and 1605, see Reiter 1938:199) illustrates
this striking disparity.[40] The average floor area of rooms constructed after
the Revolt of 1680 was notably larger, and exhibits a considerably greater
range of variation than those of the pre-Colonial era (figure 5.5). This conclusion is based on CAD-derived measurements of the floor area of 99 rooms at
Unshagi (mean = 8.04 m^2, sd = 2.50 m^2), compared with 65 rooms in the
Pueblo Revolt–era component at Boletsakwa (mean = 11.13 m^2, sd = 3.59).
This larger room size seems to index an aspect of Pueblo resistance to Spanish colonization that had a significant impact on Jemez social organization.

In the early seventeenth century, the Spaniards levied exorbitant taxes on
Pueblo Indians in New Mexico on a household-by-household basis, regardless of the number of family members living under one roof. Fray Alonso
de Benavides described the situation in 1630:

> it has been established by the first governors of New Mexico, and is being
> continued by order of the viceroy that each house pay a tribute consisting
> of a cotton blanket, the best of which are about a yard and a half square,
> and a fanega of corn. This is understood to be for each house and not for
> each Indian, even though many Indian families live in such houses. It
> often happens that the pueblos increase or decrease in houses, or, if one
> tumbles down, its dwellers move to that of their relatives, and none of
> these pay tribute, except for the house in which they live.[41]

In an attempt to subvert the colonial system of taxation, Pueblo families con-
solidated their households in the early seventeenth century, combining more
members under fewer roofs (Anderson 1985:365). Over time, this appears to
have resulted in the construction of larger rooms in order to accommodate the
increased numbers of persons living in each structure. Additionally, Steven

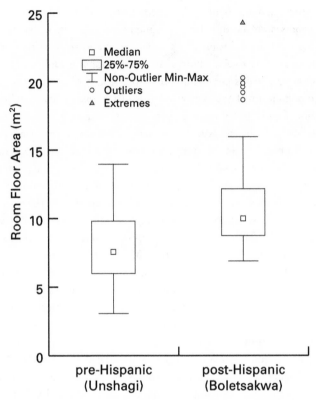

FIGURE 5.5. Box-and-whiskers plot comparing room sizes at Boletsakwa (LA 136) and Unshagi (LA 123).

James (1997:437) suggests that the introduction of metal axes, draft animals, and wagons resulted in the cutting and transport of larger trees for vigas, producing larger rooms in post-1600 pueblos than in their pre-Colonial predecessors. Tribute regulations were reassessed in 1643 as a result of declining Pueblo populations, and the burden of encomienda shifted from households to individuals (Forbes 1960:139). But the impact on Pueblo social organization was lasting, and the Jemez continued to utilize these larger rooms into the late seventeenth century at Boletsakwa.

Population at Boletsakwa

There are no known historical records regarding the population of Boletsakwa, but the numbers of rooms and floor area provide useful data for preliminary demographic calculations of the Pueblo Revolt–era population. Assuming that all rooms were occupied contemporaneously (a reasonable hypothesis considering the brief duration of occupation at the Revolt-period component of Boletsakwa—just twelve short years), and applying Dohm's (1990:212) average of 0.60 persons per room to the total count of 215 rooms yields an estimated population of 358 persons. An alternative assessment can be derived by applying figures based on Preucel's Kotyiti data (5.1 m² per person) to the total floor area of the Revolt era component of Boletsakwa, including the second story rooms (2298.9 m²), resulting in an estimated population of 451 inhabitants. A reasonable approximation of the Revolt-era population of Boletsakwa based on extant archaeological data, then, would suggest that the village housed somewhere between 350 and 450 residents in the early 1680s.

Included in these figures are a number of non-Jemez people, however. The Jemez splinter faction was not alone in their construction work at Boletsakwa. Shortly after arriving at San Juan Mesa, they were joined by a group of Keres-speaking refugees who had journeyed from their home village of Kewa, located about thirty-two kilometers (twenty miles) to the southeast on the opposite flank of the Jemez Mountains. Spanish documents of the 1690s repeatedly refer to Boletsakwa as a multiethnic community comprising both Jemez and Kewa peoples.[42] However, there are no outlying rooms or roomblocks separated from the main plazas of Boletsakwa (as appeared at numerous other Revolt-era pueblos, including Patokwa, most likely to accommodate an influx of new refugees). This suggests an integrated community that coalesced more or less at the same time, with little subsequent immigration following its initial establishment. The documentary record implies that the Kewa population of Boletsakwa was not an itinerant populace receiving temporary shelter at the site or an outside group of interlopers, but rather that these people were permanent residents of the pueblo, living side-by-side with the local Jemez population.

In the three years following the Pueblo Revolt, two new villages were constructed in the Jemez Province. Both shared a remarkable similarity in architectural layout, with two plazas and two kivas. Both display evidence of strong centralized leadership, intentional planning, and coordination of a communal labor pool. And both are located directly adjacent to the remains of earlier pueblos. This similitude is more than a mere coincidence. As we shall see, the correspondences between these villages are the material manifestations of the ideology of revitalization originally espoused by Po'pay in 1680, embodying the nativism and revivalism that reshaped the Pueblo world in the wake of the Pueblo Revolt.

6

Dismembering and Remembering

THE SIMULACRA OF POST-REVOLT SETTLEMENTS

WITH THE SUN HANGING LOW IN THE SOUTHERN SKY of late 1681 the Spaniards questioned Pedro Naranjo, an eighty-year-old "sorcerer and idolater" from San Felipe Pueblo. The octogenarian was an esteemed holy man in his home community and had been sent to the southern Pueblos by the leaders of the Revolt to "teach superstitions" during the lingering nights of mid-December in 1681.[1] The Spaniards took Naranjo into custody at Isleta, where under interrogation the old man provided the most comprehensive testimony of all of the Pueblo prisoners captured and questioned by Otermín in the wake of the Revolt. Not only did he report the motives, factors, and historical circumstances underlying the rebellion stretching back over more than three decades, but he also provided expansive details regarding the dyadic nature of Po'pay's orders. More than any other witness, Naranjo laid bare the two complementary halves of Po'pay's mandate: first, to eliminate Spanish contagion from the Pueblo world; and second, to reestablish traditional, pre-Hispanic Pueblo practices. According to Naranjo, once they had razed the churches, washed away the oils of baptism, and dissolved the sacrament of Christian marriage, Po'pay had assured the people that "they would live as they had in ancient times . . . this was the better life and the one they desired, because the God of the Spaniards was worthless and theirs was very strong, the Spaniards' God being rotten wood."[2]

In anthropological parlance, directives demanding the elimination of all foreign accoutrements and influences are classified as *nativism*, while the introduction of cultural practices thought to have been characteristic of previous generations (but not recently practiced by a social group) is known as *revivalism*. At the most basic level, both nativism and revivalism are bound up in the phenomenon of "social memory"—the ways in which shared ideas about the past are revived, referenced, dismissed, ignored, selectively utilized, and amended (Van Dyke 2009:220). Nativism frequently involves acts of intentional forgetfulness, as when Po'pay ordered the Pueblos to purge all evidence that Spaniards had ever set foot into the sands of New Mexico, wiping their very existence from the collective Pueblo consciousness. Likewise, revivalism inherently involves a process of remembering, as when the Tewa prophet attempted to stoke memories of a utopian past before the foreigners had appeared in the lands of their ancestors.

In recent years investigations of social memory have proliferated in the discipline of archaeology, with studies of "the past in the past" utilizing material culture to investigate acts of commemoration and collective amnesia in distant times (Bradley and Williams 1998; Joyce 2000; Alcock 2002; Bradley 2002; Van Dyke and Alcock 2003; Golden 2005; Jones 2007; Yoffee 2007; Mills and Walker 2008a; Van Dyke 2009). Many of these studies have built on pioneering work on social memory by social theorists Maurice Halbwachs (1992 [1925]) and Paul Connerton (1989; 2006). Halbwachs's (1992:43) contention that "no memory is possible outside frameworks used by people in society to determine and retrieve their recollections" served to shift the analysis of memory from individual psychology to the realm of collective interaction. Likewise, Connerton's (2008:59) distinction between "inscribed memories" and "incorporated memories" has proven particularly influential in anthropological analyses in recent years. Inscribed memories, glossed here as intentional commemorations of the past, have been rebranded as "citation" in archaeological literature recently. Conversely, incorporated memories can be defined as habitual practices that recursively, and often unconsciously, create and reference the past. Archaeological studies have begun to break down the distinction between inscribed and incorporated memories of late, focusing on the ways in which habitual practices and intentional memorializations work in concert to form social memories (Van Dyke 2009:222; Mills and Walker 2008b:6–7).

The Jemez people combined processes of remembering and forgetting after the Pueblo Revolt in the construction of Patokwa and Boletsakwa. At both of these new villages, architecture was used to reference ancestral lifeways, which were combined with habitual practices to allude to the pre-Hispanic past. This amalgamation of nativism, revivalism, and architecture comes as no surprise, as Naranjo's testimony directly linked the built environment to the ideology of cultural revitalization espoused by the leaders of the 1680 Revolt. According to Naranjo, after the Revolt Po'pay "saw to it that [the Pueblo people] at once erected and rebuilt their houses of idolatry . . . and that they could erect their houses and enjoy abundant health and leisure." This testimony marked the first time the Spaniards were told that

Po'pay's message was not exclusively one of destruction, but included a mandate to create anew as well—to build new kivas and pueblos, in addition to tearing down the churches. On reviving their traditional architecture, Naranjo noted that "the people were very much pleased, living at ease in this life of antiquity," much to the Spaniards' chagrin.[3] The Jemez took these edicts to heart, constructing new homes, storerooms, and kivas at the villages of Patokwa and Boletsakwa. From the beginning, the builders of these new settlements enacted the tenets of nativism and revivalism through architectural design and the construction process, attempting to revitalize their culture by purging their world of Spanish influence and returning to traditional, pre-Hispanic ways of life.

Forgetting the Saints, Remembering the Ancestors

Although much of the recent archaeological work dealing with social memory has focused on processes of commemoration and citation, often the first step in the creation of shared memories is an act of forgetting. As Connerton notes, remembering is commonly valued in contemporary Western societies, while forgetting is considered a deficiency (Connerton 2008:59). Yet the absence of memory is not always a limitation. Forgetting can be a constructive process, as well as an essential part of the creation of new cultural and social formations. In fact, omission, intentional neglect, and the denial of the colonial past were crucial elements in the reconfigurations of Pueblo culture that occurred after 1680 in the northern Rio Grande.

This desire to forget seems to have worked in concert with the attempt to emulate their ancestors when the Jemez chose the locations in which to build Patokwa and Boletsakwa: on the tops of mesas rather than in the canyon bottoms. Prior to Spanish colonization, the majority of large Jemez villages were located on mesa tops scattered throughout the province.[4] As noted in chapter 2, beginning in the 1620s the Franciscans began to implement a policy of congregación in the Jemez region. Congregación pulled the Jemez out of their mesa-top villages and forcibly resettled them in the lower elevations at the southern end of the valley.[5] As Fray Alonso de Benavides remarked in his 1630 *Memorial*:

> The Jemez nation . . . had been scattered all about this kingdom when I arrived as custodian, and their lands were nearly deserted due to hunger and war. These two plagues were finishing them off. Then I began to settle them, with tremendous effort, in a place where some had already been

baptized, and had their churches, which were tended by several priests. I got them all together in the same province.

I put a cleric in charge who supported all these efforts very attentively. We gathered this tribe into . . . San Diego de la Congregación, which for our purposes we founded anew, taking to it the Indians who had been part of that nation but had gone astray. We gave them houses already built, along with food and sustenance for several days and plowed fields for their seed plots.[6]

Through this policy the Franciscans congregated the Jemez in the lower elevations at the southern end of the Jemez valley, physically below the mesatop villages they had inhabited prior to the arrival of the Spaniards. When the Jemez people moved out of the riverside flats and back to the northern mesas to build Patokwa and Boletsakwa, they were rejecting both the Spanish mission and the policy of congregación. At the same time, the mesa-top locations of Patokwa and Boletsakwa mimicked the primary settlement pattern of their pre-Hispanic forebears.

The Cultural Landscape of Revitalization

Twice in the early 1680s, Jemez refugees surveyed their rugged territory in search of a new place to live—first after burning the mission and village of San Diego de la Congregación, then again two years later when the splinter faction left Patokwa after the Ute raid of 1683. On both occasions the migrants were greeted with seemingly boundless options. A virtually uninhabited landscape stretched for miles before their eyes, with acres of enticing lands on the tops of sprawling mesas with southerly exposures, perfect for growing the bountiful harvests that Po'pay had assured would follow the ouster of the Spaniards. With the large-scale depopulation of the landscape that had occurred over the previous half-century and the Spaniards now out of the picture, the Jemez could build their new villages anywhere they wished.

Although the mesas and canyons of the Jemez Province were essentially uninhabited at this time, it would be wrong to think of this terrain as a tabula rasa. It was not empty. Scattered across the landscape were the crumbling remains of a dozen large ancestral villages (all with five hundred rooms or more) and approximately twenty medium-sized pueblos (containing between fifty and four hundred rooms each), in addition to hundreds of one- to four-room field houses (Elliott 1986; Kulisheck and Elliott 2005). These vacant settlements, sprinkled across the mesa tops like spots on the back of a white-tailed fawn, would have been conspicuous to anyone journeying across the Jemez Province in the 1680s (as they are to contemporary visitors today). The crumbling remains of these sites probably served then, as they do now, as mnemonicons: places of visitation, wonder, remembrance, and history for the descendants of those who once lived there (Connerton 2006:321; Fowles 2009:457). In the late seventeenth century, the stone masonry of their ancestors' homes would still have been visible to the Jemez, with collapsed and broken vigas straining to keep the walls from toppling in on themselves. The ground surrounding these villages was (and still is) littered with tens of thousands of pieces of broken pottery in an astounding spectrum of whites, yellows, grays, and reds. Mixed in among the potsherds were a seemingly endless number of obsidian and chert stone flakes flickering black and white in the sun, the by-products of the production of knives, scrapers, and arrowheads in years gone by. All these relics would have served as prominent reminders to the seventeenth-century Jemez that the terrain stretching before them had not always been depopulated. In the centuries before the Spaniards arrived, the mesa tops had teemed with life.

When the Jemez struck out to make a fresh start by founding first Patokwa and later Boletsakwa, they choose to build these new pueblos not in a "pristine," previously unoccupied area, but instead placed them directly adjacent to the crumbling remains of their ancestors' villages (figure 6.1), on the tops of mesas. The choice to situate their new settlements in this way seems not to have been a coincidence. In fact, in addition to Patokwa and Boletsakwa, Kotyiti (constructed between 1683 and 1685) was similarly situated on a

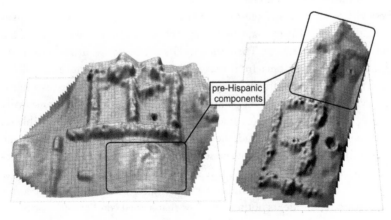

pre-Hispanic components

FIGURE 6.1. Contiguity of pre-Hispanic and Revolt-era components at Patokwa and Boletsakwa.

mesa top that shows clear evidence of an earlier occupation (Preucel et al. 2002:81–83).[7] Thus the construction of new villages in the immediate wake of the Revolt seems to have followed a consistent pattern: they tended to be located on mesa tops in direct proximity to the remains of sites that were occupied (and vacated) in pre-Hispanic times (Liebmann et al. 2005). These settlements were not examples of the reoccupation of previously inhabited buildings or simple architectural remodeling. Patokwa and Boletsakwa were constructed anew, and deliberately placed directly next to the remains of settlements that had probably been deserted for nearly two centuries. In both cases, the mesas on which these sites are located are vast. The builders of Patokwa and Boletsakwa could have placed their villages virtually anywhere, yet they chose to locate them directly adjacent to the homes of their ancestors.

To be sure, practical and functional considerations likely influenced the selection of these locales to some degree as well. From a purely pragmatic perspective, it was easier to scavenge building materials from the earlier structures than it would have been to quarry entirely new masonry. Stone-robbing does appear to have contributed to the construction of the post-Revolt component at Boletsakwa, where much of the masonry of the 1680s village appears to have been salvaged from that of the earlier, pre-Hispanic settlement. (All the tree-ring dates that have been recovered from Boletsakwa thus far date to the latter seventeenth century, however, indicating that roof beams were probably not scavenged from the older site. See table 5.1.) Defensibility clearly played a role in the selection of the mesa-top locations as well, particularly in the case of Boletsakwa, which appears to have been founded as a direct result of the Ute raid of 1683.

Utilitarian considerations alone cannot account for the similarities among these villages in terms of their placement in the landscape, however. This is particularly true of Patokwa, where stone-robbing of the older village did not take place on a large scale. There the pre-Hispanic remains utilize a different type and style of masonry from that of the 1680s component. The walls of the earlier village are largely composed of unshaped river cobbles, while the brickwork of the post-Revolt component consists primarily of intentionally shaped, tabular sandstone (as evidenced by wall alignments still visible on the ground surface today and those exposed in looters' pits). Neither can defensibility solely account for the selection of these locations; while protection from attack clearly played a role in the settlement of Boletsakwa, it was probably not the sole determining factor. In fact, when in 1694 it became apparent to the residents of these pueblos that armed conflict with the Spaniards was inevitable and imminent, both villages were evacuated in favor of a third, much more defensible locality (see chapter 9).

The choice to locate these villages directly next to the remains of the earlier settlements was thus not purely coincidental nor wholly pragmatic. Rather, the positioning of these villages within the existing cultural landscape seems to have been influenced in part by the ethos of revivalism that pervaded the northern Rio Grande in the 1680s, particularly the call to revitalize Jemez society by returning to pre-Hispanic patterns of culture. The emplacement of these villages was but one way that the Jemez followed Po'pay's call to "live as they had in ancient times." In other words, after the Revolt, the residents of Patokwa and Boletsakwa returned to the ways in which their ancestors lived by returning to the places in which their ancestors lived.

By building their new villages adjacent to the crumbling remains of older architecture, the Jemez may have been resuming an earlier settlement pattern on the intrasite level as well. Recent detailed investigations of occupational histories at other Rio Grande pueblos have determined that the remains of these settlements are not necessarily the result of sizeable, long-lived, deeply sedentary populations. Rather, the number of people living at these pueblos waxed and waned over time. Ann Ramenofsky's recent studies at San Marcos Pueblo in the Galisteo Basin have demonstrated that the populace of that village was highly itinerant, practicing a form of residential mobility in the centuries leading up to 1680 that involved frequent emigration from and return to that site throughout the centuries between 1200 and 1700 (Ramenofsky et al. 2009:506–507). This appears to have been the case at many of the pre-Hispanic ancestral Jemez pueblos as well; preliminary analysis of surface ceramics, augmented by dendrochronological evidence from roof beams, indicates that discrete architectural areas of these large sites were settled at different times throughout the 1300s–1600s. As the Jemez circulated among these previously inhabited villages, leaving one pueblo to take up residence at another, they would have become accustomed to constructing new architecture in direct proximity to the crumbling remains of prior occupations.

This pattern was broken, however, when the Franciscans founded the mission of San Diego de la Congregación, building an entirely new village where none had been located previously. Spanish mission policies such as congregación and reducción "pinned the Pueblos like butterflies to a mounting board," in the words of Steve Lekson (1990:336–37). In doing so, they inhibited the frequent migrations into and out of large villages that had characterized Jemez settlement in the pre-Hispanic era. In the 1680s, when the Jemez were finally presented with the opportunity to build a new community virtually anywhere they wished, they settled among the remains of earlier villages, just as their forebears had done in previous times. The fact that this move coincides with an overtly nativist/revivalist revitalization movement is likely more than mere coincidence. This configuration was a resumption of earlier settlement patterns and was another manner in which the Jemez chose to remember the ways of their ancestors in the years following 1680.

Whether or not the establishment of these new villages among the remains of the old was an example of "citation" or "inscribed memory"—that is, whether or not this was a deliberate attempt to reference the past by the founders of Patokwa and Boletsakwa—by their very nature, these locations must have created incorporated memories, shaping the thoughts and activities of the Jemez with reference to their past. Every day the residents of Patokwa and Boletsakwa would have walked among the evidence of their ancestors, over the crumbling walls and around and through the detritus of past lives. Daily activities such as refuse disposal would have created an awareness of the past as the 1680s residents dumped their household rubbish on top of that of their forefathers. This regular interaction with the past would have influenced their behaviors and mental processes, even if this influence was not entirely conscious.

Restoring Balance: The Architecture of Revitalization

Of the seven types of forgetting identified by Connerton, the most brutal, conspicuous, and typically violent form is that of "repressive erasure." This particular kind of communal amnesia (often associated with totalitarian regimes) involves the intentional destruction of monuments to previous rulers and prominent signs of the past. Repressive erasure is frequently employed to bring about a break with the past at the start of a new era, in an attempt to wipe the slate clean and build an improved society (Connerton 2008:60). The most comprehensive example of repressive erasure in New Mexico following the Pueblo Revolt was the destruction of the Jemez mission of San Diego de la Congregación. The razing of the mission village and subsequent construction of Patokwa and Boletsakwa represented a rejection of Franciscan mission culture—an overt example of repressive erasure in an attempt to remove the memory of the Spaniards.

The twin ideologies of nativism and revivalism played central roles in shaping the physical forms of Patokwa and Boletsakwa. As noted in chapter 5, the builders of these dual-plaza villages clearly utilized corresponding arrangements of architectural units, resulting in pueblos with strikingly similar spatial organization. These compact pueblos were a significant departure from that of the mission village that the Jemez reduced to ashes following the Revolt. Although no maps of the San Diego de la Congregación mission village are known to exist, a few tantalizing hints regarding the layout of the pre-Revolt village are contained in Spanish documents. A 1693 description of the ruined pueblo by Vargas suggests that the village consisted of numerous disconnected room blocks with up to a dozen small plazas, signifying a highly dispersed spatial plan.[8] As Fray Benavides noted a half-century before the Revolt, it was the Spaniards who had originally constructed this village, not the Jemez, with the friars giving the Natives "houses already built" in the 1620s.[9]

Going Off the Grid

Because San Diego de la Congregación was "founded anew" by the Spaniards and not constructed among the buildings of a previously existing pueblo, it is likely that the original layout of the mission village followed a grid pattern. Throughout the colonial New World, Spaniards often employed the grid plan when designing new villages and cities. Beginning as early as 1502 the grid plan was utilized in laying out new settlements in the Caribbean, soon to be followed by those in the Yucatan peninsula, Central Mexico, and the Andes (Oviedo y Valdés 1959 [1535]:11; Kubler 1978:327; Clendinnen 1987:39–40; Cummins 2002:205–206). When laying out the colonial capital of New Mexico in 1610, the founders of Santa Fe followed a grid plan as well, in accordance with the Laws of the Indies (Snow 1988:40–45). Viceroy Luís de Velasco instructed the governor to establish the new capital in six districts, with a central square block for civic structures and a chapel.[10] The missions of New Mexico were typically established at previously existing Pueblo settlements, however, obviating the need for geometric civic plans. Thus, while patterned, geometric grid plans were not generally utilized at Pueblo missions in the northern Rio Grande, such an arrangement was used at other settlements founded anew in the Kingdom of New Mexico.[11] Furthermore, the Jemez mission of San Diego de la Congregación bears the distinction of being the only Pueblo mission village founded entirely anew by the Spaniards in seventeenth-century New Mexico. In this light it seems probable, based on Benavides's and Vargas's descriptions, that the original layout of San Diego de la Congregación followed a grid plan as well.[12]

As Tom Cummins (2002:205) notes, the grid was "more than merely an architectural plan." It was also "a model for creating Christian order" in a world of barbarism and infidels. The grid embodied the triumph of civilized culture over the savage nature of unplanned settlements, a visual manifestation of Augustine's City of God. For this reason the grid-town plan, "built under the direction of Spaniards throughout their colonial domain, has been interpreted as an architectural representation of colonial control and oppression," according to Setha Low (Low 1995:749; see also Foster 1960). In their destruction of San Diego de la Congregación, then, the Jemez rejected not only the religion of the friars, but Christian order and colonial control more generally.

When the Jemez constructed the new settlements of Patokwa and Boletsakwa they eschewed the dispersed spatial arrangement of the Spanish mission, adopting a more aggregated, contiguous architectural plan. In addition to the nativist element of these new villages, their builders were utilizing a revivalist return to a traditional Puebloan form of settlement. Contiguous, plaza-oriented layouts were the norm at all ancestral Jemez villages prior to Spanish colonization. Although the pueblos built and occupied in the Jemez region between 1300 and 1600 display a wide range of variation in terms of overall size, organization of roomblocks, and numbers of rooms, plazas, and kivas (figure 6.2), all pre-Hispanic ancestral Jemez villages larger than twenty rooms were minimally composed of a combination of contiguous roomblocks and at least one plaza (Elliott 1986:176–77). It is true that the remains of these villages as they appear today represent an architectural palimpsest, collapsing centuries of settlement into a single, two-dimensional form. But even if only parts of these settlements were occupied during any given period of time, the people who did so all lived in rooms connected to those of their neighbors, and very near a central plaza. After the Revolt of 1680, the Jemez chose to return to this type of settlement. The aggregated forms of Patokwa and Boletsakwa represent not only a rejection of the gridded and dispersed plan of the mission, they also signal a return to the architecture of their ancestors.

Icons of Revivalism

The builders of Patokwa and Boletsakwa were not content to move away from the grid plan back to just any random form of contiguous, plaza-oriented village. As noted earlier, both Patokwa and Boletsakwa share very similar layouts. Each has two, roughly equal-sized plazas bisected by a central roomblock, with two associated kivas and open entrances at the corners of the plazas.

Were it only the Jemez who had utilized this distinctive twin-plaza site plan it might be easy to chalk this up to an interesting coincidence of history, or simply the imitation of Patokwa's layout by the builders of Boletsakwa (who had, after all, recently migrated from the former village). But this correspondence is no accident. A third pueblo is known to have been constructed

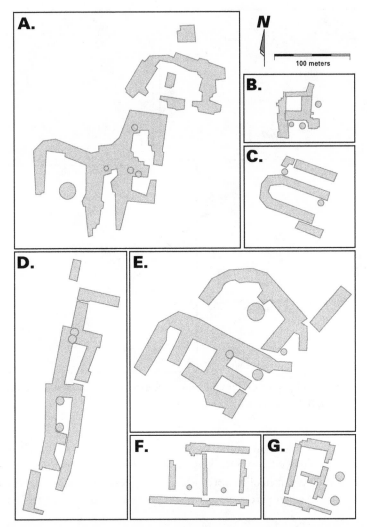

FIGURE 6.2. Architectural layouts of ancestral Jemez pueblos. (A) Kwastiyukwa (AD 1350–1650); (B) Unshagi (AD 1375–1620); (C) Nanishagi (AD 1350–1500); (D) Seshukwa (AD 1350–1650); (E) Amoxiumqua (AD 1350–1600); (F) Patokwa (AD 1681–1694); (G) Boletsakwa (AD 1683–1695).

in the early 1680s by a different ethnolinguistic group (the Keresans of the Pueblos of Cochiti, San Felipe, and San Marcos), located less than 33 kilometers (about 13.5 miles) east of Boletsakwa. Named Kotyiti, this village also displays a strikingly similar dual-plaza, central-roomblock, two-kiva form (figure 6.3; Preucel 1998, 2006). Thus between 1680 and 1685, three pueblos were

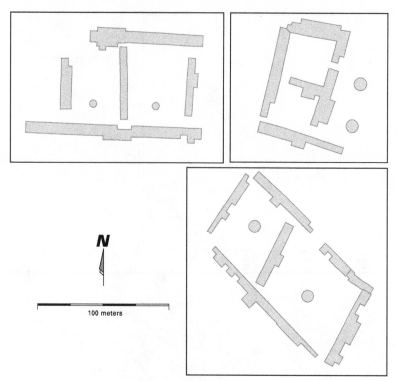

FIGURE 6.3. Twin-plaza, two-kiva pueblos of the early 1680s. Clockwise from upper left: Patokwa, Boletsakwa, Kotyiti.

constructed with the same iconic layout, all within a day's walk of each other. The fact that three villages were constructed with this distinctive layout—by multiple different ethnolinguistic groups—suggests that this pattern was not random. And in patterns such as this we can expect to find embedded meaning.

In retrospect, it is not entirely surprising to find the repetition of similar forms during a period of overt revivalism. In semiotic terms the twin-plaza, dual-kiva pattern is *iconic*. That is, this layout is a sign whose meanings are grounded in mimesis, or the repetition of formal resemblance (Peirce 1992:143–144; Parmentier 1994:17). Icons inherently refer to the past, because they rely on repetition and replication to transmit meaning (Keane 2003:414; Rogers 2005:342). For this reason revivalist discourses commonly employ iconic signs in the spread of their messages, as revivalism by definition refers to the past—specifically, to cultural practices thought to have been characteristic of previous generations (Wallace 1956:237). Following this line of reasoning, the iconic forms of Patokwa, Boletsakwa, and Kotyiti appear to reference their builders' conceptions of the past. The Pueblo people living at these sites followed Po'pay's call to return to the ways of their ancestors by adopting an architectural form that explicitly referenced the past.

It may be that the twin-plaza, two-kiva plan represents an idealized form of what the builders of these pueblos considered to be an archetypal traditional pre-Hispanic village. Preucel has suggested that the layout of Kotyiti embodies fundamental cosmological principles of the Keres worldview (Snead and Preucel 1999; Preucel 2006). He links the plan of Kotyiti and its open "gateway" corners with that of "White House," the primordial village of mythological time where Pueblo people lived after emerging into this world from the underworld (White 1932, 1964:80). If this was the case, the very architectural shape of Kotyiti would have reminded its inhabitants (and visitors from other Pueblos) of their enduring connections to the pre-Hispanic world, while affirming their renewed commitment to a traditional life, living "as they had in ancient times."[13]

Elements of the iconic plan utilized at the Revolt-era villages are characteristic of archetypal Tewa pueblos as well. According to Alfonso Ortiz, "all peoples try to bring their definitions of group space somehow into line with their cosmologies, but the Pueblos are unusually precise about it" (1972:142). Among the Tewas, this precision was ideally manifested through the construction of pueblos "in four parts in which the corners are always kept open" (Ortiz 1969:26). The Spaniards' 1598 description of Ohkay Owingeh states that it utilized an open-cornered layout similar to Patokwa and Kotyiti (and, to a lesser extent, Boletsakwa) suggesting that this structural plan dates back to the pre-Colonial era (Bandelier 1892:59). And while the specifics of Jemez cosmology may differ from that of their Keres and Tewa neighbors, the replication of the same iconic twin-plaza, two-kiva form at all three pueblos suggests that their designers shared a common ideological template, even if the specific meanings may have varied locally (Liebmann and Preucel 2007:200).

In any case, the layouts of all three pueblos embody two concepts central to much of Eastern Pueblo thought: balance and dualism (Parsons 1929:28, 279–280; Eggan 1950:316; Ortiz 1969:4–5). The plazas at each of these sites are not only divided into complementary pairs, they are also roughly equal in size. This symmetry suggests that the builders were concerned with the establishment of a structural equilibrium at Patokwa, Boletsakwa, and Kotyiti. The emphasis on architectural balance seems related to the ethos of nativism and revivalism that pervaded the northern Rio Grande in the early 1680s, which was itself a response to the disruptions Spanish colonialism had foisted on the Pueblos. In particular, Franciscan missionaries had intentionally disrupted ritual practices among the Puebloans in the eight decades preceding 1680, serving to throw the Natives' intricate ritual calendar and political organization out of balance. The razing of kivas, banning of masked dances, and destruction of ritual paraphernalia by zealous friars—all of which was practiced with particular intensity in the two decades leading up to the Revolt—served to disturb the maintenance of the Puebloans' ritual practices and internal politics (Spicer 1962:160–161; Kessell 1979:110; Riley 1995:261). Furthermore, the asymmetry of Roman Catholicism's emphasis on the Holy Trinity may have clashed with the Eastern Pueblo tendency to group the world into twos and fours, further tilting the Pueblo world out of sync.

The construction of villages with these iconic twin-plaza, two-kiva architectural plans represents an attempt to counter the disparities of colonial life through the reestablishment of duality and symmetry. At the very least, the layouts of Patokwa, Boletsakwa, and Kotyiti suggest that the persons who designed and oversaw the construction of these villages valued the concept of balanced dualism. It is unlikely that this emphasis was lost on the inhabitants of these settlements, either. But regardless of whether this balanced dualism was an explicit conviction or merely an implicit unspoken code, the construction of new villages with this iconic binary layout could not help but affect the social lives of those who lived within.

Moieties Redux?

The iconic nature of Patokwa, Boletsakwa, and Kotyiti suggest that ideology and cosmology played a significant role in the design of these new pueblos, with the thoughts and beliefs of the builders reflected in their architectural layouts. But the form of these villages represents more than just some vague mythical ideological connection to the "ways of the ancestors." Their architectural layouts likely correspond to a shift in behavior, daily practice, and social organization that occurred among these communities in the wake of the Revolt of 1680 as well. Pueblo public architecture such as plazas and kivas are not merely emblems of a traditional ideology; they are communal gathering places that provide a locus for the performance of shared social practices, rituals, and beliefs (Rautman 2000:275; Adams 1991). The significance of the twin-plaza, dual-kiva form is not only that it may have evoked notions of balance and symmetry among the residents of these villages as it does for modern Pueblo peoples, according to Ortiz (1969:5, 18, 22–26). Rather, the architectural ordering of space has social consequences, giving rise to, transforming, and ordering people's actions (Keane 2005:186).

In other words, the layouts of these villages did more than simply reflect their builders' revivalist tendencies. This architecture also shaped the daily practices of the inhabitants—thus affecting their social and ritual lives. As Winston Churchill noted, "We shape our buildings; thereafter they shape us."

The twin-plaza plans of these villages unavoidably ordered their residents into complementary halves, a fact that may provide a glimpse into the social organization of these communities as well. Southwestern archaeology has a long history of interpreting architecture as an index of social organization (Bandelier 1884; Cushing 1886, 1888; Kidder 1927; F. Roberts 1939; J. N. Hill 1970a, 1970b; Longacre 1970; Dean 1970; Hegmon 1989; Lipe and Hegmon 1989; Ferguson 1996). Specifically, duality in architecture has been argued to reflect moietal social organization, or the division of a community into ritual pairs (each of which is known as a *moiety*) (J. N. Hill 1970b:36; Vivian 1970:80–82; Rohn 1971:39–40; Clemen 1976:127–128; Fritz 1978; Lowell 1996:77; Fowles 2005). Communities utilizing a dual system of social organization require physical space in which the two groups (or their representatives) can perform their respective activities, although this physical space is not always manifested as architectural duality (Lowell 1996:82). In historical Rio Grande pueblos the influence of moietal social organization on architecture and settlement is well documented, with dwellings sometimes arranged around two plazas or in two groups, one for each moiety (Fox 1967:12, 14; Brown 1979:273; Jorgensen 1980:191–92, 239; Fowles 2005:28–29). Although architectural duality is not essential for moietal social organization, where it does occur in modern Pueblo communities, the presence of binary spatial organization strongly correlates with dual organization (Parsons 1929:91; White 1962:183; Dozier 1970:155; Ortiz 1979:281). By analogy to modern Keres and Jemez pueblos the duality evident at Patokwa, Boletsakwa, and Kotyiti likely indexes a social division partitioned into Turquoise and Pumpkin moieties, or at the Jemez villages, possibly the two Jemez men's societies, the Eagle and Arrow (Ellis 1964:11).

The emphasis on duality exemplified by the Revolt-era pueblos was likely linked to Po'pay's call for revivalism. Dualism has been identified as a fundamental organizing concept of modern Rio Grande Pueblo culture and is related to the maintenance of balance in the ritual and cosmological realms (Parsons 1929:279–280; Dozier 1961:107; Ortiz 1969:4–5). Elsie Clews Parsons, the doyenne of Pueblo ethnography, noted that "the most significant habit" of the Tewa mind is "the tendency to dichotomize." All Tewa beliefs, she claims, are "fitted into this dual pattern" (Parsons 1929:278–280). Archaeologists and ethnologists agree that dual organization has a deep antiquity among the Pueblos, stretching back to at least the thirteenth or fourteenth centuries, if not earlier (Eggan 1950:316; Vivian 1970:78–83; Lowell 1996; Fowles 2005). Oral traditions from Ohkay Owingeh maintain that the dual-division system practiced there was disrupted by the arrival of the Spaniards in 1598. Moieties are cited as the basis for the spatial separation that existed between the villages of Ohkay (home of the winter moiety) and Yungue (home of the summer moiety) prior to colonization, with the inhabitants of Ohkay displaced by the arrival of the Oñate party (Ortiz 1979:281; Ellis and Ellis 1992; Riley 1999:75). Yet moietal social organization was still practiced at Ohkay Owingeh in the generations preceding the Revolt, as suggested by the summer moiety associations of Po'pay's name (Ortiz 1980:20).

The architecture of Patokwa, Boletsakwa, and Kotyiti indicates that dual divisions were fundamental organizing principles of these communities when these pueblos were designed and constructed in the early 1680s. Ethnographic analogy suggests that moietal forms of social organization commonly arise when multiple groups coalesce into a single community, a common occurrence in Pueblo villages during the 1680s (Lowie 1948:247; Smith 1960: 39–40; Schroeder 1972:56–59; Fowles 2005:39–40). This was definitely the case at Boletsakwa, which was inhabited by an amalgamation of people from Jemez and Kewa, as well as at Kotyiti, which was composed of people from Cochiti, San Felipe, and San Marcos.[14] At Patokwa the situation is less clear; even though it was inhabited primarily by Towa-speaking Jemez, "Apaches" (probably Navajos) and people from Kewa were reportedly lodged there in 1692 as well, although this may have been a temporary arrangement.[15] Nevertheless, it is interesting that the name "Patokwa" has been translated as "turquoise-moiety place" (Sando 1979b:419), a direct reference to the importance of moietal social organization at that pueblo. Dualism serves to unite such segmented communities, mending the seams between various factions by providing balancing mechanisms and institutionalized power sharing. As described by Ortiz, "while only one of the moieties may provide the leader during any given year, this asymmetry is only temporary, for it is erased the following year when the opposite moiety provides the leader" (1969:124). In this way, tensions that may have arisen between the disparate ethnic groups gathered together in these new, post-Revolt communities could have been mitigated by the balancing nature of moietal social organization.

Creating Traditions

While the construction of these iconic twin-plaza, two-kiva pueblos would seem to be a relatively unambiguous example of revivalism, interpreting these plans as a straightforward return to an unaltered, pre-Hispanic tradition would be a mistake. Although the spatial organization of Patokwa and Boletsakwa appears to have played a role in Jemez revivalism, the form of these communities was not a direct resumption of earlier architectural conventions, and the residents did not return to live exactly "as they had in ancient times," as Po'pay had prophesied.[16] Rather, Pueblo people—and particularly the Jemez—constructed new forms of material culture in the wake of the Revolt that resourced and referenced their perceptions of the past, but did not replicate pre-Hispanic practices directly.

That innovations such as these took place during a revivalist movement should come as no surprise, as psychological studies conducted over the past century have repeatedly emphasized the creative nature of long-term memory (Bartlett 1932; Neisser 1967, 1994; Roediger 1980, 2008). These studies demonstrate that recollection is reconstructive, not photographic. That is, contrary to the popular conception of memory as a simple process of storage-and-retrieval, memory is not an exact facsimile of past events. The human mind operates very differently from a computer hard-drive or a Xerox machine; it alters what it reproduces. As pioneering cognitive psychologist Frederic Bartlett notes, "Remembering is not the re-excitation of innumerable fixed, lifeless, and fragmentary traces. It is an imaginative reconstruction, or construction. . . . It is thus hardly even really exact, even in the most rudimentary cases of role recapitulation" (1932:213). All acts of memory are acts of creation and not merely a process of unaltered data retrieval. Although we draw on conceptions of the past in creating remembrances, each instance of recollection is also unavoidably an act of innovation. Thus we don't access memories; we create them. And the constructive aspects of memory are especially apparent in the phenomena of communal traditions (Hobsbawm and Ranger 1983). The creation of tradition is an essential component of revivalist revitalization movements, which often espouse images of the past that include novel innovations (Wallace 1956:276). Here I use the phrase "creation of tradition" in contrast to Eric Hobsbawm's "invented tradition," which is sometimes taken to mean traditions fabricated from whole cloth, without any prior antecedents (Hobsbawm 1983; Sahlins 1999:403).

The use of the twin-plaza, two-kiva plan at Patokwa and Boletsakwa appears not to have been a resumption of earlier architectural practices, but rather an example of the creation of tradition. Although the large pre-Hispanic pueblos of the Jemez Province were compact and plaza oriented, the distinctive twin-plaza layout was not utilized by Jemez communities prior to 1680 (see figure 6.2).[17] (Admittedly, however, it is difficult to determine the original layouts of these earlier villages as most were occupied for far longer than Patokwa and Boletsakwa, and subsequent architectural modifications often obscure the initial layouts.) Regardless of the specific iconic meanings the dual-plaza plan may have evoked for the residents of Patokwa and Boletsakwa, this distinctive spatial organization did not directly reproduce pre-Hispanic Jemez architectural plans in a literal way. As such, the plans of Patokwa and Boletsakwa may be *simulacra*—exact representations of an ideal type that did not previously exist.

Neither is there any clear evidence in the archaeological record of the Jemez Province to suggest that the concept of duality or moietal social organization were important organizing principles in Jemez culture prior to the Pueblo Revolt era. Moreover, Jemez oral tradition records that the moietal pattern was introduced into Jemez society from their Pueblo neighbors at some (unspecified) point in the past.[18] At the time of the 1680 Revolt, moieties may not have been considered a "traditional" aspect of Jemez culture at all. If this was the case, the architecture of Patokwa and Boletsakwa may signal the initial establishment of dual organization in Jemez culture, an innovative tradition that persists down to the present day. The twin-plaza, two-kiva plans of Patokwa and Boletsakwa thus meld elements of pre-Hispanic spatial organization (compact, plaza-oriented pueblos) with new types of social organization (moieties), creating new "traditions."

But if the twin-plaza, two-kiva plan and moietal social organization were not in fact characteristic of pre-Hispanic life in the Jemez Province, why then did the builders of Patokwa and Boletsakwa adopt these conventions? After all, the Jemez Province hosted a permanent and sustained Spanish presence for only about sixty years prior to the Revolt, so it seems unlikely that the Jemez would have simply forgotten all remnants of pre-Hispanic social organization in just three short generations (Liebmann 2006:147–148). Almost surely there would have been persons living at Patokwa and Boletsakwa who were born prior to the establishment of permanent Franciscan missions in the valley, and who would have retained firsthand knowledge of pre-Hispanic Jemez lifeways. How then could communal memories have been so easily manipulated in the wake of the Revolt?

It is tempting to speculate that the idea of moietal social organization as a "traditional" practice may have originated outside the Jemez Province, and was presented to the Jemez only after the Revolt of 1680. This emphasis on duality may have been introduced via their Keres neighbors from Kewa, who took refuge with the Jemez after 1680.[19] The functional aspects of moietal social organization (mitigating conflict in newly formed communities), may have aided its adoption at Patokwa and Boletsakwa as well. Alternatively, the emphasis on duality could have come from the Tewa pueblos, with whom the

Jemez interacted with increasing frequency after the Pueblo Revolt (Liebmann and Preucel 2007:203–204; see chapter 8).

It is even conceivable that the architect of the iconic twin-plaza plan may have been the Tewa prophet Po'pay himself. The layout of these villages strongly resembles idealized traditional Tewa spatial (and social) organization (Ortiz 1969:26). For Po'pay, twin-plazas and moieties represented the ways of *his* ancestors, and although they were probably not characteristic of pre-Hispanic Jemez communities, he may have advocated these innovations for his followers as the archetype of "traditional" Pueblo life. Considering his autocratic tendencies, it is conceivable that Po'pay would have offered specific instructions regarding the construction of these pueblos when he ordered his followers to destroy the churches and build new villages while on his victory tour in 1680–81.[20] If this were the case (and granted, this is purely conjectural), the twin-plaza design may have been initiated at Patokwa and Kotyiti directly at Po'pay's behest. The builders of Boletsakwa could have simply been imitating the layout of the village they had recently vacated (Patokwa) when they constructed their new home, even though Po'pay had already been deposed by the time its foundation was laid in 1683.

Out with the New, in with the Old? The Revival (and Termination) of Pre-Hispanic Ceramic Traditions

At the same time that the people of Patokwa and Boletsakwa were reconfiguring their notions of "traditional" spatial and social organization through architecture, the women of these villages were instituting radical changes in ceramic production and trade that appear to have been linked to Po'pay's calls for nativism and revivalism as well. The fact that the Tewa prophet's commands were manifested in media other than architecture is not surprising, as one of the primary characteristics of revitalization movements is the appearance of rapid, intentional changes in multiple categories of material culture (Liebmann 2008:369). But Jemez potters were not alone in inaugurating these changes to their traditional craft after 1680. New ceramic styles and technologies were adopted across the Pueblo world in the wake of the Revolt.

Archaeologists have documented numerous changes to Pueblo pottery production and trade during the late seventeenth century that appear to be directly related to Po'pay's charge to return to the ways of the ancestors. Ideologies of nativism and revivalism influenced ceramic production at ancestral Hopi, Zuni, and Keres pueblos (Adams 1981, 1989; Capone and Preucel 2002; Mills 2002). In the post-Revolt ceramic assemblage at the Hopi village of Walpi, for example, E. Charles Adams found that "all trappings of Spanish form and design were eliminated. . . . The manufacturers were reasserting traditions in ceramic production and use, which symbolized the 'conquest' of the Spaniards and their material culture by Pueblo values and beliefs" (1989:85). The influx of Rio Grande émigrés to the Hopi pueblos during the Revolt period influenced ceramic production as well, as reflected in post-1690 Hopi vessel forms and design motifs that resemble Tewa Wares and late Rio Grande Glaze Ware pottery (Adams 1981:325–326).

Zuni ceramics display strong evidence for nativism and revivalism during the post-Revolt era as well, with potters reviving traditional wares after the ouster of the Spaniards. Prior to the arrival of Franciscan missionaries in the 1630s, the dominant ceramic types produced by Zuni potters were matte-painted wares. Beginning around 1630, however, glaze-paint technologies were reintroduced to Zuni potters, probably resulting from the arrival of Franciscan missionaries who brought Rio Grande ceramic technologies with them (Mills 2002:89–90). Following the Pueblo Revolt, Zuni women ceased the production of Franciscan-inspired glaze-painted pottery entirely, shifting back to the manufacture of matte-painted polychromes. These earlier traditions "would still have been in the memory of aging potters at the time of the Pueblo Revolt," according to Barbara Mills, suggesting that the revival of matte-painted ceramics was "an intentional act" on the part of Zuni women (2002:93).

Revivalism played a prominent role in the ceramic production of the northern Rio Grande after the Revolt as well, as evidenced by the pottery assemblage of Kotyiti. According to Preucel, the Glaze Wares there display evidence for the revival of archaic design elements, embodied most prominently in the double-headed key motif (Capone and Preucel 2002:108). This motif has considerable antiquity in the Rio Grande Glaze Ware sequence, first appearing during the Glaze B period (AD 1400–1450), and lasting through Glaze F times (AD 1625–1700). However, A. V. Kidder and Anna O. Shepard note that its appearance is relatively rare during the Glaze E period (AD 1515–1625) at Pecos (Kidder and Shepard 1936:227). Following the Pueblo Revolt, use of the double-headed key motif became frequent and widespread among glaze ware potters, appearing in more than one-third (36 percent) of all identified designs on Kotyiti Glaze Ware. This design element has been noted on glaze-painted pottery at other Revolt-era sites as well, including that of Patokwa and Boletsakwa as well as the refugee pueblos of Old San Felipe, Cerro Colorado, and Astialakwa (which were constructed between 1689 and 1694; see chapters 8 and 9). Additionally, this motif is present on contemporaneous ceramics produced outside of the Jemez and Keres districts, including those of Hopi and Zuni.[21] The revival of the hooked triangle motif on Tewa wares follows a similar pattern; it appears in the Kotyiti Tewa Ware assemblage, and also on contemporaneous Kotyiti Glaze Wares and Ashiwi Polychrome vessels (Capone and Preucel 2002:108–110).

The general trends of the ceramics of Revolt-era pueblos outside of the Jemez Province include evidence for increased interaction among tradition-ally distinct regions, the revival of archaic designs, and the creation of new styles throughout the Pueblo world. In some areas nativism seems to have played a prominent role in the shaping of post-Revolt material culture, inau-gurating entirely new vessel types in an attempt to wash away all elements of Spanish colonialism; in others, the resumption of designs employed by the ancestors seems to have been the rule. Not surprisingly, the potters of Patokwa and Boletsakwa followed similar patterns to those of their Hopi, Zuni, and Keres neighbors after 1680, signaling a significant break with their long-established ceramic practices.

A Study in Black and White: The Pottery of the Jemez Province

Prior to 1680, the pottery of the Jemez Province had remained remarkably consistent and seemingly invariable for more than three hundred years. In fact, to speak of "the ceramics of the Jemez Province" is a bit tautological, given that the region is defined primarily by the spatial extent of Jemez Black-on-white pottery (Elliott 1986:1). The ubiquitous presence of this distinctive type has been noted since the earliest days of archaeological inves-tigations in the area (Holmes 1905:206), and to this day, the existence of large quantities of Jemez Black-on-white pottery remains one of the central defining characteristics of ancestral Jemez archaeological sites.

Jemez Black-on-white is characterized by a thick white slip (described as "oyster white"), and organic matte paint ranging from deep black to brown. It is almost exclusively tempered with rhyolitic (or as Anna O. Shepard called it, devitrified) tuff. Estimates for the dates of the inception of this type range from AD 1300 to 1375, but the first secure dates come from the pueblo of Unshagi at around 1400.[22] Jemez Black-on-white dominates the ceramic assemblage of every large pueblo in the Jemez Province dating from AD 1350 to 1680 that has been subjected to systematic analyses to date, com-prising around 90 percent of the decorated ceramics at these villages, on average (table 6.1). Reiter and Shepard's 1938 investigations of the ceram-ics at Unshagi—the earliest, most comprehensive, and still best analysis of

Table 6.1. Jemez Black-on-white ceramics as a percentage of the decorated ware assemblage at ancestral Jemez pueblos

LA Number	Site Name	Jemez Black-on-white percentage of decorated assemblage	Reference
LA 123	Unshagi	93.6	Reiter 1938:189–192
LA 679	Giusewa	94.1	Lambert 1981; Elliott 1991:80, 2005:24
LA 132/133	Kiatsukwa	99.5	Futrell 1998:290; Morley 2002:124
LA 482	Kwastiyukwa	82.0	Futrell 1998:290
LA 130	Pejunkwa	99.0	Morley 2002:124
LA 541	Nanishagi	86.6	Futrell 1998:290
LA 483	Tohwakwa	88.2	Morley 2002:124
LA 478	Wabakwa	98.6	Morley 2002:124
LA 484	Tovakwa	85.8	Morley 2002:124
LA 189	Kiabakwa	98.2	Morley 2002:124

Jemez ceramics to date—found that Jemez Black-on-white comprised more than 90 percent of the decorated wares at that village (that is, all ceramics except the undecorated Utility wares; Reiter 1938:189–192).

The distinctive Black-on-white pottery of the Jemez Province appears to have been a significant sign of ancestral Jemez ethnic identity for at least three centuries leading up to 1680. So it stands to reason that after the Revolt, in a time of overt revivalism, Jemez potters would return to the ways of their ancestors by emulating pre-Hispanic patterns through a resumption of "traditional" designs and a renewed emphasis on the production of Jemez Black-on-white—particularly considering the renaissance of archaic styles among their Hopi, Zuni, Keres, and Tewa brethren. Yet rather than continuing the customs of their Jemez ancestors, the potters of Patokwa and Boletsakwa instead made a radical and unexpected break with tradition. After the Revolt of 1680, they ceased the manufacture of Jemez Black-on-white pottery entirely.

A comparison of the ceramics from Patokwa and Boletsakwa with those of the Jemez pre-Revolt pueblos of Giusewa and Unshagi provides a dramatic illustration of the radical shift that occurred after 1680 (figure 6.4). At Unshagi (AD 1325–1620) and Giusewa (AD 1300–1650), Jemez Black-on-white comprises more than 40 percent of the combined ceramic assemblage (Reiter 1938:103; Elliott 1991:80). In contrast, at the Revolt-era components of Patokwa and Boletsakwa the amount of Jemez Black-on-white dropped to less than 2 percent of the total.[23] If the comparison is limited

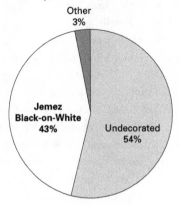

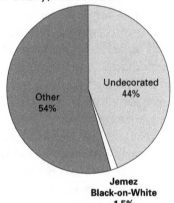

FIGURE 6.4. Pre- and post-Revolt ceramic assemblages at ancestral Jemez pueblos. Pre-Revolt data from the Jemez pueblos of Unshagi (Reiter 1938) and Giusewa (Elliott 1991; Lambert 1981). Post-Revolt data from Patokwa and Boletsakwa (see tables 7.1 and 7.2).

solely to decorated wares the disparity is even more striking: Jemez Black-on-white constitutes nearly 94 percent of the painted ceramics at the pre-Revolt sites (Reiter 1938:189–192; Elliott 1991:80), but just 3.2 percent at Patokwa and Boletsakwa.

Considering the patterns of revivalism exhibited in the ceramics of other post-Revolt communities, the decrease in manufacture of Jemez Black-on-white at Patokwa and Boletsakwa is particularly striking. Plainly this does not demonstrate a revival of traditional Jemez ceramic production at all, and raises an obvious question: why did Jemez potters cease the production of traditional ceramics after the Pueblo Revolt, even as the contemporary potters of Keres, Tewa, Zuni, and Hopi pueblos were resurrecting the pottery of their ancestors?

Clearly the termination of Jemez Black-on-white was not associated with revivalism. Rather, Jemez oral traditions suggest that the cessation of their traditional craft was influenced by the nativist component of the revitalization movement—Po'pay's call to eradicate all Spanish contagion from the Pueblo world. Admittedly, a nativist-driven purgation of Jemez Black-on-white sounds at first counterintuitive. Why, after all, would Jemez women stop making their traditional pottery as a way to expunge the *Spanish* contagion from their world? Yet previous research has clearly documented the marked influence that the European presence had on the production of Jemez Black-on-white between 1600 and 1680. Excavations at the mission component of Giusewa have unearthed a number of Jemez Black-on-white artifacts exhibiting Spanish-introduced forms, including soup plates, cups, candlestick holders, a nearly complete chalice (figure 6.5), and even a Jemez Black-on-white cross. Furthermore, many of the Black-on-white vessels from Giusewa exhibit "Greek cross" motifs and other European-derived design elements (Lambert 1981; Elliott 1991).

Taking into account the effects of colonization on the production of traditional Jemez pottery, the termination of Jemez Black-on-white ceramics at Patokwa and Boletsakwa may have been motivated by a desire to expel all memory of the Franciscan missionaries, who had appropriated the local ware during their tenure in the region. After the Revolt, Jemez potters may have viewed Jemez Black-on-white pottery as a "contaminated" style. That is, between 1601 and 1680 Jemez women had been forced to produce European and ecclesiastical forms of Black-on-white ceramics, and by the time of the Revolt they may have associated the production of Jemez Black-on-white pottery more with life in the Christian missions than with that of their pre-Hispanic ancestors. Following the calls of Po'pay to purge their world of all Spanish influence, Jemez potters drastically reduced the manufacture of the type they had previously been compelled to make into foreign and ecclesiastical accoutrements. Contemporary Jemez oral traditions support this interpretation, asserting that the manufacture of Black-on-white pottery was intentionally terminated during the Revolt era in a direct response to Spanish influences (Whatley and Delaney 1995:207–208).

A similar nativist response occurred among Zuni potters of the post-Revolt period. After 1680, Zuni women stopped using the glaze paint technology that had been reintroduced to the region by Franciscan missionaries in the

FIGURE 6.5. Jemez Black-on-white chalice from Giusewa (LA 679), circa 1601. Image courtesy of the Museum of New Mexico.

1630s. Mills (2002:93) interprets this as "an intentional act to mark a break with earlier ceramic production," an expression of nativism that appears to be a direct analogue to the termination of Jemez Black-on-white pottery. Her basis for this interpretation stems in part from the fact that glaze ware was not only reintroduced to Zuni potters by the Franciscans, but used in the mission church at Hawikuu as well (Smith et al. 1966). The baptismal font, for example, was reportedly a glaze-decorated vessel. Mills suggests that "the association of the mission with this vessel type [Glaze Ware] may have been one that the Zunis would want to leave behind" (2002:93), just as the association of the Jemez Black-on-white with the Franciscans may have been one that the potters of Patokwa and Boletsakwa wanted to leave behind as well.

Through the construction of Patokwa and Boletsakwa and the cessation of Jemez Black-on-white ceramics, the Jemez people created new traditions in the aftermath of the Revolt, employing a nativist dismembering of the Spanish colonial past while simultaneously reviving perceived memories of their ancestors. The Jemez were not alone in the practices; dramatic changes in settlement and ceramic traditions also occurred at Zia, Santa Ana, Kewa, Zuni, Acoma, Kotyiti, and among the Tanos of the Galisteo Basin (Walt 1990; Capone and Preucel 2002; Ferguson 2002; Mills 2002; Lippard 2010). The vigorous performance of Po'pay's directives that is embodied in these pots and villages was not to last, however. Within just a few years, Pueblo peoples began to employ creative modifications to the nativist and revivalist doctrines that spawned the Revolt, resulting in syncretic amalgamations of pre- and post-Revolt material culture.

7

Catachresis and Catechesis

PUEBLO APPROPRIATIONS OF COLONIAL CULTURE DURING
THE SPANISH INTERREGNUM

IN A REMOTE CAVE DWELLING IN FRIJOLES CANYON, about thirty-four
kilometers (twenty-one miles) northeast of Boletsakwa, a series of anthropomorphic figures incised in mud plaster dance nimbly along the walls. This
cavate was last occupied in the late seventeenth century,[1] most likely during the Pueblo Revolt era (Hendron 1943:ii–iv; Turney 1948:70), and its
corpus of etchings comprise exactly the sort of traditional Puebloan designs
we might expect to have been produced during a period of overt revivalism:
masked kachina figures, stepped clouds and mountains, geometric feather
designs, intricately carved serpents, and even a striped *koshare* (sacred clown)
(figure 7.1). On the west wall of the cavate, however, one spectral figure
stands out from the crowd, its hollow eyes reflecting light like two shining
patens. Unlike the rest of the characteristically Puebloan images in the cave,
this solitary effigy is conspicuous in its unorthodox nature, bearing evidence
of obvious Spanish influence. The facial features (the eyes, eyebrows, and
nose) are rendered in an undeniably European style. And the halo or crown
adorning its pate is similar to seventeenth-century depictions of Catholic
saints. A single curved line reminiscent of a veil circumscribes the head,
evoking Spanish colonial portrayals of one particularly significant Catholic
figure: Santa Maria (figure 7.2).

What is this image doing in this cavate? A seemingly Christian figure
such as this is not the type of image we might expect in post-Revolt contexts,
surrounded by traditional Pueblo etchings of kachinas, clowns, and serpents.
According to most textual sources regarding life in the Rio Grande during the 1680s, this curious Virgin-of-the-Cavate seems utterly out of place,
militating as it does against Po'pay's overtly nativist agenda. According to
the prophet's decree, all semblance of Spanish influence was to be purged
from Pueblo culture following the Revolt—particularly anything associated
with Roman Catholicism. Those who did not comply with this order risked

FIGURE 7.1. Images incised in Cavate M-100, Frijoles Canyon.

penalty of death, with Po'pay banning even the utterance of "the name of God, of the most holy Virgin, or of the Saints."[2]

How are we to explain this persistence of Catholic imagery, not to mention the other elements of Spanish culture that thrived among the Pueblos during the twelve years of their colonial independence between 1680 and

FIGURE 7.2. West wall, Panel B, Cavate M-100 (top), with Spanish colonial depictions of the Virgin Mary (bottom, left to right: *Santa Rosa de Lima* [detail], *Virgin of Guadalupe* [detail], *Coronation of the Virgin* [detail]).

1692? Aside from this intriguing saint among the kachinas, other trappings of Christianity were curated among the Pueblos during the Spanish interregnum, as well as many European crops, livestock, and technological innovations, such as metal tools. It would be easy to write these off as examples of the failure of Po'pay's plan, as incomplete nativism, or as backsliding on the part of his followers. Alternatively, it could be interpreted as a sign of Pueblo acculturation or the extent of Spanish cultural dominance, so pervasive that it continued even in the colonizers' absence. Yet such facile explanations overlook the agency of Pueblo actions following the Revolt. Furthermore, they assume that the meanings of "Spanish" objects and symbols remained stable during this tumultuous period, conveying the same messages to all people at all times. Ultimately, these interpretations oversimplify the complex relationships that exist among signs and their interpreters (Preucel and Bauer 2001; Preucel 2006; Spielmann et al. 2006).

By the mid-1680s, many of the elements of Hispanic culture that had been purged in the immediate aftermath of the Revolt were once again a regular part of Pueblo lives. However, the foreign characteristics that persisted were often altered by the Pueblos, taking on new forms and meanings in the absence of the Spaniards, and were used in very different ways in the post-Revolt world than they had been under Spanish dominion. Despite what we might expect, the appropriation of Spanish culture played an integral role in the revitalization of Pueblo societies that occurred between the Revolt of 1680 and the return of the Spaniards in 1692. In fact, these types of appropriation occur frequently in newly liberated contexts around the world. Postcolonial scholars have labeled this phenomenon *catachresis*, referring to the processes by which colonized populations seize elements of imperial culture and reinscribe it with new meanings.

According to the *Oxford English Dictionary* "catachresis" was originally defined as "the application of a term to a thing that it does not properly denote." But the word itself was appropriated by Gayatri Spivak, who redefined it more broadly to refer to the "reversing, displacing, and seizing the apparatus of value-coding" by subaltern and colonized peoples (1990:225). Catachresis can be a particularly empowering and potent form of colonial resistance. Among the Pueblos of the 1680s, catachresis was employed through the manipulation of Spanish religion, technologies, foods, architecture, and ethnic categories, all of which were invested with new meanings after the Revolt and were not perceived as contrary to notions of "traditional" indigenous culture.

The Virgin-Kachina

Although clearly imbued with Christian characteristics, the intriguing Santa Maria-of-the-cavate is not a straightforward Catholic icon. It has been infused with traditional Pueblo traits as well. While the eyes, eyebrows, and nose appear to follow European artistic conventions, it wears the distinctive rectangular mouth of a masked figure, characteristic of kachina depictions throughout the Pueblo world. And although the crown of radiating

FIGURE 7.3. Cavate icon with masked Puebloan images. Far left: petroglyph from Cochiti Reservoir District (after Schaafsma 1994:plate 16). Far right: Jeddito spattered ceramic motif (after Hays 1994:58).

triangles may resemble a saint's halo, it is also reminiscent of the feathered or horned headdresses worn by masked Pueblo dancers and some kachinas, particularly depictions of the sun kachina found in nearby rock art (figure 7.3). In short, this portrait is anything but a conventional depiction of the mother of Christ. More accurately, it is a hybrid fusion, welding Christianity with kachina ceremonialism—a transformation of Santa Maria into the Virgin-Kachina.

This composite cavate petroglyph is an archetypal example of the reinterpretation of Spanish culture that occurred after the Revolt in the Pueblo world. The cavate itself is located in a remote area that is difficult to access, hewn into the base of a towering cliff. The rooms attached to its entrance, which have long since collapsed, would have balanced precariously atop a loose scree slope that falls away at a precipitous angle. Inside, the room contains the remains of a hearth near the eroded doorway. Smokeholes overhead served as a chimney, but this didn't prevent the plastered walls and ceiling from darkening with the soot that later served as the canvas for the Revolt-era artisans. In the rear of the room, two metate bins bear silent witness to long hours spent grinding maize. The heels of the maidens assigned to this task abraded two telltale recesses into the west wall, just beside and below the Virgin-Kachina figure. The etchings adorning the walls spread around three sides of the room, and are located at eye level for a person kneeling at the grinding stone. It is easy to imagine two women rhythmically milling corn in this room, intermittently chatting and singing softly, gazing up occasionally to admire the artwork decorating the dark, womblike cave.

Rock art is notoriously difficult to date, and even harder to assign attribution. The enigmatic Virgin-Kachina cavate petroglyph is no exception.

How can we be sure that a Pueblo person created this image, much less that he or she etched it during the narrow window of two decades that followed the Pueblo Revolt? While the cavate was originally carved out generations, if not centuries, before 1680, the ceramics associated with its final substantial occupation (including Kapo Black, Tewa Polychrome, and Glaze F pottery) have led investigators to conclude that Pueblo people reoccupied it sometime between 1680 and 1700 (Turney 1948:70; Liebmann 2002:136). This is consistent with the larger pattern of "returning to the places of the ancestors" that guided settlement during the 1680s, as observed at Patokwa, Boletsakwa, and Kotyiti. Furthermore, the hidden and protected nature of this cavate made it an ideal refuge from attacks (be they from Natives or Spaniards) in the wake of the Revolt.

Yet in addition to this final permanent occupation, historical and archaeological evidence suggests that local Hispanic shepherds also used these cavates periodically throughout the eighteenth and nineteenth centuries as well. Couldn't the Santa Maria image have been carved by one of these herdsmen, who were notably devout Catholics themselves? The evidence suggests that this was not the case. Aside from the obvious Puebloan characteristics of the image itself (including, most conspicuously, the mouth), this figure appears to have been carved using the same sharp tool—and probably by the same hand—that inscribed the dozens of kachinas, clowns, snakes, feathers, stepped cloud designs, and other images that grace the walls. Persons with intimate knowledge of Pueblo ritual life and traditional design indubitably carved these figures. In other words, they are pictures that only a Pueblo hand could have created.

As for the dating of this art, the *terminus post quem* is supplied by the images of two horses incised into the same (outermost) layer of plaster as the rest of the figures, again apparently by the same hand and using the same instrument, indicating a date of post-1539. More specifically, I argue that these images were drawn during the late seventeenth-century occupation of the cavate—and not after its abandonment—based on their intramural locations. The figures in question are all located in a band 30 to 90 cm above the floor, in other words, in the field of vision of a person sitting or kneeling inside the cavate. By contrast, post-seventeenth century etchings in this and nearby cavates, including modern graffiti and images probably drawn by itinerant Hispanic shepherds, tend to be located 120 cm above the floor or higher—that is, in the field of vision of a person standing upright in the cavate. During the late seventeenth century–era occupation, people carved images on the walls at the lower level because they tended to sit or kneel in this room. After abandonment, visitors to the cavate tended to make their marks while standing.

Assuming that the Pueblo Revolt–era chronology and attribution I've assigned here are in fact correct, two questions immediately arise: why does the Virgin-Kachina appear in this context? And what did it mean to the seventeenth-century people who created and viewed it? While attempts to interpret the meanings of archaeological art typically generate more heat than light, there are some notable contextual cues contained within the cavate that provide valuable insights. For example, the fact that the Virgin-Kachina is surrounded exclusively by Puebloan imagery and not other Christian figures suggests that this is anything but an expression of Catholic piety—there are no crucifixes, Christian fish, or rosary beads inscribed on the walls of this cavate. There are, however, kachinas, serpents, a koshare, and stepped cloud and mountain forms. Based on this context, it seems safe to presume that a Puebloan artist was appropriating and manipulating the imagery of the Spaniards when creating this figure, transforming colonial iconography to serve the needs of Pueblo peoples in the post-Revolt period.

The conscious appropriation of outside elements and influences has a long history among Pueblo peoples. From the Tlaloc and horned serpent (Quetzalcoatl) iconography that spread from Mesoamerica to the Rio Grande in centuries past to the more recent adoption of the Hemis kachina at Hopi and the Hopi Dance at Jemez, Pueblo cultures are inherently accommodative (Parsons 1925:87–90; Brew 1943; Dockstader 1954:13; Riley 1987:169; Schaafsma 1994). In contemporary times, Pueblo people have referred to images of Christ as "the Jesus Kachina" (Fergusson 1931:33). The Pueblos have long "allowed alien patterns to enter the weave," states Hopi Bear Clan member Hartman Lomawaima (1989:97), but in doing so have "incorporated them into a truly Pueblo pattern." In this way, the integration of European religious imagery after the Revolt may have been experienced as a very traditional Puebloan thing to do. By transforming the Virgin Mary into a kachina, the cavate artist was adhering to the long-held Pueblo practice of assimilating outside religious influences into Pueblo culture.

Alternatively, the Virgin-Kachina illustration may represent a conscious usurpation of Spanish power by the cavate artist. After the friars' ouster, elements of the church may have been thought to retain the power of the colonizers' God(s), and were appropriated in the same way that the Pueblos sometimes venerated the scalps of brave enemies—to be used in ceremonies to call rain and blessings down on the people (Kessell and Hendricks 1992:16). Rather than emphasizing a symbiotic merger of the two religious traditions, the cavate figure could be viewed as a jarring collision between differing belief systems with Santa Maria being hijacked from the Franciscans and dragged into the Pueblo pantheon. This type of resistance-via-appropriation is a common occurrence in colonial and post-colonial contexts the world over, particularly where Christianity has been forcibly imposed on a subaltern populace (Liebmann 2002:141; Comaroff 1985; Scott 1990).

Frijoles Canyon was not the only locale in which elements of Catholicism persisted after the Pueblo Revolt. As noted in chapter 4, ecclesiastical paraphernalia were curated and reinterpreted at many Pueblos after 1680 by such notable figures as Alonso Catití and even Po'pay himself (Sanchez 1983:134–135). At times, these trappings were used in dramatic spectacles of ritual mockery, such as Po'pay and Catití's feast.[3] In other cases, Pueblo people preserved Christian accoutrements throughout the 1680s in an apparently reverential fashion. The most famous example of this careful curation took place at the Zuni refuge of Dowa Yalanne, where an altar was maintained throughout the 1680s, along with two bronze statues of Christ hanging on wooden crosses, paintings of the crucifixion and St. John the Baptist, a small library of religious texts, candlesticks, bells, numerous chalices, and a monstrance.[4]

Still, the motivations behind this preservation effort remain unclear. After the Revolt, proselytizers of Po'pay's doctrine strove to bring Christianized Native peoples back into the fold of traditional Pueblo spirituality. The elements of Catholicism that persisted may have been used accordingly, as a means to entice baptized Indians back to the old ways. After all, leaders of the Revolt would not have needed to convince more "traditional" members of their villages to return to Pueblo spirituality—it was only those who had adopted the Christian faith who needed to be brought back to the (ostensibly) ancient ways.

Whatever the reasons behind the preservation of specific objects and the creation of hybrid Pueblo-Catholic images, it is clear that in at least some cases, the Pueblos turned the semiotic weapons of the colonizers back on the Spaniards after the Pueblo Revolt. The persistence of Catholic imagery and artifacts and the reestablishment of traditional Pueblo spirituality during the 1680s is not necessarily mutually exclusive. As anthropologist Igor Kopytoff observes, "What is significant about the adoption of alien objects—as of alien ideas—is not the fact that they are adopted, but the way they are culturally redefined and put to use" (2000:377).

Profane Appropriations

The selective appropriation of Christianity after the Revolt appears to have varied among the different Pueblos. While the trappings of Catholicism continued to be used (albeit in new ways and forms) among the Eastern Pueblos and at Zuni, archaeological research at Hopi suggests that the rejection of the Spaniards' religion may have been more comprehensive (Adams 1981:326; Dongoske and Dongoske 2002). Secular items and products that had been introduced by the Spaniards continued to be employed widely across the Pueblo world, however. Spanish-introduced plants, animals, technologies, and architecture maintained significant roles in Pueblo life following the expulsion of the Spaniards in 1680, no matter how vigorously Po'pay had decried their use. Simply put, tangible and substantial benefits could still be reaped from Spanish innovations, flora, and livestock, and the Pueblos were not about to give them up.

Foremost among the things banned by the leaders of the Revolt that the Pueblos refused to relinquish were the Spanish-introduced foods to which they had grown accustomed over the previous eighty years. When Po'pay ordered his followers "to burn the seeds the Spaniards sowed and to plant only maize and beans, which were the crops of their ancestors," the Pueblos balked. As one resident of Tesuque confessed, "all the nations obeyed in everything except in the command concerning Spanish seeds."[5] While the order to cease speaking Spanish and the prohibition against baptismal names could be carried out without much hardship, the Pueblos would not (or could not) go without the wheat, tomatoes, chile peppers, and melons the Spaniards had brought into their fields. In addition, they continued to tend their orchards of peaches, apricots, plums, and cherries, and to cultivate the new forms of tobacco that the Spaniards had introduced. The last of these is evidenced by a historic Tewa Red bowl from the Revolt-era occupation of Frijoles Canyon that was found still full of *Nicotiana rustica*, nearly three centuries after the cavates were last occupied (Ford 1987:81).

This less-than-comprehensive nativism was at least partially unconscious, however. Po'pay himself was apparently confused as to which plants were foreign and which were indigenous in the profoundly creolized world of the late 1600s. During his tour of the province, he reportedly assured the people "that living thus in accordance with the law of their ancestors, they would harvest a great deal of maize, many beans, a great abundance of cotton, calabashes, and very large watermelons and cantaloupes."[6] Ironically, melons (watermelon and cantaloupe) are Old World crops, introduced to the Americas by the Spaniards. While Po'pay unwittingly incorporated elements of European influence into his depiction of "traditional" Pueblo life, he can be excused for his mistake. Watermelons and cantaloupes were growing in Pueblo fields even before don Juan de Oñate established the first permanent colonial settlement in New Mexico in 1598, apparently reaching the northern Rio Grande via the indigenous trade routes that linked the northern Rio Grande to Mexico.[7]

Given this particular history, it is perhaps unsurprising that Po'pay considered watermelon to be an aboriginal crop. It was, after all, other Natives who
introduced *sandia* to the Pueblos, not the Spaniards. Even today, watermelon
is afforded special status and is used as a symbol of a prosperous harvest in
ritual dances among the Pueblos (Ford 1987:78–84).

Plants were not the only foreign foodstuffs retained by the Pueblos during the Spanish interregnum. Flocks of animals brought first by the Europeans continued to be tended in their absence. Sheep, cattle, and goats were
carefully cared for, along with horses, mules, and oxen. Additionally, the
technologies that accompanied these animals were widely retained. Fine
woolen textiles continued to be produced, and the use of wheeled carts persisted throughout the 1680s (Adams 1981:325). A tradition of metal work
was maintained as well, with Pueblo ploughshares beat hastily into swords
in the Spaniards' absence. Near Santa Fe a Pueblo blacksmith set up shop,
supplying the Tewas with lances and other weaponry throughout the 1680s.[8]
Farther south, the people of Sandia Pueblo valued metallurgy enough to set
up a crude forge in the cloister of their former priest, complete with a bellows
and an anvil formed from a plow.[9]

Architectural Annexations

Spanish buildings, both sacred and profane, were similarly adapted for Pueblo
use throughout the Kingdom of New Mexico during the 1680s. The Hopis
of Awat'ovi moved into the mission facilities located on Antelope Mesa following the Revolt, remodeling the rooms into smaller, more traditionally
pueblo-sized dwellings and retaining some Spanish elements, such as corner
fireplaces. The Zunis at Hawikku did the same. At Sandia, the refectory and
the priests' private oratory were converted into a "seminary of idolatry" by
1681. And at the pueblo of Sevilleta, the residents destroyed the "hermitage
where the holy sacraments were administered," reusing its wooden frame in
the construction of a new subterranean kiva.[10] In these latter cases, resistance
was expressed through "symbolic inversion," with uses opposed to those
originally expected and intended by the Spaniards (Scott 1990:162–182).
Rather than a new syncretic form of hybrid Pueblo-Christian practice, the
people of Sandia and Sevilleta appropriated sacred Catholic spaces for the
opposite of the (sacred, Christian) purpose for which they were built, using
them instead for "pagan idolatry," the absolute contradiction of Christianity
(in the eyes of Franciscan missionaries, that is).

Because these mission facilities were all built on lands originally occupied by the Pueblos, their reoccupation by the local populace in the Franciscans' absence is not entirely surprising. That the Puebloans would want to take back the space within their villages after the eviction of the Spaniards seems eminently reasonable. Yet the Pueblos did not limit their appropriation of Spanish architecture just to the mission facilities within their existing villages. In the case of the Tanos of the Galisteo Basin, many left their long-established homes and migrated to the north, occupying the haciendas and fields of ousted colonists. In the wake of the Revolt these Pueblos were left isolated and vulnerable to attack by the nomadic tribes prowling the eastern plains, causing the peoples of San Cristóbal and San Lazaro to vacate the region in 1682 or shortly thereafter (Snow 1994:20). They sought immediate refuge with their Tewa kinfolk, and after a brief stay at San Juan these Tanos established two new pueblos about thirteen kilometers (eight miles) from Yungue along Santa Cruz Creek, apparently drawn there by the fields already broken and tilled, and the acequias that had been abandoned by the exiled Spaniards. Each of these new pueblos consisted of four roomblocks and a central plaza.[11] "New San Lazaro," also known as Tewige (or Tewege) was built directly inside of the plaza of the former Spanish settlement of Santa Cruz—a bold annexation of the colonizers' village, sending the unambiguous message that these were again Pueblo lands, and the once-conquerors were now the conquered (Lippard 2010:217–218).

Other Tanos from Galisteo Pueblo were even more brazen in their appropriation of Spanish space, moving directly into the casas reales in Santa Fe, the principal building of the colonial administration and the (former) home of the Spanish governor himself. Here the Galisteo Tanos were joined by northern Tewa allies, with a total population numbering in the thousands (Espinosa 1942:66). The new residents wasted no time in transforming the Governor's Palace to fit their needs, building pueblo rooms on top of the existing buildings and subdividing the space below with new adobe walls. Yet in doing so they retained a number of Hispanic traits as well, installing Spanish-style corner fireplaces, using Spanish-sized adobe bricks in the new construction, and installing a Spanish-style wood- and sand-lined irrigation system, designed to bring running water into their residences.[12] They also incorporated European architectural conventions in their attempts to fortify their new homes against attack. In essence, they turned the casas reales into a walled medieval castle, constructing towers at each of the four corners and sealing up all the entrances except for the main gate. Some windows were barred with timbers, with others bricked up entirely. Near the gate they constructed a ravelin in the shape of a half-moon (a defensive fortification consisting of two angled walls behind a ditch) to guard against a frontal attack (Leonard 1932:64; Snow 1974:8).

The new Tewa-speaking residents did not retain all the Spanish architecture of the capital, however. Unsurprisingly, they tore down the church (which they had attempted to set aflame during the siege of Santa Fe in 1680) and reduced many of the houses surrounding the Governor's Palace "down to the foundations," turning these areas into cultivated farmland.[13] They also converted the living quarters to more closely resemble their conventional abodes, sealing the exterior doorways and opening new, ladder-accessed rooftop entrances. (These renovations also aided in the protection of the new residents, allowing the inhabitants to pull up the ladders in case of attack, concealing themselves inside.) As at the missions of Awat'ovi and Hawikku, the Pueblos remodeled the larger Spanish quarters, subdividing the rooms into a beehive of smaller, more traditionally Pueblo-sized chambers (Chávez 1980:32). On top of the former seat of government they erected a traditional pueblo village consisting of four main roomblocks, three to four stories tall.[14]

Within the walls, the new inhabitants apparently carried on with daily life much as they had in the Galisteo Basin: flaking arrowheads and knives from stone; grinding corn with manos and metates; working turquoise into beads; sewing with bone awls and needles; and forming pottery, figurines, and pipes from clay. All these activities are documented through artifacts that were unearthed in the casas reales in excavations directed by Cordelia Snow (1974:17). More recent excavations in the Santa Fe plaza by Stephen Lentz have turned up items thought to be associated with the 1680 siege, including a broken knife or sword tip, gunflints, impacted musket balls (one fired from a pistol), nails (possibly from shoeing horses), broken arrowheads of both Pueblo and Apachean types, and a significant amount of late-seventeenth-century pottery (Lentz 2004:49–55, 63, 70).

But it was inside the plaza that the Tanos and Tewas made the most radical changes, transforming the Palace of the Governors into a traditional Pueblo village. In addition to the four *cuarteles* (roomblocks) they built (or modified) around the open space, the Puebloans bisected the Spanish plaza by erecting a central roomblock down the center. This had the effect of dividing the plaza in two, effectively turning the casas reales into a twin-plaza pueblo—replicating the form of Patokwa, Kotyiti, and Boletsakwa. In each plaza they erected a kiva, further reinforcing the importance of dual-organization in the new, post-Revolt world.[15] Thus, even while appropriating the most central place in the colonial Kingdom of New Mexico, the Natives manipulated the Spaniards' villa to bring it in line with their conception of traditional Puebloan spatial and social organization.

Hoisted on Their Own Petard: Pan-Pueblo Ethnogenesis

The appropriation and transformation of Spanish iconography, foods, technologies, and architecture played significant (and sometimes surprising) roles in the remaking of the Pueblo world that occurred in the wake of the Revolt. But possibly the most noteworthy element of colonial culture borrowed by the Pueblos—one that played a crucial role in their victory in August of 1680—was the appropriation of the Spaniards' ethnic classifications. More accurately, Po'pay's partisans seized and transformed one category of identity in particular: that of a monolithic group of *indios de pueblos*. During the 1680s this appropriation would foster profound changes in Pueblo material culture and social life, with the dawn of a pan-Pueblo consciousness the likes of which has not been known before or since (Spicer 1962:163).[16]

Although the indigenous farmers of the northern Rio Grande share broad similarities in ideology, material culture, and subsistence strategies, the term "Pueblo" masks the variability that existed (and continues to exist) among these peoples. On the eve of the Spanish colonization of New Mexico, the people who came to be known as Pueblo Indians did not seem to think of themselves as a unitary group. Living in an estimated seventy-five to a hundred separate villages and speaking at least seven different mutually unintelligible languages (many with multiple dialects), the maize farmers of the northern Rio Grande classified themselves according to discrete ethnolinguistic village clusters at the time of first contact (Ford et al. 1972; D. Wilcox 1981).[17] Under the colonial regime the Spaniards lumped these disparate groups together for the first time, developing and deploying the ethnic category of indios de pueblos to differentiate the so-called "civilized" sedentary agriculturalists from their supposedly "barbaric" nomadic neighbors, while simultaneously maintaining a boundary between colonizer and colonized that served to naturalize power asymmetries between the two groups (Preucel et al. 2002).

Part of Po'pay's genius was the appropriation of the ethnic category of "Pueblo" to coalesce and mobilize multiple autonomous Native communities, banding together in resistance toward their common enemy (Preucel 2000b). Crucial to the success of the 1680 Revolt was Po'pay's ability to unite the formerly disparate villages of the northern Rio Grande under the banner of a unified pan-Pueblo identity. In doing so, he drew on an ethnic category invented by the colonizers themselves, hoisting the Spaniards on their own petard. Out of this ironic appropriation grew one of the most significant social consequences of the 1680s: the creation of new identities among the Pueblos that blurred the traditional ethnolinguistic boundaries that had defined Native ethnicity for centuries before the arrival of the white men.

The formation of new ethnic identities in the face of colonial oppression and dispossession is not a phenomenon unique to the post–Pueblo Revolt world, of course. The appropriation of colonial categories by colonized populations, who subsequently reinvest these categories with new meanings to serve their own needs, is common to situations of conquest and occupation the world over, particularly among Native American communities in the seventeenth century (Comaroff 1987; Voss 2008:16). Michel de Certeau (1984:xiii) notes that Native Americans subverted Spanish colonial regimes "not by rejecting or altering them, but by using them with respect to ends and references foreign to the system they had no choice but to accept," akin to Lévi-Strauss's concept of *bricolage* (Lévi-Strauss 1966). Similarly, Gerald Sider (1994:112) notes that Native Americans in the colonial Southeast utilized "forms of differentiation imposed 'from above' . . . as part of processes of asserting their own interests and of resisting" Spanish domination.

This particular form of ethnic judo, whereby subaltern groups consolidate and appropriate forms of identification formerly used in their oppression, is a common variant of the anthropological phenomenon of ethnogenesis (Voss 2008:34). Ethnogenesis has been defined as "not merely a label for the historical emergence of culturally distinct peoples but a concept encompassing peoples' simultaneously cultural and political struggles to create enduring identities in general contexts of radical change and discontinuity" (J. D. Hill 1996:1). The formation of shared ethnic identities is a creative adaptation particularly common among indigenous groups that have been drastically impacted by colonial institutions and agendas, and is often spawned by military conflicts, economic exploitation, and/or imperialism (Singer 1962; Sturtevant 1971; Roosens 1989). In her superlative study of ethnogenesis in colonial San Francisco, Barbara Voss asserts that the concept of ethnogenesis should not be reduced to the creation of new identities out of thin air. Rather, ethnogenesis refers to the emergence of new classifications based on notions of shared lineage. The creation of new ethnicities "draws attention to the ongoing transformations of social identities," emphasizing the cultural creativity of ethnogenetic processes. Ethnogenesis, then, does not happen according to predictable, unilinear models of identification. Ethnicities are in a constant state of transformation and interaction, and ethnogenesis (like revitalization), occurs through practices that "reference the past and anticipate the future" (Voss 2008:33–37).

The pan-Pueblo identity that emerged in New Mexico during the 1680s combined an idealized collective pre-Hispanic lineage with the shared experiences of life in the missions. This unification of the Pueblos occurred hand-in-hand with a dramatic increase in intervillage migration in the years following the Revolt (Herr and Clark 1997). Whole communities vacated their mission

pueblos and established new "refugee" villages after 1680, including the
Jemez who moved to Patokwa and Boletsakwa, and the Keresans who gathered at Kotyiti (Schroeder 1972; Liebmann et al. 2005). These communities
initiated a new form of settlement composed of people from several different, often linguistically diverse home villages. As noted in chapter 6, while
Patokwa was inhabited primarily by the Towa-speaking Jemez, people from
(Keres-speaking) Kewa Pueblo and Navajos lodged there too. Similarly,
Boletsakwa was occupied by people from both Jemez and Kewa, and the
population of Kotyiti comprised residents from Cochiti, San Felipe, and San
Marcos, and probably Tewa-speaking refugees as well (as suggested by Preu-
cel's archaeological research and ceramic analysis).[18]

Material culture played a vital role in the development of this pan-Pueblo
ethnogenesis, mending the seams among the formerly discrete Pueblos that
coalesced during this period by emphasizing similarities among these groups.
The iconic dual-plaza layouts of Patokwa, Kotyiti, Boletsakwa, and Pueblo-
occupied Santa Fe emphasized the similarities shared among the various
different groups living at these new pueblos, even if some of these social
formations were recent innovations (e.g., the concepts of duality and moietal
social organization for the Jemez). Material culture did not just passively
reflect the thoughts and actions of these new multiethnic communities, however. Objects mediated the social processes of this ethnogenesis as well. In
other words, artifacts and architecture performed active roles in fostering this
new pan-Pueblo identity (Liebmann 2008). In particular, pottery played an
especially vital part in mediating Po'pay's revitalizing discourse, aiding in
the creation of this new pan-Pueblo identity by emphasizing similarities and
shared cultural formations among the previously distinct groups that now
thought of themselves as "Pueblo Indians."

From Black-on-white to Red All Over

As noted in chapter 6, after 1680 the potters of Jemez abruptly ceased the
production of Jemez Black-on-white ceramics at Patokwa and Boletsakwa.
While no single type came to dominate the ceramic assemblage as completely as Jemez Black-on-white had in pre-Revolt times, after 1680 Jemez
women began to produce entirely new wares that had never before been
made in this region. Most prominent was a new type of pottery known simply as "Plain Red," an appropriately prosaic label to describe this austere,
unadorned ware (Kidder and Kidder 1917:338). Characterized by smooth,
polished surfaces ranging from brick red to orange and generally lacking in

slip or painted decoration, Plain Red pottery could be described as "glaze ware without the glaze" (as David Snow characterized its sister type, Salinas Red).[19] Similar undecorated redwares have been identified in late seventeenth-century contexts throughout the northern Rio Grande and have been called by a variety of labels, including "Historic Red," "Polished Red," and "Jemez River Plain."[20] Kidder originally described this type at Pecos pueblo, where Shepard hypothesized that it was a post-Revolt innovation.[21]

Plain Red pottery makes up a substantial proportion of the Patokwa and Boletsakwa ceramic assemblages (tables 7.1 and 7.2). At both sites, Plain Red is the most abundant type outside of the Utility series, comprising 41.1 percent of the "decorated" ceramics at the Revolt-era component of Patokwa and 47.4 percent at Boletsakwa.[22] But unlike Jemez Black-on-white, Plain Red ceramics were not an endogenous Jemez innovation. Rather, unadorned redwares were first developed and used outside of the Jemez Valley (similar vessels were produced in the Salinas District as early as the 1620s; Hayes et al. 1981), and their adoption by the potters of Patokwa and Boletsakwa coincided with production of homologous wares at other Pueblo villages. After the Pueblo Revolt, Plain Red pottery was adopted across the middle

Table 7.1. Patokwa (LA 96) ceramic summary (1680s component)

Type	Number	Weight (g)	Percent of total (based on weight)
Rio Grande Blind Corrugated	1	3.1	0.1
Santa Fe B/w	2	5	0.1
Jemez Plain	634	2661.6	46.8
Jemez Black-on-white	18	85.8	1.5
Glaze B	1	14.9	0.3
Glaze C	1	7	0.1
Glaze E	2	18.6	0.3
Glaze F (runny)	186	817.9	14.4
Unidentified Glaze	3	7.6	0.1
Jemez River	32	143.7	2.5
Plain Red	278	1241.2	21.8
Puname Poly	37	149	2.6
Tewa Poly	28	102.4	1.8
Tewa Red	44	151.2	2.7
Kapo Black	1	7.2	0.1
Kapo Grey	3	7.4	0.1
Micaceous	6	26.5	0.5
Ashiwi Poly	1	5.4	0.1
Unidentified	68	229.8	4.0
Totals	1346	5685.3	99.9

Table 7.2. Boletsakwa (LA 136) ceramic summary (1680s component)

Type	Number	Weight (g)	Percent of total (based on weight)
Rio Grande Blind Corrugated	3	9.6	0.5
Jemez Plain	446	1342.9	73.8
Jemez B/w	9	26.4	1.5
Plain Red	74	220.9	12.1
Glaze F (runny)	31	116.2	6.4
Tewa Wares	29	65.1	3.6
Unidentified	12	37.4	2
Totals	604	1818.5	99.9

Rio Grande region. From Patokwa in the west to Pecos in the east, plain redwares dominate the ceramic assemblages of most (if not all) of the pueblos occupied from 1680 to 1700, including those inhabited by the Keresan peoples of Zia, Santa Ana, San Felipe, Cochiti, Kewa, and San Marcos pueblos, the Tewas and Tanos in Santa Fe, and of course the Towas of the Jemez Province and Pecos.[23] Not only did plain polished redwares constitute the majority of non-utility sherds at Patokwa and Boletsakwa, they also comprised the largest percentage of sherds unearthed from the Revolt-era Santa Fe plaza excavations (33 percent of the assemblage), and they outnumber Glaze Wares at Kotyiti (Warren 1979:239; Lentz 2004:51). Plain Red vessels from the Tewa region have been found among the cavates occupied after 1680 in Frijoles Canyon as well (Ford 1987:81). Like the similarities in architecture that characterize many of the Revolt-era pueblos in this region, the adoption of shared ceramic styles during this period is more than mere coincidence. For the first time in more than three hundred years, a single ware was produced across the traditional ethnolinguistic boundaries that had long separated the Jemez, Keres, Pecos, and Tewa. After the Revolt of 1680, Pueblo potters downplayed their historical heterogeneity by producing very similar types of pottery across the Pueblo world, manifested most clearly in the production of Plain Red ceramics.

The manufacture and use of nearly identical redware pottery throughout the northern Rio Grande after 1680 blurred the traditional boundaries that had previously separated Pueblo village clusters during the first eight decades of Spanish colonialism (and likely for at least three centuries before the arrival of the Europeans, if not more). The production of plain redware ceramics thus played an important role in the emergence of a new pan-Pueblo consciousness after 1680, mending the seams between these formerly distinct communities. The rise to prominence of Plain Red during a period of overt nativism and revivalism is somewhat surprising, however, as the origins of this type date to the early mission era of the 1620s (Ivey 1998:135; Hayes et al. 1981:101; Warren 1981:70).[24] Ironically, during a period when the mnemonicons of colonial life were ostensibly being purged, a pottery type that rose to prominence in the missions came into widespread use. This is particularly interesting in the Jemez case, where the production of Jemez Black-on-white seems to have ceased because of its association with life in the mission. The potters of Patokwa and Boletsakwa did not balk at the adoption of Plain Red despite its mission origins, however—probably because it was not produced in large numbers in the Jemez Province until *after* the ouster of the Spaniards (and thus would not have been associated with the Franciscan presence among the Jemez).

Nonetheless, the fact that Plain Red pottery is found in large numbers at sites outside of the Jemez Province raises a significant question about its presence at Patokwa and Boletsakwa: was Plain Red actually manufactured at these villages? Or was it produced outside of the Jemez Province, and obtained by the people of Patokwa and Boletsakwa exclusively through trade? Compositional and petrographic analyses of the Plain Red ceramics from these sites indicate that they were in fact produced locally, but that Jemez potters also adopted new technologies of ceramic manufacture hand-in-hand with the creation of these new types (Liebmann 2006:363–71).[25] These changes in technology were likely influenced by the increase in migration among Pueblo peoples that characterized life in the wake of the Pueblo Revolt (Liebmann and Preucel 2007:204–6). Large-scale shifts in ceramic production are linked to residential mobility, because moving leads to new and increased interaction among communities, brings potters into contact with new materials, and facilitates coresidence (which in turn leads to the transfer of technological knowledge from immigrants to local potters; Zedeño 1995). And in fact all these circumstances—increased interaction, movement to new locations, and coresidence—characterize the situations at Patokwa and Boletsakwa following the Pueblo Revolt.

The mixing of populations and potters from different Pueblos that occurred in the Jemez region during the 1680s resulted not only in the adoption of Plain Red pottery at Patokwa and Boletsakwa but in the creation of other new types of pottery as well. New styles of decorated wares were created during this period that blended elements of the recently discontinued Jemez Black-on-white with the traditions of their Keres neighbors to the south and east. Although not nearly as numerous as Plain Red, small amounts of a matte-painted decorated ware known as Jemez River Polychrome appear in the ceramic assemblages of Patokwa and Boletsakwa (Harlow and Lanmon

2003:31–32; Harlow et al. 2005:65–75).[26] These vessels are generally unslipped, with polished bodies ranging from brick red to orange, and are decorated with matte painted designs in black, red, and occasionally white. Tempering materials occur in two main varieties, basalt and tuff.

In general, Jemez River Polychrome vessels resemble the Glaze Wares manufactured at the Puname pueblos (ancestral Zia and Santa Ana) prior to the Pueblo Revolt. The local (Puname) variety of Glaze F pottery, known as San Diego Polychrome, is broadly similar to Jemez River Polychrome, with the exception that the lead-glaze paint of San Diego Polychrome was replaced by organic matte paints on Jemez River vessels (Harlow and Lanmon 2003:31–32; Harlow et al. 2005:50–65). After 1680, the San Diego Glaze Polychrome tradition appears to have merged with that of matte-painted Jemez Black-on-white, resulting in the production of matte-painted polychromes and the cessation of glaze paint production among the Punames. The watery black and gray organic paints that characterize Jemez River Polychromes "resemble the pigment used on Jemez Black-on-white," observes Francis Harlow, "and may indeed have been borrowed from Jemez Potters during refugee-site occupation" (Harlow et al. 2005:66). The merger of these two traditions is not entirely surprising, as Zia and Santa Ana refugees are known to have moved into the Jemez Province during the late 1680s, increasing the interactions among Jemez and Puname potters (see chapter 8). One result of these interactions was the production of Jemez River Polychrome ceramics not only at Patokwa and Boletsakwa, but also at the Zia-Santa Ana sites occupied during the Revolt era.[27]

Unity in Design: Feathers, Keys, and Sacred Mountains

The designs that Jemez and Keres women applied to Jemez River Polychrome vessels document the ethos of pan-Puebloism that pervaded the northern Rio Grande after 1680 as well. In the wake of the Revolt, these potters participated in the creation of regionally shared styles stretching from the Rio Grande across the Puname and Jemez regions to the western pueblos of Acoma and Zuni. At least four dominant design elements spread across the Pueblo world in the 1680s, uniting the pottery made by women from Jemez, Zia, Santa Ana, San Felipe, Cochiti, Kewa, Pecos, Acoma, and Zuni (and, to a lesser extent, among the Tewas): feather motifs, the hooked triangle/F figure design, the double-headed key theme, and the cap step/sacred mountain motif (figure 7.4). Like the production of Plain Red pottery, the shared use of these designs documents the emergence of the pan-Pueblo ethnogenesis of

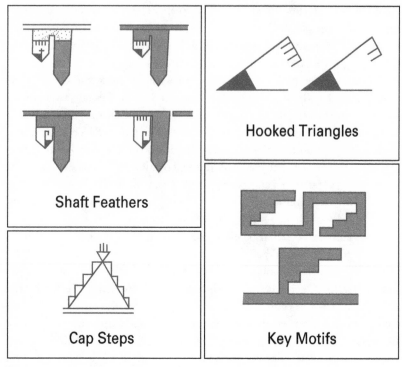

FIGURE 7.4. Common ceramic motifs of the Pueblo Revolt era.

this period, as well as the increased interaction among potters who were able to move more freely from village to village without being monitored by the Spaniards' watchful eyes.

Feather motifs played a particularly important role in ceramic decoration throughout the Pueblos in the 1680s, appearing on pottery from Zuni, Acoma, Zia, Santa Ana, Cochiti, the Jemez Province, and the Tewa region.[28] Although feather icons had been used on pottery as far back as the 1300s (Harlow et al. 2005:63), after the Pueblo Revolt they became more widespread in ceramic design, and more homogenous in execution, possibly related to the revivalist ethos of the period. Feathers play essential roles in Pueblo religion, and have long been used in the preparation and planting of prayer sticks, the construction of altars, as decoration on ritual costumes, and on shields (Mills 2002:91). Yet according to one twentieth-century Pueblo potter, "women do not prepare prayer sticks, and that is why we always put feathers on the jars" (Bunzel 1972 [1929]:106). On matte-painted pottery from Acoma and Zuni, feathers often appear in pairs after the Revolt, with a similar paired-feather motif (dubbed the "shaft feather") depicted on con-temporaneous pottery of the Zia-Santa Ana region (Harlow et al. 2005:64). "The use of feathers across the Pueblo area," observes Mills, is "evidence for a region-wide stylistic horizon," resulting from the pan-Pueblo ethnogenesis of the period. "The similarities at the regional scale in the use of feathers is quite striking," she notes, suggesting "a unity that cross-cuts language groups and other social differences among the Pueblos" (2002:95). The use of common design elements such as feathers helped to reflect and reinforce the more homogenous Pueblo identity that emerged in the period immediately following the Revolt.

Similarly, the "hooked triangle," also known as the "F figure" motif has considerable antiquity in Tewa design, with its popularity reaching a cre-scendo in the wake of the Revolt. Preucel identifies this motif on one-quarter of the Tewa ceramics analyzed from Kotyiti (Capone and Preucel 2002:109–110). One particular variant of the F figure, in which the end turns back toward the triangular base, has been identified as particularly characteristic of Zia-Santa Ana ceramics found at Jemez Revolt-era sites and is also typical of Kotyiti Glazeware jars of this period. According to Harlow, Anderson, and Lanmon this motif "is much less characteristic at other places and times" (Harlow et al. 2005:63). The spread of this motif from the Tewas south to the Keres of Kotyiti, the Punames, and the Towa-speaking Jemez is further evidence for the formation of shared identities through shared images among Pueblo potters in the 1680s.

As noted in chapter 6, the double-headed key motif is one of the most commonly depicted designs on post-Revolt decorated pottery, and has been identified at pueblos occupied during the 1680s by people from Jemez, Kewa, Cochiti, San Marcos, San Felipe, Zia, Santa Ana, Pecos, Hopi, and Zuni pueb-los (Capone and Preucel 2002:108–109). The popularity of this motif among the potters of the post-Revolt pueblos seems clearly linked to revivalism.

Another common decorative element appearing on pottery across the Pueblo world after the Revolt is known variously as the "cap step" or "sacred mountain" theme (Capone and Preucel 2002:109–110; Harlow et al. 2005:62). This iconography was shared among the eastern and western Keres, Zunis, and Jemez during this period. Unlike the feather, hooked triangle, and double-headed key motifs, however, the cap step appears to have originated in the latter seventeenth century, and may have been invented only after 1680.[29] According to Harlow and his colleagues (2005:61–62), it appears on Jemez River and San Diego Polychromes found at (unnamed) "Jemez refuge sites," as well as on Ashiwi Polychromes from Zuni, on Glaze F jars from Kotyiti, and on Tewa polychromes (Carlson 1965:Plate 34f; Capone and Preucel 2002:109–110).

Not coincidentally, the cap step/sacred mountain design is also etched into the wall of the Virgin-Kachina cavate in Frijoles Canyon. And like the feather, F-figure, and double-headed key, the cap step was involved in the creation of a common pool of images on which potters drew, emphasizing the unity of the Pueblos in the process.

New Alliances

The appropriation of Spanish ethnic categories and the resulting pan-Pueblo ethnogenesis of the 1680s is also reflected in the new patterns of exchange that emerged among the Pueblos during this period. Following the Pueblo Revolt, inter-Pueblo trade increased dramatically, and new trading partnerships were forged between previously dissociated communities. Nowhere are these changes more apparent than in the ceramic assemblages of Patokwa and Boletsakwa, which clearly document an explosion of interaction among the Jemez and neighboring Pueblos during the 1680s, the likes of which had never before occurred in the Jemez Province.

Prior to the 1680s the Jemez appear to have been a fairly xenophobic lot, at least in terms of ceramic trade. Nonlocal ceramics are found in relatively meager amounts at ancestral Jemez sites. Pre-Revolt Jemez ceramic assemblages display a remarkable lack of trade wares: at Unshagi (occupied from 1375 to 1620), just 3.2 percent of the assemblage was classified as nonlocal; similarly, at Giusewa (1300–1640) 3.0 percent of the sherds were identified as trade wares (Reiter 1938:103; Elliott 1991:80). The majority of these nonlocal types were Rio Grande Glaze Wares, and petrographic analyses indicate that the most common tempering material was basalt, suggesting exchange primarily with the Puname area to the south, albeit infrequently and in low quantities (Shepard 1938:211; Warren quoted in Lambert 1981:228). Stylistic studies of Jemez and Tewa wares support the notion that there was remarkably little interaction between these regions before 1680 (Graves and Eckert 1998:276; Morley 2002:237–239). According to Fray Alonso de Benavides, in the early seventeenth century relations between the Tewas and Jemez were so hostile that in 1634 one of the Jemez leaders was said to wear proudly around his neck a string of ears from the Tewa warriors he had killed.[30] Additionally, Jemez ceramics are not found in significant quantities at ancestral Pueblo sites outside of the Jemez Province (Futrell 1998:289–290; Kulisheck and Elliott 2005:5; Kidder and Amsden 1931). Jemez Black-on-white may have been traded to Athapaskan-speaking peoples to the west and northwest of the Jemez Province with somewhat greater frequency, however (Reed and Reed

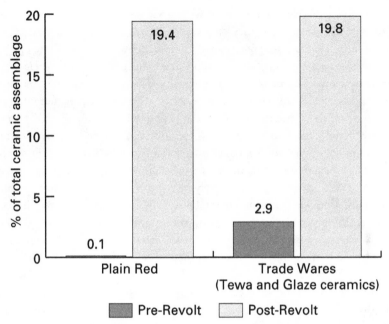

FIGURE 7.5. Comparison of pre- and post-Revolt Plain Redware and trade wares at Jemez pueblos. Pre-Revolt data from the Jemez pueblos of Unshagi (Reiter 1938) and Giusewa (Elliott 1991; Lambert 1981). Post-Revolt data from Patokwa and Boletsakwa (see tables 7.1 and 7.2).

1992). Overall, trade between the Jemez and neighboring regions occurred rarely and in low quantities between 1300 and 1680.

These centuries-old patterns of exchange shifted drastically during the 1680s, with trade wares at the Jemez Pueblos increasing nearly sevenfold over pre-Revolt levels (figure 7.5). More specifically, quantities of Keres-produced Glaze Wares jumped from less than 3 percent before the Revolt to 13.1 percent of the total combined ceramic assemblage at Patokwa and Boletsakwa. Similarly, trade between Jemez and Tewa pueblos (which was nearly non-existent prior to 1680) surged after Po'pay's victory tour, with Tewa pottery jumping from just 0.1 percent in pre-Revolt contexts to 4.4 percent of the ceramics at Patokwa and Boletsakwa (Reiter 1938:103, 189–92; Elliott 1991:80; Liebmann 2008:366).

This dramatic increase in exchange among previously disparate Pueblo communities was fostered by the formation of pan-Pueblo identities and the increased mobility of Pueblo peoples during the 1680s. The sense of shared identity that Po'pay promoted among the Pueblos ultimately encouraged the rise in trade that is reflected in the ceramic assemblages of Patokwa and Boletsakwa. But the ceramics of the post-Revolt Pueblos (nonlocal trade wares as well as Plain Red pottery and the newly created matte-painted polychromes) do not only *reflect* this pan-Pueblo ethnogenesis. They also helped to actively *cultivate* a sense of collective identity. The use of communal ceramic types, motifs, and the sharing of wares among spatially segregated villages emphasized the similarities among the people who made and used them, strengthening the bonds between these communities and furthering the development of the pan-Pueblo ethnicity that the adherents had appropriated from their Spanish colonizers. In the same way, the correspondence in layout of the dual-plaza pueblos likely served to foster a sense of pan-Pueblo community among travelers moving between these various refugee villages. As Pueblo people visited neighboring communities during the 1680s, the similarities they experienced through the shared materiality of revitalization would have actively promoted the notion of pan-Pueblo unity. Thus the distinctive types of material culture produced in the aftermath of the Pueblo Revolt were not epiphenomenal of Po'pay's nativism and revivalism; rather, the dual-plaza pueblos and new ceramic types were crucially constitutive of revitalization processes, recursively shaping the creation of new, pan-Pueblo identities (Liebmann 2008:368).

Despite Po'pay's calls to eradicate all elements of Spanish culture after the Revolt, Pueblo people appropriated colonial ideas, foods, technologies, and material culture throughout the 1680s. They did so not as loyal subjects of the Spanish crown, however, nor as zealous followers of the Catholic faith. Rather, the Pueblos usurped and transformed the things the Spaniards had introduced to their world, reworking them in innovative ways that promoted a pan-Pueblo cultural revitalization during that decade. By seizing the tools of the colonizers—their religion, technology, architecture, and classifications—the Pueblos were able to remake their world as they saw fit, emphasizing a newfound homogeneity among historically heterogeneous communities. At times, this appropriation of foreign concepts was accomplished via indigenous means, as when the pan-Pueblo identity that had been invented by the Spaniards was promoted and shaped through the production, trade, and consumption of Pueblo ceramics. Indeed, the pan-Pueblo ethnogenesis of the 1680s was arguably the most important outcome of all the colonial appropriations that occurred during the Spanish interregnum.

8

From Apostates to Compadres

COLONIAL AMBIVALENCE IN A TIME OF "UNCEASING WAR," 1687–1692

AS THE JEMEZ RIVER EXITS THE SOUTHERN END of the Jemez Province, its meanders merge with the Rio Salado and fan out across a sun-baked plain to the southeast. The waters warm as they flow over red sands, past the pueblos of Zia and Tamaya (Santa Ana), before merging one last time with the Rio Grande. The land between these two confluences is the territory of the Puname Pueblos, a name meaning "people of the west" in Keresan (White 1962:20; see figure FM.2). When the Spaniards first passed through these lands there were at least five Puname villages in the region,[1] but by the 1680s only Zia and Tamaya remained. The mercurial actions of these two Pueblos during the late 1680s-early 1690s remain one of the enduring paradoxes of the Revolt era. In the decade that followed 1680 the Punames first participated in the initial uprising, then offered their allegiance to the Spaniards in 1681. They were twice attacked and resisted, taking up arms against the Spaniards in 1687 and 1689, but then welcomed the colonizers back with open arms in 1692, accepting the waters of baptism and pledging their loyalty to the Crown and Christ. Ultimately they even joined their former enemies in battle, marching side by side with the colonial militia against their Pueblo brethren (chapter 9). In the course of a dozen years, then, the Punames vacillated between hostile resistance and cordial compliance with the Spaniards, transforming repeatedly from hated enemies to loyal allies and back again.

Why the Punames chose such radically different courses of action during the various stages of the Pueblo Revolt era is a question that has long beguiled scholars of New Mexican history (Liebmann 2011:201). What led the Zias and Santa Anas to first resist colonial efforts at virtually all costs, only to form an alliance with the Spaniards a few years later? Although the Punames' repeated oscillations between colonial opposition and alliance might seem at first unusual, such apparent inconsistencies are remarkably common among colonized populations. Postcolonial scholarship of the past two decades has repeatedly emphasized the profound *ambivalence* inherent in colonial societies, highlighting the simultaneous desire for and repulsion from foreign objects, persons, or actions experienced by parties on all sides of the colonial encounter (Young 1995:161; Bhabha 1985, 1994:110; Prakash 1994:1489). This concurrent appeal of and aversion to colonialism has often been overlooked in romanticized accounts of anticolonial resistance (Abu-Lughod 1990; Liebmann and Murphy 2011:6–8). Since the earliest encounters between Europeans and Native Americans, binary classifications of Indians have served as convenient but often inaccurate shorthand, with entire tribes pigeonholed as friendly or hostile, progressive versus conservative, and savage or civilized. The reality is often far more complicated, however, and many of the seventeenth-century Pueblos were clearly more ambivalent than exclusively opposed to Spanish rule, particularly the Punames.

The pueblos of Zia and Tamaya did not exist in isolation, of course, and their actions were enmeshed within the larger web of events and social processes that took place in northern New Spain during this tumultuous period. Between 1687 and 1692 the Spaniards made repeated attempts to reconquer the Pueblos, efforts which coincided with a slow unraveling of the pan-Pueblo fabric that had been woven in the immediate aftermath of the Revolt. The ethnogenesis of the early 1680s proved neither comprehensive nor long-lasting, and after a few years the Pueblos began to fall back into a more familiar—and, it could be argued, more traditional—pattern of rivalries marked by inter- and intra-Pueblo factionalism. By all accounts, this was a time of conflict throughout the northern Rio Grande. In sharp contrast with the preceding era of attempted utopian unification, the latter part of the 1680s saw the Pueblo world torn asunder and rife with bloodshed, with the Pueblos fighting against not only the nomadic Native groups who surrounded them and the returning Spaniards, but also against other Pueblos. It was in this climate that the Punames calculated their actions, allegiances, and ambivalence, both opposing and allying with reconquering colonists and other Pueblos alike. While there are no simple explanations for the Punames' ambivalence and alliance-switching throughout the 1680s, the roots of those fateful decisions stretch back to the earliest interactions between the Punames and the Spaniards, 140 years before the Pueblo Revolt.

Strategic Subjects, Ambivalent Rebels:
The Puname Pueblos, 1540s–1680s

From their first encounters with the conquistadores in the 1540s, the Punames displayed an ambivalence toward the Spaniards that contrasted sharply with the defiance and opposition displayed by many of the other Pueblos in the vicinity. When the Coronado expedition laid siege to the neighboring Tiguex pueblos in 1541, the Punames cautiously observed events from afar. Rather than taking up arms against these new arrivals, they offered to Vasquez de Coronado their preemptive submission in order to avoid a fate similar to that of the Tiguex. Their gambit paid off, and for their promised vassalage the Pueblo of Zia was rewarded with a gift of four bronze cannon.[2]

Yet despite their best efforts, no amount of appeasement could stave off the diseases that swept through their villages over the next century. Like the rest of the Pueblos, by 1680 the population of the Punames had been reduced by possibly as much as 80 percent (White 1962:20; Schroeder 1979:244). Adding insult to this injury was the grant of encomienda that was awarded for the Puname Province in the early 1600s, compounding the woes of the local populace (Hordes 2005:145). When Po'pay's plot presented the opportunity to free themselves from the Spanish yoke, the Punames participated in the rebellion with telltale apprehension. At Zia they did not kill their priest, burn their village, or pillage their church. Instead they focused their efforts on the estancias of nearby colonial settlers, seizing livestock and other valuables. They allowed the Franciscan minister, Fray Nicolás Hurtado, to flee, ringing the mission bells and mocking him in derision as he made his escape.[3] Fray Nicolás was one of only twelve priests in New Mexico to survive the Revolt of 1680. The friar fled to Tamaya, which he found mostly vacant, its occupants already marching north to aid in the siege on Santa Fe. (There was no priest in residence at Tamaya in 1680, and the fate of the church itself was not recorded.) Asking the women where all the men had gone, they replied "very volubly and boldly that they had gone to kill all the Spaniards," he reported. Soon thereafter the Zia warriors joined the men of Tamaya, fighting side-by-side to cast the Spaniards out of the colonial capital.[4]

The Zia church of Nuestra Señora de la Asunción de Zia was one of the few left standing after Po'pay's victory tour.[5] And unlike their Towa, Keres, and Tano neighbors, the residents of Zia and Tamaya did not leave their villages or destroy their homes, but carried on living at these pueblos throughout the 1680s.[6] In fact, Tamaya was the locale chosen to host Po'pay and Alonso Catití's feast of mockery in 1680–81, in which they mimicked the recently banished Spanish governor and the head of the Franciscan order in New Mexico. The motives behind the Punames' continued occupation of their pueblos and the destruction of mission villages by other Pueblos, such as the Jemez, were likely rooted in the differing histories of these settlements. As noted in chapters 5 and 6, the Jemez mission village was founded by a Franciscan priest in the 1620s, with the Jemez enticed to settle there subsequently— thus the pueblo of Walatowa/San Diego de la Congregación had its origins in the missionary effort.[7] But both Zia and Tamaya were occupied prior to Spanish colonization and the establishment of mission facilities. Archaeological excavations by Florence Hawley Ellis of the middens at Zia establish a founding date in the fourteenth century, with continuous occupation stretching through the 1680s (Ellis 1966a:810). And while the antiquity of Tamaya has yet to be established archaeologically, it was almost certainly occupied prior to 1598 when Oñate described a village known as Tamy or Tamaya that was inhabited by Keresan-speaking peoples in the Puname region.[8] Thus while the Jemez seem to have associated their village with a recent history of dislocation and forced removal from their ancestral lands, the villages of Zia and Tamaya likely evoked a sense of rootedness and the continuation of long-held pre-Hispanic traditions for their residents. It makes sense, then, that the Zias and Santa Anas chose not to abandon (much less destroy) their villages when Po'pay called for the return to traditional Pueblo life.

During Otermín's attempted reconquest in December 1681 the Punames seem to have reconsidered their rebellious ways. In response to a letter offering peace from the Spaniards, a Puname leader appeared in the Spaniards' camp offering his people's submission. As one of the Spanish officers testified at the time, "the Indians of Zia replied to me through one of their principal Indians named El Pupiste, who came into my presence and that of the whole camp with his cross at his neck, saying in behalf of his pueblo of Zia, and also of Santa Ana, that they had obeyed, and that everyone in the said pueblos was waiting to give obedience to both majesties."[9] The Punames appear to have been alone among all the Pueblos in their willingness to accede to the Spaniards so quickly after the Revolt—if in fact El Pupiste's words were sincere. At the same time that the Zias and Santa Anas were pledging their allegiance, Alonso Catití was outwardly feigning submission as he surreptitiously conspired to lure the Spaniards into his trap (using "all the prettiest, most pleasing, and neatest Indian women" of Cochiti).[10] Thus the Punames' 1681 pledge is difficult to interpret; whether their capitulation was earnest or a ruse is open to debate.

As at other villages, Puname potters appear to have participated in region-wide stylistic horizons related to pan-Pueblo ethnogenesis during the early 1680s. In addition to the production of Plain Red ceramics, the women of

Zia and Santa Ana produced matte-painted polychromes (Jemez River Polychrome) in increasing numbers after the Pueblo Revolt, similar to the pattern
at Zuni and Acoma (Mills 2002:92–93; Harlow et al. 2005:65–75; Liebmann 2006:355). Unlike the Zunis, however, the Punames do not appear to
have abandoned the production of Glaze Ware pottery completely during this
period. Rather, like their Keres neighbors at Kotyiti, the Zias and Santa Anas
continued their pre-Revolt tradition of glaze paint decoration on ceramics,
albeit on a reduced scale.[11] This raises the question of why the dramatic shift
in ceramic production after 1680 that is observed among the Jemez pueblos—
presumably related to the nativist agenda of the period—was not replicated
among the Punames or their neighboring Keres brethren at Kotyiti? The
answer, I suspect, is again related to the process of ethnogenesis. The Jemez
were the only ethnic group producing Jemez Black-on-white prior to the
Revolt, thus their participation in any regionwide ceramic tradition necessitated the production of new and different pottery types. But even before
1680, Rio Grande Glaze Wares were already being produced among the eastern Keres, Tano of the Galisteo Basin, and Pecos. In other words, Glaze Wares
had a preexisting tradition of crossing linguistic and ethnic boundaries before
1680. After the Revolt, potters at Zia and Santa Ana (not to mention Kotyiti,
Pecos, and those lodged in the Governor's Palace in Santa Fe) continued this
tradition, with the production of glaze-paint ceramics acting to reinforce the
pan-Pueblo ethnogenesis of the period in much the same way that the production and consumption of Plain Red ceramics did during the 1680s.

The Dissolution of the Pueblo Confederacy

Despite efforts by Pueblo potters throughout the region to cultivate this ethnogenesis during the early 1680s, the pan-Pueblo identity fostered by their
handiwork proved tenuous and fleeting. This dissolution of Pueblo unity
probably began in the mid-1680s, with the death of Alonso Catití. After
Po'pay was deposed in 1681 Catití had assumed the office of deputy lieutenant
of the Pueblos, overseeing all the villages of the Rio Abajo. He was apparently
second-in-command under Luis Tupatú (a.k.a. Luis el Picurí), who served, as
one Tano reportedly put it, as "supreme head of all the rebellious nations,"
but presided over the day-to-day operations of the pueblos of the Rio Arriba.
Catití in turn handled daily management of the Rio Abajo.[12] The untimely
and ghastly death of Catití occurred sometime in late 1684 or early 1685,
when he reportedly descended into a kiva and "burst asunder suddenly, all his
intestines coming forth in view of many other Indians." Following Catití's

demise, the witness reported, "thereafter each pueblo of the Keres governed itself independently," indicating that the pan-Pueblo alliance began to break down with the end of the power-sharing coalition between Tupatú and Catití.[13] Ultimately, Catití's passing provided the first tug on a loose thread that would eventually unravel the Pueblo confederacy completely.

With the delicate balance of this paired leadership disrupted, so too was the limited security that the pan-Pueblo coalition had provided. The Piro pueblos of Senecú, Socorro, Alamillo, and Sevilleta were reportedly "finished off" by the Jemez and Keres.[14] The abandonment of these southernmost pueblos, combined with the (temporarily) uninhabited state of the southern Tiwa villages of Isleta, Alameda, Puaray, and Sandia sparked a chain reaction of migration and relocation throughout the northern Rio Grande.[15] Without the buffer that had been provided by the Piros and southern Tiwas, the pueblos of the Galisteo Basin were suddenly more isolated and vulnerable to attack than ever before. Understandably uncomfortable with this situation, the people of San Marcos, Galisteo, San Lazaro, and San Cristóbal fled the region.[16] With their departure the Puname pueblos of Zia and Santa Ana found themselves in an entirely new position on what had become the southern frontier of the Pueblo world, with no buffer between them and whatever armies might appear from the south.

Pyrrhic Victories: The Puname Campaigns, 1687–1689

Unfortunately for the Punames, their mettle was tested in 1687 when the newly appointed governor of New Mexico, don Pedro Reneros de Posada, attempted to reclaim the "apostate Pueblos" for the Crown and Christ. Records of this expedition are scant and murky at best. All that is known is that Reneros led a column from El Paso del Norte up the Rio Grande, attacking the first occupied pueblo at which they arrived, Santa Ana, on October 8 of that year.[17] Jack Forbes (1960:208) notes that the record of this raid "appears suspiciously like a slaving expedition." Reportedly the Santa Anas were offered peace if they surrendered; when they refused, the Spaniards attacked, overrunning the village.[18] According to a 1693 account, colonial soldiers "leveled the tiny pueblo of Santa Ana," burning it to the ground.[19] An untold number of residents died in the flames. Yet the skirmish must have proved difficult for the Spaniards, as Reneros's forces immediately beat a hasty retreat back to El Paso, taking with them four Santa Ana leaders and ten other captives they had captured in the battle. The four leaders were quickly tried and condemned to public execution. The rest were accused of "murder, sacrilege, and active

FIGURE 8.1. Landscape surrounding Canjilon Pueblo (LA 2049).

participation in the 1680 Revolt," and sold into slavery in Nueva Vizcaya, never to return to their homeland again (Kessell 2008:136).

Where the Santa Anas lived in the immediate wake of the destruction of their village is unclear. Some of the survivors probably took up residence with their Puname cousins at Zia. But others may have migrated to a small mesa-top refuge east of old Santa Ana, on a basalt outcrop overlooking the confluence of the Jemez River and the Rio Grande (figure 8.1). This site, known to archaeologists as Canjilon Pueblo (LA 2049), contains less than twenty rooms arranged in an "L" shape, with an associated kiva located south of the roomblocks. Ceramics at Canjilon date to the latter seventeenth century; H. P. Mera (1940:26) notes that "this site appears to have been inhabited solely during the production of [Rio Grande Glaze] Groups E and F." As expected, "plain undecorated sherds predominate" the assemblage, including large amounts of Plain Red, according to Helene Warren's analysis of ceramics from the site held at the Museum of New Mexico's Laboratory of Anthropology.[20] Revolt-period ceramics from the Tewa region are present as well, consisting of Tewa Polychrome, Tewa Red, and Kapo Black sherds.

Twenty-three kilometers (fourteen miles) upriver from Canjilon Pueblo, the Zias carried on living at their hilltop village. If they had not fortified their pueblo previously, they almost certainly erected new defensive architecture of

adobe and stone following the Spaniards' attack on Santa Ana. In 1688 Reneros returned to the Puname District, and this time the Punames were prepared. The Spanish column retraced their route from the previous year up the
Rio Grande to its junction with the Jemez River. Continuing past Canjilon
and the charred ruins of Santa Ana, they followed the riverbed west to Zia.
There Reneros apparently intended to "reduce the rebels by force of arms,"
as he had done a year before at Santa Ana. This time, however, he succeeded
only in reducing their livestock. "The strength of the enemy," according to an
account recorded five years later, "led him to depart after having captured the
sheep and goats and some horses and mules."[21] Reneros and his forces turned
tail once again and "without accomplishing another thing," as the documents
state, they retreated ignominiously back to the colonial capital-in-exile at El
Paso del Norte.[22] The proud Spaniards of the seventeenth century were not
quick to admit defeat, prompting one particularly generous chronicler to
boast that Reneros had "succeeded in getting back from the village of Zia,"
surely the brightest spin possible on this failed attempt at reconquest.[23]

Reneros's lackluster (and possibly illegal) accomplishments on the Puname
campaigns may have contributed to his dismissal as governor. In February
1689 he was succeeded by don Domingo Jironza Petrís de Cruzate, a brash
young man in his thirties, fresh off the boat from Spain in 1680. Before leaving Mexico City for El Paso, Jironza boasted that he would succeed in reconquering the Pueblos, at his own expense, despite having yet to set foot in New
Mexico. And when the dejected El Paso *cabildo* (municipal council) begged
him to abandon the poverty-stricken capital-in-exile—three times, no less—
Jironza refused each time, maintaining his unswerving focus on restoring the
abandoned colony to glory for God and empire (Kessell 2002:152, 2008:135).

The Siege of Zia: August 1689

On the Feast of San Lorenzo in 1689, Jironza set out to accomplish the task
that had eluded both Otermín and Reneros. The date, August 10, was carefully chosen to coincide with the anniversary of the Native rebellion that had
occurred nine years prior. Leading a militia consisting of 80 men-at-arms and
120 Pueblo allies who had been living in El Paso (hailing originally from the
southern Tiwa and Piro pueblos), the column proceeded north out of El Paso
del Norte with the intent of reconquering the Kingdom of New Mexico.
It took them nearly three weeks to make their way up the Rio Grande to
the Puname District, dragging a rehabilitated bronze cannon at the rear.
Stopping outside Zia Pueblo, Governor Jironza made plans for a siege that

would begin at dawn, a common Spanish battle tactic known as an *alborada* (Kessell 2008:136). As the first rays of sunlight struck the hilltop on August 29, the blasts of muskets and cannon ripped open the morning air. According to accounts prepared in El Paso more than a year later, the battle raged from daybreak until ten o'clock at night, with more than seventy Indians captured alive.[24] The Zias reportedly "defended themselves with such valor and desperate courage that many let themselves burn alive on the tops of their houses rather than surrender." As the fighting ceased, four of the Pueblo's religious leaders were marched into the main plaza of the village and executed before a firing squad. Six hundred Punames were purportedly killed that day, a number that included not only Zias but also "those from Santa Ana and others who came to the aid of the besieged . . . of both sexes and of different ages."[25]

Jironza's force had prevailed, but the victory proved pyrrhic. More than fifty of his eighty men-at-arms were wounded in the fighting and six were killed, with an untold number of casualties among his Native allies. Recognizing that his brigade could ill afford another triumph of that sort, Jironza and his tattered militia limped back to El Paso del Norte, leaving the still-smoldering remains of Zia behind.[26]

There are, however, reasons to doubt the veracity of the official reports of Jironza's 1689 battle at Zia. John Kessell points out that chronicles of the siege bear remarkable similarities to the account of an attack on Acoma Pueblo ninety years earlier that appears in Gaspar Pérez de Villagrá's *Historia de la Nueva México* (1992 [1610]). Both claim more than six hundred Indians killed, with "many preferring death in flames to surrender" (Kessell 2008:136). Furthermore, interviews with Zia survivors recorded five years after the battle suggest that reports of Jironza's crushing victory were greatly exaggerated. According to these Native versions, the attacking forces inflicted relatively few casualties in 1689 as the majority of the Zia populace was "away from the pueblo, hunting, fishing, and gathering fruit in the forest" on that day.[27] Zia and Santa Ana oral traditions recorded in the twentieth century concur with these accounts, maintaining that many villagers were out on a communal hunt when the pueblo was attacked. These oral traditions also relate some interesting details not included in Spanish documents, stating that the invaders intentionally timed their invasion to a date when the men would be absent, with the specific goal of capturing all the Zia children. When the men returned to the pueblo the Spaniards used the little ones as human shields, preventing the Punames from launching a counterattack. After a stalemate lasting three or four days, the Zias sent one adult male with the children back to El Paso with instructions to "watch and learn all that the Spaniards taught them. Then he would return to the pueblos with news of the children," according to Santa Ana oral tradition. "Having no other choice, the pueblos agreed, and the Zia man went to [the Spaniards'] camp. The next day, the soldiers left, taking the children with them."[28]

The Spoils of War: Bartolomé de Ojeda

While Spanish documents make no mention of child captives, they do contain references to one particularly valuable item that Jironza plundered from the battlefield: a Zia war captain named Bartolomé de Ojeda. The Spaniards later recalled how valiantly Ojeda had fought against them at the Battle of Zia, even after his flesh was torn by a musket ball and an arrow. As he lay on the battlefield bleeding and "thinking he could not survive with such wounds," the Puname warrior "surrendered, impelled by fear of hell, in order to confess before dying" according to an eighteenth-century account.[29] Ojeda begged for a priest to administer his last rites and was taken prisoner. To his surprise he did not die, however, and was transported to El Paso del Norte where he was nursed back to health. (Communal memories of Ojeda persist to this day among the Punames, as he appears to be the Zia man who accompanied the captive children to the south, mentioned in the contemporary oral traditions noted above.)

Ojeda would eventually become a crucial asset in the Spaniards' reconquest campaigns of the 1690s. Born of Pueblo and Hispano parentage, the Castilian-speaking indio ladino was educated by the Franciscans as a child and could read and write—skills rare among the seventeenth-century Pueblos. Like many of the other mestizos and coyotes of the northern Rio Grande, Ojeda was a supporter of the Pueblo Revolt of 1680 as well (Riley 1999:219). As his wounds healed over the following months in El Paso, Ojeda transformed himself from a fierce enemy of the Spaniards into one of their strongest Native allies. While in El Paso he revealed shocking details to his captors regarding life in the Pueblos during the 1680s, including gruesome descriptions of the deaths of Franciscans during the Pueblo Revolt as well as an account of his own grandmother, a Christian mestiza, being stripped naked and executed for her faith.[30] These fantastic reports served to further stoke the desires of the exiled El Paso colonists to restore Christian order to the Pueblos.[31]

Maybe most valuable to the Spaniards was Ojeda's testimony regarding the political turmoil that had beset the Pueblos in the aftermath of Alonso Catití's death. Needing no interpreter, he took an oath in the name of God and the holy cross to testify in all honesty. According to his sworn statement (as related by Fray Silvestre Vélez de Escalante, who wrote in the late 1770s with access to documents that have not survived to the present day), by the late 1680s:

> The rebellious pueblos of New Mexico became inflamed one against the other and began to wage war. The Keres, Taos, and Pecos fought against the Tewas and Tanos. . . . [Luis Tupatú] governed the Tewas and Tanos until the year 1688, in which the same Po'pay was again chosen; soon after he died and the said don Luis Tupatú was chosen for a second time. . . . Thereafter each pueblo of the Keres governed themselves independently. The Apaches were at peace with some of these pueblos and in others inflicted all the damage they could. The Utes, when they heard of the misfortune of the Spaniards, waged unceasing war upon the Jemez, Taos, and Picuris, and even with greater vigor upon the Tewas. Not alone in this and with their civil wars were all the apostates afflicted but also by famines and pestilence. The Keres and Jemez finished off the Piros and Tiwas who remained after the invasion by Otermín because they considered them friendly to the Spaniards. Of the Tiwas there only escaped some families which retired to the Province of Hopi; of the Piros none whatever.[32]

Ojeda went on to relate that the pueblo of Acoma had split into factions, and the Zunis and Hopis battled each other as well. Thus the picture of the Pueblo world provided by the Zia war captain in 1689 was one of chaos and unremitting turmoil. This information proved to be almost as valuable as the informant himself in the coming years, as the Spaniards laid yet another set of plans to reconquer the Kingdom of New Mexico.

Puname Refuge: Cerro Colorado

Following the 1689 battle, the people of Zia left the charred ruins of their razed pueblo, turning upstream to seek refuge in the Jemez Province. They migrated approximately 12.5 kilometers (7.7 miles) to the northwest, settling on a mesa just west of the crumbling remains of the Jemez mission pueblo of San Diego de la Congregación (Kessell et al. 1995:117; Elliott 2002:56–57). Their Puname allies from Santa Ana joined them there, along with some refugees from Kewa who shared their Keres tongue.[33] The Jemez strongholds of Patokwa and Boletsakwa were located just 7.3 and 15.5 kilometers (4.5 and 9.6 miles) to the north, respectively, and the mutual protection provided by these neighboring villages was likely an important factor in the Zia's decision to settle this location. While the Punames would still occupy the southernmost of the Rio Grande pueblos during this era, they were also now located the farthest west, and would no longer be in the direct line of fire of any future Spanish entradas that might penetrate their lands.

On this mesa the Punames constructed a new village (LA 2048), known variously as Cerro Colorado, Tutiqua, or Saiyatukikyokwa (meaning "Old Zia Pueblo" in Towa; Liebmann 2006:261–265). The pueblo sits approximately 150 meters (500 feet) above the surrounding basin on a sandstone mesa formed by an anticlinal uplift along the Nacimiento fault line (Smith et al. 1970). The architecture of the village consists of four main roomblocks arranged around two long plazas on an east-west axis (figure 8.2). The southern plaza is rectangular while the northern plaza is irregularly shaped due to the topography of the mesa and the northernmost, curvilinear roomblock. The east ends of both plazas are open (that is, they are not bounded by enclosing roomblocks). A detached, L-shaped roomblock bearing a striking similarity to Canjilon Pueblo lies to the south and downslope from the plazas. Additional detached one- to three-room structures are scattered to the south, southwest, and southeast of the main roomblocks. A stone scatter in the west end of the north plaza may represent the remains of a shrine, but no apparent kiva depressions exist on the mesa top. Walls consist of simple biflagged uncoursed masonry made from unshaped, roughly shaped, and irregularly shaped red sandstone quarried from the immediate vicinity of the mesa top. Today, no mortar remains in any of the standing walls, and no in-situ wall stands higher than 50 centimeters. Although no tree-ring dates have been recovered from this pueblo, documentary evidence dates its occupation to a narrow, five-year window between September 1689 and July 1694.[34] Associated ceramic dates corroborate this occupation, and the general dearth of the ceramic assemblage is consistent with a short, one-time occupation (Liebmann 2006:255).

In 2002–3, the Pueblo of Jemez Department of Resource Protection and I performed an architectural survey and ceramic sampling at Cerro Colorado. Our noninvasive mapping used the same techniques we developed at Patokwa and Boletsakwa, documenting 167 ground-floor rooms based on the presence of in-situ walls and/or room depressions as well as the dispersion and location of masonry rubble. In order to account for second-story architecture, we performed an analysis of intra-site topography to determine the existence and probable locations of the multistoried rooms mentioned in Spanish documents.[35] We documented evidence for 11 second-story rooms, resulting in a total estimate of 178 rooms at Cerro Colorado. The average floor area of these rooms is 12.0 square meters (3.2 m² sd), with an average length of 4.7 meters (1.2 m sd) and an average width of 2.5 m (0.3 m sd).

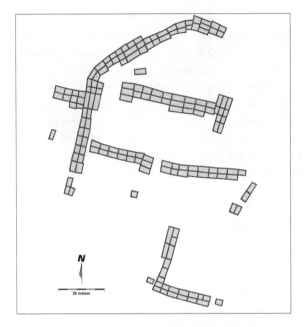

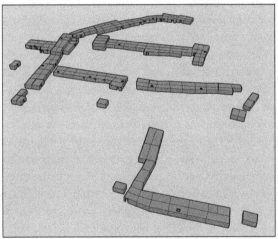

FIGURE 8.2. Cerro Colorado (LA 2048), plan and reconstruction circa 1689–93.

Spanish documents contain no count of the total population of Cerro Colorado,[36] but the number of rooms and measurements of floor area can be used to produce conjectural estimates of the number of residents living there in the early 1690s. Assuming that all rooms were occupied contemporaneously (a reasonable hypothesis considering the brief duration of occupation

at Cerro Colorado) and applying Dohm's (1990:212) average of o.60 persons
per Pueblo room to the total count of 179 rooms at Cerro Colorado yields an
estimate of 298 persons. Alternatively, applying figures based on Preucel's
Kotyiti data of 5.1 m² per person to the total floor area of Cerro Colorado
(including second-story rooms: 2156.8 m²) results in an estimated population of 423 inhabitants (Preucel 1998:74; Liebmann 2006:233). Based
on these calculations, the population of Cerro Colorado likely numbered
between 300 and 425 persons. If Jironza's claim of 600 killed at the Battle of
Zia is accurate, this would mean that more than 60 percent of the populace
was massacred during the 1689 skirmish.[37]

The Architecture of Immigration

Documentary evidence and oral traditions from Zia, Santa Ana, and Jemez
all concur that Cerro Colorado was settled by a mass migration of Puname
peoples into the Jemez Province in 1689.[38] Cerro Colorado displays the long
narrow roomblocks surrounding proportionally large plazas characteristic of
linear-plaza pueblos, a construction style linked to large-scale, well-organized
communal migration events. Indications of ladder construction are restricted
to the roomblocks surrounding the south plaza, however (e.g., rooms of similar size and walls with shared azimuths). Additionally, the right angles that
define the northwest, southwest, and northeast corners of the southern plaza
suggest that this was an intentionally designed space, and that construction
in this area followed a master plan. Based on these features, it seems likely
that the roomblocks around the south plaza were the first constructed at
Cerro Colorado, with the rooms circumscribing the north plaza and the outlying roomblocks added in subsequent episodes of construction.[39]

Linear-plaza plans such as this result from preconstruction planning, and
typically require coordination of labor above the household level, suggesting that a leader (or a small group of leaders) coordinated the planning and
construction of the south plaza (Cordell 1998:27; Kidder 1958:63). At Cerro
Colorado, one of those leaders was a man named Antonio Malacate. Active in
the planning of the 1680 Revolt, Malacate was identified as the "captain and
leader" of Cerro Colorado.[40] His name derives from the Nahuatl term *mala-
catl*, meaning spindle or winch, suggesting that he was a person in constant
motion—a perennial attribute of political leaders.[41]

In contrast to the intentional design of the south plaza, the rooms defining the north plaza at Cerro Colorado appear to have formed primarily
through agglomerative construction, added on bit-by-bit and room-by-room.

Variability in room sizes, orientations, and wall azimuths suggest that the majority of the rooms in this section are the result of discrete episodes of building activity in which one to six rooms were erected at a time. Unlike the rooms surrounding the south plaza, they do not display evidence of communal organization of labor. Rather, these suites were likely built by individual households or kin-based work groups. This type of agglomerative construction has been linked to longevity of occupation at Pueblo sites as well as the immigration of new groups into previously existing communities (Cameron 1999a:111). Because Cerro Colorado was occupied for a total span of less than five years, longevity can safely be eliminated as an explanation for the agglomerative construction of the northern roomblock (Liebmann 2006:263–265). More likely, the northern and outlying roomblocks resulted from the immigration of individual households into the Cerro Colorado community following the initial establishment of the village.

The numerous outlying rooms and roomblocks to the west, east, and south of the plaza architecture provide further evidence for a substantial amount of immigration into the Cerro Colorado community. Outlying rooms are common features in Pueblo sites, and form a unique architectural category indicative of population growth (Cameron 1999a:105). Like agglomerative construction, outlying rooms have been linked to the occasional establishment of a new house for a new family, and are consistent with both internal population growth and the immigration of new persons into a community. Again, the short duration of occupation of this site supports the latter as the most plausible explanation for the construction of the outlying rooms and roomblocks by the residents of Cerro Colorado.

The presence of rooms indicative of agglomerative construction and the numerous outlying structures at Cerro Colorado may also be related to the multiethnic populace of the village. Spanish documents refer to persons from Kewa living with the Punames of Zia and Santa Ana at Cerro Colorado, with individuals from Hopi and Zuni present as well.[42] The architectural data suggest that individuals or small groups of immigrants trickled into Cerro Colorado over time, with the spatial organization of the village maintaining subtle boundaries among social groups, while integrating others into the larger community.

The End of Revivalism

The architecture of Cerro Colorado provides a window into the Pueblo world during the final years of the Revolt era, allowing a glimpse of the changes to Pueblo culture and society that occurred between the construction of the twin-plaza pueblos (1681–1685) and the well-documented reconquest campaigns of 1692–94. Like Patokwa, Boletsakwa, and Kotyiti, Cerro Colorado was constructed in a defensive, mesa-top location. But unlike the three villages built earlier in the Revolt era, the mesa on which Cerro Colorado sits bears no evidence of previous occupation. In archaeological parlance, Cerro Colorado is a "single component" site, meaning there was no substantial earlier (or later) occupation of this area. For the people of Zia and Santa Ana, the move to Cerro Colorado was not a move back to the places of their ancestors. In fact, this mesa is located entirely outside of the ancestral Puname district, far away from the homes of their forefathers. Unlike the sites occupied earlier in the Revolt era, then, the selection of this locale was not motivated by an ideology of revivalism.

Similarly, revivalism does not seem to have played a role in the architectural design of Cerro Colorado, at least not in the same way it did at Patokwa, Boletsakwa, and Kotyiti. All four villages are similar in size, with 167 ground-floor rooms at Cerro Colorado, 168 at Boletsakwa, an estimated 219 at pre-1694 Patokwa, and 137 at Kotyiti (Liebmann 2006:227, 252, 272; Preucel 1998:47). And while all four pueblos are composed of long narrow roomblocks defining two proportionally large plazas bisected by a central roomblock, Cerro Colorado is not a proper "twin-plaza" pueblo. Its plazas are not mirror images of each other, varying in both shape and size. And they do not seem to have been created in simultaneous construction events, as were the plazas of the other three pueblos. The builders of Cerro Colorado did not follow the same iconic twin-plaza template as did their neighboring Jemez and Keres brethren, suggesting that either the revivalist agenda driven by the revitalization movement of the early 1680s was waning (if not entirely absent) among the Punames by 1689, or that it was employed in a very different manner.

The most striking architectural difference between Cerro Colorado and the three earlier Revolt-era pueblos, however, is the apparent absence of kivas at the Puname refuge. This lack of subterranean architecture is not entirely surprising as the pueblo sits on exposed sandstone bedrock, and the excavation of an underground chamber would prove extremely difficult in this location, involving untold months of grueling labor. Kivas are not always subterranean, however, nor are they necessarily circular. In fact, quadrilateral kivas were sometimes constructed above ground and included within roomblocks, particularly during the Spanish colonial period among the Eastern Pueblos (Hayes et al. 1981:47–48, 61; Ivey 1998:136). The rectangular, above-ground kivas were indistinguishable from the domestic spaces surrounding them, hiding these "houses of idolatry" from the watchful eyes of disapproving Franciscans.

So while there are no circular, subterranean chambers at Cerro Colorado, this does not necessarily mean that there were no kivas; a particularly large rectangular room might have served as such a communal gathering place.

At Boletsakwa and Kotyiti, the (round, subterranean) kivas exhibit floor areas more than three times the size of the residential room mean (Liebmann 2006:245–257; Preucel 1998:58). Yet Cerro Colorado exhibits a relatively even distribution of room sizes with no extreme outliers (figure 8.3), suggesting that there were no rooms that served a unique or specialized function. In fact, no rooms at Cerro Colorado exhibit a floor area large enough to have served as a kiva or more general communal gathering space. If one of the rectangular, aboveground rooms of Cerro Colorado served as a kiva, it should have a floor area of 36 square meters or more (as the average room size is 12.0 m^2). But the largest room at Cerro Colorado has a floor area of just 23.2 square meters. By comparison, the north kiva at Boletsakwa and the west kiva at Kotyiti have floor areas of 60.4 and 43.0 square meters, respectively. Based on these data, it is safe to conclude that the Zias constructed no kivas at their post-1689 refuge, either subterranean or aboveground, circular or square. Any suprahousehold gatherings that did take place at Cerro Colorado were likely extramural, occurring in the plazas.

The lack of kivas at Cerro Colorado suggests a difference in the ritual activities that occurred there between 1689 and 1694 as compared with those that took place among the Jemez at Patokwa and Boletsakwa or the Keres at Kotyiti. Without an enclosed space in which to carry out the secretive ceremonies commonly performed in kivas (rites which are today directed by high-ranking religious specialists who commonly comprise the elites of Pueblo society), the ritual leaders of Cerro Colorado would have faced significant obstacles in the maintenance of their ritual practices, spiritual traditions, and social positions within the Puname community.

Why then did Cerro Colorado lack kivas? One possibility is that the Punames truly were the committed Christians the Spaniards asserted them to be in 1680, when they referred to the Zias as their "Christian enemy."[43] Yet given their participation in the Revolt that year as well as their armed resistance to the Spaniards in 1687 and 1689, this seems an unlikely scenario. Rather, the Punames appear to have been profoundly ambivalent—and strategic—regarding Christianity in the late 1600s, fluctuating between acceptance and aversion in a manner typical of colonized persons the world over (Young 1995:161). And while this ambivalence may have tipped to the side of traditional Pueblo religion in the early 1680s (at Po'pay's nativistic behest), the tide seems to have turned by 1692. It is possible that the lack of kivas at Cerro Colorado is related to the execution of Puname religious leaders

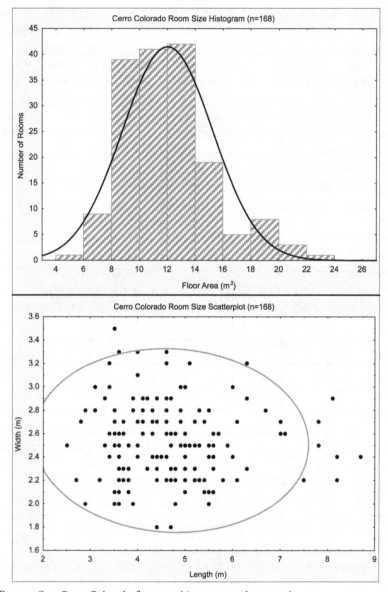

FIGURE 8.3. Cerro Colorado floor area histogram and scatterplot.

in the late 1680s (four by Reneros at Santa Ana in 1687, and another four at
Zia by Jironza in 1689). With those keepers of sacred knowledge dead, gone
too was the leadership that might have guided the construction and consecra-
tion of new kivas at Cerro Colorado.

Alienation and Alliance

The ambivalence of the Punames during the early 1690s was not limited solely to their attitudes toward the Spaniards or their religion. The residents of Cerro Colorado also had ambivalent relationships with the other Pueblos during this period. Interactions among the Punames and their neighbors between 1689 and 1694 are reflected in the ceramics found at Cerro Colorado, which display patterns that are both similar to and very different from the other Revolt-era pueblos and those of their pre-1680 ancestors.

At first glance, the pottery of Cerro Colorado appears pretty much the same as that of the other Revolt-period pueblos (table 8.1). The assemblage displays many of the general trends observed at Patokwa, Boletsakwa, and Kotyiti: Plain Red ceramics dominate—even more so than at any of the other Revolt-period villages, in fact. Basalt-tempered Glaze Wares, produced in abundance among the pre-Revolt Puname pueblos, still comprise 10 percent of the post-1689 assemblage. But matte-painted polychromes (Jemez River and Puname Polychrome) show a marked increase in production as well, constituting 6.9 percent of the pottery at Cerro Colorado. As expected, Jemez Black-on-white is nonexistent. Of course, this does not necessarily signify the absence of trade between the Jemez pueblos and Cerro Colorado. In fact, the adoption of traditional Puname basalt-tempering technology by potters at Patokwa suggests that significant interaction occurred between the Zia/Santa Anas and the Jemez women during this period (Liebmann 2006:361–364).

The biggest changes in trade occurred not in the Punames' relations with the Jemez after their move to Cerro Colorado, but rather in their interactions with the Tewas. Prior to the Pueblo Revolt, the Zias seem to have maintained steady if not voluminous trade relations with the Tewas, with Tewa wares

Table 8.1. Cerro Colorado (LA 2048) ceramic inventory

Type	Number	Weight (g)	Percent of total (based on weight)
Plain	401	1293.2	38.9
Jemez River	43	120.1	3.6
Plain Red	418	1378.8	41.4
Puname Poly	54	109.4	3.3
Glaze F (runny)	104	331.4	10.0
Unidentified Glaze	2	2.3	0.1
Tewa B/w	2	4.4	0.1
Unidentified	27	88.1	2.6
Totals	1051	3327.7	100

comprising between 2 and 4 percent of pre-Revolt Zia ceramic assemblages (Ellis 1966a:807–10). After 1689, however, Tewa ceramics are virtually non-existent at the Puname refuge, accounting for just 0.1 percent of all sherds at Cerro Colorado. This pattern is the opposite of that exhibited by the Jemez Pueblos (chapter 7), where Tewa pottery jumped from just 0.1 percent in pre-Revolt contexts to 4.4 percent of the ceramics at Patokwa and Boletsakwa.

These patterns suggest that at least some of the pan-Pueblo ties forged in the immediate aftermath of the Revolt had been all but severed by 1689. The Tewas seem to have maintained ties with the inhabitants of Patokwa and Bolet-sakwa (as well as Kotyiti) throughout the 1680s. In fact, interaction between these two regions was stronger in the sixteen years following the Revolt than it had been for three centuries prior to 1680. By contrast, all the available evidence—from both Ojeda's testimony and archaeological sources—suggests that the Punames had become alienated from the Tewas by the late 1680s. Although we do not have ceramic data to assess the relationship between these two groups during the early years of the Revolt period, by the time the Punames were living at Cerro Colorado (between 1689 and 1694) they were no longer in regular contact with the Tewa pueblos, as evidenced by the nearly complete lack of Tewa pottery found at Cerro Colorado. The exact causes of this rift is unknown, although it is tempting to speculate that the Zias' desultory partici-pation in the 1680 uprising and subsequent reluctance to follow Po'pay's com-mands (leaving their church intact and not killing the priest, for example) may have earned their reprobation from the staunchly resistant Tewas. Furthermore, the Punames' purported offer of obedience to the Spaniards in 1681 (if not a ruse) would almost certainly have garnered the Tewas' reproach and may have put a strain on relations between the two regions. Whatever the cause of the Puname-Tewa rift, the attitudes of the Cerro Colorado populace toward other Pueblo communities—trading with some, alienated from others—was clearly ambivalent, much the same as their attitude toward the Spaniards would be when they returned in the autumn of 1692.

The archaeology of Cerro Colorado paints a bleak picture of life in the Pueblo world during the early 1690s: the revitalization movement initiated by Po'pay was on the wane, if not completely defunct by this time. No longer were Pueblo peoples explicitly attempting to emulate the ways of their ances-tors. Lapsed too was the ethos of *communitas* and ethnogenesis that had spread throughout the Pueblos in the 1680s, with rifts developing among some communities, and outright hostilities occurring between others. Indeed, as Bartolomé de Ojeda had observed, by the 1690s the Pueblo world was in chaos. The time was ripe for the Spaniards to return once again.

Part III

Return of the Castyilash: 1692–1696

9

Reconquista de Sangre

IT WAS THE TIME OF YEAR WHEN THE PEOPLE OF Cerro Colorado began to awake with cold noses. The aspen leaves were turning the colors of fire, and smoke spiraled through the rungs of the ladders as it rose out the rooftop hatchways. Three years had passed since the last time the *españoles* had appeared, torched their pueblo, and vanished again into the night. Now a solitary figure came into view at the edge of Red Mesa. As he drew closer, the beads swinging around his neck clicked softly against a crucifix. Although he carried a cross in one hand, he was not wearing the blue robes of the friars. Yet there was something familiar in his limping gait. It wasn't until he had entered the plaza that the Zias and Santa Anas finally recognized the man's face as that of the war captain the Spaniards had dragged off the battlefield in 1689. Bartolomé de Ojeda had returned.

As his fellow Punames crowded around that late September day in 1692, the women of the village touched his arms and torso to ensure that he was not an apparition. His family wept with joy at his return. "What happened to you?" they asked. "How did you escape from the blue-eyes? Did they torture you? How many did you have to kill?" On the contrary, Ojeda replied, the Spaniards were his saviors. They had nursed him back to health at their village in the south, and the friars had redeemed him in the face of the Lord, his Savior. He had atoned for his sins of the past. Moreover, he met a good woman at the Spaniards' village and had made her his wife. She was still in the south, and yes, they would meet her soon. But there would be plenty of time to tell his tales of life among the people-with-hair-like-corn-tassels in the coming days. For now, he needed to speak with Antonio Malacate.

They directed Ojeda to Malacate's house, at the west end of the main plaza. The leader of Cerro Colorado had aged much in the past three years. Now he was a thinning shadow of his former self. The two men embraced, and Ojeda hung a rosary around the old man's neck. He explained to Malacate that he had

come from El Paso, and he had been sent by a great Spanish warrior named don
Diego de Vargas. The foreigners were returning to these lands, and they wished
for the Punames to join them in peace. This time things would be different,
Ojeda promised. Vargas was a careful and judicious man, not like the hotheads
who had attacked Santa Ana and Zia in recent years. The friars would return
too, bringing with them the powers of their many saints. Then Ojeda unrolled
a letter. Knowing that Malacate could not decipher the foreigners' script he
read it aloud, translating from Spanish into Keresan. It said that the Spaniards had not returned to fight, but to pardon the Indians so they could again
become Christians. All that needed be done was for the Punames to accept this
offer of peace and once again acknowledge the authority of the two majesties,
the King and Christ. The Zias and Santa Anas should begin to prepare to move
back to their home villages, according to the letter, and they should be assured
of the Spaniards' good intentions. In order to discuss these words further,
Vargas ordered Malacate to come to Kewa to parley in three weeks' time.[1]

Return of the Conquistadores: The Reconquista of New Mexico

By the time of Ojeda's meeting with Malacate in late September 1692, the
Pueblos had been monitoring the Spaniards' reentry into New Mexico for
weeks. They hadn't heard the initial announcement of the armed reconnaissance when it was publicly proclaimed in the streets of El Paso del Norte
on the twelfth anniversary of the Pueblo Revolt. But when Vargas's column
arrived at the deserted pueblo of Cochiti a month later, word of the Spaniards'
return quickly spread throughout all the villages of the northern Rio Grande.
Now the Pueblos prepared their defenses, expecting another round of brutal
attacks like those visited on the Punames in 1687 and 1689. In early October
a council was convened to discuss the recent turn of events, with leaders from
the pueblos of Zuni, Hopi, Jemez, San Felipe, Kewa, Cochiti, and Pecos all
gathered at Acoma, where they were joined by their Faraón Apache allies.
(The Tewas, Tanos, and northern Tiwas were notably absent from this meeting, however.) For three days and nights the junta deliberated their next steps.
The general consensus was that this entrada was different from those of previous years. These Spaniards had not yet attacked any village; rather than a one-
day blitzkrieg, the foreigners seemed intent to stay among the Pueblos for
some time. Yet it was clear that they were not prepared to settle these lands
permanently at this time, either. Their small numbers, as well as the lack of
women, children, and livestock necessary to reestablish a permanent presence

in New Mexico suggested that this was an expedition, not an attempt at resettlement. In any case, the Pueblos were taking no chances. They devised a plan to "lie in ambush along the road to fall upon the horses, the camp, and . . . the governor and captain general." The attack would take place at the Jemez pueblo of Patokwa. "In the interim," the council recommended, "they should prepare their supplies."[2]

To the Pueblos' collective surprise, the Spanish harquebusiers never fired a single shot as they made their tour of the northern Pueblos. Their forty-eight-year-old leader, don Diego José de Vargas Zapata Luján Ponce de León y Contreras, was a master politician. Unlike his predecessors Reneros and Jironza, Vargas preferred to lead with diplomacy rather than brute force. After cajoling the rebel Tewas and Tanos out of their fortress in Santa Fe, Vargas secured the obedience of Luis Tupatú and all those under his jurisdiction. The column proceeded to visit the pueblos of the Tewas and northern Tiwas, a tour which made the coalition of southern Pueblos understandably nervous. At each stop, don Diego secured the alliance of the northern villages, with whom the Hopis, Zunis, Keres and Jemez had been feuding in recent years.

Whether the 1692 capitulation of the Tewas, Tanos, and northern Tiwas was sincere or feigned is open to debate. Certainly the fact that Luis Tupatú had attempted to convince Vargas to return to El Paso when the two met in Santa Fe suggests that the northern Pueblos were less than enthusiastic about receiving the Spaniard and his retinue. Rather than visiting the Tewa and Tano pueblos to the north, Tupatú had suggested that "what [Vargas] could do, since this villa [Santa Fe] had now surrendered, was go to El Paso and within a year, return once and for all with the fathers. Then [Tupatú] would have everyone back together at their pueblos, and they would render the obedience he said they would."[3] Although Vargas declined the Picuris chieftain's offer, Tupatú's alternative plan proved ironically prescient.

October 1692: Castyilash Return to the Jemez Province

Vargas's newly cozy relationship with the Pueblos of the Rio Arriba served only to heighten the anxieties of those south of Santa Fe, who watched nervously as the Spaniards made their way from village to village.[4] In early October, Jemez leaders from Patokwa paid a visit to Antonio Malacate at Cerro Colorado to try to convince him to join in their planned attack on the Spaniards, enlisting the aid of the Punames in their cause. The fearsome Faraón Apaches had already signed on and were lying in wait for the Spaniards within the houses of Patokwa. All the Jemez needed now was ancillary support from the Zias and Santa Anas. But a vocal contingent of Punames thought it a bad idea. They had already prepared Cerro Colorado for Vargas's visit, erecting arches and crosses on all their houses as signs of their peaceful intent. Besides, Bartolomé de Ojeda had assured them that the better plan was to appease the Spaniards. The people of Cerro Colorado decided they would not join the Jemez in their plot. Not this time. They were made to pay dearly for their participation in the 1680 attacks by Reneros and Jironza, and they wouldn't make the same mistake again.[5]

On October 24, 1692, the Spaniards reentered the Jemez Province and found that much had changed since their last visit a dozen years prior. When they approached Cerro Colorado, they were relieved to find that the Puname residents met them with arms that were open, and not at the ready. Vargas described the encounter in his military journal:

> I, the governor and captain general, entered this Keres pueblo of Zia, which is on the mesa of the Cerro Colorado, whose ascent is very steep and rocky. After the Indians saw me and the camp, most of them came down to the first mesa to receive me. Having gone up, I found that they had set up arches and crosses, in accord with the message and letter I had sent them and Antonio Malacate, the captain and leader whom they obey.
>
> With the other captains and elders, he received me with all reverence. They all had crosses in their hands and on most of the houses of the cuarteles of the plaza, where they had prepared a ground-level room for me. With the people of the pueblo on the plaza, I told them through the Indian Bartolo [de Ojeda], who acted as interpreter, about my coming and took possession for his majesty, as in the other pueblos. . . . It was seen that 123 of all ages, male and female, were baptized.[6]

Among those baptized was Antonio Malacate's newest son. Vargas served as the child's godfather, naming him Carlos "in honor of the king, our lord (may God keep him)."[7] This simple act was motivated by more than mere kindness, however. By taking part in the sacrament of baptism, Vargas was establishing ties of *compadrazgo* with Malacate, a fictive kinship meant to bind the two together and ultimately to make Malacate indebted to the new governor. Following the ceremony Vargas took leave of his newfound Puname allies, spending the night below the mesa among the charred ruins of the destroyed Jemez mission of San Diego de la Congregación.

When the Spaniards journeyed to the Jemez stronghold of Patokwa the next morning, the reception they received was markedly different from that to which they had been treated at Cerro Colorado. The Spanish column proceeded warily, as Vargas had been warned of the planned ambush against him.[8] As they approached the mesa, Vargas and his army were met by five hundred armed Pueblo warriors, who greeted them with battle cries. The Native warriors quickly surrounded the Spaniards, "throwing dirt in their eyes and making all the gestures they use in their fighting." When the Spanish captain Roque Madrid (who spoke Towa and Keresan) told the Jemez to cease their taunting,[9] "they replied that it was in token of celebration of my coming," Vargas scoffed.[10] In fact, this may have been another example of the appropriation and catachresis of Spanish culture by the Pueblos. In their conquest of the New World, the Virgin was said to intercede on the part of the conquistadores by throwing dust in the eyes of rebellious Indians (Taylor 1987:10; Simmons 1991b:18). Now the Pueblos turned the tactic back on the soldiers who marched under the banner of Our Lady of Remedies.

The general continued up the mesa on horseback. When he reached the pueblo he encountered a man named Sebastián that he identified as the leader at Patokwa, waiting at the entrance to the village with a cross in his hand. Mindful of the warnings regarding the plot to kill him, Vargas dismounted and ventured into the plaza:

> I entered, followed by the people of the pueblo. I saw that it has two plazas, one with an entrance that leads to the other, garrisoned and closed, and each with four cuarteles. In this way, I found myself afoot and hemmed in by the crowd. Because they were suspicious, some had not laid down their weapons. Others were bewildered, while others prepared a great war dance.
>
> Presently, I said to Captain Sebastián, who had the holy cross in his hand, as well as to the other elders who accompanied him, that I saw in their faces a troubled look. Despite the fact that I was the one who should have been and was troubled because I entered with so few men, I neither spoke a word nor made a gesture that might cause them to think I was afraid of them and knew their evil intention.[11]

Clearly unnerved by the situation, Vargas later found Apaches lodged in the "second plaza" at Patokwa, confirming to him that the rumors he had heard regarding a planned ambush were true.

Vargas then addressed the crowd with his words translated into Towa and Keres (the latter for the Natives of Kewa who were apparently living with the Jemez), notifying them of his reclamation in the name of the king "both of the land and of his vassals, which they are." The priest who accompanied him then granted the people of Patokwa absolution, and 117 persons were baptized. The general remained wary during this process "in case they gave me cause to begin fighting." He and the friars were invited into a second-story room to dine with the Jemez leaders and war captains, an invitation he obliged "so that they would not suspect the bad opinion I had formed and was forming of them."[12] Following the meal Vargas instructed the Jemez to move back to Walatowa. He then left Patokwa, preferring to spend the night outside of the vacant and ruined Jemez mission village because he was still leery of their plot to assassinate him and his men.[13]

The Spaniards had appeared and vanished in a single day once again, just as they had in 1687 and 1689, although this time, no village was sacked. Within six weeks Governor Vargas and his retinue were back in El Paso. If and when they would return again remained to be seen. For the people of Patokwa, Boletsakwa, and Cerro Colorado, little had changed as a result of the Spaniards' visitation. Life in the Jemez Province continued much as it had in previous years, with one major difference. With the Punames' decision to side with the Spaniards, their last remaining ties to the other Pueblos were severed. Tensions between the Jemez and their Zia/Santa Ana neighbors simmered. While the Punames had originally chosen Cerro Colorado's location for defense against the Spaniards, they now needed it for protection from the other Pueblos.

1693: Retreat, Return, Resettlement

After the Spaniards' departure, the Pueblos met again to discuss the most recent turn of events. They needed to decide on a strategy in the event that the foreigners returned as they had promised. Many of the Pueblos were determined to keep the Spaniards at bay, urging the others to take up the bow and lance, come what may. Those who supported armed resistance agreed to settle their feuds with one another and revive the coalition that had thrived during the first half of the 1680s. The Tewas, Tanos, northern Tiwas, Pecos, Jemez, and most of the Keres agreed to oppose the Spaniards (although pro-Spanish factions continued to thrive at some of these Pueblos, most notably at Pecos). At Ohkay Owingeh a coyote named Pedro de Tapia rallied Pueblo warriors with conspiratorial rhetoric. He had served as an interpreter for Vargas the year before, and now he told the Pueblos that although the Spaniards claimed to have pardoned them, the next time Vargas returned he planned to "kill them and run every one of them through with a knife." Consequently, in Tapia's view the Pueblos had no choice but to band together and organize a preemptive strike on the españoles. After all, he reasoned, "they were only preparing for their defense and protection by seeking the union of all." In Santa Fe, the Tanos and Tewas schemed with the Pecos over the summer, their leaders ordering the people to make many extra arrows in preparation for the Spaniards' return.[14]

Back in El Paso, the Spaniards celebrated their reconquista with pride, rejoicing "because of the conversion of so many apostates reduced to the faith and the many baptized children." The bells of the Cathedral in Mexico City announced news of the reconquest to the people of New Spain, and Vargas's superiors praised the general for "the wise decision of demanding peace from the Pueblos before bloodying weapons."[15] But while Vargas's resettlement of New Mexico is commonly referred to today as the "Bloodless Reconquest," this term is a misnomer on two accounts. Firstly, it was initially more of what John Kessell and Rick Hendricks (1992:507) term a "ritual repossession" than a reconquest, as the Spaniards did not remain in the territory but returned to El Paso del Norte after securing the Pueblos' (supposed) submission. Secondly, the blood of Apache warriors was shed during the 1692 reconquest (and when they did finally return to permanently resettle the northern Rio Grande more than a year later, their recolonizing efforts were anything but bloodless).

For most of 1693 Vargas and his staff remained in their southern capital-in-exile, organizing the resettling expedition that was to follow. They recruited weavers, tailors, and cobblers to provide them with clothing. Masons, carpenters, painters, and cabinetmakers were brought on to rebuild their houses. Blacksmiths, coppersmiths, and cutlers joined the expedition to make their tools. And chandlers, barbers, and musicians were drafted to keep them comfortable, well groomed, and entertained.[16] By October 1693 they were ready to forge back up the Rio Grande to settle New Mexico once again.

In their absence only the Zias, Santa Anas, San Felipians, and a faction at Pecos remained loyal to King Carlos II. When these Pueblos balked at joining the coalition of resistance, the Jemez, Tewas, and Tanos repeatedly harassed them, promising the trio of sympathizers that the other Pueblos "were coming to destroy them during the first quarter of the moon."[17] When the Spaniards returned in November 1693 the Santa Anas apparently left Cerro Colorado to reinhabit Tamaya, the village next to the Jemez River that had been destroyed by Reneros six years prior.[18] Whether this move was because of or in spite of the threats from other Pueblos is unclear, but the Santa Anas were not alone in their choice to relocate during this period. Their allies from San Felipe did likewise, taking to the mesa top above their old village on the Rio Grande. There they constructed a pueblo known today as Old San Felipe or Basalt Point Pueblo (LA 2047; figure 9.1). This new

FIGURE 9.1. Landscape surrounding Old San Felipe/Basalt Point Pueblo (LA 2047).

village was composed of 55–65 rooms in a classically defensive layout. With three roomblocks enclosing a central plaza, Old San Felipe was built in the shape of a square with one side missing. The open edge faces the Rio Grande to the east, and abuts the steep slope of the mesa on which it sits. Thus the plaza is shielded from attack by inward-facing roomblocks on three sides and the cliff edge on the fourth. There appear to be no circular, subterranean kivas associated with this village, but the Spaniards identified a "large, spacious kiva" (presumably above ground and rectangular) that was turned into a chapel in 1694.[19] The remains of this renovated mission church are still visible in the northeast corner of the pueblo today.

Antonio Malacate left Cerro Colorado in 1693 as well, but for very different reasons. In typically ambivalent fashion, Malacate wavered in his support of the Spaniards even after becoming the *compadre* of Vargas at his son's christening. When he chose to side with the resistors he was forced out of Cerro Colorado, taking up residence at Kotyiti. There he was reported to be "worshipping the things of the devil every night in order to kill [Vargas] and the Spaniards," according to Bartolomé de Ojeda.[20] As Malacate left his Puname compatriots, he advised his Zia brothers and sisters "neither to make peace nor be friends with the Spaniards." The Zias responded by telling him, "If you

go, you will be our enemy, because we made peace last year and must keep it."
When Vargas and the colonists reappeared in November, Malacate, keeping
true to his name, had yet another change of heart and seemingly returned to
the Spanish fold. Six weeks later Vargas ordered his arrest for secretly fomenting another rebellion, with the help of the Jemez and their Navajo allies.[21]

Almost immediately on his reentry into the northern Rio Grande, Vargas received word of the precarious position in which the Pueblos of Zia,
Santa Ana, and San Felipe found themselves. When the Native allies relayed
their concerns regarding an imminent Jemez attack on their villages, Vargas
responded that they should not be afraid because if their enemies attacked,
he "would make mincemeat out of them."[22] When he reached Cerro Colorado in late November, the Zias held a dance in Vargas's honor. They erected
crosses on the summit of the mesa, in the plaza of the pueblo, and on most
of their houses—a testament to their acceptance of the Spaniards' return.
With the Santa Anas already back in their original village, Vargas instructed
the Zias to follow suit and return to the pueblo that Jironza had sacked (Zia
Pueblo, LA 28). He even promised soldiers to provide for their security. The
continued harassment of the Jemez, combined with the fact that locusts had
recently ravaged their crops, made the Zia people eager to return to their old
village. So they agreed to leave the mesa posthaste, vowing to rebuild the old
church at their former pueblo.[23]

After visiting his Zia allies at Cerro Colorado, Vargas returned once again
to Patokwa. There he was greeted "with great pleasure and humility" by the
Jemez, who "recogniz[ed] their vassalage" (or so he thought) and had even
erected a cross in one of the plazas. But when the Spaniards attempted to
acquire provisions, the residents of Patokwa handed over only a meager quan-
tity of maize. The worms had eaten the rest, the Jemez explained regretfully.
Vargas suspected otherwise, having seen signs of an abundant harvest in their
fields below the mesa. After a few rounds of hard bargaining, a deal was struck
and the Jemez promised to hand over additional maize. But their reluctance
to acquiesce to Spanish demands suggests that, like Malacate, the Jemez had
adopted a strategy of outward compliance that masked their hidden resistance. The cross they had erected in the plaza and the phantom worms in
the corn were mere props in their ploy to appease Governor Vargas. In fact,
the Jemez were already readying for what they saw as an inevitable conflict
with the Spaniards. Following Vargas's second visit, their preparations for war
accelerated precipitously.[24]

Similar acts of token compliance greeted Vargas at the other Pueblos
as he made his way from village to village up the Rio Grande. But when

his ragged cavalcade of a thousand colonial settlers reached the fortress the Pueblos had erected inside the Governor's Palace in Santa Fe, conditions worsened considerably. The Tewas and Tanos refused to vacate, holding the settlers at bay outside the villa. Emissaries shuttled back and forth between the temporary encampment and the fortified villa for days on end, attempting to convince the occupants to clear out. But the Pueblos, "shameless and sneering at the Spaniards," refused to give up their stronghold in the casas reales. They were prepared to wait out the foreigners, having dug at least nine huge bell-shaped storage pits (two meters deep and two meters across at their midsection) inside one of the plazas, and filling them with corn in anticipation of the Spaniards' siege. (Excavations by Cordelia Snow at the Palace of the Governors uncovered these pits in 1973, finding them filled with the detritus of later years; Snow 1974:16.) When the swirling snows of December closed in, twenty-two of the colonists' children died in the encampment. As the days grew into weeks and their straits grew increasingly dire, the settlers convinced the general to abandon diplomacy and reconquer the Pueblos by force.

When Vargas awoke amidst the long morning shadows of December 29 he found the ladders of the fortress drawn up, and Pueblo archers manning the ramparts. Battle lines had been drawn, so he called on 140 Pueblo allies from the pro-Spanish faction at Pecos to aid his militia. The attack on Santa Fe commenced as soon as they arrived. After a full day of fighting Vargas's forces finally managed to dislodge the Tewas and Tanos and retake the capitol.[25] The bloodless stage of the reconquest was officially over, aided in no small part by the Spaniards' Pueblo allies.

A few days later, on New Year's Eve, Vargas intercepted a knotted cord of maguey fiber that was being sent from pueblo to pueblo—an eerie echo of the 1680 rebellion. There were four knots in it, and Vargas was well aware of their meaning.[26] The Pueblos were ready for war. In the spring of 1694, the Spaniards began to march on the Pueblo strongholds that housed the "rebellious" Natives. In late February Vargas rallied 115 armed colonists and an unspecified number of Pecos allies to attack the Tewa stronghold at Black Mesa near San Ildefonso. The eighteen-day siege was ultimately unsuccessful, leaving the Spaniards embittered and ever more irritated with the Pueblo "apostates."[27] In April Vargas led another force of 90 Spaniards in a far more devastating attack on Kotyiti, this time aided by Bartlomé de Ojeda and 100 Zia, Santa Ana, and San Felipe warriors. Colonial forces killed 21 and captured 342 noncombatants—mainly the women, children, and elderly inhabitants of the mesa-top refuge.[28] With this victory under his belt General Vargas turned his eyes to the backsliding rebels of the Jemez

Province, who had been harassing his *compadre* Ojeda and his Puname kin in recent weeks.

1694: The Construction of Astialakwa

Months before Vargas's attacks on Santa Fe, Black Mesa, and Kotyiti, the Jemez had recognized the forebodings of war and had begun readying themselves accordingly. As early as November 1693 they began to cache food and supplies on the towering peñol that loomed above Patokwa. There they initiated construction on a new stronghold where they could take refuge against the Spaniards' muskets and cannon, a fortress-pueblo known as Astialakwa (figure 9.2).

The meaning of *Astialakwa* is obscure. Jemez historian Joe Sando (1982:12) translates it as "grinding-stone lowering place," a name quite possibly referring to the throwing of metates down at the Spaniards when they attacked the mesa in 1694 (a strategy recorded at the other Revolt-era refuge battle sites; Espinosa 1942:61). Other Towa speakers gloss it as "place where they all line up," possibly a reference to the sheer cliffs surrounding the village.[29] The peñol on which the Jemez built Astialakwa is sometimes called *Mashtiashinkwa*, meaning something akin to "big thumb hilltop place" or "place of the thumb" in Towa (because its profile is similar to that of a pointing index finger with the thumb resting on top of the hand).[30] In plan view the peñol resembles a footprint, with the heel to the north and the village of Astialakwa located around the base of the big toe. Perennial rivers flow in the valleys on the east and west sides of the mesa, approximately 300 meters (1000 feet) below the cliffs.

Although no tree-ring dates have yet been recovered from Astialakwa,[31] documentary evidence suggests that the Jemez constructed and occupied the pueblo within a narrow window of just eight months (or less). Between November 26, 1693, and July 23, 1694, the people of Patokwa and Boletsakwa left their villages and joined together to construct this new refuge.[32] They hurriedly threw up the walls of 190 rooms, all single-story, in 62 discrete roomblocks dispersed haphazardly across the top of the peñol. The friable tuff stone of the surrounding cliffs provided a ready source of building materials. Irregularly shaped masonry, roughly cut and hastily laid, attests to the anxiety that surrounded the construction of the village. To bolster the already stout natural defenses of the mesa they erected ramparts along access points on the north and south ends of the peñol. In their haste to erect the new stronghold they cannibalized Patokwa on the mesa below, robbing out

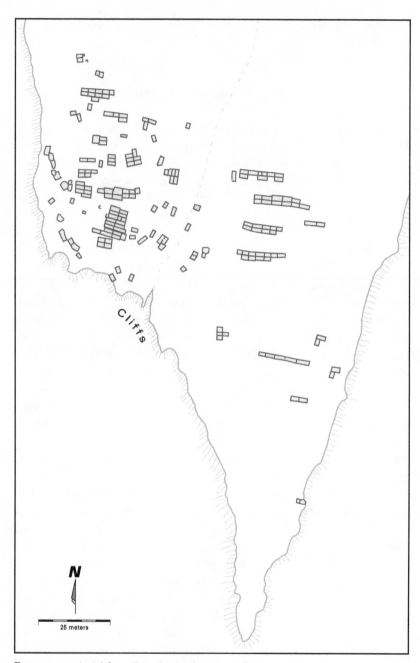

FIGURE 9.2. Astialakwa (LA 1825), plan circa 1694.

the vigas and doorways to be reused at Astialakwa, leaving the twin-plaza village scalped and toothless.[33]

Mapping Astialakwa

The mapping of Astialakwa was a very different process from that of Patokwa, Boletsakwa, and Cerro Colorado. Simply gaining access to the site is far more difficult than at any of these other sites. Entry to the top of the imposing peñol is granted only after completing a grueling 2.4 kilometer (1.5 mile) hike up the mesa, with an elevation gain of 317 meters (1040 feet) Each summer morning over the course of four field seasons I set out with one or two interns at 7 a.m. to scale the equivalent of a 100-story building, carrying a total station and tripod with us as we navigated the switchbacks of the narrow footpath up the mesa. The trail is loose and rocky throughout, and requires scaling a small, 3 meter (10 foot) cliff at one point. In all likelihood, we were scrambling up the same paths used by the Jemez who constructed the village in the spring of 1694.

Those who brave the arduous climb are rewarded when they reach the mesa top. In addition to the awe-inspiring 360-degree views of the surrounding mesas, canyons, and mountain peaks, the architectural remains of Astialakwa are remarkably well preserved. The stone walls of the village still stand up to 1.5 meters in places. Many rooms retain intact doorways, with earthen mortar still clinging to the stone masonry. Even in areas where the walls have crumbled entirely, the foundation stones are often plainly apparent on the ground surface. Fallen masonry is scattered throughout the site, interspersed with broken pottery lying among the roomblocks. Because nearly all the rooms retain elements of the original architecture, we were able to record the original footprint of the site with a high degree of confidence and accuracy.

Within each of the sixty-two individual roomblocks, we began by first recording all in-situ masonry features and standing walls. Interns marked the locations of the interior and exterior extents of all walls, which I then recorded with the total station, along with the locations of any additional architectural features, such as doorways, vents, and benches. After we fixed the location of each room using the total station, we recorded digital images of each room in plan view by mounting a digital camera on a specially designed photo tripod (built by Bill Whatley, former director of the Jemez Department of Resource Protection). This tripod raised the camera five meters above the ground, and once aloft we tripped the shutter on the camera using an infrared remote control (figure 9.3). We then slid the camera along the top bar of the

FIGURE 9.3. Plan view digital image documentation at Astialakwa.

tripod, so that we could record three successive images, covering the length of each room. Each evening we would download these pictures and merge them, using image-stitching software to produce a seamless single image of each room in plan view. We were then able to georectify these images by aligning them with the total station data using a computer-aided drafting (CAD) software package, in which we then traced each in-situ wall and foundation.

Following the total station recording and plan view digital image documentation of each architectural feature, we completed a written architectural survey form for each room, which recorded additional characteristics including masonry size and type (flagged/biflagged vs. tabular, simple vs. compound), style of coursing (uncoursed, semi-coursed, or fully coursed), and type of construction (wet-laid, dry-laid, or dry-laid/mudded). We also noted any additional architectural elements and features, dimensions of all walls, number of remaining courses, patterns of corner bonding and abutment, and any evidence of looting activity.

The scattered layout of Astialakwa contrasts starkly with the compact, orderly, and intentional plans of Patokwa and Boletsakwa. No dual-plaza, two-kiva prototype was used to carefully model the 1694 village. Astialakwa evolved organically, room-by-room and apparently without any overarching design. While all the walls were raised across the mesa top over the same eight-month period, this was not a task shared by communitywide work groups. Instead individual households each took it on themselves to construct their new homes independently from one another. Unlike the cookie-cutter roomblocks typical of Patokwa and Boletsakwa, Astialakwa's architecture is much more diverse, with rooms displaying heterogeneous floor areas, disparate orientations, and walls with variable azimuths (figure 9.4). Patterns of corner bonding and abutment reveal that dwellings were erected in groups of one to four rooms at a time, rather than the 10- to 20-room clusters typical of ladder-constructed architecture.

The haphazard arrangement of Astialakwa's architecture is not at all what archaeologists have come to expect from rapidly constructed, defensive Pueblo villages founded in the wake of communal migrations. Rational economic models of Pueblo architecture predict that when builders seek to maximize security and the speed of construction while minimizing labor expenditures, the result should be compact, contiguous, multistoried architecture with inwardly-facing roomblocks on a central plaza, employing ladder-construction techniques and shared labor in the process (Cameron 1999b:207; LeBlanc 1999:56–66). In other words, in situations of rapidly built, defensive pueblos, we expect villages with layouts similar to Patokwa, Boletsakwa, and Kotyiti. Yet Astialakwa bears none of these hallmarks, even though it was constructed in haste, as a result of mass migrations, with defense as a primary consideration. Why then did the builders of Astialakwa settle on such a seemingly counterintuitive design—or more correctly, lack thereof? And why does the spatial organization of Astialakwa differ so radically from that of Patokwa and Boletsakwa, particularly considering the fact that the same social group constructed all three sites in a span of less than thirteen years?

The answer, of course, is that the layout of Astialakwa was not a plan but a process, resulting from a host of related factors. Based on architectural evidence alone, the revivalist element of the revitalization movement that played such a strong role in the early years of the Revolt era appears to have dissipated by the time Astialakwa was constructed in 1694. Throughout the latter 1680s the movement apparently lost momentum as many of the leaders who championed revivalism early on lost their influence and then died— Po'pay and Alonso Catití being the prime examples. As with the Punames at Cerro Colorado, revivalism was evidently no longer a central tenet of the Jemez when Astialakwa was constructed in 1694, as no effort was made to build this new village in the iconic twin-plaza, dual-kiva style, ostensibly in the manner of their pre-Hispanic ancestors.

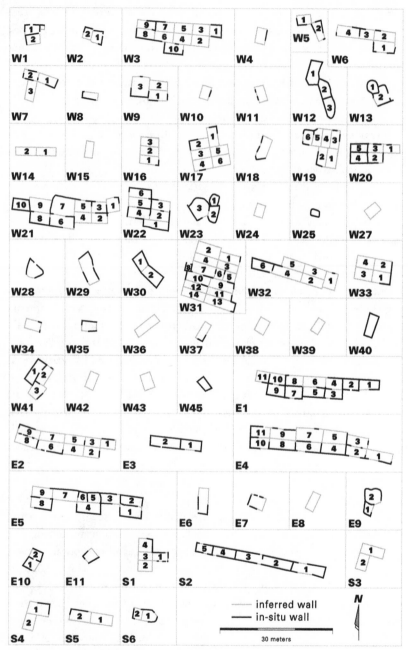

FIGURE 9.4. Architectural units at Astialakwa.

Associated with the breakdown of revivalism was a shift in the organization of labor away from communal work groups to construction organized on the household level. The relatively indiscriminate arrangement of rooms and roomblocks at Astialakwa points to the fact that there was no single leader (or group of leaders) directing the overall construction of the village. The centralized leadership exhibited early in the Revolt era through the architecture of Patokwa, Boletsakwa, and Kotyiti was lacking in 1694. Authority at Astialakwa seems to have been more diffuse, possibly a by-product of the coming together of two communities with a shared history of factionalism. The convergence of the people of Patokwa and Boletsakwa at Astialakwa presumably brought together two previously separate village-level political systems (with two caciques, multiple war chiefs, four war captains, society leaders, and their multiple attendants). The dispersed site plan may be the result of the political and social negotiations that would have been necessary for these two groups to coexist.

A related factor contributing to the dispersed spatial organization of Astialakwa was the increase in migration of Pueblo peoples that characterized the end of the Pueblo Revolt era. With the return of the Spaniards, many Pueblo people chose to leave their home villages, moving from one refuge to another in an attempt to avoid the crushing attacks of colonial forces (and their Native allies). At the same time, anti-Spanish warriors often joined refuge communities in anticipation of impending attacks in order to aid Pueblo defense efforts. The scattered layouts of pueblo villages constructed and occupied in the early 1690s—including Astialakwa, the Tewa stronghold of Tunyo at Black Mesa (a.k.a. San Ildefonso Mesa), and the Zuni redoubt of Dowa Yalanne—reflect the social experimentation that accompanied the incorporation of new persons and groups into a single village (Ferguson 1996:145; Liebmann et al. 2005:57).

In fact, the architecture of Astialakwa is not completely devoid of structure. Rooms and roomblocks cluster into three main units—a western group, separated by a five- to ten-meter deep arroyo from the eastern and southern architectural groups. This clustering may reflect the need to incorporate two separate factions of Jemez people (from Patokwa and Boletsakwa) with the Kewas who lived at Boletsakwa and any other newcomers into a single village. The tripartite spatial organization may also index the subtle social boundaries maintained between these groups through architecture and the manipulation of open space. T. J. Ferguson (1996:30; 2002) documents a similar pattern at Dowa Yalanne, where six previously autonomous Zuni villages coalesced into a single community during this period, involving a major reorganization of Zuni society in order to accommodate the unification of clans, medicine societies, and priesthoods from formerly separate pueblos. A comparable strategy seems to have been utilized at Kotyiti, where a second, more dispersed site was constructed nearby to integrate newcomers yet maintain boundaries between differing ethnic groups (Preucel 2000b:66–71).

A Time of Anxiety and Foreboding: Life at Astialakwa, Early 1694

Between 500 and 600 persons occupied Astialakwa during the first half of 1694, based on the tallies in various Spanish documents of that year (which add up to at least 527 persons).[34] The majority of the population comprised the Jemez from Patokwa and Boletsakwa, along with their Kewa allies. Additionally, an indefinite number of temporary residents probably gathered at Astialakwa as the summer progressed, primarily warriors from other Pueblos who came to aid in the battle that loomed so ominously on the horizon.

While living on the peñol the inhabitants of Astialakwa attempted to maintain some semblance of normal life—no doubt a difficult task under such extreme conditions. They built corrals and tended a flock of 175 sheep and goats on the mesa top, penning them in enclosures at the edges of the cliffs on the west and east sides of the mesa.[35] The men worked their fields in the valleys below, descending the peñol to tend to the maize they cultivated in riverside *milpas* on either side of the mesa.[36] The women ground corn for tortillas in workshops along the mesa edge, where an intact mano and metate were discovered in 2002. They also cached vast quantities of maize in caves and hollows along the mesa edge that were modified to serve as storerooms. As they settled into the rhythms of daily life, they tended to their ritual obligations as well. Two u-shaped stone shrines (identified as such by contemporary members of Jemez Pueblo) are located among the western group of roomblocks and appear to have been constructed contemporaneously with the surrounding roomblocks based on the size of the masonry, their locations relative to the surrounding architecture, and the accretion of soil in and around these features. While the people of Astialakwa dug no circular, subterranean kivas (like at Cerro Colorado, the shallow topsoil and exposed bedrock on which the village sits would have made this a difficult prospect at best), they did establish a plaza among the western roomblocks where they could gather and perform ritual dances.

Two areas of rock art are associated with the site as well, and although there is no way to be sure that these panels were created during the 1690s, the fact that the only substantial occupation of this area occurred during the Pueblo Revolt era suggests that the figures were probably pecked at that time.

FIGURE 9.5. Warrior petroglyph at Astialakwa.

On the eastern edge of the mesa are two large panels displaying petroglyphs of corn plants, animal tracks, birds, and geometric figures. Across the peñol, on the cliffs below the western cluster of rooms, is a solitary anthropomorphic figure holding a bow in one hand and an arrow in the other (figure 9.5). This appears to be a depiction of one of the famed culture heroes of Pueblo mythology: the elder brother of the hero twins, called *Masewi* by the Jemez. Identified by his distinctive pointed cap and the battle paraphernalia in his hands (White 1942:304; Schaafsma 2000:125–126), Masewi is associated with warfare and lightning. As such, his presence at a village constructed in anticipation of attack is appropriate. Among the Keres Pueblos, Masewi is said to be the founder of the Opi (scalp takers) Society. According to Parsons (1925:125), at Jemez the Opi are one of three male war societies and in the past were known as the killers of humans (as opposed to killers of animals). The presence of an image of Masewi at Astialakwa thus makes sense, as warfare became a part of the rhythm of daily life for the Jemez throughout the first half of 1694.

By May, tensions between the Jemez and their Puname neighbors had reached the breaking point. Threats from the warriors of Astialakwa forced the Zias out of Cerro Colorado, its proximity to the Jemez now a liability despite the defensive nature of the mesa. The Zias moved back to their old village, but were not content to wait idly until the other Pueblos attacked. They launched a preemptive strike, ambushing the Jemez near their old mission pueblo, killing five and capturing five others. A few weeks later the Jemez retaliated, attacking Zia and Santa Ana with help of their Tewa and Keres allies. Applying a bit of psychological warfare, the Jemez and their partisans took to assaulting individuals when they ventured out to tend their corn fields or cut wood in the forest. Soon the Punames were unable to leave their villages without an armed escort. Feeling their enemies' grip tighten around their throats, they sent an urgent call to Governor Vargas requesting Spanish troops to be stationed at their pueblos, and that the general himself come "as soon as possible to make offensive war against their enemies," the Jemez, "who are rebels against the royal crown."[37]

The governor responded by issuing an edict declaring a military campaign against the "rebellion and backsliding of the Jemez nation, the Keres from Santo Domingo, and their partisans." His decree was posted in the twin plazas of Santa Fe, alerting the men of the capital to prepare themselves for battle. On July 21, Vargas mustered ninety soldiers and thirty militiamen from the local vecino population. Word of the imminent attack had already reached the warriors of Astialakwa, and as Vargas gathered his forces in Santa Fe, the Jemez once again raided Zia, aided by their confederates from Kewa, Cochiti, the Tewa pueblos, and some Navajos.[38] The Spaniards made their way to Zia too late to aid in the defense of the village, arriving on July 23. Nonetheless, the Punames were more than willing to contribute to Vargas's cause, and one hundred warriors from Zia, Santa Ana, and San Felipe joined the column, under the leadership of Bartolomé de Ojeda. That evening a storm rolled in, shrouding Astialakwa in misty clouds. Taking full advantage of the cover provided by this proverbial dark and stormy night, the Spaniards marched to the base of the peñol and prepared for battle.

The Battle of Astialakwa: July 24, 1694

On top of the cliffs, the warriors of Astialakwa danced throughout the night as part of a ritual preparation for battle. Jemez oral traditions recorded in the nineteenth century recall that "whilst engaged in their dances, they were told that the Spaniards were below; but they did not believe it, and continued dancing."[39] Presumably these dances took place in the plaza among the western roomblocks of the village. In the valley below the Spaniards readied themselves for the attack. At 1:00 a.m., Vargas split his forces in two, employing the same multipronged "pincer" tactic he had successfully used in the raid on Kotyiti a few months prior (Preucel 2000a; Hendricks 2002:190). Ojeda knew of a trail leading up the back (north) side of the peñol that they could climb without being detected. Armed with this information, Vargas sent the Zia and Santa Ana warriors with twenty-five of his men (led by a Spaniard named Eusebio de Vargas, no relation to the governor) around the back of the mesa, while the Santa Anas and the rest of the Spaniards planned to ascend up the well-worn path on the southern end of the mesa that led directly to the village.

When the morning star appeared, Vargas gave the signal to begin the assault. As first light broke over Astialakwa, the opening volley from a Spanish harquebus cracked the morning silence and the Jemez warriors scrambled to defend their village. The Spaniards on the south trail quickly reached a section that was too steep to ascend on horseback. Clawing their way up the scree, they struggled to dodge the rocks and arrows raining down on them from above. Meanwhile on the north end of the peñol, the combined Puname-Spanish brigade exacted a hefty toll on its defenders, breaching the mesa top early in the fight and killing between twelve and fifteen of the warriors stationed there.[40] Pueblo versions of the battle (differing slightly from those recorded by the Spaniards) survive at Jemez today, as related by Jemez historian and tribal council member Joshua Madalena (2003:21):

> According to Jemez oral tradition, when the Jemez warriors on the north end heard the loud noises of the cannons [sic], some of the defenders abandoned their post to investigate, leaving their allies to protect their post, unaware that some of the allied warriors entrusted were actually a part of Governor Vargas's military. These few warriors had arrived on the mesa the previous night and had insisted they watch the north end of the mesa. These warriors were said to have worn white bandanas on their foreheads. When the Spanish troops on the north end heard the echo of the cannons, they immediately attacked. The warriors with the white bandanas assisted the Spanish troops as they assaulted their way up the mesa. Eusebio de Vargas and his troops succeeded to the top of the mesa, then attacking the Jemez village of Astialakwa.

The details of this account echo that of a sixteenth-century battle in which the Zuni allies of Antonio de Espejo reportedly wore red headbands to differentiate them from hostile Indians in battle.[41] Spanish chronicles of the skirmish at Astialakwa make no mention of this tactic, however. Instead, Vargas recorded the events of that morning as follows:

> The rebels, having detected the men coming from two directions—those of Capt. Eusebio de Vargas, who were already on the mesa, and those of the present captain, who were winning their way up the ascent—began to defend it. They knew it was very rough and steep and were well prepared with their ramparts. Although they hurled some large stones and rocks, as well as shooting many arrows, they were valiantly resisted. Our men responded with several shots, with God Our Lord encouraging us. Although the path up was long and straight, they were soon masters of the mesa. In this way, both squadrons were favored.[42]

The defensive ramparts mentioned by Vargas still remain piled on the ends of the peñol today, in linear arrangements of unshaped, dry-laid tuff stones 50 cm and higher in some places. These parapets protected the archers who hid behind them, leaving clear views of the trails leading to the top of the peñol. Nearby lay piles of fist-sized granite cobbles (manuports from the Permian geological stratum below the peñol) stacked at the trailheads on each end of the mesa. The people of Astialakwa carried these river cobbles to the mesa top, storing them as ammunition for their slings. (The friable tuff of the mesa top is unsuitable for slingstones, as it shatters on impact with hard surfaces, such as metal armor.) Vargas recounted that the Jemez "shot many arrows, threw stones, and tumbled boulders down" on his soldiers, and these piles are the remnants of these tactics.[43] Their locations indicate that the inhabitants of Astialakwa anticipated the multiple fronts of Vargas's pincer-style attack, and even correctly predicted where the opposing forces would gain access to the peñol.

   Once the advancing forces breached the top of the mesa, the defenders retreated into the village, barricading themselves inside their houses. They continued to fire on the Spaniards through the arrow slits ("loopholes") they had prepared in the walls of the newly constructed pueblo, injuring some of the attackers.[44] The Spaniards and their Keres allies returned these volleys, with skirmishes occurring throughout the village. Vargas states that he "found both squadrons in combat with the rebels who were fortified in the houses. From their loopholes, they had wounded and injured many, though not seriously. The rebels were also lanced, shot, and some set afire."[45] We recovered pieces of chain mail and copper plating that probably served as armor for the Spaniards from among the roomblocks of Astialakwa, attesting to the Spaniards' sweep of the village. At one point, two warriors—an Apache and a Jemez—were captured. As the harquebusiers prepared to execute them, the Apache man begged for mercy, asking to be baptized. Vargas assented, allowing a Franciscan to administer the sacrament. Surely their two hearts leapt as their heads were anointed, believing their lives had been spared. But moments later the hopes of the neophytes were dashed. Vargas's mercy proved fleeting, and with holy water still dripping from their heads, the governor ordered the firing squad to take aim. With a flash of smoke and gunpowder, the bodies of the Apache and the Jemez crumbled under the noonday sun.

The rest of the defenders proved stubbornly difficult to dislodge from their houses, so the Spaniards opted to smoke them out by setting fire to the village. Room by room and house by house, Vargas's troops lit the vigas of Astialakwa aflame. At least four men and one woman were burned alive in the blaze, and evidence of this conflagration is still apparent in the burned plaster, tuff, and charred material found in the fill of nearly every room at Astialakwa today. With the pueblo in flames and their escape routes blocked, the warriors were trapped, and they started to jump from the cliffs. Later reports suggest that at least eighty-two others escaped the Spaniards' grasp and lived to tell the tale.[46]

Throughout the afternoon the Spaniards picked off the remaining resistors one by one. By 4:00 p.m. the smoke had dissipated, the cannon were quiet, and the musket barrels cool. Vargas and his Keres allies had carried the day. In total, 84 residents of Astialakwa were killed in the battle. Another 361 women, children, and elders were taken prisoner, along with 172 head of sheep and some horses.[47]

Floating Like Butterflies

Different versions of the story of the battle at Astialakwa and the events surrounding those that jumped from the cliffs have been recorded over the past 160 years. Jemez historian Joe Sando (1982:120) writes that "some people jumped over the cliffs to avoid capture; at that moment a likeness of San Diego appeared on the cliff, and the people who had jumped simply landed on their feet and did not die." Similar versions note that when the saint appeared, he "eased the jumpers gently through the air so that they landed upon the rocks like birds" (Ellis 1956:38). Other reports attribute the miraculous escape of these warriors to a visitation of the Virgin, under whose guidance the men "floated like butterflies" to safety (Dougherty and Neal 1979:14). In 1849, Jemez Governor Francisco Hosta related a version of the story that included apparitions of both the Virgin and San Diego (Simpson 1852:22). A generation later his son recounted: "When the Spaniards came up . . . the despair of the people was great; many threw themselves headlong into the frightful depths below, preferring suicide to humiliating death at the hands of their conquerors. Suddenly the Spirit of Guadalupe, who is the custodian of the cañon, made his [*sic*] appearance, and from this moment the people could jump down without any danger" (Loew 1875:343–344).

While these accounts may sound fantastic (and even fictitious) to skeptical modern ears, more than likely they do have a basis in actual events. Some of the warriors of Astialakwa undoubtedly did jump from the cliffs and survive to tell the story. Two days after the battle, a Kewa captain (who had been living at Boletsakwa before the Spaniards' return) climbed out of the rocks below the top of the peñol. According to Vargas, "it could be seen from his wounded, bruised shoulder and right elbow and his damaged leg and thigh that this man had thrown himself from the peñol on the day of the combat and survived, hiding among the rocks in the area where he fell."[48]

Images of both San Diego (on the east side of the peñol) and the Virgin (on the west side) are said to be visible on the cliffs of the mesa today, and are still venerated by the contemporary people of Jemez (as well as the non-Native residents of the Jemez Valley). Confusingly, the image purported to represent San Diego (St. Didacus, patron of Franciscan laity) actually seems to be that of Santiago (St. James, patron of the Spanish empire, soldiers, and the reconquista). The likeness emblazoned on the side of the cliff (comprised of a series of cracks, variations in the color of the stone, and water stains) resembles a bearded man in profile standing above a distinctively equine shape. Colonial representations of Santiago commonly depicted him with a flowing white beard astride a magnificent steed (Simmons 1991b:16–18); thus the apparition on the peñol is probably more appropriately termed that of Santiago, not San Diego. Significantly, the battle at Astialakwa occurred just one day prior to the feast of Santiago (July 25) as well. "Doubtless, it was his patronage and intercession," opined Vargas, "since it was the eve of his glorious day, that played a large part in the triumph."[49]

Ultimately, the historicity of these apparitions is less significant than the fact that the oral traditions surrounding the battle exemplify yet another instance of postcolonial catachresis, in which the colonizer's culture is usurped and redeployed by the colonized. Even allowing for the fact that the apparition element(s) of this tale may have been added long after the last shots of the battle were fired, it is noteworthy that the source of the salvation of the Pueblo warriors is found in Catholic iconography. Spanish colonial armies typically marched under the banners of Santa Maria and Santiago, with Vargas himself calling on the protection of La Conquistadora ("Our Lady of the Conquest"), a statue of the Virgin that he carried back to New Mexico during the reconquest and is famously venerated to this day in Santa Fe's Cathedral (Chávez 1954; Simmons 1991b:24). The intercessions of the saints—particularly Santiago and the Virgin—were commonly invoked to account for Spanish victories during the reconquista in Iberia and the New World. Specifically, the Virgin and Santiago (aka Santiago *Matamoros*, the Moor-killer) had reportedly appeared to the people of Acoma when they were attacked by Oñate's forces in 1599, and this legend would have been well known to warriors on both sides of the battle lines at Astialakwa. In fact, there are a number of parallels between the 1694 battle at Astialakwa and the 1599 battle at Acoma. In both skirmishes, a small group of men jumped from the cliffs (Indians at Astialakwa, Spaniards at Acoma). In both, some of these men survived. In both, it was the Indians who reportedly witnessed the apparitions of the Virgin and Santiago (Lamadrid 2002:457). And ultimately, in both the Spaniards proved victorious.

The appropriation of Catholic saints by the Jemez, while counterintuitive, is thus not entirely surprising. Throughout the Spanish interregnum the Pueblos had usurped and transformed the Spaniards' most potent symbols. The apparitions of Santiago and the Virgin that appear in oral traditions in aid of the warriors of Astialakwa represent the continuation of the practice of catachresis down to the present day.

Following the battle, Vargas spent nine days collecting the spoils of war from Astialakwa. He forced the Jemez women and children to carry down the vast stores of maize they had cached on top of the peñol and allowed his allies from Zia, Santa Ana, and San Felipe to take as much as they could carry. In total the Spaniards alone collected 420 fanegas (about 58,800 pounds) of corn from Astialakwa; the amount seized by their Keres partners went unrecorded. As Vargas prepared to leave he ordered his men-at-arms to set fire to the remaining roomblocks "and leave them completely in ashes, burned down as a warning and reminder of the punishment and that the triumph had been obtained by fire and sword against the rebels for the Divine and human majesty." As they exited the Jemez Province, Vargas stopped at the ruins of the mission pueblo at Walatowa to perform one final task. He forced a Jemez couple to guide him to the place where they had buried the bones of Fray Juan de Jesus, the Franciscan who had been martyred at the mission of San Diego de la Congregación during the uprising fourteen years prior. In the main plaza, next to the wall of a kiva, they exhumed the skeleton of the friar and found an arrow still lodged in his spine. The symbolism of the disinterment was not lost on the Jemez, who watched as the Spaniards reclaimed control of the clergyman's body and in so doing, spirited away the remnants of their 1680 uprising.[50]

The exhumation of Fray Juan de Jesus would seem a fitting end to the saga of the Pueblo Revolt in the Jemez Province, but Vargas provided one final, paradoxical twist. In order to secure the release of the more than 350 Jemez women, children, and elders he held captive, Vargas required the men of Astialakwa to aid the Spaniards in their upcoming raid on the Tewa stronghold at Black Mesa. In order to coordinate the timing of the attack, the General presented the Jemez with a knotted cord to signify the number of days remaining before the siege.[51] It was an ironic—and calculated—gesture. For the Jemez, the Pueblo Revolt era ended in much the same way it began, with the loosing of the final knot in a fateful cord.

IO

Conclusion

ON AUGUST IO, 2005, I STOOD LOOKING ACROSS the central plaza of the ancestral Jemez pueblo of Giusewa in northern New Mexico. An army of piñon, juniper, and ponderosa pines stood sentinel over the stone walls and kivas of the long-vacant village, while nearby the Jemez River slipped between the cliffs of the adjacent mesas. Overhead the sun pushed us fair-skinned tourists into the last strip of shade cast by the façade of the seventeenth-century Spanish mission church. Backs pressed to the wall, we watched as two Buffalo Dancers from Jemez Pueblo performed in the center of the plaza. The fur and horns of their bison headdresses undulated with each dusty step, bells tied to their waists softly jingling with every movement. All of us had gathered together on this August day to commemorate the anniversary of the Pueblo Revolt of 1680, or as the organizers had dubbed it, "Pueblo Independence Day." As the first round of singing and dancing ended, the governor of Jemez Pueblo stepped to a microphone to deliver a short speech about the importance of the Pueblo Revolt in his tribe's history: "It is because our ancestors were brave enough to declare their independence 325 years ago, in 1680, that we are here today," he affirmed. "And we honor them now by once again proclaiming that we are *Hemish*. We are a sovereign nation. And our descendants will be here in another 325 years to proclaim the same thing."

Six weeks later, on September 23, a marble figure of Po'pay was installed in the National Statuary Hall of the U.S. Capitol building in Washington, D.C. After a decade-long effort of garnering political support, fundraising, and planning for the statue, spearheaded by Herman Agoyo of Ohkay Owingeh, the Po'pay sculpture filled the final spot in the 100-member gallery. The assembled audience of dignitaries and invited guests applauded as the statue was unveiled, and rightly so, as this was a momentous occasion. Po'pay's monument is the only work in the national collection carved by a Native American artist, Cliff Fragua of Jemez. One of the more interesting aspects of the ceremony was the positioning of Po'pay within the hall. Over the Tewa prophet's right shoulder hung John Vanderlyn's giant, eighteen-foot-wide oil painting, *Landing of Columbus* (1846). On the canvas, Christopher Columbus holds a sword in his right hand and the banner of his Spanish sovereigns in his left. The placement of Po'pay in front of this work of art was thus both ironic and appropriate; with Columbus looming in the background, the Pueblo holy man had his back turned to the explorer, focused on a distant horizon. Fingering a knotted cord in his left hand, Po'pay pondered a future with Spaniards behind him, both literally and figuratively.

The Penumbra of the Pueblo Revolt

In a provocative 1979 essay, French philosopher Michel Foucault (1981 [1979]) asked, "Is it useless to revolt?" His question hints at the seemingly overwhelming forces of history that serve to stifle resistance time and time again. Indeed, Foucault's own work documents the ubiquitous, insidious, and paralyzing nature of power and domination in social life. Given the seemingly unstoppable march of global capitalism in the modern world, the revolts of the past can appear to be little more than quaint and idealistic interludes. It is perhaps surprising, then, that Foucault answers his own question in the negative: "I am not in agreement with anyone who would say, 'It is useless for you to revolt; it is always going to be the same thing,'" he writes. "People do revolt, that is a fact. And that is how subjectivity (not that of great men, but that of anyone) is brought into history, breathing life into it." In this Foucault is in rare accord with Karl Marx, who was of course profoundly attuned to the vital role of revolutions in larger historical perspective. The agreement of these two giants of social theory (often read as counterpoints to one another) illustrates why the study of rebellion and revolution has played a central role in the social sciences for more than 150 years. The forcible overthrow of the social order in favor of a new system raises classic questions regarding the relationship between agency and structure, event and process, and the individual versus society.

As the annual observance of "Pueblo Independence Day" and the installation of the Po'pay statue in the U.S. Capitol demonstrate, the Pueblo Revolt of 1680 was certainly not fruitless. For contemporary Pueblo peoples, Po'pay's rebellion is more than merely a historical footnote. It was vital in the formation of the modern Pueblo world, and it persists in shaping contemporary Pueblo cultures down to the present day (Ortiz 1980, 1994; Suina 2002; Sando and Agoyo 2005; Liebmann and Preucel 2007:206–09). Perhaps the

most significant outcome of the Pueblo Revolt was the breakdown of traditional boundaries and creation of new, shared identities among the formerly distinct Pueblos. According to Alfonso Ortiz, Po'pay cemented among
the Pueblos "the sense of unity and common purpose necessary to defend
Pueblo cultural integrity against Spanish onslaughts" (1994:300). Although
it would be misleading to say that a monolithic, pan-Pueblo ethnic identity
exists today (indeed, it did not even persist through the late 1680s), the
bonds first forged during the Pueblo Revolt era endure in modern institutions such as the All Indian Pueblo Council, the Indian Pueblo Cultural
Center, and the Eight Northern Pueblos Council.

One of the most important outcomes of the Pueblo Revolt was the new
rapprochement that tacitly emerged between the Pueblos and Spaniards
in the eighteenth century. No longer were Pueblo people subjected to the
exploitive practices of encomienda and repartimiento. The termination of
these Spanish policies had a profound impact on Pueblo communities in the
eighteenth and nineteenth centuries. As historian H. Allen Anderson notes,
"Indeed, it has been argued that had it not been for the uprising . . . a settlement pattern similar to that which subsequently appeared in Nueva Vizcaya
and other provinces to the south" would have occurred in New Mexico, "with
the labor of dependent Indians or poor meztizos supporting widely scattered
large holdings" (1985:372). Franciscan missionaries became more accom-
modating of Pueblo religion after the Revolt as well, and less inclined to
demand strict allegiance to Christianity (Norris 2000). While the friars did
not approve of the kachina religion, after the reconquest of the 1690s, they
did tolerate it. This newfound accommodation helped to ensure the continuation of Pueblo religion, or as Joseph H. Suina (2002) of Cochiti Pueblo has
termed it, "the persistence of the Corn Mothers."

Normalizing the Exotic: Anthropological Perspectives

The main goal of this book has been to tell a more complete version of the
Pueblo Revolt story through the lenses of historical archaeology and anthropology. This process has uncovered some unexpected elements to add to the
tale, many of which challenge the classic metanarratives that have attached
themselves to this chronicle over the past three centuries. The most prominent of these "stories about the story" have cast the Pueblo Revolt era as either
a romanticized Native victory or a tragic indigenous defeat. But the brand-
ing of Native American revolts as a success or a failure based primarily on
Euro-American models of revolution is, of course, profoundly ethnocentric.

It militates against the core tenets of anthropology, a discipline that strives above all else to understand cultural formations (and transformations) on their own terms. A myopic focus on the end game of indigenous resistance distracts attention from the negotiated processes that constitute these remarkable phenomena. In fact, many of the practices that seem most curious, unanticipated, and irrational to modern readers are repeated elements of Native insurrections, cropping up again and again in colonial contexts around the world over the past five hundred years. Indigenous revolutionaries often appropriate elements of the colonizer's culture; they employ imperfect mimicry of colonial institutions; they engage in factionalism and intertribal warfare; they form alliances with former enemies. In turn, it is just these elements that are frequently cited as evidence for the "failed" nature of these uprisings. Rather than asking why Native revolts so frequently "failed," then, the preceding pages have sought to give meaning to these seemingly strange behaviors. And rather than passing judgment on the "success" of the Pueblo Revolt, this book has attempted to unmask the cultural logics underlying the peculiar patterns and choices made by the Pueblos, showing how Native revolutionaries made sense of their world between the Revolt of 1680 and the battles of the reconquista in 1694.

According to twenty-first century "common sense," these actions are curious and often inexplicable, seemingly working against the very goals Po'pay had set forth when he first emerged from the Taos kiva. It would be easy to dismiss them as acts of irrational, deluded "Others"; or as the Spaniards did, as those of persons possessed by the devil in a mass hysteria. But to do so overlooks the larger patterns into which this behavior falls. The goal of anthropology, it could be said, is to normalize the exotic (and to exoticize the normal). Things that seem at first anomalous, strange, and illogical are often revealed to be commonplace and recurring aspects of larger processes when we look at them through the lens of anthropology. For this reason, this book has examined the Pueblo Revolt story not as a "success" or "failure," based on twenty-first century wishes and expectations. Rather, in the preceding pages I have attempted to view the actions of the Pueblos between 1680 and 1694 on something like their own terms, in an attempt to grant validity and meaning to these experiences.

Postcolonial Amnesia and Re-membering

What then does the specific historical example of the Pueblo Revolt tell us about the larger anthropological phenomena of subaltern resistance and revitalization movements more generally? Like many Native rebellions, the Revolt of 1680 began with acts of destruction, in which the most conspicuous signs of colonial domination were attacked with fierce abandon. Catholic churches, mission bells, and the friars themselves were frequent targets of the Pueblos' nativist fury. In the parlance of postcolonial theorists, such practices are known as acts of "decolonizing amnesia," and they occur repeatedly among societies undergoing the transition from occupation to emancipation. The emergence of independence is often accompanied by a desire to forget the colonial past, a desire manifested through destruction of the most prominent signs of colonization (Gandhi 1998:4). While Native enmity toward these overt signs of colonial domination is perhaps understandable, non-Native observers of this "decolonizing amnesia" are frequently baffled by the additional and corresponding destruction of other elements that they would not have associated with the colonizers' culture. Among the Jemez, examples include the burning of their own homes along with the mission church after the Revolt, and the termination of production of their traditional Black-on-white pottery. Similar acts of renunciation were recorded among the nineteenth-century Creeks, Shawnees, Delawares, and Cherokees during periods of prophetic revitalization, where they destroyed even their own crops in the initial stages of rebellion. As ethnohistorian Joel Martin notes, these acts of destruction and purification were necessary "as a kind of prelude, an opening phase within a larger transformational drama," serving as a rite of passage to affirm the transformation of colonized peoples to a new, post-colonial status, frequently accompanied by the inauguration of new pan-Native identities (1991:691–92).

The initial desire to erase colonial memories among subaltern revolutionaries is typically followed by what Homi Bhabha (1994:63) calls a re-membering of the past, in which new cultural forms are created in an attempt to forge a reparative continuity with previous times. The creation of iconic dual-plaza pueblos directly adjacent to the remains of pre-Hispanic villages is an archetypal example of this re-membering process. Postcolonial re-membering is never simply an act of straightforward revivalism, however. Following initial attempts to repress and repudiate the colonial past, decolonizing societies typically adopt new, hybrid forms of culture that index the fundamental changes that occurred to them through the process of colonization. This hybridization is an essential part of the re-membering process. At the ancestral Jemez villages of the Pueblo Revolt era, the adoption of Plain Red pottery is an example of this postcolonial hybridity. Plain Red was introduced to Jemez potters through interactions with Franciscan missionaries but was transformed into a marker of new, pan-Pueblo identities in the wake of the Pueblo Revolt.

One of the primary contributions of this study has been to emphasize the novelty inherent in the material culture of revitalization. In the Jemez Province, new settlement plans, patterns of ceramic production, and community interactions during the Revolt era all departed from pre-1680 practices. The creative nature of this materiality should come as no surprise, as ethnohistorians have long recognized that revitalization movements cultivate innovation, rather than the replication of past practices. Wallace himself identifies innovation as one of the primary consequences of revitalizing rituals, noting its role in such famous examples as the Ghost Dance, the Handsome Lake religion, and the Native American Church (1966:209–10). Furthermore, recent archaeological studies of the role of social memory in communal action (the basis of most revivalist discourse) stress its variable, mutable, and selective nature, suggesting that we should not expect antiquated forms of material culture to (re)appear unaltered in the course of revitalization (Golden 2005:271; Hodder and Cessford 2004:31; Mills 2004:238; Van Dyke and Alcock 2003:2–3).

Signs of Struggle and the Struggle over Signs

Maybe the most puzzling aspect of the Pueblo Revolt story for modern audiences is the persistence of Christian imagery during this period of overt nativism. It would be easy to dismiss the images of saints, the curated ecclesiastical paraphernalia, and the crosses that adorned Pueblo houses during the Spanish interregnum as examples of acculturation in the classic sense of the word, or as that of a "false consciousness" that had taken root among the Pueblos through eight decades of colonization. But to view the persistence of Christian imagery as evidence of the straightforward displacement of indigenous beliefs by those of the colonizers is simply too facile. If this were the case, why bother to revolt at all? If the ideas of the colonizers' culture were so appealing, why not simply convert wholeheartedly to Christianity (Cave 2006:245)? Such easy explanations overlook the abilities of subalterns to transform and redeploy the signs of colonial culture, inscribing them with new and different meanings. The persistence of Christian imagery is not evidence of the "failure" of Po'pay's movement or of incomplete nativism. To read these signs as such ignores the new meanings that the Pueblos invested in them as they merged with traditional Pueblo cultural formations or were used to augment indigenous power structures.

In fact, the transformative process of catachresis is a common strategy of subaltern resistance in colonized (and newly liberated) contexts the world over.

In his classic study of peasant insurgency in colonial India, Ranajit Guha documents the inversion of prominent signs of colonial authority in more than one hundred cases of subaltern rebellion between 1783 and 1900 (1983:18–76). Guha masterfully shows how the peasantry inverted the codes by which their colonizers dominated them—deploying forms of dress, speech, and behavior that appropriated and re-interpreted colonial symbols of authority in new ways. To dismiss these acts as "merely symbolic" or evidence of Marxian false consciousness overlooks their repeated and centrally important role in subaltern resistance. As Guha notes, the struggle over signs is "at the heart of insurgency. Inversion was its principal modality. It was a political struggle in which the rebel appropriated and/or destroyed the insignia of his enemy's power and hoped thus to abolish the marks of his own subalternity" (1983:75). Although this persistence of colonial imagery may not be what modern Western audiences expect (or desire) of the heroic Native revolutionaries of the past, to read these signs as antithetical to the cause of anticolonial resistance is to rob them of the meanings invested in them by subalterns, and in so doing, to rob Native subalterns of agency in the construction of their social worlds.

Previous analyses of anticolonial resistance have often downplayed the roles of religious signs in these movements, viewing them as "merely symbolic" and epiphenomenal to the real-world, material instantiations of rebellion (Martin 1991:668). Yet as we have seen in the case of the Pueblo Revolt and its aftermath, religion is not secondary to indigenous resistance, but a primary motivating factor. As Foucault notes, throughout history revolts against oppression "have easily been able to find their expression and mode of performance in religious themes: the promise of beyond, the return of time, the waiting for a savior or the empire of the last days, the indisputable reign of the good." Such themes, he suggests, "have furnished throughout the centuries not an ideological cloak but the very way to live revolts" (quoted in Cave 2006:9). As we have seen, religion played a central role (if not *the* central role) in the Pueblo Revolt, both in the initial motivation for the rebellion and in the ways in which Pueblo peoples negotiated their newfound freedom.

Decentering Resistance

Finally, the historical anthropology of the Pueblo Revolt draws our attention to the importance of indigenous politics in shaping subaltern resistance. In the analysis of Native American revolts, the scholarly gaze tends to fall on the colonizer-colonized relationship above all else, reinscribing the primary importance of the colonial dyad. While undoubtedly significant, this privileging of relations between foreign and indigenous can distract attention from the importance of intraindigenous politics in shaping the alliances that are forged during this era. But as the archaeology of the Pueblo Revolt era demonstrates, there is a need to look to additional factors outside of the colonizer-colonized relationship if we are to develop better understandings of subaltern resistance and revitalization. In other words, we need to "decenter" the study of Native revolts by shifting the focus away from the traditional Indian versus European dichotomy, affording a central role to the internal politics of Native communities in the reconstruction of subaltern resistance (Beck et al. 2011).

As the archaeology of the Pueblo Revolt era demonstrates, the phenomena of cultural revitalization welds previously separate groups together, forging new alliances and identities among Native communities. Anthropological studies of revitalization in varied contexts worldwide have documented time and time again the fact that these processes enable groups from disparate backgrounds to recognize and develop a common identity (Worsley 1957:228; Gill 1983:144–45; Martin 1991:690–91). During the Pueblo Revolt era, this merging of previously separate (and sometimes previously hostile) communities occurred multiple times and was manifested in and promoted by the material culture produced by the Pueblos. The formation of a pan-Pueblo identity and the related new patterns of ceramic production and trade, changes in settlement patterns, and development of shared site layouts are the most obvious examples of this process. Even the alliance that formed among the Punames and the Spaniards during the reconquest was shaped in large part by the internal politics of the Pueblos. Conceptualizing of subaltern resistance and cultural revitalization merely as responses to the actions of colonizers risks flattening the archaeology of colonial encounters. In order to develop more nuanced and detailed histories, we must pay attention to the actions that occurred off the colonial stage. Often those actions went unrecorded, sentencing Native actors of the past to subaltern roles. As this book has strived to demonstrate, however, archaeology can be used to work against this subalternity, helping to re-create the Native worlds that set the stage for the dramas recorded in historical documents.

Epilogue

THE PUEBLO REVOLT OF 1696

FOLLOWING THE BATTLE AT ASTIALAKWA, the Jemez returned to their homes at Patokwa and Boletsakwa. In late September 1694, Vargas visited Patokwa and installed Fray Francisco de Jesús María Casañas as the new missionary there. The Jemez had constructed a mission complex in the northwest corner of Patokwa (figure E.1), with an associated convento complex located south of the church. A low wall enclosed the *claustro* (church yard) to the east of the convento rooms. Vargas christened the church *San Diego del Monte y Nuestra Señora de Remedios* (Elliott 2002). His journal entry notes that the living quarters for Fray Francisco were large enough "that four religious could have lived in it with everything they needed." During this visit Vargas also issued the canes of office to the new officials of both Patokwa and Boletsakwa. Although he did not visit Boletsakwa during this trip (nor did he station a priest there), Vargas reported that a group of Jemez people and their Keres allies from Kewa once again inhabited San Juan Mesa at that time.[1] In January 1695 Vargas prepared a puzzling report indicating the status of the Jemez Province, noting, "Half the mesa of San Juan is occupied by the Keres nation from the pueblo of Santo Domingo and the other half by the Jemez nation, which has its pueblo on the mesa of San Diego with its minister. Its parish is made up of 405 people."[2]

Sometime in 1695 the mission at Walatowa was reestablished. This church was dubbed San Juan de los Jemez,[3] possibly because it was built to minister to the Jemez people who had recently been living on San Juan Mesa (at Boletsakwa) and had returned to resettle Walatowa by this time. Thus by late 1695 there were two missions in the Jemez Province: San Diego del Monte at Patokwa and San Juan de los Jemez at Walatowa. Not long after the founding of the new mission at Walatowa, rumors of another unified Pueblo revolt began to circulate in New Mexico, first planned for Christmas Eve 1695,

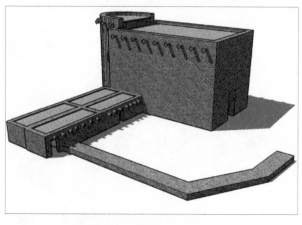

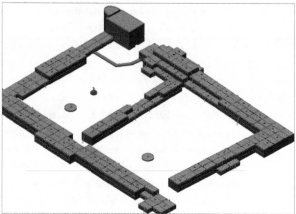

FIGURE E.1. San Diego del Monte mission complex (top), Patokwa 1695–96 (bottom).

and later during the full moon in March 1696. Again the Natives used a knotted cord to communicate the date of the battle from one village to the next.[4] Neither of these predicted uprisings materialized, however, partially because the Franciscans discovered the plans beforehand. Over the following months the Friars noted an increase in impudence and insolence by Pueblo neophytes, and they petitioned Vargas for soldiers to be stationed at the missions for the priests' protection. "To place myself at the mouth of the wolf, so that he may swallow me and drink my blood, my mother did not bear me . . . for that purpose," complained Fray Francisco, writing from the mission at Patokwa. "For I did not come to seek death but rather the lives of these miserable ones."[5]

At San Juan de los Jemez, Fray Miguel Trizio was saved from martyrdom when "a few of the good ones" removed him from the mission for his own protection. Following the foiled murder plot, many of the residents of Walatowa reportedly fled the pueblo because, in the words of the friar, "they were so malevolent."[6] During this turbulent period Fray Miguel notified Vargas that in order to carry out his priestly duties he needed protection. "Neither 12 nor 14 men are sufficient," he complained, "but if your lordship gives 50 men to Jemez," Fray Miguel promised to serve with great pleasure.[7] Vargas rebuffed these requests for reinforcements, replying that he "did not have enough bread for a wedding that big."[8] The Franciscans responded to the governor with indignation and dire predictions. In a letter dated April 18, 1696, Fray Francisco forecasted: "If they do not revolt today, they will tomorrow."[9]

Unfortunately for Fray Francisco, tomorrow came on June 4, when the Jemez joined in the Pueblo Revolt of 1696, along with the Tewa, northern Tiwa, Tano, and some of the Keres.[10] Once again the Puebloans and their Athapaskan allies rose up against the Spanish oppressors, killing five priests and twenty-one other españoles throughout New Mexico.[11] At San Diego del Monte, the Jemez lured Fray Francisco from the church under the pretense that a sick woman needed him to hear her confession. Once outside the chapel door the priest reportedly "called out to God Our Lord and the most holy Virgin to help and favor him." His calls went unheeded, however, and two Jemez men clubbed him to death next to a cross he had erected in the cemetery (figure E.2). According to the Franciscan Custodio of New Mexico, "on many occasions the said religious was heard to say, and I heard him say, that he had [the cross built] so that they could crucify him on it, and although these wishes were not attained, he succeeded in expiring at the foot of the cross."[12] Oral traditions of this event were still maintained at Jemez a century and a half later, as told by Governor Hosta in 1849: "When living on the mesa between the cañons of Guadalupe and San Diego, there came another padre among them, whom, whilst on his way to receive the confessions of a sick man, they killed" (Simpson 1852:22). Fray Francisco's body was disposed of at the door of the church. The Jemez then enticed the Spanish captain stationed at Patokwa to take a stroll in a nearby orchard, killing him along with three other soldiers. Two women and two boys were also seized as captives and made to serve the Jemez leaders. The church of San Diego del Monte may have been damaged at this time as well; a decade later "the mission of San Diego" reportedly still "had no bell" and was being rebuilt.[13]

At Walatowa the Jemez killed two other soldiers and a Jemez native named Cristóbal, who spoke Castilian and was suspected of spying for the Spaniards.[14] In the mission of San Juan de los Jemez they smashed the images

FIGURE E.2. *The Martyrdom of Fray Francisco de Jesus Maria*, by Diego de Sanabria (late 1700s or early 1800s), depicting the death of the friar stationed at Patokwa in 1696.

of the saints and shattered the crosses in a display of nativist rage that would have made Po'pay proud. Inside the church they tore the rosaries from their necks, symbolically throwing off the fetters of their oppressors once again. They cast the beads and crucifixes in the dirt, covering them with offerings of feathers, ashes, and rabbit skins in yet another demonstration of the triumph of Pueblo tradition over Christianity. Other "articles of divine worship" were removed from the convent and buried or stashed in the houses of Walatowa. Luckily for Fray Miguel, he happened to be visiting a sick *compadre* at Pecos that day and once again escaped the martyrdom that his parishioners had planned for him.[15]

Seven days later one of the Jemez leaders from Patokwa, Luis Cunixu, appeared at Pecos. Cunixu had been instrumental in the planning of the Revolt of 1680, and was probably a member of Po'pay's inner circle of war captains (Riley 1999:219). He carried with him a reliquary that belonged to Fray Francisco de Jesús as proof of his death, and urged the people of Pecos to join Jemez and the other pueblos in their upcoming attack on the Spaniards. Cunixu was accompanied by the cacique of Nambé Pueblo, Diego Xenome, "the main rabble-rouser among the Tewa." Cunixu and Xenome were captured by the pro-Spanish faction at Pecos and brought to Vargas for questioning in Santa Fe. There Cunixu testified that the Zuni, Hopi, and Acoma warriors were gathering at Jemez to plan their siege. Following their questioning, Cunixu, Xenome, and another captive named Alonso Guigi (identified as the governor of Kewa but originally from Jemez) were executed by a firing squad.[16]

Two more weeks had passed when reports reached Vargas of more Indians gathering at Jemez. He dispatched an additional eight soldiers to Zia, with instructions to reconnoiter the area with a militia of warriors from Zia and Santa Ana. On June 29 this force left Zia, making their way to Patokwa at dawn. They found the village empty, with the Jemez and their allies (including people from Acoma, Zuni, Hopi, and Cochiti, as well as Tewas, Tanos, and Navajos) once again fortified at Astialakwa.[17] As soon as they arrived at the peñol, the Spaniards and Keres were attacked "with powder and ball." The Jemez and their allies won the initial skirmish, forcing the Spaniards to retreat to Patokwa. As they passed through the mission, the Spaniards recovered Fray Francisco's remains,[18] but the Jemez attacked again, forcing the Spaniards and their Keres allies to retreat once more. This time they withdrew to a location near the mission of San Juan de los Jemez at Walatowa (Kessell et al. 1998:796). Later Vargas (who was not present at the battle) would characterize these retreats as "a stratagem of fleeing to draw them to more suitable terrain." Near Walatowa the colonial force was ambushed. Apparently the Jemez and their allies had learned from the battles of 1694, and they now turned the Spaniards' military strategies back upon them by utilizing a two-pronged battle strategy as "they attacked [the Spaniards and Keres] on horseback from both sides." The Spaniards apparently held their ground, and a bloody two-hour battle ensued. Initial reports indicated that twenty-eight of the Jemez-allied forces were killed, with two captured alive and one member of the colonial militia wounded.[19]

What happened to the Jemez after the Revolt of 1696 is unclear. Most seem to have left the Jemez Province, traveling to Hopi, Zuni, Acoma, Taos, and the Gobernador region (Hendricks and Wilson 1996; Brugge 2002).[20] By August 1696 the Jemez Province was effectively depopulated, and remained largely vacant for the next six years. In November 1696 and again in March 1697 Vargas lists the Jemez pueblos as "absent." But by 1703 some Jemez had apparently returned to resettle the province. It has often been assumed that Walatowa was the only Jemez village reinhabited at this time.[21] However, in a report dated August 18, 1706, the governor of New Mexico listed both "San Diego and San Juan de los Jemez" in a record of settlements occupied in the Jemez Province.[22] The same year don Luis Conitzu (a relative of the rabble-rousing Cunixu?) was appointed governor of "San Diego de los Jemez," where it was said that 300 Christian Indians resided, "and others keep coming down from the mountains, where they are still in insurrection."[23] A decade later the mission at Walatowa was still referred to as San Juan de los Jemez, when 113 Jemez refugees were forcibly removed from Hopi and resettled there. Two missions were still operating in the Jemez valley as late as 1716 at Patokwa and Walatowa (Bloom 1931:159–60). Sometime in the mid-eighteenth century the residents of Patokwa left that village and moved back to Walatowa, coalescing into a single Jemez village once again.

Jemez settlement at Walatowa proudly continues to the present day.

Notes

Chapter 1

1. Diego de Vargas, Edict, Santa Fe, 26 June 1694 (Kessell et al. 1998:283–84). On the dancing at Astialakwa, see Simpson 1852:22. On the participation of Ojeda and the Zia, Santa Ana, and San Felipe warriors, see Jones 1966:50–53.

2. Diego de Vargas, campaign journal, 22 July–10 August 1694 (Kessell et al. 1998:325–27). On La Conquistadora, see Chávez 1954. On Santiago, see M. Simmons 1991b:24.

3. Accounts of this legend can be found in Simpson 1852:22; Loew 1875:343–44; Ellis 1956:38; Dougherty and Neal 1979:14; and Sando 1982:120.

4. Hackett and Shelby 1942, 2:247, 289, 300; Riley 1999:215.

5. Hackett and Shelby 1942, 1:5, 15; 2:232–253, 328–330, 342–346, 359–362; De Marco 2000.

6. Declaration of Josephe, Spanish-speaking Indian (Place of the Rio del Norte, December 19, 1681) (Hackett and Shelby 1942, 2:239–40).

7. In recent years the translation and publication of many of the primary texts relating to the Spanish reconquest has further advanced knowledge of this era in important new directions, see Kessell and Hendricks 1992; Kessell et al. 1995, 1998; De Marco 2000.

8. See also Sando 1998:3.

9. Hackett and Shelby 1942; Espinosa 1988; Kessell and Hendricks 1992; Kessell et al. 1995, 1998; De Marco 2000.

10. The use of "subaltern" in the place of "proletariat" was an example of self-censorship necessitated by Gramsci's incarceration in Italian prison during the 1920s and 1930s.

11. Although not the first to recognize the existence and importance of deliberate attempts to stimulate rapid culture change (see Barber 1941; Linton 1943; Hallowell 1945), Wallace's work did initially identify the fundamental commonalities in cause and process shared by rapid culture change phenomena that had previously been considered under disparate rubrics.

Chapter 2

1. Hammond and Rey 1940:244. Castañeda, chronicler of the Vasquez de Coronado expedition, provides a list that includes an entry of "Hemes, seven villages" immediately followed by "Aguas Calientes, three villages." The latter probably refers to an additional cluster of villages in the Jemez Province, most likely Unshagi, Nanishagi, and Giusewa (Bloom 1922:22–23; Reiter 1938:24; Elliott 1986:189; Liebmann 2006:144–45). Therefore, there were likely a total of at least ten large villages occupied in the Jemez Province in 1541.

2. Hackett 1937:110, 120; Hammond and Rey 1953, 2:653; Riley 1999:162

3. Hammond and Rey 1953, 2:210, 680, 1089.

4. Scholes 1944:340–341; Hodge et al. 1945: 171; Simmons 1980:13; Anderson 1985:363.

5. I suspect that Santiago may have been another name for Giusewa (LA 679). In 1581 the Rodriquez-Chamuscado expedition visited a valley they called Santiago, apparently referring to the upper Jemez Valley, a.k.a. San Diego Canyon (Hammond and Rey 1966:6–15, 86–87). If this is correct, it would make sense that they might refer to the entire canyon by the name of the first major settlement they encountered when venturing up the valley, which would have been Giusewa.

6. Scholes 1938:63.

7. Hammond and Rey 1953, 2:610, 687.

8. Scholes 1942:26; Hammond and Rey 1953, 2:679–680.

9. M. Simmons 1979:181; Riley 1999:110; D. Weber 1999b:4.

10. Scholes 1942:55–57; Broughton 1993; Knaut 1995:88–117.

11. Scholes 1942:59; Hodge et al. 1945:43; Spicer 1962:160–161; Kessell 1979:110.

12. Kidder 1932:86–88, 96; 1958:236–240; Montgomery et al. 1949:157; Smith et al. 1966:42–44; Wiget 1982:186; Riley 1999:124.

13. Scholes 1936:151–156; Riley 1999:96.

14. Scholes 1942:12–13.

15. Hackett 1937, 3:141.

16. Ibid., 234; Hackett and Shelby 1942, 2:226.

17. Hackett 1937, 3:170, 202, 214–16, 259–60; Scholes 1942:7; Gutiérrez 1991:76, 123–24; Riley 1999:91–92, 171.

18. Hopi Dictionary Project 1998:607.

19. Wiget 1982:184–86.

20. Hodge et al. 1945:69.

21. A general census of the province was reportedly conducted in 1660 (Vetancurt 1971 [1697]), but no copies of this survey have surfaced to date.

22. Scholes 1930:97; Simmons 1979:192; Riley 1999:203.

23. Hammond and Rey 1953, 1:485.

24. Hackett 1937, 3:108.

25. In his critique of studies of Native American depopulation as Eurocentric and colonialist, Wilcox overlooks the work of indigenous scholars on Native American demography, most notably that of Russell Thornton (Cherokee) (Thornton 1981, 1982, 1986, 1987, 1990a, 1990b).

26. Wilcox states that the presence of Rio Grande Glaze Ware ceramics at ancestral Jemez sites "supports the notion that ancestral Jemez settlements were periodically resettled during periods of conflict" (2009:175). This may be the case, but the data are insufficient to support this conclusion at the present time. The presence of Glaze Ware ceramics (Glaze E and F specifically) does document the presence of people at these sites in the early-to-mid seventeenth century. However, we do not yet have an idea of the size of these populations, nor whether this was a reoccupation of these sites or was a continuation of earlier, uninterrupted settlement. Wilcox's argument is based on studies that document only the presence/absence of late Glaze Wares at these sites, but not their frequencies in these assemblages. An analysis of relative frequencies of Glaze Ware ceramics at the sites in question would help to clarify this picture significantly. Furthermore, if production of Glaze F begins in the first half of the seventeenth century (possibly as early as 1625), as suggested by the most recent chronologies cited by Wilcox (2009:163)—those of Sundt (1987) and Schaafsma (1995, 1996)—then the presence of these ceramics could support the Spanish documentary evidence noting that multiple large Jemez pueblos were occupied in the region in the early 1600s, but were depopulated by the 1630s–50s (see Liebmann 2006:144–48).

There are other problems concerning Jemez archaeology in Wilcox's 2009 analysis, including the grouping of Jemez Black-on-white in the Tewa Series (2009:170) and the identification of LA 2049 and 2048 as Jemez sites (Wilcox 2009:173). LA 2049 is not located in the Jemez Region. This site is an ancestral Santa Ana village located more than thirty-two km (approximately twenty miles) outside of the archaeologically defined Jemez Province. Cerro Colorado (LA 2048), while located in the Jemez Province, is not an ancestral Jemez site. All the available documentary, oral traditional, and archaeological evidence concurs that Cerro Colorado was constructed and occupied by Zia and Santa Ana peoples, possibly with some Kewa residents as well (see chapter 8, infra).

27. Winship 1922:105.
28. Hammond and Rey 1953, 2:1059.
29. Hackett 1937, 3:186–187; M. Simmons 1979:184.
30. Hackett 1937, 3:204.
31. Ibid., 3:271–272.
32. Ibid., 3:17, 299; Kessell 1979:221; Schroeder 1979:241; M. Simmons 1979:184.
33. M. Simmons 1980:12; Hackett and Shelby 1942, 2:245.
34. Malotki 1993:288.
35. Ibid.:341, 357–359, 375. This oral tradition refers to social conditions leading up to the destruction of Awat'ovi in 1700. Like many oral traditions it does not specify absolute (calendar) dates, resulting in an undefined temporal scale (i.e., whether it refers to pre-1680 contexts or events that occurred between 1680 and 1700 is uncertain).
36. Scholes 1938:63, 68–69, 95–96; Hackett and Shelby 1942, 2:299; Sando 1982:118; Ivey 1991:10; Kessell and Hendricks 1992:42 n9; Riley 1999:21.
37. Hackett and Shelby 1942, 2:289–90, 300–301.

Chapter 3

1. Kessell 1979:238; Sando 1992:179; Agoyo 2005:xii.
2. Ortiz 1980:20–21; Hackett and Shelby 1942, 2:246–248, 385.
3. Hackett and Shelby 1942, 1:5, 14–15; 2:246–248.
4. Reff 1995:64, 76–77; Perez de Ribas 1645:685.
5. Hackett and Shelby 1942, 2:308.
6. Ibid., 1:117, 2:305–18; Chávez 1967:88–89; Reff 1995:68.
7. Hackett and Shelby 1942, 1:4, 2:236; Riley 1999:218–219.
8. Hackett and Shelby 1942, 1:59.
9. Ibid., 1:13–14.
10. Catití is identified both as a mestizo and as a coyote in Spanish records (Hackett and Shelby 1942, 1:66, 2:236, 241, 270).
11. Hackett and Shelby 1942, 2:241, 247, 263; De Marco 2000:4152.
12. Knaut 1995:140.
13. Hackett 1937, 3:217.
14. Hackett and Shelby 1942, 2:299; Kessell 1980.
15. Ibid., 2:234.
16. Ibid., 2:246.
17. Ibid., 1:xxxviii, 3; Kessell 1979:232.
18. Hackett and Shelby 1942, 2:234; De Marco 2000:389.
19. Hackett and Shelby 1942, 1:16, 25, 2:234, 247, 382.
20. Ibid., 1:3.
21. Catua and Omtua named the superiors who gave them these orders: Pedro Situ and Diego Misu. The fact that they gave two names suggests that Situ and Misu were the war captains at Tesuque at that time (following the tradition of paired appointments, one from each moiety). This corroborates later testimony, which noted that Po'pay assigned the war captains the responsibility for distributing the knotted cords among the pueblos (Ibid., 2:234). Situ and Misu were thus likely part of Po'pay's inner circle.
22. Sanchez 1983:144.
23. Hackett and Shelby 1942, 1:4–5. There is considerable confusion regarding the date planned for the uprising (see discussion in Hackett and Shelby 1942, 1:xxv n. 10), which seems to have originally been set for August 13. Shortly before the capture of Catua and Omtua the date seems to have been changed to August 11.
24. Hackett and Shelby 1942, 1:7; 2:246–247.
25. Ibid., 1:6.
26. Riley 1999:48, 77, 109.
27. Hackett and Shelby 1942, 1:21.
28. Espinosa 1988:35–36.
29. Wiget 1982:186–187.
30. Adams n.d.:160–161.
31. Hackett and Shelby 1942, 1:26, 177–178, 2:231.
32. Ibid., 1:21.
33. Kessell and Hendricks 1992:549.

34. Hackett and Shelby 1942, 1:66–67, 80–81.
35. Cushing 1896:331.
36. Wiget 1996:476–77.
37. Cushing 1896:330.
38. Wiget 1996:478–479.
39. Hackett and Shelby 1942, 1:8–10.
40. Ibid., 1:71–72, 2:170–171.
41. Ibid., 1:10, 97, 151, 2:115.
42. Ibid., 1:64–66.
43. Ibid., 1:81, 2:330.
44. Ibid., 1:96.
45. Ibid., 1:7–8.
46. Ibid., 1:11, 18.
47. Ibid., 1:13, 98.
48. Ibid., 1:12–17, 98–103.
49. Ibid., 2:233.

Chapter 4

1. Hackett and Shelby 1942, 1:20.
2. Ibid., 1:73–74. The factors behind the initial exclusion of the Piros from Po'pay's plans remains an enduring mystery, particularly in light of their history of anticolonial resistance and rebellion prior to the 1680s. See Ibid., 2:299.
3. Ibid., 2:233–53; Sanchez 1983:138.
4. Twitchell 1914, 2:272; Silverberg 1970:133; Sanchez 1983:134–35.
5. Twitchell 1914, 2:272–73.
6. Ibid., 2:272.
7. Hackett and Shelby 1942, 2:235; Ortiz 1980:19.
8. Sanchez 1983:135.
9. Hackett and Shelby 1942, 2:247.
10. Bloom and Mitchell 1938; Hackett and Shelby 1942, 1:96, 2:240; Montgomery et al. 1949; Smith et al. 1966; Hayes 1974.
11. Hackett and Shelby 1942, 1, 13, 2:203–9.
12. Ibid., 2:203–6, 260; Montgomery et al. 1949:56; Ellis 1956:32; Kessell and Hendricks 1992:549–50; Lippard 2010:202.
13. Adams n.d., 39–40.
14. Hackett and Shelby 1942, 2:286; Hayes 1974; see Ivey 1998 for a discussion of the case at Pecos.
15. Hackett and Shelby 1942, 2:286.
16. Ibid., 2:215–31; 260–69.
17. Ibid., 2:207.
18. Sanchez 1983:134–37. When Baltasar and Tomás arrived in El Paso in late March, they denied that this conversation ever took place to the Spaniards, saying "There was no such convocation; it was an invention of Shimitihua's to save himself."

19. Hackett and Shelby 1942, 2:239, 247; Sanchez 1983:138.
20. Hackett and Shelby 1942, 2:274, 296; Sanchez 1983.
21. Hackett and Shelby 1942, 1:cxxi–cxxiv.
22. Ibid., 2:207–8, 218–19.
23. Ibid., 2:226, 236.
24. Ibid., 1:cli, 2:269.
25. Initial reports to the Pueblos (carried by two Tiwas who fled the scene) indicated erroneously that Otermín's takeover of Isleta had resulted in the deaths of all Isleta's Native inhabitants (Ibid., 2:236).
26. Ibid., 2:274.
27. Ibid., 2:308–10.

Chapter 5

1. Hackett and Shelby 1942, 1:80, 110.
2. Gutiérrez 1991:131; Kessell et al. 1998:237, 371.
3. Adams n.d. 158–159; Espinosa 1988:35; Kessell et al. 1998:342–343.
4. Kessell et al. 1998:237.
5. Pueblo testimonies delivered to the Spaniards in 1681, 1682, and again in 1692 stated that the Jemez left their mission village when the Spaniards returned in 1681 (Hackett and Shelby 1942, 2:236, 360; Kessell et al. 1995:203).
6. Bloom and Mitchell 1938:108.
7. Kessell et al. 1995:113, 1998:352.
8. Morrow 1996:29.
9. Translation from Sando 1979b:419; The prefix of "LA" denotes "Laboratory of Anthropology," and is the nomenclature utilized in the State of New Mexico's Archaeological Records Management Section's database.
10. Any remains of vigas recovered from Patokwa in the future may reflect post-1694 repairs as well as the original 1680s construction, as many of the original vigas were removed and reused in the construction of another village, Astialakwa (which was subsequently burned following a 1694 battle, see chapter 9). In a letter dated September 1, 1694, Vargas notes that on "entering into the pueblo on the mesa [Patokwa], that not only had the enemies abandoned it, but they also had taken the doors from most of their houses, and the metates from all of them. From others they had taken some beams for construction on the peñol" (Kessell et al. 1998:367).
11. Kessell and Hendricks 1992:520–522; see also Elliott 2002:57.
12. This older village may have been called *Ka'atusekwa* (translation: "place where they hit or ring the stones" [Harrington 1916:397]).
13. Anecdotal reports suggest that this damage was done in hopes of recovering a golden mission bell believed to have been buried on the site by Spanish priests, a legend popular at seventeenth-century mission sites throughout the Southwest United States (Elliott 2002:50).
14. Roney 1996:150; Cameron 1999b:207; see also Creamer et al. 1993:16; LeBlanc 1999:65; Liebmann 2006:277.

15. Benavides 1916 [1630]:121.

16. These entrances were noted by the Spaniards in the 1690s, but three of the four (the northeast, northwest, and southwest entrances) were sealed when colonial forces under Diego de Vargas garrisoned Patokwa in 1694 (Kessell et al. 1998:328, 335, 370), see chapter 9.

17. The room estimates listed here pertain only to the seventeenth-century component of Patokwa. Because of the degraded nature of the Classic Period architecture and the fact that no quantitative measurements of room sizes could be attained from surface remains in this area, no estimates of individual room dimensions or counts were attempted for the earlier component.

18. Based on these assumptions, I created the reconstruction of Patokwa by superimposing a CAD-generated architectural model consisting of 2.5 × 5.0 meter rooms on a plan view of the Patokwa topographic data. These calculations yield an estimate of 192 ground-floor rooms (plus two kivas) in what is presumed to be the original, 1681 component of Patokwa. In order to account for second- and third-story rooms I analyzed the topographic variation within individual room blocks to determine the intrasite differences in room elevations. Based on analogies with other ancestral pueblo sites, I assumed that as pueblo stone masonry architecture degrades, each story results in 0.75 to 1.0 meters of rubble. In other words, mounded remains of pueblo architecture one meter in height or less are assumed to have originally stood one story tall, mounds one-and-a-half to two meters are thought to have stood two stories; and mounds two to three meters in height are assumed to have been originally three stories tall. By applying these estimates to the spatial information collected at Patokwa and projecting the plan view of ground-story rooms onto the topographic data, I was able to infer the height of individual rooms. Assuming the rooms damaged by the bulldozer cut in the northern and central roomblocks were two stories tall, these techniques yield an estimate of 359 total rooms (excluding the kivas) constructed at Patokwa in 1681 (additional rooms were added later in the Revolt era and after the Spanish reconquest, as described below). The final model of Patokwa as it might have appeared following the initial construction in 1681 was created by merging the estimated room count data with the room height projection.

19. Vetancurt 1971 [1697]; see also Bloom and Mitchell 1938:96.

20. Hackett and Shelby 1942, 2:361.

21. Ibid., 2:236.

22. D. Weber 2005:72.

23. see Schaafsma 2002:242–245 for an extended treatment of the derivation of the term *Navajo*.

24. Scholes 1938:63, 95–96.

25. Hackett 1937, 3:186; Sando 1982:118; Brugge 2002:7.

26. Brugge 2002:8.

27. Kessell et al. 1995:203.

28. Twitchell 1914, 2:277; Reiter 1938:36; John 1975:120–121.

29. Walz 1951:126.
30. Linton 1940; Norcini 2005:544.
31. Hackett and Shelby 1942, 1:cc; 2:357; Kessell et al. 1995:113, 416, 445.
32. Kidder 1917; 1958:108; Kessell 1979:7, 26, 232, 241, 246.
33. Hackett and Shelby 1942, 2:235.
34. Ibid., 2:240.
35. Kessell et al. 1998:402.
36. Bloom 1922:25.
37. Kessell et al. 1998:402–403.
38. Walz 1951:126.
39. Room estimates pertain to the seventeenth-century component of Boletsakwa only. Because of the degraded nature of the Classic Period architecture and the fact that no quantitative measurements of room sizes could be attained from surficial data in this area, no estimates of individual room dimensions or counts were attempted for the earlier component.
40. Unshagi was chosen for comparison because it is the only pre-Colonial pueblo in the Jemez Province for which accurate data regarding the room size of more than eight rooms has been published.
41. Hodge et al. 1945:169–170.
42. Kessell et al. 1995: 416, 445; Kessell et al. 1998: 403, 406, 586; Espinosa 1988:129, 149.

Chapter 6

1. Hackett and Shelby 1942, 2:212.
2. Ibid., 2:248; De Marco 2000:416.
3. Hackett and Shelby 1942, 2:248.
4. There are a few notable exceptions to this rule, including LA 123 (Unshagi), LA 499 (Setukwa), LA 541 (Nonishagi), LA 679 (Giusewa), and LA 403, which were all built in valley-bottom locations. However, this is just a small minority of the thirty-two documented large (50+ rooms) ancestral Jemez villages in the Jemez Province (Elliott 1986:178–181).
5. Hodge et al. 1945:69.
6. Morrow 1996:29.
7. A significant amount of Kwahe'e Black-on-white ceramics at Kotyiti (20 percent of the total assemblage) indicates an earlier, pre-Hispanic (Coalition period, AD 1025–1175) occupation existed at that site (Preucel et al. 2002:81–83).
8. Kessell et al. 1995:203.
9. Morrow 1996:29.
10. Hazen-Hammond 1988:21.
11. Although the plan of Santa Fe was probably conceived as a grid, the streets and buildings evolved to modify this plan significantly within the first 150 years of settlement. "Rather than stay in compact settlements," notes Chris Wilson, "Spanish settlers across northern New Mexico instead moved their houses closer to their

fields. . . . In Santa Fe by 1766, houses built beside their owner's fields stretched for three miles up and down the valley" (1997:34). See also M. Simmons 1969.

12. Unfortunately this hypothesis is difficult to disprove at the present time, as the modern settlement of Walatowa/Jemez Pueblo presumably sits atop the ruins of the original mission settlement.

13. Hackett and Shelby 1942, 2:248; De Marco 2000:416.

14. Kessell and Hendricks 1992:515; Kessell et al. 1995: 416, 445.

15. Kessell and Hendricks 1992:521–522.

16. De Marco 2000:416.

17. One possible exception is the southern portion of LA 132/133, Kiatsukwa; but this pueblo also contains at least three kivas (Elliott 1986:176).

18. Jemez tribal representative, personal communication 2007.

19. Kessell et al. 1995:416, 445; 1998:403–406, 586.

20. Hackett and Shelby 1942, 2:248.

21. Smith et al. 1966:Figures 75, 78, 79; Harlow 1973:Plate 32e; Frank and Harlow 1974:Plate X.

22. Reiter 1938; Elliott 1994; Whatley and Delaney 1995.

23. Liebmann 2008:366. The small percentage of Jemez Black-on-white at Patokwa and Boletsakwa likely represents vessels produced prior to the Revolt of 1680 and curated for a time after the Spaniards' ouster.

Chapter 7

1. A *cavate* is a human-made cave dwelling carved into a stone (volcanic tuff) cliff face. Although the cavates are typically all that remain today, many would have originally been fronted by free-standing pueblo rooms, including the cavate described here (M-100, Bandelier National Monument).

2. Hackett and Shelby 1942, 2:235.

3. Twitchell 1914, 2:272–273; Kessell 2002:148.

4. Kessell and Hendricks 1992:549–550.

5. Hackett and Shelby 1942, 2:235.

6. Ibid., 2:248.

7. Hammond and Rey 1953:484, 626, 634, 645, 660.

8. Kessell and Hendricks 1992:392.

9. Hackett and Shelby 1942, 2:225.

10. Hodge 1937; Hackett and Shelby 1942, 2: 207, 225, 259; Montgomery et al. 1949:80; Smith et al. 1966.

11. Kessell et al. 1995:444–446.

12. Chávez 1980:32; Seifert n.d.:11–14; Kessell and Hendricks 1992:393.

13. Kessell et al. 1995:495.

14. Ibid.:190.

15. Ibid.:482.

16. Although it could be argued that some form of pan-Pueblo identity accompanied the Chaco Phenomenon between AD 850–1150 in the American Southwest, I argue

that while a singular Chacoan identity (if in fact such a concept existed) may have incorporated greater numbers of ancestral Pueblo peoples, Chacoan ethnicity was not as comprehensive as Po'pay's pan-Pueblo identity. Although much shorter lived, the ethnogenesis of the 1680s incorporated nearly every Pueblo person and community in the Pueblo world at the time, whereas small but not insignificant populations of Puebloan peoples persisted outside of the Chacoan sphere of influence between the ninth and thirteenth centuries in what is now the Southwestern United States.

17. Today the base level of identification for most "Pueblo Peoples" is that of their individual home village (i.e., Jemez, Acoma, Cochiti, Zia, Santa Clara, etc.), with Hopi persons often identifying first with their clan. Above that, some will identify according to ethnolinguistic divisions (Tewa, Tiwa, Keres, Hopi). Only after these, if pressed, will these people identify as "Pueblo," typically in opposition to other regional tribes or groupings (Navajo, Apache, or Ute).

18. Kessell and Hendricks 1992:515, 521–22; Kessell et al. 1995: 416, 445; Preucel 2006:232.

19. Pecos Archaeological Survey 1996:52.

20. Kidder and Amsden 1931:131; Lambert 1981; Harlow et al. 2005:66

21. Kidder and Kidder 1917:338; Kidder and Shepard 1936:287–290, 541–547. Plain Red pottery is also sometimes equated with "Salinas Red," previously reported in the Salinas and Cochiti districts (Toulouse 1949; Warren 1979:239; Hayes et al. 1981:101). This type of unpainted pottery increased in frequency through the seventeenth century in the latter levels at the Salinas Pueblos of Abó, Quarai, and Las Humanas (Hayes et al. 1981:101). The excavators of these pueblos "considered Salinas Redware at Abó to be virtually the same as Kidder's 'Plain Red' ware at Pecos" (Ivey 1998:135).

22. Due to the polished exteriors of these vessels, I characterize Plain Red pottery as a decorated ware in distinction to the rough-surfaced Utility wares, even though it lacks any other decorative elements.

23. Kidder and Shepard 1936:547; Warren 1979:239; Lentz 2004:51; Liebmann 2006:355.

24. Undecorated redware ceramics may have been produced in small quantities prior to the Spanish colonization of the northern Rio Grande, but extensive production began only in the early to mid seventeenth century (Pecos Archaeological Survey 1996:52–54).

25. It is possible to determine the probable locus of the production of these Plain Red pots through an examination of the tempering materials used in their production. As noted by Shepard, tempering traditions among the Rio Grande pueblos were generally conservative and geographically localized: "Extreme conservatism in the selection of temper is illustrated by the customs of some Pueblo potters. The Rio Grande potters of San Ildefonso, Santa Clara, and San Juan use fine volcanic ash, and the prehistoric pottery of the region shows a continuous use of this temper for certain types back to the earliest times. Zia pottery is tempered with ground basalt, and the same temper occurs in the prehistoric Glaze-paint ware of this area. Again, Acoma

and Zuni potters use potsherd, which carries on the tradition of the prehistoric peoples in these localities" (Shepard 1956:164). In the Jemez Province, volcanic tuff was used to temper Jemez Black-on-white vessels throughout its 350-year history, as well as a large portion of pre-Revolt Utility wares (Shepard 1938; Warren quoted in Lambert 1981:220). The majority of the Glaze Wares found at pre-1680 Jemez sites were tempered with basalt, however, and are thought to have been obtained in trade from pueblos in the Puname region (Shepard 1938:207; Warren quoted in Lambert 1981:228).

Analysis of the tempering materials of the Plain Red pottery at Patokwa and Boletsakwa reveals two primary tempering traditions: tuff and basalt. Of the total combined Plain Red assemblage from both sites, slightly more than one-quarter (25.9 percent) was tempered with tuff, identical to the temper used in the Jemez Black-on-white manufactured prior to 1680 (D. Hill in Liebmann 2006:458–467). This strongly suggests that at least one-quarter of the Plain Red vessels used at Patokwa and Boletsakwa were locally made within the Jemez Province. And in fact, at Boletsakwa the tuff-tempered variety comprises more than half of the assemblage (56 percent), indicating that the majority of Plain Red found there can be reasonably assumed to have been made within the walls of that village.

At Patokwa, the pattern is slightly different: 20.8 percent of the Plain Red is tempered with tuff, but more than 78 percent was not (with basalt used instead). As basalt was the favored tempering material of the Puname pueblos of Zia and Santa Ana prior to 1680, it might stand to reason that the basalt-tempered pottery at Patokwa represents vessels obtained in trade from their Zia and Santa Ana neighbors. But the assumption that the samples exhibiting basalt temper were made exclusively by Zia/Santa Ana potters and the tuff-tempered variety were made by the Jemez is problematic; the simple correlation of basalt temper with non-Jemez manufacture is complicated by the fact that basalt outcrops occur naturally in the immediate vicinity of Patokwa. Thus it seems reasonable to entertain the possibility that Jemez potters at Patokwa may have incorporated new tempering materials—specifically basalt—after 1681 in order to take advantage of local resources. As Shepard (1956:164) notes: "Changes in paste composition are often found when a stratigraphic sequence of pottery types is followed through. In all such instances the cause of change, whether a native development or the result of the influence of people with a different ceramic tradition or change in population, should be sought. Premature generalizations regarding conservatism should not be allowed to limit or discourage such investigations."

Such a shift in tempering technology has precedence in the Jemez Province, where the patterns of Utility ware production prove particularly instructive. Utility wares are thought to have been locally manufactured and not widely traded at ancestral Jemez pueblos (Kidder and Shepard 1936:297; Reiter 1938:103; Shepard 1938:209). At Unshagi, the temper of Utility wares changed from predominantly tuff in the earliest (fourteenth century) levels to predominantly andesite in the latest (seventeenth century) strata (Shepard 1938:207). It is not entirely surprising, then, that the Utility wares of Patokwa bear similar evidence of a shift in tempering technology. As with Plain Red, tuff and basalt are the two main varieties of temper exhibited among the Utility wares at Patokwa, comprising 17.5 percent and 80 percent, respectively. Assuming that Utility wares continued to be locally made after the Revolt (as they were before 1680), the fact that the majority was tempered with basalt suggests that Jemez potters adopted this new method after moving to Patokwa in 1681. The tuff-tempering tradition persisted as well, albeit to a lesser extent. But basalt tempering is present in the Utility wares of Patokwa in nearly identical frequencies as that of the Plain Red assemblage (Liebmann 2006:368), suggesting that, like Utility wares, Plain Red was made locally at Patokwa as well. This shift to basalt-tempering was likely effected in part by the easy availability of basalt at their new home, but may have also been influenced by the increase in migration among Pueblo peoples that characterized life in the wake of the Pueblo Revolt (Schroeder 1972; Herr and Clark 1997).

26. Harlow, Anderson, and Lanmon (2005:67) suggest that "fragments of Jemez River Polychrome and cognate types . . . occur in significant proportions at the Jemez refugee sites," based presumably on their collections of whole and partially reconstructed vessels from "Jemez refugee sites." However, controlled ceramic sampling from all four known "refugee sites" in the Jemez Province reveals that decorated Jemez River ceramics comprise just 0.1 to 3.6 percent of these assemblages (see tables 7.1, 7.2, and 8.1; Liebmann 2006:350–355). Were we able to establish definitively at which of the "Jemez refugee sites" these vessels were found, we would have a much better understanding of the frequency and spatio-temporal boundaries of this type.

27. Although Harlow, Anderson, and Lanmon note numerous similarities among Jemez River Polychrome and Jemez Black-on-white ceramics (most notably paint styles and temper types), they do not seem to entertain the possibility that Jemez River Polychromes could have been made by Jemez potters themselves, despite the fact that the majority of examples they discuss and/or illustrate were found at one or more unidentified "Jemez refugee site[s]" (Harlow et al. 2005:66–75).

28. Capone and Preucel 2002; Mills 2002; Mobley-Tanaka 2002:81; Harlow et al. 2005:42–43.

29. The cap step motif may be derivative of earlier "capitan" and "hand" figures, however (Harlow et al. 2005:62).

30. Hodge et al. 1945:70.

Chapter 8

1. Pérez de Luxán 1929:83–85.
2. Hammond and Rey 1940:233.
3. Hackett and Shelby 1942, 1:66–67.
4. Ibid., 1:81; Kessell et al. 1995:145.
5. Kessell and Hendricks 1992:519.
6. The Punames did temporarily withdraw from their villages during Otermín's attempted reconquest in 1681 (Hackett and Shelby 1942, 2:236, 360, 382, 394),

but returned to their homes in early 1682 when the Spaniards left the northern Rio Grande (Sanchez 1983:145). In contrast, the pueblos of Jemez, Kewa, San Felipe, Cochiti, and San Marcos were all unoccupied for most of the Pueblo Revolt era, with San Lazaro, Galisteo, and San Cristóbal permanently depopulated during this period (Lippard 2010:213).

7. Morrow 1996:29.

8. Hammond and Rey 1953:337–339, 346.

9. Hackett and Shelby 1942, 2:263.

10. Ibid., 2:241.

11. By the early 1700s, glaze-paint technology ceased to be used among all Pueblo potters. Rather than a nativistic response (à la Zuni), this cessation appears to have been related to colonial restrictions on the Pueblos' access to lead mines (Dillingham and Elliott 1992:128–130; Snow 1982:260).

12. Hackett and Shelby 1942, 2:295; Sanchez 1983:145.

13. Vélez de Escalante 1983 [1778]:8; Walz 1951:180.

14. Twitchell 1914, 2:277.

15. Many Isletans were taken to El Paso del Norte with the retreating Spaniards in 1681, while other southern Tiwas had migrated to various refugee villages after the pueblos of Alameda, Puaray, and Sandia were destroyed by Otermín's forces after the Revolt (Hackett and Shelby 1942, 2:357–361).

16. Lippard 2010:213.

17. Bayer 1994:307 n.72.

18. Kessell and Hendricks 1992:24. There is some controversy regarding which ancestral Puname site the Santa Anas occupied in 1687, and thus which site was destroyed by the Spaniards that year (Ellis 1956:30; Bayer 1994:70–71). Santa Ana oral tradition holds that it was the site of Tamaya (LA 8975; Ellis 1956:30), and the historical references to the battle present no obvious reason to doubt that this was the case.

19. Bayer 1994:71.

20. Accurate assessments of the frequency of various types of pottery in the LA 2049 assemblage are not possible based on the collections currently held at the Laboratory of Anthropology in Santa Fe. These collections were made with an attempt to demonstrate the variability of the ceramics at LA 2049, not to provide representative frequencies.

21. Kessell et al. 1995:145.

22. Adams n.d.:156.

23. Sigüenza y Góngora 1932 [1692]:58.

24. Kessell and Hendricks 1992:25–26.

25. Twitchell 1914, 2:277; Sigüenza y Góngora, 1932 [1692]:57–58.

26. Kessell and Hendricks 1992:25–26; Kessell et al. 1995:217.

27. Kessell et al. 1995:117, 145, 201, 217.

28. Bayer 1994:71; see also Ellis 1956:32, 1966b:100.

29. Adams n.d.:157.

30. Ibid.:159–161; Kessell 1994:34.
31. Flint and Flint 2008.
32. Twitchell 1914, 2:276–277.
33. Kessell and Hendricks 1992:557, 609.
34. Ibid.:518–20; Kessell et al. 1998:234, 323–24.
35. Kessell and Hendricks 1992:518; Kessell et al. 1995:435.
36. The Spaniards do mention baptizing "123 men, women, and children of all ages" at Cerro Colorado on October 24, 1692 (Ibid.:518), and an additional 24 children born between October 1692 and November 25, 1693 (Kessell et al. 1995:435).
37. This is a conservative estimate, as it does not account for the Santa Anas and Kewas that were reportedly lodged at Cerro Colorado as well.
38. Ellis 1956:31–32; Kessell and Hendricks 1992:431, 518; Kessell et al. 1995:113–117, 201, 434; 1998:234, 323–324; Pueblo of Jemez tribal representative, personal communication 2004.
39. In the absence of evidence concerning wall bonding and abutment patterns (D. Wilcox 1975), wall-facing (Reid and Shimada 1982:14), or dendrochronology, however, it is impossible to definitively determine the construction sequence at Cerro Colorado.
40. Kessell and Hendricks 1992:431, 513, 518–19, 557, 608; Riley 1999:218.
41. Kessell and Hendricks 1992:488n68.
42. Ibid.:431, 557–58, 609; Kessell et al. 1995:113, 408.
43. Hackett and Shelby 1942, 1:66–67.

Chapter 9

1. Kessell and Hendricks 1992:431, 513–14.
2. Ibid.:454.
3. Ibid.:409.
4. Ibid.:415–416.
5. Ibid.:518–519, 608.
6. Ibid.:518–519.
7. Ibid.:519.
8. Ibid.:601.
9. Hendricks and Wilson 1996:114–115.
10. Kessell and Hendricks 1992:521.
11. Ibid.:521.
12. Ibid.:522.
13. Ibid.:601; Kessell et al. 1995:203
14. Kessell et al. 1995:406.
15. Kessell and Hendricks 1992:467–468.
16. Kessell et al. 1995:6–7.
17. Ibid.:405.
18. Ibid.:401, 429–434.
19. Kessell et al. 1998:400.

20. Ibid.:33.

21. Kessell et al. 1995:404, 427, 540.

22. Ibid.:405.

23. Ibid.:404, 408, 434–436.

24. Ibid.:404, 441–42.

25. Ibid.:503–533; Kessell 2008:154.

26. Ibid.:538.

27. Kessell et al. 1998:139–170.

28. Ibid.:192–194.

29. Paul Tosa, personal communication, 2003.

30. Reiter 1938:21; Sando 1982:12. Bloom (1931:162n5) translates Mashtiashinkwa as "place of the index finger," but Jemez tribal members concur that this translation is incorrect (Jemez tribal representative 2005).

31. Any remains of vigas recovered from Astialakwa in the future could be expected to return dates in the early 1680s as well as (or instead of) the mid-1690s. Vargas reported that some of the original vigas from Patokwa were removed and reused in the construction of Astialakwa (and subsequently burned following the 1694 battle). In a letter dated September 1, 1694, Vargas notes that on "entering into the pueblo on the mesa [Patokwa], that not only had the enemies abandoned it, but they also had taken the doors from most of their houses, and the metates from all of them. From others they had taken some beams for construction on the peñol" (Kessell et al. 1998:367).

32. Kessell et al. 1995:404, 441–442; 1998:367. The ceramic assemblage confirms that Astialakwa is a single-component site, with no significant settlement of the peñol either before or after the 1690s occupation, with the exception of a brief, three-week reoccupation of Astialakwa in 1696 (Liebmann 2006:321, 350; see Epilogue).

33. Kessell et al. 1998:367.

34. Ibid.:349–50, 368, 374; Liebmann 2006:297–300. Using the reported figures, the average floor area per person at Astialakwa can be calculated at 3.3 m^2 per person (total floor area: 2020.5 m^2). This figure is lower than the 5.1 m^2 estimated at Kotyiti (Preucel 1998), a result that is to be expected considering Dohm's (1990) assertion that houses in nucleated pueblos such as Kotyiti typically allocate more floor area per person than houses in dispersed villages such as Astialakwa.

35. Kessell et al. 1998:327, 368; Liebmann 2006:315–17.

36. Kessell et al. 1998:323, 366.

37. Ibid.:234, 279–81.

38. Ibid.:320.

39. Simpson 1852:22.

40. Kessell et al. 1998:324–366.

41. Hammond and Rey 1966:187–188; Kessell 2010.

42. Kessell et al. 1998:325.

43. Ibid.:367; note also that the reference to throwing large stones down upon the Spaniards could relate to the name of the pueblo, "grinding-stone lowering place."

44. Ibid.:368.
45. Ibid.:325.
46. Ibid.:325–327, 374.
47. Ibid.:325–327.
48. Ibid.:332.
49. Ibid.:369.
50. Ibid.:337, 342–43, 369.
51. Ibid.:354, 376.

Epilogue

1. Kessell et al. 1998:402–406.
2. Ibid.:586.
3. Espinosa 1988:149, 158, 170. There is some confusion regarding the original name of the 1690s mission at Walatowa. Espinosa (who also confuses San Diego de la Congregación with San Diego del Monte [Espinosa 1988:19]) published notes written in the margin of a document dated December 20, 1695, acknowledging that both San Diego de Jemez and San José [sic] de Jemez had seen the document (Espinosa 1988:158). The name San José presumably refers to the mission at Walatowa later identified as San Juan; regardless, this note verifies the existence of two Jemez missions in 1695.
4. Ibid.:157, 167; Kessell et al. 1998:673, 679.
5. Espinosa 1988:200.
6. Ibid.:233.
7. Kessell et al. 1998:688.
8. Espinosa 1988:200.
9. Ibid.:229.
10. Kessell et al. 1998:723.
11. Ibid.:861.
12. Espinosa 1988:250; Kessell et al. 1998:750.
13. Bloom and Mitchell 1938:108n54; Espinosa 1988:244; Kessell et al. 1998:750–511. There is some confusion as to which San Diego mission this refers. The mention of the existence of San Juan de los Jemez in the same year suggests that it does in fact refer to San Diego del Monte at Patokwa (Bloom and Mitchell 1938:108n54). However, Sando (1982:121–122) and Elliott (2002:58) have proposed that it refers to San Diego de la Congregacion at Walatowa.
14. Kessell et al. 1998:751.
15. Espinosa 1988:252.
16. Kessell et al. 1998:748–51, 761, 879.
17. Espinosa 1988:271; Kessell et al. 1998:778, 792, 796–98, 881.
18. In a report dated July 21, 1696, the Custodio stated that animals had consumed the flesh of Fray Francisco's corpse. This suggests that he was never buried, and thus that Patokwa was likely vacated immediately after the uprising on June 4, 1696 (Espinosa 1988:245).

19. Ibid.:271; Kessell et al. 1998:792, 796, 881.

20. Ibid:969, 978, 984, 1004, 1030, 1103.

21. Bloom and Mitchell 1938:107–108; Sando 1982:121; Kessell et al. 1998:1064, 1102; Elliott 2002:58.

22. Bloom and Mitchell 1938:108 n54.

23. Hackett 1937, 3:369–76.

Bibliography

Abu-Lughod, Lila

1990   The Romance of Resistance: Tracing Transformations of Power through Bedouin
        Women. *American Ethnologist* 17(1):41–55.

Adams, E. Charles

1981   The View from the Hopi Mesas. In *The Protohistoric Period in the North Ameri-
        can Southwest, AD 1450–1700*, edited by D. R. Wilcox and W. B. Masse,
        pp. 321–35. Arizona State University Anthropological Research Papers No. 24,
        Tempe.

1989   Passive Resistance: Hopi Responses to Spanish Contact and Conquest. In *Colum-
        bian Consequences: Vol. 1. Archaeological and Historical Perspectives on the Spanish
        Borderlands West*, edited by D. H. Thomas, pp. 77–91. Smithsonian Institution
        Press, Washington, DC.

1991   *The Origin and Development of the Pueblo Katsina Cult.* University of Arizona
        Press, Tucson.

Adams, E. Charles, and Andrew I. Duff, eds.

2004   *The Protohistoric Pueblo World, A.D. 1275–1600.* University of Arizona Press,
        Tucson.

Adams, Eleanor B.

n.d   Translation of Velez de Escalante's "Extracto de Noticias." Box 13, Folder 21.
        Center for Southwest Research, University Libraries, University of New Mexico,
        Albuquerque.

Adas, Michael

1979   *Prophets of Rebellion: Millenarian Protest Movements against the European Colonial
        Order.* University of North Carolina Press, Chapel Hill.

Agoyo, Herman

2002   The Holy War. In *Archaeologies of the Pueblo Revolt*, edited by R. W. Preucel,
        pp. xi–xiv. University of New Mexico Press, Albuquerque.

2005   The Tricentennial Commemoration. In *Po'pay: Leader of the First American
        Revolution,* edited by J. S. Sando and H. Agoyo, pp. 93–106. Clear Light,
        Santa Fe.

Alcock, Susan E.

2002   *Archaeologies of the Greek Past: Landscape, Monuments, and Memories*. Cambridge University Press, Cambridge, UK.

Althusser, Louis Pierre

2005   *For Marx*. Translated by B. Brewster. Verso, London.
[1962]

Anderson, H. Allen

1985   The Encomienda in New Mexico, 1598–1680. *New Mexico Historical Review* 60(4):353–77.

Ashcroft, Bill, Gareth Griffiths, and Helen Tifflin

2000   *Post-Colonial Studies: The Key Concepts*. Routledge, London.

Baldwin, Louis

1995   *Intruders Within: Pueblo Resistance to Spanish Rule and the Revolt of 1680*. Franklin Watts, New York.

Bandelier, Adolph F.

1884   Reports by A. F. Bandelier on His Investigations in New Mexico during the Years 1883–84. *Archaeological Institute of America, Fifth Annual Report*, pp. 55–98. John Wilson and Son, Cambridge, MA.

1892   *Final Report of Investigations among the Indians of the Southwestern United States, Carried on Mainly in the Years from 1880–1885. Part II*. Papers of the Archaeological Institute of America, American Series, Vol. IV. University Press, Cambridge, MA.

Barber, Bernard

1941   Acculturation and Messianic Movements. *American Sociological Review* 6:663–69.

Barrett, Elinore M.

2002a   *Conquest and Catastrophe: Changing Rio Grande Settlement Patterns in the Sixteenth and Seventeenth Centuries*. University of New Mexico Press, Albuquerque.

2002b   The Geography of Rio Grande Pueblos in the Seventeenth Century. *Ethnohistory* 49(1):123–69.

Bartlett, Frederic C.

1932   *Remembering: A Study in Experimental and Social Psychology*. Cambridge University Press, Cambridge, UK.

Baugh, Timothy G.

1991   Ecology and Exchange: the Dynamics of Plains-Pueblo Interaction. In *Farmers, Hunters, and Colonists: Interaction between the Southwest and the Southern Plains*, edited by K. Spielmann, pp. 107–27. University of Arizona Press, Tucson.

Bayer, Laura, with Floyd Montoya and the Pueblo of Santa Ana

1994   *Santa Ana: The People, the Pueblo, and the History of Tamaya*. University of New Mexico Press, Albuquerque.

Beck, Robin A., Christopher B. Rodning, and David G. Moore.

2011   Limiting Resistance: Juan Pardo and the Shrinking of Spanish La Florida, 1566–68. In *Enduring Conquests: Rethinking the Archaeology of Resistance to Spanish Colonialism in the Americas*, edited by M. Liebmann and M. S. Murphy, pp. 19–40. SAR Press, Santa Fe.

Benavides, Alonso de

1916   *The Memorial of Fray Alonso de Benavides.* Translated by E. A. B. Ayer. R.R.
[1630] Donnelley and Sons Co., Chicago.

Beninato, Stefanie

1990   Popé, Pose-yemu, and Naranjo: A New Look at Leadership in the Pueblo
        Revolt of 1680. *New Mexico Historical Review* 65:417–35.

Bhabha, Homi K.

1985   Signs Taken for Wonders: Questions of Ambivalence and Authority under a
        Tree outside Delhi, May 1817. *Critical Inquiry* 12:144–165.

1994   *The Location of Culture.* Routledge, London.

Bloom, Lansing B.

1922   The West Jemez Culture Area. *El Palacio* 14:14–20.

1931   A Campaign against the Moqui Pueblos. *New Mexico Historical Review*
        6:158–226.

Bloom, Lansing B., and Lynn Mitchell

1938   The Chapter Elections in 1672. *New Mexico Historical Review* 13:85–119.

Boas, Franz

1928   *Keresan Texts.* American Ethnological Society, New York.

Bohrer, Vorsila L.

1968   Girl Scout Archaeology Unit. Manuscript on file, Archaeological Records Man-
        agement Service, Laboratory of Anthropology, Museum of New Mexico.

Bourdieu, Pierre

1987   Legitimation and Structured Interests in Weber's Sociology of Religion. In
[1971] *Max Weber, Rationality and Modernity,* edited by S. Lash and S. Whimster,
        pp. 119–36. Translated by C. Turner. Allen and Unwin, London.

1991   Genesis and Structure of the Religious Field. *Comparative Social Research*
        13:1–44.

Bradley, Bruce A.

1996   Pitchers to Mugs: Chacoan Revival at Sand Canyon Pueblo. *Kiva* 61(3):
        241–55.

Bradley, Richard

2002   *The Past in Prehistoric Societies.* Routledge, London.

Bradley, Richard, and Howard Williams

1998   The Past in the Past: The Reuse of Ancient Monuments. *World Archaeology*
        30(1):90–108.

Bray, Tamara L., ed.

2001   *The Future of the Past: Archaeologists, Native Americans, and Repatriation.* Garland
        Publishing, New York.

Brew, John Otis

1943   On the Pueblo IV and on the Kachina-Tlaloc Relations. In *El Norte de Mex-
        ico y el sur de Estados Unidos, tercera Reunion de Mesa Redonda sobre Problemas
        Anthropologicos de Mexico y Centro America,* pp. 241–245. Sociedad Mexicana de
        Anthropologia.

Brooks, James F.

2002 *Captives and Cousins: Slavery, Kinship, and Community in the Southwest Border-lands*. Published for the Omohundro Institute of Early American History and Culture, Williamsburg, Virginia, by the University of North Carolina Press, Chapel Hill.

Broughton, William H.

1993 The History of Seventeenth-Century New Mexico: Is It Time for New Interpretations? *New Mexico Historical Review* 62(2):85–126.

Brown, Barton McCaul

1987 Population Estimation from Floor Area: A Re-Study of Naroll's Constant. *Behavior Science Research* 21(1):1–49.

Brown, Donald Nelson

1979 Picuris Pueblo. In *Handbook of North American Indians: Southwest*, edited by A. Ortiz, pp. 268–77. Vol. 9. Smithsonian Institution, Washington, DC.

Brugge, David M.

2002 Jemez Pueblo and the Navajos: Relations Prior to 1800. In *Forward into the Past: Papers in Honor of Teddy Lou and Francis Stickney*, edited by R. N. Wiseman, T. C. O'Laughlin, and C. T. Snow, pp. 5–16. Archaeological Society of New Mexico Papers No. 28, Albuquerque.

Brumfiel, Elizabeth M.

2003 It's a Material World: History, Artifacts, and Anthropology. *Annual Review of Anthropology* 32:205–33.

Bruwelheide, Karin S., Douglas W. Owsley, and Richard L. Jantz

2010 Burials from the Fourth Mission Church at Pecos. In *Pecos Pueblo Revisited: The Biological and Social Context*, edited by M. E. Morgan, pp. 129–60. Papers of the Peabody Museum of Archaeology and Ethnology Volume 85. Peabody Museum of Archaeology and Ethnology, Cambridge, MA.

Bunzel, Ruth L.

1972   *The Pueblo Potter: A Study of Creative Imagination in Primitive Art*. Columbia
[1929] University Press, New York.

Cameron, Catherine M.

1999a *Hopi Dwellings: Architectural Change at Orayvi*. University of Arizona Press, Tucson.

1999b Room Size, Organization of Construction, and Archaeological Interpretation in the Puebloan Southwest. *Journal of Anthropological Archaeology* 18:201–39.

Capone, Patricia H., and Robert W. Preucel

2002 Ceramic Semiotics: Women, Pottery, and Social Meanings at Kotyiti Pueblo. In *Archaeologies of the Pueblo Revolt*, edited by R. W. Preucel, pp. 99–113. University of New Mexico Press, Albuquerque.

Carlson, Roy L.

1965 *Eighteenth Century Navajo Fortresses of the Gobernador District: The Earl Morris Papers, No. 2*. University of Colorado Studies in Anthropology No. 10. University of Colorado Press, Boulder, CO.

Casselberry, Samuel E.

1974   Further Refinements of Formulae for Determining Population from Floor Area. *World Archaeology* 6:118–22.

Cave, Alfred A.

2006   *Prophets of the Great Spirit: Native American Revitalization Movements in Eastern North America*. University of Nebraska Press, Lincoln.

Chakrabarty, Dipesh

2000   Subaltern Studies and Postcolonial Historiography. *Nepantla: Views from South* 1(1):9–32.

Chávez, Angelico

1954   *La Conquistadora: The Autobiography of an Ancient Statue*. St. Anthony Guild Press, Patterson, NJ.

1967   Pohé-yemo's Representative and the Pueblo Revolt. *New Mexico Historical Review* 42:85–126.

Chávez, Thomas E.

1980   But Were They All Natives? *El Palacio* 86:32.

Clark, G. A.

1998   NAGPRA, the Conflict between Science and Religion, and the Political Consequences. *SAA Bulletin* 16(5).

1999   NAGPRA, Science, and the Demon-Haunted World. *Skeptical Inquirer* 23(3):44–48.

2001   Letter to the Editor. *The SAA Archaeological Record* 1(2):3.

2003   American Archaeology's Uncertain Future. In *Archaeology is Anthropology*, edited by S. Gillespie and D. Nichols, pp. 51–68. Archaeological Papers of the American Anthropological Association. Vol. 13. AAA, Arlington, VA.

Clarke, Steven

1974   A Method for the Estimation of Prehistoric Pueblo Populations. *Kiva* 39(3–4): 283–87.

Clemen, Robert T.

1976   Aspects of Prehistoric Social Organization on Black Mesa. In *Papers on the Archaeology of Black Mesa*, edited by G. J. Gumerman and R. C. Euler, pp. 113–35. Southern Illinois University Press, Carbondale.

Clendinnen, Inga

1987   *Ambivalent Conquests: Maya and Spaniard in Yucatan, 1517–1570*. Cambridge University Press, Cambridge, UK.

Colwell-Chanthaphonh, Chip, and T. J. Ferguson

2006   Memory Pieces and Footprints: Multivocality and the Meanings of Ancient Times and Ancestral Places among the Zuni and Hopi. *American Anthropologist* 108(1):148–62.

2008   *Collaboration in Archaeological Practice: Engaging Descendant Communities*. Altamira Press, Lanham, MD.

Comaroff, Jean

1985   *Body of Power, Spirit of Resistance*. University of Chicago Press, Chicago.

Comaroff, Jean, and John Comaroff

1991   *Of Revelation and Revolution*. University of Chicago Press, Chicago.

1992   *Ethnography and the Historical Imagination*. Westview Press, Boulder, CO.

Comaroff, John L.

1987   Of Totemism and Ethnicity: Consciousness, Practice, and the Signs of Inequality. *Ethnos* 52(3–4):301–23.

Connerton, Paul

1989   *How Societies Remember*. Cambridge University Press, Cambridge, UK.

2006   Cultural Memory. In *Handbook of Material Culture*, edited by C. Tilley, W. Keane, S. Kuchler, M. Rowlands, and P. Spyer, pp. 315–24. Sage, London.

2008   Seven Types of Forgetting. *Memory Studies* 1(1):59–71.

Cook, Sherburne F.

1972   *Prehistoric Demography*. In Addison-Wesley Module 16. Addison-Wesley, Reading.

Cordell, Linda S.

1998   *Before Pecos: Settlement Aggregation at Rowe, New Mexico*. Maxwell Museum of Anthropology Anthropologica Papers No. 6. University of New Mexico Press, Albuquerque.

Creamer, Winifred, with Catherine M. Cameron and John D. Beal

1993   *The Architecture of Arroyo Hondo Pueblo, New Mexico*. Arroyo Hondo Archaeological Series 7. School of American Research Press, Santa Fe.

Cummins, Tom

2002   Forms of Andean Colonial Towns, Free Will, and Marriage. In *The Archaeology of Colonialism*, edited by C. L. Lyons and J. K. Papadopoulos, pp. 199–240. Getty Research Institute, Los Angeles.

Cushing, Frank Hamilton

1886   A Study of Pueblo Pottery as Illustrative of Zuni Culture Growth. In *Fourth Annual Report of the Bureau of Ethnology to the Secretary of the Smithsonian Institution 1883–1884*, pp. 467–521. Government Printing Office, Washington, DC.

1888   *Preliminary Notes on Origin, Working Hypotheses, and Primary Researches of the Hemenway Southwestern Archaeological Expedition*. Congres International des Americanistes, Berlin.

1896   Outline of Zuni Creation Myth. In *Thirteenth Annual Report, Bureau of American Ethnology*, pp. 321–447. U.S. Government Printing Office, Washington, DC.

Dahlin, Bruce H.

1986   Los rostros del tiempo: un movimiento revitalizador en Tikal durante el periodo clasico tardio. *Mesoamerica* 11:79–112.

Dawdy, Shannon Lee

2008   *Building the Devil's Empire: French Colonial New Orleans*. University of Chicago Press, Chicago.

Dean, Jeffrey S.

1970   Aspects of Tsegi Phase Social Organization: A Trial Reconstruction. In *Reconstructing Prehistoric Pueblo Societies*, edited by W. A. Longacre, pp. 140–74. University of New Mexico Press, Albuquerque.

de Certeau, Michel

1984   *The Practice of Everyday Life*. Translated by S. F. Rendall. University of California Press, Berkeley.

de Kock, Leon

1992   Interview with Gayatri Chakravorty Spivak: New Nation Writers' Conference in South Africa. *ARIEL: A Review of International English Literature* 23(3):29–47.

De Marco, Barbara

2000   Voices from the Archives, Part 1: Testimony of the Pueblo Indians in the 1680 Pueblo Revolt. *Romance Philology* 53:375–448.

Dietler, Michael

2010   *Archaeologies of Colonialism: Consumption, Entanglement, and Violence in Ancient Mediterranean France*. University of California Press, Berkeley.

Dillingham, Rick, and Melinda Elliott

1992   *Acoma and Laguna Pottery*. School of American Research Press, Santa Fe.

Dirlik, Arif

1997   *The Postcolonial Aura: Third World Criticism in the Age of Global Capitalism*. Westview Press, Boulder, CO.

Dockstader, Frederick F.

1954   *The Kachina and the White Man: The Influences of White Culture on Hopi Kachina Religion*. Bulletin 35. Cranbrook Institute of Science, Bloomfield Hills, MI.

Dohm, Karen

1990   Effect of Population Nucleation on House Size for Pueblos in the American Southwest. *Journal of Anthropological Archaeology* 9:201–239.

Dongoske, Kurt E., and Cindy K. Dongoske

2002   History in Stone: Evaluating Spanish Conversion Efforts through Hopi Rock Art. In *Archaeologies of the Pueblo Revolt*, edited by R. W. Preucel, pp. 114–131. University of New Mexico Press, Albuquerque.

Dougherty, Julia D., and William R. Neal

1979   Guadalupe Mesa. U.S. Forest Service, Santa Fe National Forest Report, Santa Fe.

Dozier, Edward P.

1961   Rio Grande Pueblos. In *Perspectives in American Indian Culture Change*, edited by E. H. Spicer, pp. 94–186. University of Chicago Press, Chicago.

1966   Factionalism at Santa Clara Pueblo. *Ethnology* 5(2):172–185.

1970   *The Pueblo Indians of North America*. Holt, Rinehart, and Winston, New York.

Dunnell, Robert C., and William S. Dancey

1983   The Siteless Survey: A Regional Scale Data Collection Strategy. In *Advances in Archaeological Method and Theory*, edited by M. B. Schiffer, pp. 267–87. Vol. 6. Academic Press, New York.

Duwe, Samuel

2010   Coalescence and Population Movement in the Rio Chama Drainage. Paper presented at 75th Annual Meeting of the Society for American Archaeology, St. Louis, Missouri.

Eggan, Fred

1950   *Social Organization of the Western Pueblos.* University of Chicago Press, Chicago.

Elliott, Michael L.

1982   *Large Pueblo Sites near Jemez Springs, New Mexico.* Cultural Resources Document No. 3, Santa Fe National Forest.

1986   *Overview and Synthesis of the Archaeology of the Jemez Province, New Mexico.* Archaeology Notes 51. Museum of New Mexico, Office of Archaeological Studies, Santa Fe.

1991   Pueblo at the Hot Place: Archaeological Excavations at Giusewa Pueblo and San Jose de los Jemez Mission, Jemez State Monument, Jemez Springs, New Mexico. New Mexico State Monuments, Santa Fe.

1994   *Jemez Area Ceramics.* Manuscript on file at USDA Forest Service, Santa Fe National Forest, Jemez Ranger District. Jemez Springs, NM.

2002   Mission and Mesa: Some Thoughts on the Archaeology of Pueblo Revolt Era Sites in the Jemez Region, New Mexico. In *Archaeologies of the Pueblo Revolt,* edited by R. Preucel, pp. 45–60. University of New Mexico Press, Albuquerque.

2005   National Historic Landmark Nomination: Giusewa Pueblo and San Jose de los Jemez Mission, Manuscript on file, United States Department of the Interior, National Park Service.

Ellis, Florence Hawley

1956   Anthropological Evidence Supporting the Claims of the Pueblos of Zia, Santa Ana, and Jemez. Manuscript on file at Archaeological Records Management Service, Laboratory of Anthropology, Museum of New Mexico, Santa Fe.

1964   *A Reconstruction of the Basic Jemez Pattern of Social Organization, with Comparisons to Other Tanoan Social Structures.* University of New Mexico Publications in Anthropology No. 11. University of New Mexico Press, Albuquerque.

1966a   The Immediate History of Zia Pueblo as Derived from Excavation in Refuse Deposits. *American Antiquity* 31:806–811.

1966b   Pueblo Boundaries and Their Markers. *Plateau* 38(4):97–105.

Ellis, Florence Hawley, and Andrea Hawley Ellis

1992   A Window on San Gabriel del Yungue. In *Current Research on the Late Prehistory and Early History of New Mexico,* edited by B. J. Vierra, pp. 175–183. New Mexico Archaeological Council, Albuquerque.

Espinosa, J. Manuel

1942   *Crusaders of the Rio Grande.* Institute of Jesuit History, Chicago.

1988   *The Pueblo Revolt of 1696 and the Franciscan Missions in New Mexico: Letters of the Missionaries and Related Documents.* Institute of Jesuit History, Chicago.

Ferguson, T. J.

1996   *Historic Zuni Architecture and Society: An Archaeological Application of Space Syntax.* Anthropological Papers of the University of Arizona No. 60. University of Arizona Press, Tucson.

2002   Dowa Yalanne: The Architecture of Zuni Resistance and Social Change during the Pueblo Revolt. In *Archaeologies of the Pueblo Revolt,* edited by R. W. Preucel, pp. 32–44. University of New Mexico Press, Albuquerque.

Ferguson, T. J., and Chip Colwell-Chanthaphonh

2006   *History Is in the Land: Multivocal Tribal Traditions in Arizona's San Pedro Valley.*
        University of Arizona Press, Tucson.

Fergusson, Erna

1931   *Dancing Gods: Indian Ceremonials of New Mexico and Arizona.* University of
        New Mexico Press, Albuquerque.

Ferris, Neal

2009   *The Archaeology of Native-Lived Colonialism: Cultural Contact from 5000 BC to the
        Present.* University of Arizona Press, Tucson.

Flint, Richard

2008   *No Settlement, No Conquest: A History of the Coronado Entrada.* University of
        New Mexico Press, Albuquerque.

Flint, Richard, and Shirley Cushing Flint

2008   Bartolome de Ojeda. http://www.newmexicohistory.org/filedetails_docs.php?
        fileID=481. Last accessed October 26, 2011.

Folsom, Franklin

1973   *Red Power on the Rio Grande: The Native American Revolution of 1680.* Follet,
        Chicago.

Forbes, Jack D.

1960   *Apache, Navaho, and Spaniard.* University of Oklahoma Press, Norman.

Ford, Richard I.

1987   The New Pueblo Economy. In *When Cultures Meet: Remembering San Gabriel del
        Yungue Oweenge,* pp. 73–91. Sunstone Press, Santa Fe.

Ford, Richard I., Albert H. Schroeder, and Stewart L. Peckham

1972   Three Perspectives on Puebloan Prehistory. In *New Perspectives on the Pueblos,*
        edited by A. Ortiz, pp. 19–39. University of New Mexico Press, Albuquerque.

Foster, George M.

1960   *Culture and Conquest: America's Spanish Heritage.* Quadrangle Books, Chicago.

Foucault, Michel

1981   Is It Useless to Revolt? *Philosophy and Social Criticism* 8(1):1–9.
[1979]

Fowles, Severin

2005   Historical Contingency and the Prehistoric Foundations of Moiety Organi-
        zation among the Eastern Pueblos. *Journal of Anthropological Research* 61(1):
        25–52.

2009   The Enshrined Pueblo: Villagescape and Cosmos in the Northern Rio Grande.
        American Antiquity 74(3):448–66.

Fox, Robin

1967   *The Keresan Bridge: A Problem in Pueblo Ethnology.* Humanities Press, New
        York.

Frank, Larry, and Francis H. Harlow

1974   *Historic Pottery of the Pueblo Indians, 1600–1880.* New York Graphic Society,
        Boston.

Frank, Ross

1998 Demographic, Social, and Economic Change in New Mexico. In *New Views of Borderlands History*, edited by R. H. Jackson, pp. 41–71. University of New Mexico Press, Albuquerque.

Frink, Lisa

2007 Storage and Status in Precolonial and Colonial Coastal Western Alaska. *Current Anthropology* 48(3):349–362.

Fritz, John M.

1978 Paleopsychology Today: Ideational Systems and Human Adaptation in Prehistory. In *Social Archaeology: Beyond Subsistence and Dating*, edited by C. L. Redman, M. J. Berman, E. V. Curtin, W. T. Langhorne, N. M. Versaggi, and J. C. Wanser, pp. 37–59. Academic Press, New York.

Fry, Robert E.

1985 Revitalization Movements among the Postclassic Lowland Maya. In *Lowland Maya Postclassic*, edited by A. F. Chase and P. M. Rice, pp. 126–141. University of Texas Press, Austin.

Futrell, Mary E.

1998 Social Boundaries and Interaction: Ceramic Zones in the Northern Rio Grande Pueblo IV Period. In *Migration and Reorganization: The Pueblo IV Period in the American Southwest*, edited by K. A. Spielmann, pp. 285–92. Arizona State University Anthropological Research Papers No. 51, Tempe.

Gandhi, Leela

1998 *Postcolonial Theory: A Critical Introduction.* Columbia University Press, New York.

Garner, Van Hastings

1999 Seventeenth-Century New Mexico, the Pueblo Revolt, and Its Interpreters. In *What Caused the Pueblo Revolt of 1680?* edited by D. J. Weber, pp. 57–80. Bedford/St. Martin's, New York.

Gill, Sam

1983 *Native American Traditions: Sources and Interpretations.* Wadsworth, Belmont.

Given, Michael.

2004 *The Archaeology of the Colonized.* Routledge, London.

Golden, Charles

2005 Where Does Memory Reside, and Why Isn't It History? *American Anthropologist* 107(2):270–74.

Gosden, Chris

2004 *Archaeology and Colonialism: Cultural Contact from 5000 BC to the Present.* Cambridge University Press, Cambridge, UK.

Graves, William M., and Suzanne L. Eckert

1998 Decorated Ceramic Distributions and Ideological Developments in the Northern and Central Rio Grande Valley, New Mexico. In *Migration and Reorganization: The Pueblo IV Period in the American Southwest*, edited by K. A. Spielmann, pp. 263–284. Arizona State University Anthropological Research Papers No. 51. Arizona State University, Tempe.

Graziano, Frank

1999   *The Millennial New World.* Oxford University Press, Oxford.

Griffen, William B.

1969   *Cultural Change and Shifting Populations in Central Northern Mexico.* University of Arizona Press, Tucson.

Grissino-Mayer, Henry D., Christopher H. Baisan, Kiyomi A. Morino, and Thomas W. Swetnam

2002   *Multi-Century Trends in Past Climate for Middle Rio Grande Basin, AD 622–1992.* Final Report submitted to the USDA Forest Service, Rocky Mountain Research Station, Albuquerque. University of Arizona Laboratory of Tree-Ring Research Report 2000/6. University of Arizona Laboratory of Tree-Ring Research, Tucson.

Guha, Ranajit

1982   On Some Aspects of the Historiography of Colonial India. In *Subaltern Studies,* edited by R. Guha, pp. 1–8. Vol. 1. Oxford University Press, New Delhi.

1983   *Elementary Aspects of Peasant Insurgency in Colonial India.* Oxford University Press, Delhi.

Gutiérrez, Ramon A.

1991   *When Jesus Came, the Corn Mothers Went Away: Marriage, Sexuality, and Power in New Mexico, 1500–1846.* Stanford University Press, Stanford.

Haas, Jonathan, and Winifred Creamer

1992   Demography of the Protohistoric Pueblos of the Northern Rio Grande, A.D. 1450–1680. In *Current Research of the Late Prehistory and Early History of New Mexico,* edited by B. J. Vierra, pp. 21–27. New Mexico Archaeological Council Special Publication No. 1, Albuquerque.

Habicht-Mauche, Judith A.

1991   Evidence for the Manufacture of Southwestern-style Culinary Ceramics on the Southern Plains. In *Farmers, Hunters, and Colonists: Interaction between the Southwest and the Southern Plains,* edited by K. Spielmann, pp. 51–70. University of Arizona Press, Tucson.

Hackett, Charles Wilson, ed.

1937   *Historical Documents Relating to New Mexico, Nueva Vizcaya, and Approaches Thereto, to 1773.* 3 vols. Carnegie Institution, Washington, DC.

Hackett, Charles Wilson, ed., and Charmion Clair Shelby, trans.

1942   *Revolt of the Pueblo Indians of New Mexico and Otermin's Attempted Reconquest, 1680–1682.* Coronado Cuarto Centennial Publications, 1540–1940. 2 vols. University of New Mexico Press, Albuquerque.

Halbwachs, Maurice

1992   *On Collective Memory.* University of Chicago Press, Chicago.
[1925]

Hallowell, A. Irving

1945   Sociological Aspects of Acculturation. In *The Science of Man in the World Crisis,* edited by R. Linton, pp. 171–200. Columbia University Press, New York.

Hammond, George P., and Agapito Rey, eds.

1940   *Narratives of the Coronado Expedition*. University of New Mexico Press, Albuquerque.

1953   *Don Juan de Oñate, Colonizer of New Mexico, 1595–1628*. 2 vols. University of New Mexico Press, Albuquerque.

1966   *The Rediscovery of New Mexico, 1580–1594*. University of New Mexico Press, Albuquerque.

Harkin, Michael E., ed.

2004a   *Reassessing Revitalization Movements: Perspectives from North America and the Pacific Islands*. University of Nebraska Press, Lincoln.

2004b   Introduction: Revitalization as History and Theory. In *Reassessing Revitalization Movements: Perspectives from North America and the Pacific Islands*, edited by M. E. Harkin, pp. xv–xxxvi. University of Nebraska Press, Lincoln.

2004c   Revitalization as Catharsis: The Warm House Cult of Western Oregon. In *Reassessing Revitalization Movements: Perspectives from North America and the Pacific Islands*, edited by M. E. Harkin, pp. 143–161. University of Nebraska Press, Lincoln.

Harlow, Francis H.

1973   *Matte-Paint Pottery of the Tewa, Keres, and Zuni Pueblos*. Museum of New Mexico Press, Santa Fe.

Harlow, Francis H., Duane Anderson, and Dwight P. Lanmon

2005   *The Pottery of Santa Ana Pueblo*. Museum of New Mexico Press, Santa Fe.

Harlow, Francis H., and Dwight P. Lanmon

2003   *The Pottery of Zia Pueblo*. School of American Research Press, Santa Fe.

Harrington, John P.

1916   The Ethnogeography of the Tewa Indians. In *Twenty-ninth Annual Report of the Bureau of American Ethnology for the years 1907–1908*, pp. 29–636. Government Printing Office, Washington, DC.

Hassan, Ferki

1981   *Demographic Archaeology*. Academic Press, New York.

Hayes, Alden C.

1974   *The Four Churches of Pecos*. University of New Mexico Press, Albuquerque.

Hayes, Alden C., Jon Nathan Young, and A. H. Warren

1981   *Excavation of Mound 7, Gran Quivira National Monument, New Mexico*. National Park Service Publications in Archaeology 16. National Park Service, Washington, DC.

Hays, Kelley Ann

1994   Kachina Depictions on Prehistoric Pueblo Pottery. In *Kachinas in the Pueblo World*, edited by P. Schaafsma, pp. 47–62. University of New Mexico Press, Albuquerque.

Hazen-Hammond, Susan

1988   *A Short History of Santa Fe*. Lexikos, San Francisco.

Hegmon, Michelle

1989   Social Integration and Architecture. In *The Architecture of Social Integration in Prehistoric Pueblos*, edited by W. D. Lipe and M. Hegmon, pp. 5–14. Crow Canyon Archaeological Center, Cortez.

Hendricks, Rick

2002   Pueblo-Spanish Warfare in Seventeenth-Century New Mexico: The Battles of Black Mesa, Kotyiti, and Astialakwa. In *Archaeologies of the Pueblo Revolt*, edited by R. W. Preucel, pp. 181–197. University of New Mexico Press, Albuquerque.

Hendricks, Rick, and John P. Wilson, eds.

1996   *The Navajos in 1705: Roque Madrid's Campaign Journal*. University of New Mexico Press, Albuquerque.

Hendron, J. W.

1943   *Group M of the Cavate Dwellings, Rooms 1, 2, 3, 4, and 5, Caves 1, 2, 3, and 4, Frijoles Canyon, Bandelier National Monument, New Mexico*. Manuscript on file, Bandelier National Monument.

Herr, Sarah A., and Jeffery J. Clark

1997   Patterns in the Pathways: Early Historic Migrations in the Rio Grande Pueblos. *Kiva* 62(4):365–389.

Hill, J. Brett, Jeffery J. Clark, William H. Doelle, and Patrick D. Lyons

2004   Prehistoric Demography in the Southwest: Migration, Coalescence, and Hohokam Population Decline. *American Antiquity* 69(4):689–716.

Hill, James N.

1970a   *Broken K Pueblo: Prehistoric Social Organization in the American Southwest*. Anthropological Papers No. 18. University of Arizona, Tucson.

1970b   Prehistoric Social Organization in the American Southwest: Theory and Method. In *Reconstructing Prehistoric Pueblo Societies*, edited by W. A. Longacre, pp. 11–58. University of New Mexico Press, Albuquerque.

Hill, Jonathan D.

1996   Introduction: Ethnogenesis in the Americas, 1492–1992. In *History, Power, and Identity: Ethnogenesis in the Americas, 1492–1992*, edited by J. D. Hill, pp. 1–19. University of Iowa Press, Iowa City.

Hill, Willard W.

1982   *An Ethnography of Santa Clara Pueblo, New Mexico*. University of New Mexico Press, Albuquerque.

Hobsbawm, Eric

1959   *Primitive Rebels: Studies in Archaic Forms of Social Movements in the 19th and 20th Centuries*. Manchester University Press, Manchester.

1983   Introduction: Inventing Traditions. In *The Invention of Tradition*, edited by E. Hobsbawm and T. Ranger, pp. 1–14. Cambridge University Press, Cambridge, UK.

Hobsbawm, Eric, and Terence Ranger, eds.

1983   *The Invention of Tradition*. Cambridge University Press, Cambridge, UK.

Hodder, Ian, and Craig Cessford

2004   Daily Practice and Social Memory at Çatalhöyük. *American Antiquity* 69(1):17–40.

Hodge, Frederick Webb

1937   *History of Hawikuh, New Mexico*. Ward Ritchie Press, Los Angeles.

Hodge, Frederick Webb, George P. Hammond, and Agapito Rey, eds.

1945   *Fray Alonso de Benavides' Revised Memorial of 1634*. University of New Mexico Press, Albuquerque.

Holmes, William Henry

1905   Notes on the Antiquities of the Jemez Valley. *American Antiquity* 7:198–212.

Hopi Dictionary Project

1998   *Hopi Dictionary, Hopìikwa Lavàytutuveni: A Hopi-English Dictionary of the Third Mesa Dialect*. University of Arizona Press, Tucson.

Hordes, Stanley J.

2005   *To the End of the Earth: A History of the Crypto-Jews of New Mexico*. Columbia University Press, New York.

Ivey, James E.

1991   *"Una Muy Suntuosa y Curiosa Yglesia": A Structural Assessment of the Mission Church of San Jose de Giusewa, Jemez State Monument, New Mexico*. National Park Service, Southwest Regional Office, Santa Fe.

1994   "The Greatest Misfortune of All": Famine in the Province of New Mexico, 1667–1672. *Journal of the Southwest* 36(1):76–100.

1998   Convento Kivas in the Missions of New Mexico. *New Mexico Historical Review* 73:121–152.

2005   *The Spanish Colonial Architecture of Pecos Pueblo, New Mexico*. Professional Paper No. 59, Division of Cultural Resources Management, Intermountain Region, Department of Interior, National Park Service.

James, Steven R.

1997   Change and Continuity in Western Pueblo Households during the Historic Period in the American Southwest. *World Archaeology* 28(3):429–456.

John, Elizabeth A. H.

1975   *Storms Brewed in Other Men's Worlds: The Confrontation of Indians, Spanish, and French in the Southwest, 1540–1795*. Texas A&M Press, College Station.

Johnson, Matthew H.

1998   Rethinking Historical Archaeology. In *Historical Archaeology: Back from the Edge*, edited by P. P. Funari, M. Hall and S. Jones, pp. 23–36. Routledge, London.

Jones, Andrew.

2007   *Memory and Material Culture*. Cambridge University Press, Cambridge, UK.

Jones, Okah L. Jr.

1966   *Pueblo Warriors and Spanish Conquest*. University of Oklahoma Press, Norman.

Jorgensen, Joseph G.

1980   *Western Indians: Comparative Environments, Languages, and Cultures of 172 Western American Indian Tribes*. W. H. Freeman, San Francisco.

Joyce, Rosemary A.

2000   Heirlooms and Houses: Materiality and Social Memory. In *Beyond Kinship: Social and Material Reproduction in House Societies*, edited by R. A. Joyce and S. D. Gillespie, pp. 189–212. University of Pennsylvania Press, Philadelphia.

Kantner, John

2004   *Ancient Puebloan Southwest.* Cambridge University Press, Cambridge, UK.

Keane, Webb

2003   Semiotics and the Social Analysis of Material Things. *Language and Communication* 23:409–425.

2005   Signs Are Not the Garb of Meaning: On the Social Analysis of Material Things. In *Materiality*, edited by D. Miller, pp. 183–205. Duke University Press, Durham, NC.

Kellner, Corina M., Margaret Schoeninger, Katherine A. Spielmann, and Katherine Moore

2010   Stable Isotope Data Show Temporal Stability in Diet at Pecos Pueblo and Diet Variation among Southwest Pueblos. In *Pecos Pueblo Revisited: The Biological and Social Context*, edited by M. E. Morgan, pp. 79–91. Papers of the Peabody Museum. Vol. 85. Peabody Museum of Archaeology and Ethnology, Cambridge, MA.

Kerber, Jordan, ed.

2006   *Cross-Cultural Collaboration: Native Peoples and Archaeology in the Northeastern United States.* University of Nebraska Press, Lincoln.

Kessell, John L.

1979   *Kiva, Cross, and Crown: The Pecos Indians and New Mexico 1540–1840.* University of New Mexico Press, Albuquerque.

1980   Esteban Clemente: Precursor of the Pueblo Revolt. *El Palacio* 86:16–17.

1994   The Ways and Words of the Other: Diego de Vargas and Cultural Brokers in Late Seventeenth-Century New Mexico. In *Between Indian and White Worlds: The Cultural Broker*, edited by M. C. Szasz, pp. 25–43. University of Oklahoma Press, Norman.

2002   *Spain in the Southwest.* University of Oklahoma Press, Norman.

2008   *Pueblos, Spaniards, and the Kingdom of New Mexico.* University of Oklahoma Press, Norman.

2010   A Long Time Coming: The 17th Century Pueblo-Spanish War. Paper presented at the Southwest Seminars 400th Anniversary Lecture Series, Santa Fe.

Kessell, John L., and Rick Hendricks, eds.

1992   *By Force of Arms: The Journals of Don Diego de Vargas, New Mexico 1691–1693.* University of New Mexico Press, Albuquerque.

Kessell, John L., Rick Hendricks, and Meredith Dodge, eds.

1995   *To the Royal Crown Restored: The Journals of Don Diego de Vargas, New Mexico 1692–1694.* University of New Mexico Press, Albuquerque.

1998   *Blood on the Boulders: The Journals of Don Diego de Vargas, New Mexico 1694–1697.* 2 vols. University of New Mexico Press, Albuquerque.

Kidder, Alfred V.

1917 *The Old North Pueblo of Pecos: The Condition of the Main Pecos Ruin*. Papers of the School of American Archaeology No. 38. Archaeological Institute of America, Santa Fe.

1927 Southwestern Archaeological Conference. *Science* 68:489–91.

1932 *The Artifacts of Pecos*. Papers of the Phillips Academy Southwest Expedition No. 6. New Haven.

1958 *Pecos, New Mexico: Archaeological Notes*. Papers of the Peabody Foundation for Archaeology No. 5. Phillips Academy, Andover.

Kidder, Alfred V., and Charles A. Amsden

1931 *The Pottery of Pecos, Volume 1: The Dull-Paint Wares* 1. Papers of the Phillips Academy Southwest Expedition No 5. Yale University Press, New Haven.

Kidder, Alfred V., and Anna O. Shepard

1936 *The Pottery of Pecos*. Vol. 2. Papers of the Phillips Academy Southwest Expedition No. 5. Yale University Press, New Haven.

Kidder, Madeline A., and Alfred V. Kidder

1917 Notes on the Pottery of Pecos. *American Anthropologist* 19:325–60.

Kintigh, Keith

1985 Settlement, Subsistence, and Society in Late Zuni Prehistory. Anthropological Papers of the University of Arizona No. 44. University of Arizona Press, Tucson.

Knaut, Andrew L.

1995 *The Pueblo Revolt of 1680: Conquest and Resistance in Seventeenth-Century New Mexico*. University of Oklahoma Press, Norman.

Kopytoff, Igor

2000 The Cultural Biography of Things: Commodization as Process. In *Interpretive Archaeology*, edited by J. Thomas, pp. 377–97. Leicester University Press, London.

Kubler, George

1978 Open-Grid Town Plans in Europe and America. In *Urbanization in the Americas from Its Beginnings to the Present*, edited by R. P. Schaedel, J. E. Hardoy, and N. S. Kinzer, pp. 327–42. Mouton, The Hague.

Kulisheck, Jeremy

2001 Settlement Patterns, Population, and Congregación on the 17th Century Jemez Plateau. In *Following Through: Papers in Honor of Phyllis S. Davis*, edited by R. N. Wiseman, T. C. O'Laughlin, and C. T. Snow. Vol. 27, pp. 77–101. The Archaeological Society of New Mexico.

2003 Pueblo Population Movements, Abandonment, and Settlement Change in Sixteenth and Seventeenth Century New Mexico. *Kiva* 69(1):30–54.

2005 *The Archaeology of Pueblo Population Change on the Jemez Plateau, A.D. 1200–1700: The Effects of Spanish Contact and Conquest*. Ph.D. diss., Southern Methodist University, Dallas, TX.

2010 "Like Butterflies on a Mounting Board": Pueblo Mobility and Demography before 1825. In *Across a Great Divide: Continuity and Change in Native North American Societies, 1400–1900*, edited by L. L. Scheiber and M. D. Mitchell, 174–91. University of Arizona Press, Tucson.

Kulisheck, Jeremy, and Michael L. Elliott
2005   A Proposed Late Prehistoric and Early Historic Phase Sequence for the Jemez
        Plateau, North-Central New Mexico, USA. Paper presented at the 70th Annual
        Meeting of the Society for American Archaeology, Salt Lake City.

Lamadrid, Enrique R.
2002   Santiago and San Acacio: Slaughter and Deliverance in the Foundational Leg-
        ends of Colonial and Postcolonial New Mexico. *Journal of American Folklore*
        115(457/458):457–74.

Lambert, Marjorie F.
1981   Spanish Influences on the Pottery of San Jose de los Jemez and Giusewa, Jemez
        State Monument (LA 679), Jemez Springs, New Mexico. In *Collected Papers in
        Honor of Erik Kellerman Reed*, edited by A. H. Schroeder, pp. 215–36. Archaeo-
        logical Society of New Mexico Papers No. 6. Albuquerque Archaeological Soci-
        ety Press, Albuquerque.

Lange, Charles H.
1979   Relations of the Southwest with the Plains and Great Basin. In *Handbook of
        North American Indians: Southwest,* edited by A. Ortiz, pp. 201–205. Vol. 9.
        Smithsonian Institution, Washington, DC.

Lange, Charles H., and Carrol L. Riley, eds.
1966   *The Southwestern Journals of Adolph F. Bandelier, 1880–1882.* University of New
        Mexico Press, Albuquerque.

Lanternari, Vittorio
1963   *The Religions of the Oppressed: A Study of Modern Messianic Cults.* Translated by
        L. Sergio. Mentor Books, New York.

1974   Nativistic and Socio-Religious Movements: A Reconsideration. *Comparative
        Studies in Society and History* 16(4):483–503.

LeBlanc, Steven A.
1971   An Addition to Naroll's Suggested Floor Area and Settlement Population Rela-
        tionship. *American Antiquity* 36(2):210–211.

1999   *Prehistoric Warfare in the American Southwest.* University of Utah Press, Salt Lake
        City.

Lekson, Stephen H.
1990   Sedentism and Aggregation in Anasazi Archaeology. In *Perspectives in Southwest-
        ern Prehistory*, edited by P. E. Minnis and C. L. Redman, pp. 333–40. Westview
        Press, Boulder, CO.

Lentz, Stephen C.
2004   *Excavations at LA 80000, The Santa Fe Plaza Community Stage Location, Santa
        Fe, New Mexico.* Archaeology Notes 343, Museum of New Mexico, Office of
        Archaeological Studies, Santa Fe.

Leonard, Irving A., trans.
1932   *The Mercurio Volante of Don Carlos Sigüenza Y Góngora: An Account of the First
        Expedition of Don Diego de Vargas into New Mexico in 1692.* The Quivira Society,
        Los Angeles.

Lévi-Strauss, Claude

1963   *Structural Anthropology*. Basic Books, New York.

1966   *The Savage Mind*. Wiedenfield and Nicholson, London.

Lewarch, Dennis E., and Michael J. O'Brien

1981   The Expanding Role of Surface Assemblages in Archaeological Research. In *Advances in Archaeological Method and Theory*, edited by M. B. Schiffer, pp. 297–342. vol. 4. Academic Press, New York.

Liebmann, Matthew

2002   Signs of Power and Resistance: The (Re)Creation of Christian Imagery and Identities in the Pueblo Revolt Era. In *Archaeologies of the Pueblo Revolt*, edited by R. W. Preucel, pp. 132–44. University of New Mexico Press, Albuquerque.

2006   Burn the Churches, Break Up the Bells: The Archaeology of the Pueblo Revolt Revitalization Movement in New Mexico, AD 1680–1696. Ph.D. diss., University of Pennsylvania, Philadelphia.

2008   The Innovative Materiality of Revitalization Movements: Lessons from the Pueblo Revolt of 1680. *American Anthropologist* 110(3):360–72.

2011   The Best of Times, the Worst of Times: Pueblo Resistance and Accommodation during the Spanish Reconquista of New Mexico. In *Enduring Conquests: Rethinking the Archaeology of Resistance to Spanish Colonialism in the Americas*, edited by M. Liebmann and M. S. Murphy, pp. 199–221. SAR Press, Santa Fe.

Liebmann, Matthew, T. J. Ferguson, and Robert Preucel

2005   Pueblo Settlement, Architecture, and Social Change in the Pueblo Revolt Era, A.D. 1680 to 1696. *Journal of Field Archaeology* 30(1):45–60.

Liebmann, Matthew, and Melissa S. Murphy

2011   Rethinking the Archaeology of Rebels, Backsliders, and Idolaters. In *Enduring Conquests: Rethinking the Archaeology of Resistance to Spanish Colonialism in the New World*, edited by M. Liebmann and M. S. Murphy, pp. 3–18. SAR Press, Santa Fe.

Liebmann, Matthew, and Robert W. Preucel

2007   The Archaeology of the Pueblo Revolt and the Formation of the Modern Pueblo World. *Kiva* 73(2):197–219.

Lightfoot, Kent G.

1995   Culture Contact Studies: Redefining the Relationship between Prehistoric and Historical Archaeology. *American Antiquity* 60(2):119–217.

2005   *Indians, Missionaries, and Merchants: The Legacy of Colonial Encounters on the California Frontiers*. University of California Press, Berkeley.

Lindstrom, Lamont

1993   *Cargo Cult: Strange Stories of Desire from Melanesia and Beyond*. University of Hawaii Press, Honolulu.

Linton, Ralph, ed.

1940   *Acculturation in Seven American Indian Tribes*. Appleton, New York.

1943   Nativistic Movements. *American Anthropologist* 45:230–40.

Lintz, C.

1991   Texas Panhandle-Pueblo Interactions from the Thirteenth through the Six-
        teenth Century. In *Farmers, Hunters, and Colonists: Interaction between the South-
        west and the Southern Plains*, edited by K. Spielmann, pp. 89–106. University of
        Arizona Press, Tucson.

Lipe, William D., and Michelle Hegmon

1989   Historical and Analytical Perspectives on Architecture and Social Integration
        in the Prehistoric Pueblos. In *The Architecture of Social Integration in Prehistoric
        Pueblos*, edited by W. D. Lipe and M. Hegmon, pp. 15–34. Crow Canyon
        Archaeological Center, Cortez.

Lippard, Lucy R.

2010   *Down Country: The Tano of the Galisteo Basin, 1250–1782.* Museum of New
        Mexico Press, Santa Fe.

Little, Barbara J., and Paul A. Shackel, eds.

2007   *Archaeology as a Tool of Civic Engagement.* Altamira Press, Lanham, MD.

Loew, Oscar

1875   Report on the Ruins of New Mexico. In *Annual Report of the Chief of Engineers to
        the Secretary of War.* Vol. 2, part 2, pp. 337–45. U.S. Government Printing Office,
        Washington, DC.

Lomawaima, Hartman H.

1989   Hopification, a Strategy for Cultural Preservation. In *Columbian Consequences,
        Vol. I: Archaeological and Historical Perspectives on the Spanish Borderlands West*,
        edited by D. H. Thomas, pp. 93–99. Smithsonian Institution Press, Washing-
        ton, DC.

Longacre, William A.

1970   *Archaeology as Anthropology: A Case Study.* Anthropological Papers of the Univer-
        sity of Arizona No. 17, Tucson.

Loren, Diana DiPaolo

2008   *In Contact.* Altamira Press, Lanham, MD.

Low, Setha M.

1995   Indigenous Architecture and the Spanish American Plaza in Mesoamerica and
        the Caribbean. *American Anthropologist* 97(4):748–62.

Lowell, Julia C.

1996   Moieties in Prehistory: A Case Study from the Pueblo Southwest. *Journal of
        Field Archaeology* 23:77–90.

Lowie, Robert H.

1948   *Social Organization.* Rinehart, New York.

Lyons, Claire L., and John K. Papadopoulos, eds.

2002   *The Archaeology of Colonialism.* The Getty Research Institute, Los Angeles.

Madalena, Joshua

2003   The Battle of Astialakwa—July 24, 1694. In *Jemez Thunder,* July 15, pp. 21.

Malotki, Ekkehart, ed.

1993   *Hopi Ruin Legends: Kiqötutuwutsi.* University of Nebraska Press, Lincoln.

Martin, Joel W.

1991   Before and Beyond the Sioux Ghost Dance: Native American Prophetic Movements and the Study of Religion. *Journal of American Academy of Religion* 59(4):677–701.

2004   Visions of Revitalization in the Eastern Woodlands: Can a Middle-Aged Theory Stretch to Embrace the First Cherokee Converts? In *Reassessing Revitalization Movements: Perspectives from North America and the Pacific Islands*, edited by M. E. Harkin, pp. 61–87. University of Nebraska Press, Lincoln.

McDavid, Carol

2002   Archaeologies that Hurt; Descendants that Matter: A Pragmatic Approach to Collaboration in the Public Interpretation of African-American Archaeology. *World Archaeology* 34(2):303–14.

McMullen, Ann

2004   "Canny about Conflict": Nativism, Revitalization, and the Invention of Tradition in Native Southeastern New England. In *Reassessing Revitalization Movements: Perspectives from North America and the Pacific Islands*, edited by M. E. Harkin, pp. 261–78. University of Nebraska Press, Lincoln.

Meighan, Clement W.

1996   Burying American Archaeology. In *Archaeological Ethics*, edited by K. Vitelli, pp. 209–13. Altamira, Lanham, MD.

Mera, H. P.

1940   *Population Changes in the Rio Grande Glaze-paint Area.* Laboratory of Anthropology Technical Series, Bulletin No. 9. Museum of New Mexico, Santa Fe.

Mihesuah, Devon A., ed.

2000   *Repatriation Reader: Who Owns American Indian Remains?* University of Nebraska Press, Lincoln.

Miller, Daniel, ed.

2005a   *Materiality.* Duke University Press, Durham, NC.

2005b   Materiality: An Introduction. In *Materiality*, edited by D. Miller, pp. 1–50. Duke University Press, Durham, NC.

Mills, Barbara J.

1998   Migration and Pueblo IV Community Reorganization in the Silver Creek Area, East-Central Arizona. In *Migration and reorganization of the Pueblo IV period in the American Southwest*, edited by K. A. Spielmann, pp. 65–80. Arizona State University Anthropological Papers No. 51, Tempe.

2002   Acts of Resistance: Zuni Ceramics, Social Identity, and the Pueblo Revolt. In *Archaeologies of the Pueblo Revolt*, edited by R. W. Preucel, pp. 85–96. University of New Mexico Press, Albuquerque.

2004   The Establishment and Defeat of Hierarchy: Inalienable Possessions and the History of Collective Prestige Structures in the Pueblo Southwest. *American Anthropologist* 106(2):238–251.

Mills, Barbara J., and T. J. Ferguson

2008   Animate Objects: Shell Trumpets and Ritual Networks in the Greater Southwest. *Journal of Archaeological Method and Theory* 14(4):338–61.

Mills, Barbara J., and William H. Walker, eds.

2008a   *Memory Work: Archaeologies of Material Practice.* School for Advanced Research
         Press, Santa Fe.

2008b   Introduction: Memory, Materiality, and Depositional Practice. In *Memory
         Work: Archaeologies of Material Practices*, edited by B. J. Mills and W. H. Walker,
         pp. 3–23. School for Advanced Research Press, Santa Fe.

Mobley-Tanaka, Jeanette L.

2002   Crossed Cultures, Crossed Meanings: The Manipulation of Ritual Imagery in
         Early Historic Pueblo Resistance. In *Archaeologies of the Pueblo Revolt*, edited by
         R. W. Preucel, pp. 77–84. University of New Mexico Press, Albuquerque.

Montgomery, Ross Gordon, Watson Smith, and John Otis Brew, eds.

1949   *Franciscan Awatovi: The Excavation and Conjectural Reconstruction of a 17th Cen-
         tury Spanish Mission Establishment at a Hopi Indian Town in Northeastern Arizona.*
         Papers of the Peabody Museum of Archaeology and Ethnology, Vol. 36. Pea-
         body Museum of Archaeology and Ethnology, Cambridge, MA.

Morgan, Michèle E., ed.

2010a   *Pecos Pueblo Revisited: The Biological and Social Context.* Papers of the Peabody
         Museum of Archaeology and Ethnology, Vol. 85. Peabody Museum of Archae-
         ology and Ethnology, Cambridge, MA.

2010b   A Reassessment of the Human Remains from the Upper Pecos Valley Formerly
         Curated at the Peabody Museum of Archaeology and Ethnology, Harvard Uni-
         versity. In *Pecos Pueblo Revisited: The Biological and Social Context*, edited by M. E.
         Morgan, pp. 27–41. Papers of the Peabody Museum of Archaeology and Ethnol-
         ogy, Vol. 85. Peabody Museum of Archaeology and Ethnology, Cambridge, MA.

Morley, Selma E.

2002   *Stylistic Variation and Group Self-Identity: Evidence from the Rio Grande Pueblos.*
         Ph.D. diss., University of California, Los Angeles.

Morrow, Baker H., ed.

1996   *A Harvest of Reluctant Souls: The Memorial of Fray Alonso de Benavides, 1630.*
         University Press of Colorado, Niwot.

Naroll, Raoul

1962   Floor Area and Settlement Population. *American Antiquity* 27(4):587–589.

Neisser, Ulric

1967   *Cognitive Psychology.* Prentice-Hall, Englewood Cliffs, NJ.

1994   Multiple Systems: A New Approach to Cognitive Theory. *European Journal of
         Cognitive Psychology* 3(3):225–41.

Nelson, Ben A., Timothy A. Kohler, and Keith W. Kintigh

1994   Demographic Alternatives: Consequences for Current Models of Southwestern
         Prehistory. In *Understanding Complexity in the Prehistoric Southwest*, edited by
         G. J. Gumerman and M. Gell-Mann. Addison-Wesley, Reading, MA.

Neuzil, Anna A., Georgiana Boyer, and Peter Boyle

2007   Comparing Surface and Excavated Collections: A Case Study from Three Sites
         in the Safford Valley, Southeastern Arizona. Poster presented at Society for
         American Archaeology 72nd Annual Meetings, Austin, TX.

Nicholas, Ralph W.

1973   Social and Political Movements. *Annual Review of Anthropology* 2:63–84.

Noel Hume, Ivor

1964   Archaeology: Handmaiden to History. *North Carolina Historical Review* 41(2): 214–25.

Norcini, Marilyn

2005   The Political Process of Factionalism and Self-Governance at Santa Clara Pueblo, New Mexico. *Proceedings of the American Philosophical Society* 149(4):544–90.

Norris, Jim

2000   *After "The Year Eighty": The Demise of Franciscan Power in Spanish New Mexico.* University of New Mexico Press, Albuquerque.

Ortiz, Alfonso

1969   *The Tewa World: Space, Time, Being, and Becoming in a Pueblo Society.* University of Chicago Press, Chicago.

1972   Ritual Drama and the Pueblo World View. In *New Perspectives on the Pueblos,* edited by A. Ortiz, pp. 135–61. University of New Mexico Press, Albuquerque.

1979   San Juan Pueblo. In *Handbook of North American Indians: Southwest,* edited by A. Ortiz, pp. 278–95. Vol. 9. Smithsonian Institution, Washington, DC.

1980   Popay's Leadership: A Pueblo Perspective. *El Palacio* 86:18–22.

1994   The Dynamics of Pueblo Cultural Survival. In *North American Indian Anthropology: Essays on Society and Culture,* edited by R. J. DeMallie and A. Ortiz, pp. 296–306. University of Oklahoma Press, Norman.

Ortman, Scott G.

2010   *Genes, Language, and Culture in Tewa Ethnogenesis, A.D. 1150–1400,* Ph.D. diss, Arizona State University, Tempe.

Osterreich, Shelley Anne

1991   *The American Indian Ghost Dance, 1870 and 1890: An Annotated Bibliography.* Greenwood Press, New York.

Oviedo y Valdés, Gonzalo Fernández de

1959   *Natural History of the West Indies.* Translated and edited by S. A. Stoudemire.
[1535] University of North Carolina Press, Chapel Hill.

Palkovich, Ann M.

1994   Historic Epidemics of the American Pueblos. In *In the Wake of Contact: Biological Responses to Conquest,* edited by C. S. Larsen and G. R. Milner, pp. 87–95. Wiley-Liss, New York.

Palmer, Gabrielle, and Donna Pierce

1992   *Cambios: The Spirit of Transformation in Spanish Colonial Art.* University of New Mexico Press, Albuquerque.

Parmentier, Richard J.

1979   The Mythological Triangle: Poseyemu, Montezuma, and Jesus in the Pueblo. In *Handbook of North American Indians: Southwest,* edited by A. Ortiz, pp. 609–622. Vol. 9. Smithsonian Institution, Washington, DC.

1994   *Signs in Society: Studies in Semiotic Anthropology.* Indiana University Press, Bloomington.

Parsons, Elsie Clews

1925　　*The Pueblo of Jemez.* Papers of the Southwestern Expedition No. 3. Phillips Academy, Andover.

1929　　*The Social Organization of the Tewa of New Mexico.* Memoirs of the American Anthropological Association 36, Menasha, WI.

1939　　*Pueblo Indian Religion.* 2 vols. University of Chicago Press, Chicago.

Peach, Wesley

2001　　*Itineraires de Conversion: Perspectives de Theologies Pratique.* Editions Fides, Quebec.

Pecos Archaeological Survey

1996　　*Pecos Archaeological Survey, 1996 Ceramic Typology Field Manual.*

Peirce, Charles Sanders

1992　　*The Essential Peirce: Selected Philosophical Writings, Vol. I (1867–1893).* Indiana University Press, Bloomington.

Pérez de Luxán, Diego

1929　　Expedition into New Mexico Made by Antonio de Espejo, 1582–1583, as Revealed in the Journal of Diego Pérez de Luxán, a Member of the Party, edited by G. P. Hammond and A. Rey. The Quivira Society, Los Angeles.

Perez de Ribas, Andres

1645　　*Historia de los triumfos de nuestra santa fe entre gentes las mas barbaras y tieras de nuevo orbe.* Ayers Collection, Newberry Library, Chicago, Madrid.

Pérez de Villagrá, Gaspar

1992　　*Historia de la Nueva Mexico, 1610.* University of New Mexico Press,
[1610]　　Albuquerque.

Philips, Caroline, and Harry Allen, eds.

2010　　*Bridging the Divide: Indigenous Communities and Archaeology into the 21st Century.* Left Coast Press, Walnut Creek, CA.

Prakash, Gyan

1994　　Subaltern Studies as Postcolonial Criticism. *American Historical Review* 99(5):1475–90.

Pratt, Boyd, and David Snow

1988　　*The North Central Regional Overview: Strategies for the Comprehensive Survey of the Architectural and Historic Archaeological Resources of North Central New Mexico, Vol. 1: Historic Overview of North Central New Mexico.* New Mexico State Historic Preservation Division, Santa Fe.

Preucel, Robert W.

1998　　*The Kotyiti Archaeological Project: Report of the 1996 Field Season.* Pueblo de Cochiti and USDA Forest Service, Santa Fe.

2000a　　Living on the Mesa: Hanat Kotyiti, a Post-Revolt Cochiti Community in Northern New Mexico. *Expedition* 42:8–17.

2000b　　Making Pueblo Communities: Archaeological Discourse at Kotyiti, New Mexico. In *The Archaeology of Communities: A New World Perspective*, edited by M. A. Canuto and J. Yaeger, pp. 58–77. Routledge, New York.

2002a　　*Archaeologies of the Pueblo Revolt.* University of New Mexico Press, Albuquerque.

2002b   Writing the Pueblo Revolt. In *Archaeologies of the Pueblo Revolt*, edited by R. W. Preucel, pp. 3–29. University of New Mexico Press, Albuquerque.

2006   *Archaeological Semiotics*. Blackwell, London.

Preucel, Robert W., and Alexander Bauer

2001   Archaeological Pragmatics. *Norwegian Archaeological Review* 34(2):85–96.

Preucel, Robert W., Loa P. Traxler, and Michael Wilcox

2002   "Now the God of the Spaniards Is Dead": Ethnogenesis and Community Formation in the Aftermath of the Pueblo Revolt of 1680. In *Traditions, Transitions, and Technologies: Themes in Southwestern Archaeology*, edited by S. H. Schlanger, pp. 71–93. University Press of Colorado, Boulder, CO.

Ramenofsky, Ann F.

1996   The Problem of Introduced Infectious Diseases in New Mexico: A.D. 1540–1680. *Journal of Anthropological Research* 52(2):161–184.

Ramenofsky, Ann F., and Jeremy Kulisheck

in press   Regarding Sixteenth-Century Native Population Change in the Northern Southwest. In *Native and Imperial Transformations: Sixteenth-Century Entradas in the American Southwest and Southeast*, edited by C. Mathers, J. M. Mitchem and C. M. Haecker. University of Arizona Press, Tucson.

Ramenofsky, Ann F., Fraser D. Neiman, and Christopher D. Pierce

2009   Measuring Time, Population, and Residential Mobility from the Surface at San Marcos Pueblo, North Central New Mexico. *American Antiquity* 74(3):505–530.

Ranger, Terence

1975   *Dance and Society in Eastern Africa, 1890–1970: The Beni Ngoma*. University of California Press, Berkeley.

Rautman, Allison E.

2000   Population Aggregation, Community Organization, and Plaza-Oriented Pueblos in the American Southwest. *Journal of Field Archaeology* 27(3):271–83.

Reed, Lori S., and Paul F. Reed

1992   The Protohistoric Navajo: Implications of Interaction, Exchange, and Alliance Formation with the Eastern and Western Pueblos. In *Cultural Diversity and Adaptation: The Archaic, Anasazi, and Navajo Occupation of the Upper San Juan Basin*, edited by L. S. Reed and P. F. Reed, pp. 91–104. Bureau of Land Management Cultural Resources Series No. 9, Santa Fe.

Reff, Daniel T.

1991   *Disease, Depopulation, and Culture Change in Northwestern New Spain, 1518–1764*. University of Utah Press, Salt Lake City.

1995   The "Predicament of Culture" and Spanish Missionary Accounts of the Tepehuan and Pueblo Revolts. *Ethnohistory* 42:63–90.

Reid, Jefferson J., and Izumi Shimada

1982   Pueblo Growth at Grasshopper: Methods and Models. In *Multidisciplinary Research at Grasshopper Pueblo, Arizona*, edited by W. A. Longacre, S. J. Holbrook, and M. W. Graves, pp. 12–18. University of Arizona Anthropological Papers No. 40, Tucson.

Reiter, Paul

1938   *The Jemez Pueblo of Unshagi, New Mexico.* University of New Mexico Bulletin, Anthropological Series, Albuquerque.

Riley, Carroll L.

1987   *The Frontier People: The Greater Southwest in the Protohistoric Period.* University of New Mexico Press, Albuquerque.

1995   *Rio del Norte: People of the Upper Rio Grande from Earliest Times to the Pueblo Revolt.* University of Utah Press, Salt Lake City.

1999   *The Kachina and the Cross: Indians and Spaniards in the Early Southwest.* University of Utah Press, Salt Lake City.

Roberts, David

2004   *The Pueblo Revolt: The Secret Rebellion that Drove the Spaniards Out of the Southwest.* Simon and Schuster, New York.

Roberts, Frank H. H., Jr.

1939   *Archaeological Remains in the Whitewater District, Eastern Arizona, Part 1: House Types.* Smithsonian Institution Bureau of American Ethnology Bulletin 121, Washington, DC.

Robins, Nicholas A.

2005   *Native Insurgencies and the Genocidal Impulse in the Americas.* Indiana University Press, Bloomington.

Robinson, William J.

1990   Tree-ring Studies of the Pueblo de Acoma. *Historical Archaeology* 24(3): 99–106.

Robinson, William J., John W. Hannah, and Bruce G. Harrill

1972   *Tree-ring Dates from New Mexico, I, O, U: Central Rio Grande Area.* Laboratory of Tree-ring Research, University of Arizona, Tucson.

Roediger, Henry L.

1980   Memory Metaphors in Cognitive Psychology. *Memory and Cognition* 8:231–246.

2008   *Cognitive Psychology of Memory.* Elsevier, Oxford.

Rogers, J. Daniel

2005   Archaeology and the Interpretation of Colonial Encounters. In *Archaeology of Colonial Encounters: Comparative Perspectives*, edited by G. Stein, pp. 331–54. School of American Research Press, Santa Fe.

Rohn, Arthur H.

1971   *Mug House, Mesa Verde National Park, Colorado.* Archaeological Research Series 7-D. Washington, DC, National Park Service.

Roney, John R.

1996   The Pueblo III Period in the Eastern San Juan Basin and Acoma-Laguna Areas. In *The Prehistoric Pueblo World, A.D. 1150–1350*, edited by M. A. Adler, pp. 145–69. University of Arizona Press, Tucson.

Roosens, Eugene E.

1989   *Creating Ethnicity: The Process of Ethnogenesis.* Frontiers of Anthropology 5. Sage Publications, Newbury Park, CA.

Rosaldo, Renato

1989   Imperialist Nostalgia. *Representations* 26:107–22.

Roth, Randolph

1992   Is History a Process? Nonlinearity, Revitalization Theory, and the Central Metaphor of Social Science History. *Social Science History* 16(2):197–243.

Rothschild, Nan

2003   *Colonial Encounters in a Native American Landscape: The Spanish and Dutch in North America*. Smithsonian Institution Press, Washington, DC.

Sahlins, Marshall

1999   Two or Three Things that I Know about Culture. *Journal of the Royal Anthropological Institute* 5(3):399–421.

Said, Edward

1988   Foreword. In *Selected Subaltern Studies*, edited by R. Guha and G. C. Spivak, pp. v–x. Oxford University Press, Oxford.

Sálaz Márquez, Rubén

2008   *The Pueblo Revolt Massacre*. Cosmic House, Albuquerque.

Salzer, Matthew W.

2000   *Dendroclimatology in the San Francisco Peaks Region of Northern Arizona, USA*. Ph.D. diss., University of Arizona, Tucson.

Sanchez, Jane C.

1983   Spanish-Indian Relations during the Otermín Administration, 1677–1683. *New Mexico Historical Review* 58(2):133–51.

Sando, Joe S.

1979a   The Pueblo Revolt. In *Handbook of North American Indians: Southwest*, edited by A. Ortiz, pp. 194–97. Vol. 9. Smithsonian Institution, Washington, DC.

1979b   Jemez Pueblo. In *Handbook of North American Indians: Southwest*, edited by A. Ortiz, pp. 418–429. Vol. 9. Smithsonian Institution, Washington, DC.

1982   *Nee Hemish: A History of Jemez Pueblo*. University of New Mexico Press, Albuquerque.

1992   *Pueblo Nations: Eight Centuries of Pueblo Indian History*. Clear Light, Santa Fe.

1998   *Pueblo Profiles: Cultural Identities through Centuries of Change*. Clear Light, Santa Fe.

2005   The Pueblo Revolt. In *Po'pay: Leader of the First American Revolution*, edited by J. S. Sando and H. Agoyo, pp. 5–53. Clear Light, Santa Fe.

Sando, Joe S., and Herman Agoyo, eds.

2005   *Po'pay: Leader of the First American Revolution*. Clear Light, Santa Fe.

Sayre, Gordon M.

2005   *The Indian Chief as Tragic Hero: Native Resistance and the Literatures of America, from Moctezuma to Tecumseh*. University of North Carolina Press, Chapel Hill.

Schaafsma, Curtis F.

1995   The Chronology of Las Madres Pueblo (LA 25). In *Of Pots and Rocks: Papers in Honor of A. Helene Warren*, edited by D. T. Kirkpatrick and M. S. Duran, pp. 155–65. Archaeological Society of New Mexico, Albuquerque.

1996   Ethnic Identity and Protohistoric Archaeological Sites in Northwestern New Mexico: Implications for Reconstructions of Navajo and Ute History. In *The*

Archaeology of Navajo Origins, edited by R. H. Towner, pp. 19–46. University of Utah Press, Salt Lake City.

2002   *Apaches de Navajo: Seventeenth Century Navajos in the Chama Valley of New Mexico.* University of Utah Press, Salt Lake City.

Schaafsma, Polly

1975   *Rock Art in the Cochiti Reservoir District.* Museum of New Mexico Papers in Anthropology No. 16. Museum of New Mexico Press, Santa Fe.

1994   The Prehistoric Kachina Cult and Its Origins as Suggested by Southwestern Rock Art. In *Kachinas in the Pueblo World*, edited by P. Schaafsma, pp. 63–80. University of New Mexico Press, Albuquerque.

2000   *Warrior, Shield and Star: Imagery and Ideology of Pueblo Warfare.* Western Edge Press, Santa Fe.

Scholes, France V.

1930   The Supply Services of the New Mexican Missions in the Seventeenth Century, 1663–1680. *New Mexico Historical Review* 5:186–210.

1936   Church and State in New Mexico, 1610–1650. *New Mexico Historical Review* 11:9–76, 145–178, 283–294, 297–349.

1938   Notes on the Jemez Missions in the Seventeenth Century. *El Palacio* 44:61–71, 93–102.

1942   *Troublous Times in New Mexico, 1659–1670.* Historical Society of New Mexico, Publications in History, vol. 11. University of New Mexico Press, Albuquerque.

1944   Juan Martínez de Montoya, Settler and Conquistador of New Mexico. *New Mexico Historical Review* 19(3):337–42.

Schroeder, Albert H.

1972   Rio Grande Ethnohistory. In *New Perspectives on the Pueblos*, edited by A. Ortiz, pp. 41–70. University of New Mexico Press, Albuquerque.

1979   Pueblos Abandoned in Historic Times. In *Handbook of North American Indians*, edited by A. Ortiz, pp. 236–254. Vol. 9. Smithsonian Institution, Washington, DC.

Scott, Eleanor

1991   Animal and Infant Burials in Romano-British Villas: a Revitalization Movement. In *Sacred and Profane: Proceedings of a Conference on Archaeology, Ritual, and Religion, Oxford 1989*, edited by P. Garwood, pp. 115–21. Oxford University Committee for Archaeology, Oxford.

Scott, James C.

1990   *Domination and the Arts of Resistance: Hidden Transcripts.* Yale University Press, New Haven.

Seifert, Donna J.

n.d   Archaeological Excavations at the Palace of the Governors, Santa Fe, New Mexico: 1974 and 1975. Museum of New Mexico, History Bureau, Santa Fe.

Shepard, Anna O.

1938   Technological Notes on the Pottery from Unshagi. In *The Jemez Pueblo of Unshagi, New Mexico, with Notes on the Earlier Excavations at "Amoxiumqua" and Giusewa*, edited by P. Reiter, pp. 205–11. Monographs of the School of

American Research Number 6. University of New Mexico and the School of American Research, Santa Fe.

1956   *Ceramics for the Archaeologist.* 5th ed. Carnegie Institution of Washington, Publication 609. Reprinted by Braun-Brumfield, Ann Arbor.

Sider, Gerald

1994   Identity as History: Ethnohistory, Ethnogenesis, and Ethnocide in the Southeastern United States. *Identities* 1(1):109–22.

Siegel, Bernard J., and Alan R. Beals

1960   Pervasive Factionalism. *American Anthropologist* 62(3):394–419.

Sigüenza y Góngora, Carlos de

1932   *The Mercurio Volante of Don Carlos de Sigüenza y Góngora: An Account of the First*
[1692]   *Expedition of Don Diego de Vargas into New Mexico in 1692.* Translated by I. A. Leonard. The Quivira Society, Los Angeles.

Siikala, Jukka

2004   Priests and Prophets: The Politics of Voice in the Pacific. In *Reassessing Revitalization Movements: Perspectives from North America and the Pacific Islands*, edited by M. E. Harkin, pp. 88–103. University of Nebraska Press, Lincoln.

Silliman, Stephen

2004   *Lost Laborers in Colonial California: Native Americans and the Archaeology of Rancho Petaluma.* University of Arizona Press, Tucson.

2005   Culture Contact or Colonialism? Challenges in the Archaeology of Native North America. *American Antiquity* 70(1):55–74.

2008   *Collaborating at the Trowel's Edge: Teaching and Learning in Indigenous Archaeology.* University of Arizona Press, Tucson.

2009   Change and Continuity, Practice and Memory: Native American Persistence in Colonial New England. *American Antiquity* 74(2):211–30.

Silverberg, Robert

1970   *The Pueblo Revolt.* Waybright and Talley, New York.

Simmons, Alan H.

1998   Exposed Fragments, Buried Hippos: Assessing Surface Archaeology. In *Surface Archaeology*, edited by A. P. Sullivan, pp. 159–67. University of New Mexico Press, Albuquerque.

Simmons, Marc

1969   Settlement Patterns and Village Plans in Colonial New Mexico. *Journal of the West* 8(1):7–21.

1979   History of Pueblo-Spanish Relations to 1821. In *Handbook of North American Indians: Southwest*, edited by A. Ortiz, pp. 178–93. Vol. 9. Smithsonian Institution, Washington, DC.

1980   The Pueblo Revolt: Why Did It Happen? *El Palacio* 86:11–15.

1991a   *The Last Conquistador: Juan de Oñate and the Settling of the Far Southwest.* University of Oklahoma Press, Norman.

1991b   Santiago: Reality and Myth. In *Santiago: Saint of Two Worlds*, edited by M. Simmons, D. Pierce, and J. Myers, pp. 1–29. University of New Mexico Press, Albuquerque.

Simpson, James H.

1852   *Journal of a Military Reconnaissance from Santa Fe, New Mexico, to the Navajo Country, Made with the Troops under Command of Brevet Lieutenant Colonel John M. Washington, Chief of Ninth Military Department, and Governor of New Mexico in 1849* Senate Ex. Doc. 1st Sess. 31st Congress No. 64. Lippincott, Philadelphia.

Singer, Lester

1962   Ethnogenesis and Negro Americans Today. *Social Research* 29:419–32.

Smith, Michael G.

1960   Kagoro Political Development. *Human Organization* 19(3):137–49.

Smith, R. L., R. A. Bailey, and C. R. Ross

1970   Geologic Map of the Jemez Mountains. *Miscellaneous Investigations Series Map I-571*. U.S. Geological Survey, Denver.

Smith, Watson, Richard B. Woodbury, and Nathalie F. S. Woodbury

1966   *The Excavation of Hawikuh by Frederick Webb Hodge: Report of the Hendricks-Hodge Expedition 1917–1923*. Museum of the American Indian, Heye Foundation, New York.

Snead, James E., Winifred Creamer, and Tineke Van Zandt

2004   "Ruins of Our Forefathers": Large Sites and Site Clusters in the Northern Rio Grande. In *The Protohistoric Pueblo World*, edited by E. C. Adams and A. I. Duff, pp. 26–34. University of Arizona Press, Tucson.

Snead, James E., and Robert W. Preucel

1999   The Ideology of Settlement: Ancestral Keres Landscapes in the Northern Rio Grande Region. In *Archaeologies of Landscape*, edited by W. Ashmore and A. B. Knapp, pp. 169–200. Blackwell, Oxford.

Snow, Cordelia Thomas

1974   A Brief History of the Palace of the Governors and a Preliminary Report on the 1974 Excavation. *El Palacio* 80(3):1–21.

1988   The Plazas of Santa Fe, New Mexico. *El Palacio* 94(2):40–51.

Snow, David

1982   The Rio Grande Glaze, Matte Paint, and Plainware Traditions. In *Southwest Ceramics: A Comparative Review*, edited by H. S. Albert, pp. 235–278. Arizona Archaeologist, No. 15.

1983   A Note on Encomienda Economics in Seventeenth-Century New Mexico. In *Hispanic Arts and Ethnohistory in the Southwest*, edited by M. Weigle, pp. 347–57. Ancient City Press, Albuquerque.

1994   *Archaeological and Historical Investigations of Barclay Ranch—La Gotera Grant, Santa Fe County, New Mexico (April–May 1993)*. Arlington, VA: Conservation Fund.

Speth, John D.

1991   Some Unexplored Aspects of Mutualistic Plains-Pueblo Food Exchange. In *Farmers, Hunters, and Colonists: Interaction between the Southwest and the Southern Plains*, edited by K. Spielmann, pp. 18–35. University of Arizona Press, Tucson.

Spicer, Edward H.

1962   *Cycles of Conquest: The Impact of Spain, Mexico, and the United States on the Indians of the Southwest, 1533–1960*. University of Arizona Press, Tucson.

Spielmann, Katherine A.

1983   Late Prehistoric Exchange between the Southwest and Southern Plains. *Plains Anthropologist* 28(102):257–72.

1986   Interdependence among Egalitarian Societies. *Journal of Anthropological Archaeology* 5:279–312.

1989   Colonists, Hunters, and Farmers: Plains-Pueblo Interaction in the Seventeenth Century. In *Columbian Consequences: Vol. 1. Archaeological and Historical Perspectives on the Spanish Borderlands West*, edited by D. H. Thomas, pp. 101–13. Smithsonian Institution Press, Washington, DC.

1991   Coercion or Cooperation? Plains-Pueblo Interaction in the Protohistoric Period. In *Farmers, Hunters, and Colonists: Interaction between the Southwest and the Southern Plains*, edited by K. A. Spielmann, pp. 36–50. University of Arizona Press, Tucson.

Spielmann, Katherine A., Tiffany Clark, Diane Hawkey, Katharine Rainey, and Suzanne K. Fish

2009   ". . . being weary, they had rebelled": Pueblo Subsistence and Labor under Spanish Colonialism. *Journal of Anthropological Archaeology* 28:102–25.

Spielmann, Katherine A., Jeannette L. Mobley-Tanaka, and James M. Potter

2006   Style and Resistance in the Seventeenth-Century Salinas Province. *American Antiquity* 71(4):621–49.

Spivak, Gayatri Chakravorty

1985   Can the Subaltern Speak? Speculations on Widow Sacrifice. *Wedge* 7(8):120–30.

1990   Poststructuralism, Marginality, Post-coloniality and Value. In *Literary Theory Today*, edited by P. Collier and H. Geyer-Ryan, pp. 219–44. Cornell University Press, Ithaca.

Stein, Gil J., ed.

2005   *The Archaeology of Colonial Encounters: Comparative Perspectives*. School of American Research Press, Santa Fe.

Stewart, Kathleen, and Susan Harding

1999   Bad Endings: American Apocalypsis. *Annual Review of Anthropology* 28:285–310.

Stodder, Ann L., and Debra Martin

1992   Health and Disease in the Southwest before and after Spanish Contact. In *Disease and Demography in the Americas*, edited by J. W. Verano and D. H. Ubelaker, pp. 55–73. Smithsonian Institution Press, Washington, DC.

Stodder, Ann L., Debra L. Martin, Alan H. Goodman, and Daniel T. Reff

2002   Cultural Longevity and Biological Stress in the American Southwest. In *The Backbone of History: Health and Nutrition in the Western Hemisphere*, edited by R. H. Steckel and J. C. Rose, pp. 481–505. Cambridge University Press, Cambridge, UK.

Sturtevant, William C.

1971   Creek into Seminole. In *North American Indians in Historical Perspective*, edited by E. Leacock and N. Lurie, pp. 92–128. Random House, New York.

Suina, J. H.

2002   The Persistence of the Corn Mothers. In *Archaeologies of the Pueblo Revolt*, edited by R. W. Preucel, pp. 212–16. University of New Mexico Press, Albuquerque.

Sullivan, Alan P. III, ed.

1998a   *Surface Archaeology*. University of New Mexico Press, Albuquerque.

1998b   Preface: Surface Phenomena in Archaeological Research. In *Surface Archaeology*, edited by A. P. Sullivan, pp. xi–xiii. University of New Mexico Press, Albuquerque.

Sumner, W. M.

1979   Estimating Population by Analogy: An Example. In *Ethnoarchaeology: Implications of Ethnography for Archaeology*, edited by K. Carol, pp. 164–74. Columbia University Press, New York.

Sundt, William M.

1987   Pottery of Central New Mexico and Its Role as Key to Both Time and Space. In *Secrets of a City: Papers on Albuquerque Area Archaeology in Honor of Richard A. Bice*, edited by A. V. Poore and J. Montgomery, pp. 116–47. Archaeological Society of New Mexico Papers No. 13. Santa Fe, Ancient City Press.

Tainter, Joseph A.

1998   Surface Archaeology: Perceptions, Values, and Potential. In *Surface Archaeology*, edited by A. P. Sullivan, pp. 169–79. University of New Mexico Press, Albuquerque.

Taylor, William B.

1987   The Virgin of Guadalupe in New Spain: An Inquiry into the Social History of Marian Devotion. *American Ethnologist* 14(1):9–33.

Thomas, David Hurst

1988   Saints and Soldiers at Santa Catalina: Hispanic Designs for Colonial America. In *The Recovery of Meaning: Historical Archaeology in the Eastern United States*, edited by M. P. Leone and P. B. Potter, pp. 73–124. Smithsonian Institution Press, Washington, DC.

Thomas, Nicholas

1994   *Colonialism's Culture: Anthropology, Travel, and Government*. Polity Press, Cambridge, UK.

Thompson, Edward Palmer

1963   *The Making of the English Working Class*. Pantheon Books, New York.

Thornton, Russell

1981   Demographic Antecedents of a Revitalization Movement: Population Change, Population Size, and the 1890 Ghost Dance. *American Sociological Review* 46:88–96.

1982   Demographic Antecedents of Tribal Participation in the 1870 Ghost Dance Movement. *American Indian Culture and Research Journal* 6:79–91.

1986   *We Shall Live Again: The 1870 and 1890 Ghost Dance Movements as Demographic Revitalization*. Cambridge University Press, New York.

1987 *American Indian Holocaust and Survival.* University of Oklahoma Press, Norman.

1990a Boundary Dissolution and Revitalization Movements: The Case of the Nineteenth-Century Cherokees. *Ethnohistory* 40(3):359–83.

1990b *The Cherokees: A Population History.* University of Nebraska Press, Lincoln.

Todorov, Tzvetan

1984 *The Conquest of America: The Question of the Other.* Harper and Row, New York.

Toulouse, Joseph, Jr.

1949 *The Mission of San Gregorio de Abó.* School of American Research Monograph 13. University of New Mexico Press, Albuquerque.

Trigg, Heather

2005 *From Household to Empire: Society and Economy in Early Colonial New Mexico.* University of Arizona Press, Tucson.

Turnbaugh, William A.

1979 Calumet Ceremonialism as a Nativistic Response. *American Antiquity* 44(4):685–91.

Turney, John F.

1948 *An Analysis of the Material Taken from a Section of Group M of the Cliffs, Frijoles Canyon, Bandelier National Monument, New Mexico,* Unpublished Masters Thesis, Adams State College, Alamosa, CO.

Twitchell, Ralph Emerson

1914 *The Spanish Archives of New Mexico.* 2 vols. The Torch Press, Santa Fe.

Upham, Steadman

1982 *Polities and Power: An Economic and Political History of the Western Pueblo.* Academic Press, New York.

Van Dyke, Ruth M.

2009 Chaco Reloaded: Discursive Social Memory on the Post-Chacoan Landscape. *Journal of Social Archaeology* 9(2):220–48.

Van Dyke, Ruth M., and Susan E. Alcock, eds.

2003 *Archaeologies of Memory.* Blackwell, Oxford.

Van West, Carla R., Thomas C. Windes, and Frances Levine

in press The Role of Climate in Early Spanish-Native American Interactions in the U.S. Southwest. In *Native and Imperial Transformations: Sixteenth-Century Entradas in the American Southwest and Southeast,* edited by C. Mathers, J. M. Mitchem, and C. M. Haecker. University of Arizona Press, Tucson.

Vélez de Escalante, fray Silvestre

1983 *Letter of the Father Fray Silvestre Vélez de Escalante Written on the 2nd of April, in*
[1778] *the Year 1778.* Acoma Books, Ramona CA.

Vetancurt, Augustín de

1971 *Teatro Mexicano: Descripcíon Breve de los sucesos ejemplares de la Nueva España en el*
[1697] *Nuevo Mundo.* Cronica de la Provincia del Santo Evangelico de Mexico, Editorial Porrúa, Mexico City.

Vivian, R. Gwinn

1970 An Inquiry into Prehistoric Social Organization in Chaco Canyon, New Mexico. In *Reconstructing Prehistoric Pueblo Societies,* edited by W. A. Longacre, pp. 59–83. University of New Mexico Press, Albuquerque.

Voloshinov, Valentin

1973   *Marxism and the Philosophy of Language.* Harvard University Press, Cambridge, MA.

Voss, Barbara L.

2005   From Casta to Californio: Social Identity and the Archaeology of Culture Contact. *American Anthropologist* 107(3):461–74.

2008   *The Archaeology of Ethnogenesis: Race and Sexuality in Colonial San Francisco.* University of California Press, Berkeley.

Wagner, Mark J.

2006   "He Is Worst Than the [Shawnee] Prophet": The Archaeology of Nativism among the Early Nineteenth Century Potawatomi of Illinois. *Midcontinental Journal of Archaeology* 31(1):89–116.

2010   A Prophet Has Arisen: The Archaeology of Nativism among the Nineteenth-Century Algonquin Peoples of Illinois. In *Across a Great Divide: Continuity and Change in Native North American Societies, 1400–1900,* edited by L. L. Scheiber and M. D. Mitchell, pp. 107–27. University of Arizona Press, Tucson.

Walker, William H.

2002   Stratigraphy and Practical Reason. *American Anthropologist* 104(1):159–77.

Wallace, Anthony F. C.

1956   Revitalization Movements. *American Anthropologist* 58:264–81.

1966   *Religion: An Anthropological View.* Random House, New York.

1970   *Culture and Personality.* Random House, New York.

1972   *The Death and Rebirth of the Seneca.* Vintage Books, New York.

2004   Foreword. In *Reassessing Revitalization Movements: Perspectives from North America and the Pacific Islands,* edited by M. Harkin, pp. vii–xi. University of Nebraska Press, Lincoln.

Walsh, Marie T.

1934   *The Mission Bells of California.* Hart Wagner, San Francisco.

Walt, Henry

1990   Style as Communication: Early Historic Pueblo Pottery of New Mexico. Ph.D. diss., University of New Mexico, Albuquerque.

Walz, Vina

1951   *History of the El Paso Area, 1680–1692,* Ph.D. diss, University of New Mexico, Albuquerque.

Warren, A. Helene

1979   Historic Pottery of the Cochiti Reservoir Area. In *Archaeological Investigations of the Cochiti Reservoir, New Mexico, Volume 4: Adaptive Change in the Northern Rio Grande Valley,* edited by J. V. Biella and R. C. Chapman, pp. 235–45. University of New Mexico Office of Contract Archaeology, Albuquerque.

1981   A Petrographic Study of the Pottery of Gran Quivera. In *Contributions to Gran Quivera Archaeology, Gran Quivera National Monument, New Mexico.* National Park Service Publications in Archaeology 17, pp. 57–73. National Park Service, Washington, D.C.

Watson, Patty Jo, Steven A. LeBlanc, and Charles L. Redman

1980   Aspects of Zuni Prehistory: Preliminary Report on Excavations and Survey in
        the El Morro Valley of New Mexico. *Journal of Field Archaeology* 7:201–18.

Weber, David J.

1999a   *What Caused the Pueblo Revolt of 1680?* Bedford/St. Martins, Boston.

1999b   Pueblos, Spaniards, and History. In *What Caused the Pueblo Revolt of 1680?*,
        edited by D. J. Weber, pp. 3–18. Bedford/St. Martins, Boston.

2005   *Bárbaros: Spaniards and Their Savages in the Age of Enlightenment.* Yale University
        Press, New Haven.

Weber, Eugen

1974   Revolution? Counterrevolution? What Revolution? *Journal of Contemporary
        History* 9(2):3–47.

Weber, Max

1947   *The Theory of Social and Economic Organization.* Translated by A. M. Henderson
        and T. Parsons. Free Press, Glencoe, IL.

Weisman, Brent R.

2007   Nativism, Resistance, and Ethnogenesis of the Florida Seminole Indian Iden-
        tity. *Historical Archaeology* 41(4):198–212.

Whatley, William J., and Robert W. Delaney

1995   Jemez: A Chronological History of the Canon de San Diego Region of the
        Kingdom and Provinces of New Mexico. Unpublished Manuscript on file,
        Pueblo of Jemez Department of Resource Protection.

White, Leslie A.

1932   *The Acoma Indians.* 47th Annual Report, Bureau of American Ethnology, Wash-
        ington, DC.

1942   *The Pueblo of Santa Ana, New Mexico.* American Anthropological Association
        Memoir No. 60, Washington, DC.

1962   *The Pueblo of Sia, New Mexico.* Smithsonian Institution Bureau of American Eth-
        nology Bulletin 184. United States Government Printing Office, Washington,
        DC.

1964   The World of the Keresan Pueblo Indians. In *Primitive Views of the World*, edited
        by S. Diamond, pp. 83–94. Columbia University Press, New York.

Whiteley, Peter

1988   *Deliberate Acts: Changing Hopi Culture through the Oraibi Split.* University of Ari-
        zona Press, Tucson.

2008   *The Orayvi Split: A Hopi Transformation.* Anthropological Papers of the Ameri-
        can Museum of Natural History No. 87. American Museum of Natural His-
        tory, New York.

Wiget, Andrew

1982   Truth and the Hopi: An Historiographic Study of Documented Oral Tradition
        Regarding the Coming of the Spanish. *Ethnohistory* 29:181–99.

1996   Father Juan Greyrobe: Reconstructing Tradition Histories, and the Reliability
        and Validity of Uncorroborated Oral Tradition. *Ethnohistory* 43:459–82.

Wilcox, David R.

1975   A Strategy for Perceiving Social Groups in Puebloan Sites. In *Chapters in the Prehistory of Eastern Arizona 4*, pp. 120–59. vol. Fieldiana: Anthropology 65.

1981   Changing Perspectives on the Protohistoric Pueblos, AD 1450–1700. In *The Protohistoric Period in the American Southwest, AD 1450–1700*, edited by D. R. Wilcox and W. B. Masse, pp. 378–409. Anthropological Research Papers No. 24. Arizona State University, Tempe.

Wilcox, Michael V.

2009   *The Pueblo Revolt and the Mythology of Conquest*. University of California Press, Berkeley.

Wilson, Chris

1997   *The Myth of Santa Fe: Creating a Modern Regional Tradition*. University of New Mexico Press, Albuquerque.

Winship, George P.

1922   *The Journey of Coronado, 1540–1542*. Allerton, New York.

Worsley, Peter

1957   *The Trumpet Shall Sound: A Study of Cargo Cults in Melanesia*. MacGibbon and Kee, London.

Yoffee, Norman, ed.

2007   *Negotiating the Past in the Past: Identity, Memory, and Landscape in Archaeological Research*. University of Arizona Press, Tucson.

Young, Robert J. C.

1995   *Colonial Desire: Hybridity in Theory, Culture, and Race*. Routledge, London.

Zedeño, Maria Nieves

1995   The Role of Population Movement and Technology Transfer in the Manufacture of Prehistoric Southwestern Ceramics. In *Ceramic Production in the American Southwest*, edited by B. J. Mills and P. L. Crown, pp. 115–141. University of Arizona Press, Tucson.

Zubrow, Ezra B.

1974   *Population, Contact, and Climate in the New Mexican Pueblos*. Anthropological Papers of the University of Arizona No. 24. University of Arizona Press, Tucson.

Index

About the Author

Matthew Liebmann is an assistant professor in the Department of Anthropology at Harvard University. He has published research in *American Anthropologist,* the *Journal of Field Archaeology, Kiva: The Journal of Southwestern Anthropology and History,* and *Plains Anthropologist,* and he is the coeditor (with Uzma Rizvi) of *Archaeology and the Postcolonial Critique* (Altamira Press, 2008) and (with Melissa Murphy) of *Enduring Conquests: Rethinking the Archaeology of Resistance to Spanish Colonialism in the Americas* (SAR Press, 2011). Liebmann received his BA in English and Theology from Boston College in 1996. Following his graduation he taught at Red Cloud High School on the Pine Ridge (Oglala Lakota) Indian Reservation before entering graduate school at the University of Pennsylvania. At Penn he was a William Penn Fellow and a member of the Kolb Society of Fellows at the University Museum of Archaeology and Anthropology. From 2003 to 2005 he worked as tribal archaeologist and NAGPRA program director at the Pueblo of Jemez Department of Resource Protection. In 2006 he received his Ph.D. in anthropology and was named a University of Pennsylvania School of Arts and Sciences Dean's Scholar. He won the Society for American Archaeology's Dissertation Award in 2007, when he was an assistant professor at the College of William and Mary. He began teaching at Harvard in 2009, and was a William and Rita Clements Fellow for the Study of Southwestern America at Southern Methodist University in 2010. Liebmann lives in Cambridge, Massachusetts, and continues to collaborate on archaeological research with the Pueblo of Jemez.

CPSIA information can be obtained
at www.ICGtesting.com
Printed in the USA
BVHW070231070921
616157BV00006B/44